ENGLAND'S HELICON

England's Helicon

Fountains in Early Modern Literature and Culture

HESTER LEES-JEFFRIES

OXFORD
UNIVERSITY PRESS

OXFORD
UNIVERSITY PRESS

Great Clarendon Street, Oxford OX2 6DP

Oxford University Press is a department of the University of Oxford.
It furthers the University's objective of excellence in research, scholarship,
and education by publishing worldwide in

Oxford New York

Auckland Cape Town Dar es Salaam Hong Kong Karachi
Kuala Lumpur Madrid Melbourne Mexico City Nairobi
New Delhi Shanghai Taipei Toronto

With offices in

Argentina Austria Brazil Chile Czech Republic France Greece
Guatemala Hungary Italy Japan Poland Portugal Singapore
South Korea Switzerland Thailand Turkey Ukraine Vietnam

Oxford is a registered trade mark of Oxford University Press
in the UK and in certain other countries

Published in the United States
by Oxford University Press Inc., New York

© Hester Lees-Jeffries 2007

British Library Cataloguing in Publication Data
Data available

Library of Congress Cataloging in Publication Data
Data available

Typeset by Laserwords Private Limited, Chennai, India
Printed in Great Britain
on acid-free paper by
Biddles Ltd., King's Lynn, Norfolk

ISBN 978–0–19–923078–5

1 3 5 7 9 10 8 6 4 2

For my family

Preface

First books have long gestations and many midwives. I began *England's Helicon* as a doctoral thesis at Cambridge University, where I was funded by a Commonwealth Scholarship from the Association of Commonwealth Universities, with additional support from the New Zealand Vice Chancellors' Committee and the University of Canterbury. A Research Fellowship at Magdalene College, Cambridge, 2003–6 allowed me to undertake a considerable amount of new research, as well as to revise the thesis. I am grateful to the staff of the Cambridge University Library, especially in the Reading Room, the Rare Books Room, and Imaging Services, for all their help over the years, and also to staff at the British Library, the National Portrait Gallery, the British Museum, the Victoria and Albert Museum, the Museum of London, Hatfield House, and the Walker Gallery in Liverpool, who have answered my queries and helped me to obtain images. But, in the words of a Maori proverb, *He aha te mea nui o te Ao? He tangata, he tangata, he tangata.* (What is the most important thing in this world? It is people, it is people, it is people.) At the University of Canterbury, New Zealand, Margaret Burrell introduced me to medieval French romance and the *hortus conclusus*, and David Gunby to *The Duchess of Malfi*; with David Carnegie and Mac Jackson, David subsequently gave me eighteen happy months of work (and invaluable experience) on *The Works of John Webster* before I came to Cambridge. In Cambridge, Pippa Berry was a doctoral supervisor of wisdom, passion, and vision; Gavin Alexander acted as an additional adviser with wit and insight, and great kindness (and went on to read the whole book in draft form). My examiners, Juliet Fleming and Blair Worden, offered much useful advice, and I have appreciated their continuing enthusiasm for the project. Anne Barton, Colin Burrow, Helen Cooper, and Raphael Lyne have always been interested and helpful; it has been a particular pleasure to have the Spenserian support of Christopher Burlinson and Andrew Zurcher, and the Jonsonian back-up of David Bevington, Martin Butler, Ian Donaldson, and Eugene Giddens. Jayne Archer and Elizabeth Goldring have been unfailingly helpful in matters Elizabethan. Paula Henderson has been tremendously generous with her time and expertise in garden history. Two anonymous readers for Oxford University Press made many useful suggestions, and I have been very grateful for the enthusiasm and support of Andrew McNeillie. I was fortunate to be a research fellow at Magdalene under the Mastership of Duncan Robinson and the Presidency of Eamon Duffy, both of them outstanding scholars, warm and witty colleagues, and men of integrity and zest. Among such a small fellowship it is invidious to single out individuals, but my life and work at Magdalene would have been much duller without the particular contributions of Simon Barrington-Ward, Andrew Brown, Aude Fitzsimons, Tim Harper, Jane Hughes, Neil Jones, Michael Keall, Silke Mentchen, Tom Nutt, Roger O'Keefe, Derek Oulton, James Rigney, and especially Carl Watkins and the inimitable Richard Luckett, as well as some of the nicest porters in Cambridge. My life would also have been duller (although the book would have been finished sooner) without my students, particularly at Magdalene, Jesus, and Christ's, and now at St Catharine's, where my colleagues Caroline Gonda and Paul Hartle have been especially welcoming and supportive. Jane Grogan, Jane Partner (who read the book in draft form), Amanda Power, Deana Rankin, Angus Vine, and Daniel Wakelin have kept me going, as has the *aroha* of Kit Grover and Keith Lewis, Christopher Bowen, Catherine Rainey, and Sue and Peter Sheriff in London, and Brigitte Murray, Nicole Moreham, Tim Smith, and Emily Ross, and my extended family, on the other side of the world. Above all, this book is for my twin sister Susannah and her husband Mark, who have given much support (and sometimes welcome distraction), my mother Sarah, who has sustained me, telephonically, electronically, and in person, ever since I left New Zealand to come to Cambridge, and for all my life before that, and my father Peter, teacher, theatrical designer, and connoisseur of beautiful things, who died when I was still at school; in many respects this is a book that only his daughter could have written.

Material in Chapters 3 and 4 appeared in an earlier form in 'Sacred and Profane Love: Four Fountains in the *Hypnerotomachia* (1499) and the *Roman de la Rose*', *Word & Image*, 22/1 (2006), 1–13, and 'Sidney's Zelmane and the *Songe de Poliphile*', *Sidney Journal*, 21 (2003), 67–75. An expanded version of part of Chapter 5 appeared in 'Location as Metaphor: *Veritas Temporis Filia* (1559) and its Afterlife', in Jayne Archer, Elizabeth Goldring, and Sarah Knight (eds.), *The Progresses, Pageants and Entertainments of Queen Elizabeth I* (Oxford: Oxford University Press, 2007), 65–85. An earlier version of some material in Chapters 5, 6, and 7 appeared in 'From the Fountain to the Well: Redcrosse Learns to Read', *Studies in Philology*, 100 (2003), 135–76, and of some material in Chapter 12 in 'A new allusion by Jonson to Spenser and Essex?', *Notes and Queries*, 50 (Mar. 2003), 63–5. Passages are quoted from *Hypnerotomachia Poliphili: The Strife of Love in a Dream* by Francesco Colonna, translated by Joscelyn Godwin © 1999 Joscelyn Godwin. Reprinted by kind permission of Thames and Hudson Ltd., London. Extracts from Martin Biddle, 'The Gardens of Nonsuch: Sources and Dating', *Garden History*, 27 (1999), 145–83 are reprinted by kind permission of the editor of *Garden History*. Images are reproduced by kind permission of the Syndics of the Cambridge

University Library, the British Library Board, the Provost and Scholars of King's College, Cambridge, the Trustees of the British Museum, the National Portrait Gallery, the Walker Art Gallery (National Museums and Galleries on Merseyside), the Trustees of the twelfth Earl of Scarborough's 1979 Settlement, and the Marquess of Salisbury.

The cover illustration shows a detail from a cushion embroidered by Bess of Hardwick, Countess of Shrewsbury, now at Hardwick Hall, © NTPL/John Hammond. It is reproduced by permission of the National Trust. I am grateful to the Master and Fellows of St Catharine's College, Cambridge, for a grant from the Fellows' Research Fund towards the cost of the illustrations.

Contents

Figures   Plates Section between pages 164–5
A Note on Translations and References   xii

    Introduction: Origins   1

PART I. SOURCES AND REFLECTIONS: THE *HYPNEROTOMACHIA POLIPHILI* (1499) AND SIDNEY'S *NEW ARCADIA* (1582–1584)

1. 'Some Fair Book': The *Hypnerotomachia Poliphili* in England   41

2. Reading Fountains in the *Hypnerotomachia*   53

3. The Fountains of Venus and Adonis: Revelation and Reflection   69

4. The Fountain of Aeneas: Sidney Rewrites the *Hypnerotomachia*   85

PART II. LIVING WATERS: SPENSER'S *THE FAERIE QUEENE* (1590)

5. *Ad Fontes*: Elizabeth and the English Bible   103

6. The Christian Knight: Redcrosse Learns to Read   122

7. The Well of Life: All Things Made New   144

8. Fountains Seen and Unseen   169

PART III. POISONED SPRINGS: JONSON'S *THE FOUNTAINE OF SELFE-LOVE* (1600)

9. The Public Fountain: Elizabethan Politics and the Humanist Tradition   197

10. A Visual Metaphor: Staging the Fountain   218

11. The Fountain of Salmacis: Self-Love and Satire   234

12. Diana's Justice: Essex, Nonsuch, and Hampton Court   255

    Conclusion   279

Bibliography   287
Index   319

A Note on Translations and References

Where translations into English are taken from a published source, I have (with one or two exceptions) not quoted the text in the original language. Where translations are my own, I have included the original text also, either in the main body of the text or in a footnote.

References for quotations from the texts that are the main subject of each chapter are given in the main body of the text, immediately following the quotation; other references are given in the footnotes. Quotations are taken from Robert Dallington, *The Strife of Love in a Dreame* (London, 1592) and *Hypnerotomachia Poliphili*, trans. Joscelyn Godwin (London: Thames and Hudson, 1999); from *The Faerie Queene*, ed. A. C. Hamilton (London: Longman, 2001); and from *The Fountaine of Selfe-Love* (London, 1601).

Introduction:
Origins

In 1596, an inventive act of vandalism temporarily transformed London's Cheapside Cross into a fountain: 'On the East side of the same Crosse, the steppes being taken thence, vnder the Image of Christes resurrection, was set vp a curious wrought frame of grey Marble, and in the same an Image in Alabaster of a woman (for the most part naked) and Thames water prilling from her breasts'.[1] The Cross was one of the twelve 'Eleanor' crosses erected by Edward I to mark the places where the funeral bier of his wife, Eleanor of Castile, had rested overnight on her funeral procession's journey from Lincoln to Westminster in December 1290. Three storeys high and covered with religious statuary, it stood in one of London's main thoroughfares, a familiar landmark for London citizens as well as a royal and religious monument. As such it was increasingly controversial and contested in the sixteenth century, and was vandalized on many occasions, as John Stow records.[2] In the second edition of his *Survay* (1603), Stow confirmed that the naked woman was Diana, familiar persona of Queen Elizabeth and the form in which she was frequently celebrated in English Renaissance literature, paintings, gardens, and fountains. When it was proposed in 1599 that the Cross be dismantled altogether, 'meaning in place therof to haue set vp a Piramis', Queen Elizabeth herself became involved, instructing that it was 'forthwith to be repaired'. A year elapsed with nothing being done,

wherevpon the said counsellors . . . wrote to William Rider then Maior, requiring him by vertue of her highnesse said former direction, and commandement, that without any further delay to accomplish the same her Maiesties most princely care therein, respecting especially the antiquitie and continuance of that monument, an ancient ensigne of Christianitie, &c. dated the 24. of December, 1600. After this a crosse of Timber was framed, set vp, coured with lead and gilded.[3]

It was vandalized again within a fortnight. By 1600 the contested iconography of the Cross had become something of a cause célèbre, witnessed by references in Ben Jonson's *The Fountaine of Selfe-Love, or Cynthias Revels*, at

---

[1] John Stow, *The Survay of London* (London, 1598), sig. R6ᵛ.
[2] It was finally demolished in 1643.
[3] John Stow, *The Survay of London* (London, 1603), sig. S7.

the end of which the dissolute courtiers are sent to the 'well of knowledge', 'That it may change the name, as you must change, | And of a stone be called *Weeping Crosse*' and, possibly, *As You Like It*, in which Rosalind assures Orlando that she 'will weep for nothing, like Diana in the fountain'.[4] The vandalized Cheapside Cross displayed, in material and monumental terms, some of the cultural preoccupations and tensions of Elizabeth's last years. Literary fountains in early modern texts can act as analogous nodal points, ways of accessing and interpreting both the aesthetic and ethical agendas of the texts in which they appear and the interpenetrations of those agendas. As real fountains attested, and as my discussion of some of their literary configurations will show, fountains in early modern England and in Renaissance literature were particularly dense signifiers, with functions that were structural and moral as well as purely aesthetic. They had an accumulated weight of symbolism, classical (especially Ovidian), religious, and humanist, and were frequently syncretic in their imagery and their associations. Both real fountains and their literary counterparts could raise questions of how to look and how to read.

England's Helicon takes its title from the hill of the Muses in ancient Boeotia and the spring located there,[5] and also from an anthology of English poetry—the first such—which appeared in 1600. The date and patriotic sentiment of the latter seems fitting, as does its intention (at the time a radical one, at least in English and in print) of assembling a new whole out of apparently disparate fragments. As one would expect of such a collection, it has fountains in abundance, but one in particular seems especially apt to the project of this second *England's Helicon*. In the poem 'The Shepheards description of Loue', a dialogue signed 'Ignoto' but sometimes attributed to Sir Walter Raleigh, Melibeus begins by posing the question 'Sheepheard, what's Loue, I pray thee tell?' to which his friend Faustus replies, 'It is that Fountaine, and that Well, | Where pleasure and repentance dwell'.[6] Similar oxymorons fill the remaining stanzas of this wholly unremarkable poem, yet in its very opening it neatly encapsulates both the copiousness and the capaciousness of the fountain figure in early modern texts.[7] *England's*

---

[4] *The Fountaine of Selfe-Love* (1601), M1; *As You Like It*, ed. Juliet Dusinberre, The Arden Shakespeare: Third Series (London: Thomson Learning, 2006), 4.1.143–4. Dusinberre cites an episode from Montemayor's *Diana* for the reference; Michael Hattaway additionally notes the London context in his Cambridge edition of the play, *As You Like It* (Cambridge: Cambridge University Press, 2000), 4.1.121–2 n. Jonson's play is the subject of Part III.

[5] The spring is properly Hippocrene, so named because it sprang out where Pegasus' hoof struck the ground, but hill and spring are in practice frequently elided.

[6] *Englands Helicon* (London, 1600), sig. L2ᵛ.

[7] The connection of the 'Well' with 'repentance' invokes the emblem tradition, which is discussed in relation to the experiences of Spenser's Redcrosse in the House of Holiness in *The Faerie Queene* 1.10 in Chapter 7.

Helicon first suggests that the fountain is a literary device that was very much of its historical moment in its capacity to syncretize a number of salient early modern concerns and cultural features. That elaborate and complex fountains were such a remarkable and important feature of the early modern English garden and city at the end of the sixteenth century suggests that their appearances in literary texts should be treated with the same interest and awareness of associative density. Hitherto, this has not been the case, perhaps because most of the fountains themselves, some of them as exotic (if on a smaller scale) as any still found in Italy, have not existed for centuries. Second, focusing on fountains in this way serves as a case study for the relocation of early modern texts in relation to their material and monumental contexts. I make a special case for fountains as figures which particularly express some early modern English cultural features and concerns, but some of the arguments regarding texts and the physical spaces in or in relation to which they were read or performed advanced here could be applied to other devices or entities which have both a significant literary and physical presence in early modern English culture. Here, I offer neither a survey nor an overview, but rather studies of texts which have not been looked at in this way before.

There are fountains in many late Elizabethan texts, and indeed in early modern texts in general they can be found in abundance. In the texts I have chosen as my focus, however—a prose romance (or two), an epic poem, and a satirical play—the fountains are central in interesting ways, above all structurally, but also ethically. As such, they exemplify the ways in which, across generic boundaries, fountains can function with great associative density, whether in structuring a narrative as physical settings for its action, or in advancing a particular political, religious, or aesthetic agenda. I draw on the works of many other writers from throughout the sixteenth century, political and religious commentators as well as writers of poetry, prose, and drama. Some become especially prominent in my discussion: George Peele, for example, in relation to Jonson's play in Chapters 9 and 10. In a study that takes in Sidney, Spenser, and Jonson, Shakespeare might seem an obvious omission. In fact, there are very few fountains 'in' Shakespeare, one notable exception being the striking fountain metaphors in *Titus Andronicus*;[8] other examples are noted in passing. Erasmus in particular is referred to throughout. The centrality of his ideas to a number of the chapters that follow will become apparent, but he is not the implicit fourth or fifth author of this author-based discussion. He is, however, a great synthesizer of ideas, about textual scholarship, political and educational theory, the Christian life,

---

[8] Discussed in Chapter 9.

and the morality of art (to identify but some of his writings upon which I draw), and himself maintained a lively interest in the interplay between the textual, the visual, and the material, paying much attention to the settings for his *Colloquies* and suggesting, for example, that *sententiae* be engraved into drinking cups and rings, walls and windows.[9] His own writings were in turn mined by those devising some of the greatest decorative schemes of the Tudor age: the windows of the chapel of King's College, Cambridge, draw many of their 'biblical' texts from Erasmus' *Paraphrases*.[10] Erasmus' influence on English intellectual, religious, political, and cultural life throughout the sixteenth century (and beyond) was profound, both as an individual writer and as a representative figure in humanist discourse; it is in both guises that he appears so often in this book.

Despite my interest in gardens and in spatiality, my choice not to discuss 'landscape entertainments' here is deliberate. To speak of 'landscape entertainments' as a genre apart suggests that they alone manifest a special relationship with the places in which they were performed. I am interested in exploring and emphasizing the points of contact and overlap between city streets and country gardens, between printed texts, dramatic performances, and the cultural and material circumstances to which they refer and in which they were produced and consumed, and will suggest here that other plays, poems, prose works, and civic pageants could exhibit, and indeed depend upon, as dynamic and integrated a relationship with their physical settings as those pieces more obviously labelled 'landscape entertainments'. These texts from Elizabeth's last decades present a literary response to and exploration of recent developments and landmarks (and I use the term deliberately) in their cultural environment, an environment which encompassed images as well as texts, and gardens and houses as well as maps. I am drawn, in describing this relationship, to the metaphor of the palimpsest, the textuality of which is similarly inextricable from its materiality. Texts accrete around the landscapes, sites, and monuments that they describe, the reality and materiality of which in turn informs the ways in which they are written about and read. In early modern England, fountains were particularly important and suggestive sites for such interplay, in the way in which they were both a real feature of the late sixteenth-century landscape and

[9] Desiderius Erasmus, *De Copia; De Ratione Studii*, trans. Betty I. Knott and Brian McGregor, ed. Craig R. Thompson (Toronto: University of Toronto Press, 1978), 671.

[10] 'Of 41 texts from the New Testament [displayed by the "messenger" figures in the windows of the north and south sides of the chapel], 12 correspond exactly with Erasmus' version, and 11 more are very close.' Hilary Wayment, *The Windows of King's College Chapel Cambridge: A Description and Commentary* (London: Oxford University Press, 1972), 35 n. 2.

a prominent metaphor in the period's discourses of religion, politics, and literature.

What follows, in the remainder of the Introduction, sets out the context for this project. First, there is a brief survey of recent developments in garden history and theory, and other pertinent cultural and critical approaches. Next, there is a more detailed account of some conceptual frameworks, especially drawing on the writings of Gaston Bachelard, and also setting out the importance of Ovid's *Metamorphoses*. A third section begins by examining how the expectations of English travellers in Italian gardens in the sixteenth and seventeenth centuries were shaped by classical texts, above all by the *Epistles* of Pliny the Younger, and goes on to explore the ways in which these English travellers reacted to—and read—the Italian gardens they visited within a classical paradigm, finishing with a consideration of the ways in which English gardening manuals of the period treated fountains and other garden ornaments. The next section surveys fountains in medieval texts—Chrétien's *Yvain*, the *Roman de la Rose*, the *Tristan*, Chaucer, and Malory—setting out the literary background. A final section makes the case for an interdisciplinary approach to early modern literature and culture, and is followed by a brief synopsis of the remainder of the book.

England's Helicon is not a simple motif study of fountains in English Renaissance literature: it is, rather, an investigation of how literary fountains both inform and are informed by real fountains in early modern literature and culture and, more, what sort of *modus legendi* might be (re)formulated that would take account of the interpenetrations and elisions of the textual, visual, material, and experiential in early modern England. While its focus remains the literature of the late sixteenth century, *England's Helicon* recognizes that intertextuality and influence can be material as well as literary. It demonstrates that the 'missing piece' needed to make sense of a passage in a play, a poem, or a prose romance could be a fountain, a conduit, a well, or a reflecting pool, in general or even in a specific, known garden. As well as considering some of the lost gardens, lost fountains, and lost landscapes of early modern England, *England's Helicon* takes objects and images that do survive—portraits, jewellery, textiles—and employs them as 'ways in', material and experiential points of access that, by soliciting ways of seeing, reading, and apprehending which are not straightforwardly (inter)textual, suggest by analogy some of the modes in which these lost gardens and their fountains and their relationships with texts might similarly be recovered. A hat-badge is not a fountain, and neither is an embroidered book-binding (even if both depict fountains)[11] but both are inextricable

---

[11] These are discussed in Chapters 7 and 5 respectively.

from ideas about reading and textuality, and demand particular strategies of interpretation that might plausibly parallel those called for in recovering some of the relationships between real and literary fountains in the English Renaissance.

Fountains, springs, wells, and 'sources' are far from being dead metaphors in Renaissance literature: they are frequently lively, complex, and concrete. To think about early modern literary texts and visual, material, and experiential culture in this way is more than simply a matter of writing good footnotes, identifying the 'real' referents of literary allusions, or broadly applying the cultural studies premiss that all cultural productions are texts. Early modern English gardens and fountains are, sadly, almost all lost, but to approach them through literary texts—sometimes through other images and objects of the period also—is often to recover them in new ways. This is the project that *England's Helicon* undertakes and, while an awareness of the vital interconnectedness between the textual, the visual, and the material is currently animating literary critical work, it is already the essence of the Renaissance garden, and one might say of the Renaissance itself.

WRITING THE HISTORY OF RENAISSANCE GARDENS

The history of Renaissance gardens, and in particular of Renaissance gardens in England, is a small and increasingly well-researched field.[12] In the last few years much has been done to reconstruct early modern English gardens, using contemporary descriptions, archival material (such as household accounts), and archaeological remains. While Roy Strong's statement in *The Renaissance Garden in England* (1979) that no gardens of the period still exist has been technically disproved (as he himself has admitted) by archaeological investigations and in particular by aerial photography, the fact remains that in England there are no equivalents of the Boboli Gardens, of Pratolino or Versailles. Because the gardens of the Italian (and the French) Renaissance are a much larger, more fertile and recoverable field, much more work has been done on them, going beyond simple reconstructive investigations. Several

[12] To write about gardens in relation to literary texts makes one aware of the extent to which such discussions must inevitably employ the metaphors of gardening: as Anne Salmond puts it, '*knowledge is a landscape*', 'Theoretical Landscapes: On a Cross-cultural Conception of Knowledge', in David Parkin (ed.), *Semantic Anthropology* (London: Academic Press, 1982), 67. A list of sources for English and Italian Renaissance gardens and fountains can be found in the Bibliography; the most recent contribution to the field is Paula Henderson's magnificent *The Tudor House and Garden* (New Haven: Yale University Press, 2005).

specialist studies have been made of their fountains, and of fountains in French and Italian urban settings, for, as Elisabeth MacDougall comments, 'fountains, or to state it more broadly, the decorations associated with water, were the most important feature of [Italian] Renaissance gardens'.[13] No comparable study has been made of early modern English fountains and, given the apparent paucity of detailed evidence, it seems unlikely that a full-length historical study will ever eventuate. In particular, this book is not one such, although it does give detailed accounts of a number of the great gardens and fountains of early modern England. It is a generation since Strong's *The Renaissance Garden in England*, and while the detail of this and his other studies may have been challenged and revised, their breadth and their awareness of the interconnectedness of Renaissance art, (material) culture, and literature have perhaps been overlooked by more recent scholars anxious to distance themselves from the 'cult of Elizabeth'.[14] Yet (to take but one small point of contact) the Queen is at the heart of Spenser's *Faerie Queene* and Jonson's *The Fountaine of Selfe-Love*, and she has a significant implied presence in Sidney's *Arcadia*, and it is not going too far to suggest that her celebration as Diana in her later years was partly responsible for the vogue for elaborate garden fountains, some of which even featured sculptural representations of Diana, in the same period.

Even before the appearance of Paula Henderson's *The Tudor House and Garden* (2005), Roy Strong's work had been supplemented and in many particulars superseded by a number of detailed archaeological and archival studies of specific Renaissance gardens, such as Kenilworth, Theobalds, and Nonsuch. Yet this recent industry has not been matched by a similar level of renewed interest in the relationship between gardens and literature. In the years following Strong, a number of such studies appeared. In 'Spenser, Sidney, and the Renaissance Garden', for example, Michael Leslie compared the moral didacticism of episodes in Sidney's *Arcadia* and Spenser's *The Faerie Queene* with the instructive nature of gardens such as Nonsuch and Kenilworth. He argued that 'the literary gardens of the English Renaissance depend upon and

[13] See in particular Elisabeth MacDougall (ed.), *Fons Sapientiae: Renaissance Garden Fountains* (Washington, DC: Dumbarton Oaks, 1978) and Naomi Miller, *French Renaissance Fountains* (New York: Garland, 1977).

[14] See the discussion of this scholarly prejudice and the need for its re-evaluation in the introduction to Julia M. Walker, *Dissing Elizabeth: Negative Representations of Gloriana* (Durham, NC: Duke University Press, 1998), 3–4. Kevin Sharpe observes that 'Thirty years ago, Strong lamented that "the study of British art during this period has suffered because of isolation from the general currents of political, religious, cultural and social history" . . . With one or two brilliant exceptions, Strong's case for such an art history of early modern England has still not been answered,' Kevin Sharpe, *Remapping Early Modern England: The Culture of Seventeenth-Century Politics* (Cambridge: Cambridge University Press, 2000), 26–7.

direct us to contemporary gardening, as well as the literary tradition of the *locus amoenus* normally adduced',[15] but he did not go much beyond the literal occurrences of gardens in literature. Terry Comito's 'Beauty Bare: Speaking Waters and Fountains in Renaissance Literature' largely referred to Italian texts, and paid more attention to the watery than the architectural component of fountains, although he gestured at some of the same points I will make here.[16] Several scholars, most prominently Michael Leslie and John Dixon Hunt, who published their first essays on Renaissance gardens and literature as literary critics, have since moved further into the area of garden history and theory. In the last decade innovative work in these areas has largely emanated from the United States, notably from Dumbarton Oaks and the University of Pennsylvania, and it has increasingly emphasized non-elite (or 'vernacular') gardens, urban gardens, and non-European gardens. But the particular field opened up by Strong, and by Leslie, Comito, Dixon Hunt, and others, has never been thoroughly explored, especially not taking into account new directions in the cultural-historical study of materiality and spatiality. The interesting and suggestive work that has recently been produced in this area, notably by Lawrence Manley, Peter Stallybrass, and Ann Rosalind Jones,[17] has largely been confined to dramatic texts, with little attention being paid to poetry or prose romance.

SOME WAYS OF THINKING ABOUT FOUNTAINS

What is it about a fountain, whether in a garden, a city street, or a literary text, that makes it any different from a statue or a tree? Some of the qualities and characteristics of fountains, and of fountains in Renaissance gardens in particular, are particularly pertinent to their literary appearances. The first is that early modern fountains were not the perpetually playing devices familiar today. Uncertainties of water supply or mechanism often meant that they were only turned on for special occasions, such as the entertainment of visitors. The sculptural component of fountains was therefore particularly important,

---

[15] Michael Leslie, 'Spenser, Sidney and the Renaissance Garden', *English Literary Renaissance*, 22 (1992).

[16] Terry Comito, 'Beauty Bare: Speaking Waters and Fountains in Renaissance Literature', in MacDougall (ed.), *Fons Sapientiae*, 15–58. See also Terry Comito, 'Caliban's Dream: The Topography of Some Shakespeare Gardens', *Shakespeare Studies*, 14 (1981), 23–54.

[17] Lawrence Manley, *Literature and Culture in Early Modern London* (Cambridge: Cambridge University Press, 1995); Ann Rosalind Jones and Peter Stallybrass, *Renaissance Clothing and the Materials of Memory* (Cambridge: Cambridge University Press, 2000).

as they frequently existed as static tableaux of statues and pools. In theory, if not in practice, their reflective quality was prominent. It seems unlikely that visitors to the great gardens of early modern England were allowed to wander them unguided, and the many similarities between the descriptions given by tourists suggest that prescribed routes were followed. Fountains therefore frequently functioned as focal points in a garden, giving it a quasi-rhetorical structure, impelling visitors through the landscape.

A fountain combines a material structure with the manipulation of an element, water. It compels attention on a number of physical levels, offering coolness, the quenching of thirst, the opportunity to gaze upon a reflection. Discussing the semiotics of sculpture in general, Michael O'Toole observes that sculpture 'makes us acutely and immediately aware of our body', through its scale, its frequent representation of the human form, and its tactility. Representational sculpture is implicitly animate, and frequently numinous,[18] and all of these qualities are enhanced and magnified by the presence of water; as Geneviève Bresc-Boutier puts it, a fountain is 'un type de monument qui existe concrètement, mais dont on rêve' (a kind of monument that exists in concrete terms, but of which one also dreams).[19] Fountains are not passive: they capture observers, drawing them into their surfaces, promising refreshment, and so involving those who gaze upon or into them in an active and sometimes demanding relationship. It is a paradox of the fountain that it can present both (reflective) surface and profundity, both the finitude of containment and concrete location and the suggestion of ceaseless flow and infinite depth. Recent work in garden theory has emphasized that gardens are, in general, experienced in motion: 'the experience of moving through the material world of the garden in present time transports visitors into the different world and temporality of a narrative'.[20] This narrative is shaped not only by shifting spatial configurations and changing visual perspectives but by overt interventions in the landscape also, such as garden buildings, sculpture, inscriptions, and fountains. But when a visitor to a garden pauses in his or her own motion to gaze at or into a fountain, his or her subjective experience continues to be one of movement, that of light and water. Terry Comito observed that, in fountains, 'the constant element is the paradoxical juxtaposition of movement and stillness . . . we see through the water and also

---

[18] See Michael O'Toole, *The Language of Displayed Art* (London: Leicester University Press, 1994), 32–8. He does not specifically discuss fountains.

[19] Geneviève Bresc-Boutier, 'Fontaines laïques de la première Renaissance française: les marbres de Tours, de Blois et de Gaillon', in *Sources et fontaines du Moyen Âge à l'Âge Baroque* (Paris: Honoré Champion Éditeur, 1998), 185.

[20] Michel Conan, 'Landscape Metaphors and Metamorphosis of Time', in Michel Conan (ed.), *Landscape Design and the Experience of Motion* (Washington, DC: Dumbarton Oaks Research Library and Collection, 2003), 302.

by means of the water'.[21] The capacity of a fountain to reflect, and to frame that reflection as the object of art or fiction, blurs the distinction between subject and object. As Gaston Bachelard put it,

Le miroir de la fontaine est donc l'occasion d'une *imagination ouverte*. Le reflet un peu vague, un peu pâli, suggère une idéalisation. Devant l'eau qui réfléchit son image, Narcisse sent que sa beauté *continue*, qu'elle n'est pas achevée, qu'il faut l'achever. Les miroirs de verre, dans la vive lumière de la chambre, donnent une image trop stable.[22]

To look into a fountain is to see oneself; its surface is the space of imagination.

It is not surprising, given their liminality and their blurring of the boundaries between art and nature, that many Renaissance gardens and fountains drew on Ovid's *Metamorphoses* for their imagery and controlling narratives.[23] Metamorphosis involving water is perhaps the 'ur-metamorphosis', for water is itself a metamorphic element. Although Bachelard mostly discusses rivers and the sea, he does suggest in general that 'L'eau est vraiment l'élément transitoire. Il est la métamorphose ontologique essentielle entre le feu et la terre' (Water is truly the transitory element. It is the essential, ontological metamorphosis between fire and earth).[24] In Linda Gregerson's useful formulation, 'The optical phenomena that make natural looking glasses of fountains and pools and springs and wells are commonly augmented in Renaissance narrative by the Ovidian tradition that makes of these kindred bodies natural repositories for the temperamental or ethical or erotic burden of fable'.[25] For my discussion of fountains here, three Ovidian episodes are particularly important: the confrontation between Diana and Actaeon, the story of Narcissus, and that of Salmacis and Hermaphroditus. All three foreground anxieties over desire, specularity, and identity; the first two in particular implicate the spectator or reader in the moral and psychological consequences of the gaze. In all

[21] Comito, 'Beauty Bare', 24.

[22] Gaston Bachelard, *L'Eau et les rêves: essai sur l'imagination de la matière* (Paris: Librairie José Corti, 1947), 33. 'The mirror that a fountain provides, then, is the opportunity for *open imagination*. This reflection, a little vague and pale, suggests idealization. Standing before the water which reflects his image, Narcissus feels that his beauty *continues*, has not come to an end, and must be completed. In the bright light of a room, glass mirrors give too stable an image.' Gaston Bachelard, *Water and Dreams: An Essay on the Imagination of Matter*, trans. Edith R. Farrell (Dallas: The Dallas Institute of Humanities and Culture, 1983), 21–2.

[23] See Charles Martindale, *Ovid Renewed: Ovidian Influences on Literature and Art from the Middle Ages to the Twentieth Century* (Cambridge: Cambridge University Press, 1988), 1.

[24] Bachelard, *L'Eau et les rêves*, 8–9; Bachelard, *Water and Dreams*, 6. The source here is Plato's *Timaeus* 49; see Chapter 7, n. 57. See also the discussion by Hélène Casanova-Robin, *Diane et Actéon: éclats et reflets d'un mythe à la Renaissance et à l'Âge Baroque* (Paris: Honoré Champion Éditeur, 2003), 216 f.

[25] Linda Gregerson, *The Reformation of the Subject: Spenser, Milton, and the English Protestant Epic* (Cambridge: Cambridge University Press, 1995), 34.

three, the water of a fountain[26] is the catalyst for the transformation or loss of identity. There are other, more minor, Ovidian episodes involving fountains which operate in a similar way, such as the stories of Biblis and Niobe and, more subtly, Python and Echidna. Elisabeth B. MacDougall notes that when looking at the fountains of Renaissance gardens, 'spectators could easily recognize the myths represented; they were also accustomed both by their religious training and by their classical education to look for a deeper meaning below the level of the myth'.[27] Considering that MacDougall made this observation a quarter of a century ago, it is surprising that so little attention has been paid to the analogous functions of real or metaphorical fountains in Renaissance texts, especially given that, as Sarah Annes Brown persuasively articulates it, concluding her discussion of the Actaeon motif, 'Although the matrix of myth is but one of the many entrances into the Renaissance docuverse, Ovid's *Metamorphoses* seems a particularly apt portal, for as well as having a fluid, open structure it presents a universe where selfhood is multiple and fractured, where all boundaries, not just textual ones, are radically unstable'.[28] Renaissance gardens and their fountains share many of these characteristics. A second strand of classical, if not specifically Ovidian, imagery further associates fountains with poetry and the act of poetic inspiration and creation, and hence (on occasion) with language in general. Poetic inspiration, personified by the Muses, is associated with the springs on Mount Helicon, Hippocrene and Aganippe, and the Castalian Spring on Mount Parnassus, home of Apollo, the god of poetry. The description of the poets of the past as pure fountains, whose works both inspire and function as a model which the modern poet can never hope to emulate, is a motif notably found in Spenser.[29]

ENGLISH TRAVELLERS IN ITALIAN GARDENS

Classical descriptions of gardens and fountains influenced both English writers and English travellers' expectations, experiences, and descriptions of Italian

[26] 'Fons' is the word for all three, translated by both Golding and Sandys as 'fountain' or 'spring'. The relevant passages in the *Metamorphoses* are 3.155 f. (Actaeon), 3.407 f. (Narcissus), and 4.306 f. (Salmacis).

[27] Elisabeth B. MacDougall and Naomi Miller, *Fons Sapientiae: Garden Fountains in Illustrated Books: Sixteenth–Eighteenth Centuries* (Washington, DC: Dumbarton Oaks, 1977), p. x.

[28] Sarah Annes Brown, 'Arachne's Web: Intertextual Mythography and the Renaissance Actaeon', in Neil Rhodes and Jonathan Sawday (eds.), *The Renaissance Computer: Knowledge Technology in the First Age of Print*, ed. (London: Routledge, 2000), 132.

[29] *The Faerie Queene*, 4.2.32; 7.7.9.

gardens. They provided them with a set of topoi around which to base their own accounts or descriptions, and they also gave them a catalogue of some of the different kinds and qualities of fountains. The *Epistolae* of Pliny the Younger, for example, are an implicit source for much writing about early modern gardens and, although they were not available in an English translation at the time, the descriptions that two of the letters in particular contain of his villas and their gardens exercised a considerable influence over Renaissance ideas about classical gardens, Italian gardens, and ideal gardens. The first of these describes Pliny's Laurentine villa, paying particular attention to the way in which the house and its garden are integrated into the surrounding landscape. Although there are apparently no fountains *per se* at this villa, the excellence of the estate is confirmed by its being well irrigated:

Only one thing is needed to complete the amenities and beauty of the house—running water; but there are wells, or rather springs, for they are very near the surface. It is in fact a remarkable characteristic of this shore that wherever you dig you come upon water at once which is pure and not in the least brackish, although the sea is so near.[30]

The Laurentum villa was primarily a winter residence, so it is not surprising that fountains were not one of its features. A second letter, however, describes Pliny's Tuscan villa, which was apparently full of fountains. As with the previous description, much is made of the ease with which one can move from garden to house, and of the sheltered garden spaces within the house itself: 'Almost opposite the middle of the colonnade is a suite of rooms set slightly back and round a small court shaded by four plane trees. In the centre a fountain plays in a marble basin, watering the plane trees round it and the ground beneath them with its light spray'.[31] In one of the bedrooms off the courtyard was 'a small fountain with a bowl surrounded by tiny jets which together make a lovely murmuring sound' and nearby there was 'an ornamental pool, a pleasure both to see and to hear, with its water falling from a great height, and foaming white when it strikes the marble'.[32] The next fountain described introduces the particular capacity of fountains for extreme artifice and hidden devices; it consists of

a curved dining-seat of white marble, shaded by a vine trained over four slender pillars of Carystian marble. Water gushes out through pipes from under the seat as if pressed out by the weight of people sitting there, is caught in a stone cistern and then held in a finely-worked marble basin which is regulated by a hidden device so as to remain full without overflowing. The preliminaries and main dishes for dinner are placed on

[30] Pliny the Younger, *Letters and Panegyricus*, trans. Betty Radice (Cambridge, Mass.: Harvard University Press, 1969), 2.17.26.
[31] Ibid., 5.6.20.   [32] Ibid., 5.6.23–4.

the edge of the basin, while the lighter ones float about in vessels shaped like birds or little boats.[33]

The device of the dining table upon which dishes were floated in a channel of water was certainly copied in Italian gardens. Pliny's descriptions of his gardens may not have had much direct influence over garden design in Renaissance England, but they were indubitably one of the *loci classici* of literary garden description.

One of the better-informed sixteenth-century accounts of travels in Italy was written by Sir Thomas Hoby, traveller, Marian exile, diplomat, and the translator of Castiglione's *The Book of the Courtier* (1561). Hoby's accounts of his travels are found in *A book of the Travaile and Lief of me, Thomas Hoby*, which covers the years from about 1550 to 1565, the year before Hoby's death at the age of 36. The passages describing or mentioning fountains have a number of features which continue to appear in similar and more elaborate descriptions over the next eighty years, and beyond. For example, Hoby used the word 'fountain' to describe a range of water features, both natural and artificial, in the space of three pages noting that the Neapolitan hinterland 'hath . . . sweete fountaynes and verie helthsom springs', commenting on 'the temperate fountaynes of Baia, Lucrino and Averno', and stating that 'Naples is a verie beawtifull citie situated betwext the seea and verie pleasant hilles, full of howses, well fortified of late dayes with a strong wall that th'Emperor hathe begonne abowt yt, replenisshed with sumptious palaces, delicious gardines, and sundrie divises of fountaynes round abowt yt'.[34] Hoby's use of the word 'divises' here is significant, identifying the capacity of fountains for the display of conspicuous artifice. Fountains can offer a kind of intellectual pleasure, as the observer attempts to understand and appreciate their symbolism and mechanics. It also suggests that fountains, like heraldry and other iconographical programmes, can be imbued with various significations and 'read' by the alert and prepared observer. In Messina,

For a new worke, and that not finisshed at my being there, I saw a fountaine of verie white marble graven with the storie of Acteon and such other, by on Giovan Angelo, a Florentine, which to my eyes is on of the fairest peece of worke that ever I sawe. This fountain was appointed to be sett uppe before the hige churche where there is an old on alreadie.[35]

Thus the idea of fountains as devices to be read is elaborated: fountains can depict narrative as well as single static images. In this case the narrative was one

[33] Ibid., 5.6.36–7.
[34] Thomas Hoby, 'The Travels and Life of Sir Thomas Hoby', ed. E. Powell, *Camden Miscellany*, 10, 3rd ser. 4 (1902), 28–30.
[35] Ibid., 45. 'Giovan Angelo' is identified by Powell as Giovanni Agnolo Montorsoli, d. 1563. 'A description of his work at Messina is given in Vasari's *Lives*', 45 n.

of Ovidian transgression and transformation itself centred on a fountain, and the Ovidian theme continued, for in Syracuse Hoby found the spring which supplied the town with water worthy of a passage of lengthy and discursive description:

Undernethe the rocke there issuethe owt suche abundance of water and so sweeftlie that it is straunge to behold: and it cumethe not xl foote from the rocke but it entrethe into the haven. This springe or litle river that I may call it findeth all the towne with water, and thither they bring asses with great earthen pottes upon their backs to fetch it home to their howses. It issueth from under the rocke as thowgh it had some trouble by the way, as the water hath that cummeth from an hige mountain emong great stones. The colour of it is like unto water when it is sodd. In drinking it hathe a tast above other waters somwhitt like unto whay. Of the origion of it there have bine sundrie opinions. For sum have ghessed that it cummeth from Arcadia, where it entrethe into the earthe and goethe under the sea and so ariseth again in this place according to Ovid, lib. v. Metamorph: Quae tibi causa fugae? Cur sis Arethusa sacer fons?[36] And again in the same place:

> Delia rupit humum: caecisque ego mersa cavernis
> Advehor Ortigiam:[37]

The Siracusani that inhabited the citie were also called Arethusides by the name of this fountain, as Ovid makethe mention 4 Fast. Utque Siracusas Arethusidas abstulit armis Claudius.[38] Sum other say it cummethe owt of the yland of Sicilia: which in my opinion is unliklie, bicause the towne or the yland of Siracusa is invironed on the land side with drie rocks and betwext those rocks and the towne there is a plaine where we enter into the towne. And again it is to great abundance of water, and issuethe owt to swiftlie, to have his beginning in the litle rocke upon the whiche the towne standethe invironed with salt water. Not farr from this fountain there are certain springes within the seea which arise owt of the bottom and discover on the toppe withowt anie tast at all of the salt water.[39]

Hoby found the spring scientifically interesting, and weighed up the various explanations for it in a measured way. But he also approached it as a place where it was possible literally to 'tap into' a different history, a different narrative; one that was, once again, Ovidian. The fountain becomes a place of intertextuality, as Hoby interweaves his own narrative with the canonical texts of Ovid, with local tradition, and with quasi-scientific speculation. Soon after visiting the Arethusa fountain, he came upon another site associated with a local tradition of transformation, near Patria/Linternum: 'Emong the ruines

---

[36] 'Why did you flee? Why, Arethusa, are you now a sacred spring?', Ovid, *Metamorphoses*, trans. Frank Justus Miller (3rd edn. Cambridge, Mass: Harvard University Press, 1977), 5.573.

[37] 'My Delian goddess cleft the earth, and I, plunging down into the dark depths, was borne hither to Ortygia', Ibid., 5.639–40.

[38] 'When Claudius carried Arethusian Syracuse by force of arms', Ibid., 4.873.

[39] 'The Travels and Life of Sir Thomas Hoby', 48–9.

here there is a fountain or spring of sowre water, which th'inhabitants saye is good for the headache, and yf a mann drink unordinatlie of yt, yt makethe him dronke as wine dothe'.[40] The element of transformation here is not specifically Ovidian, but the moral appended to it (excessive drinking of the medicinal waters will lead to drunkenness, itself a byword for excess) allows Hoby to place it very much within the same broad tradition.

As Thomas Hoby travelled through the landscape of mid-sixteenth-century Italy, apparently simultaneously (although in fact probably retrospectively) constructing his autobiography and travelogue, he was creating, participating in, and invoking a number of narratives. Like other travellers, Hoby was aware that he was in a place that was at once 'modern', 'classical', and legendary; like them he looked to understand and enhance his experience of the present by recourse to the stories of the past. Some travellers made personal compendia of the relevant classical texts to take with them before setting off from England, as an adjunct to or even a substitute for one of the more conventional guidebooks of the day; one such exhorted the traveller 'where you shall set your feet, or cast your eie: but you shall haue occasion to call into remembraunce, that which is set down in *Livie, Salust, Polibius, Plyny, Tacitus, Dion,* and *Dionisius*'.[41] Hoby himself interacted with the local people, who passed on to him their own mixtures of folklore and the classical tradition. Local Italian guides (although Hoby himself does not comment on this) were well aware that it was in their interests to show their clients what they wanted to see, generally sites associated with classical history and mythology, the distinction between the two often being difficult to draw. Virgil's tomb and Cicero's villa were great tourist attractions, however spurious they may have been: the party shown the purported site of the Elysian fields, however, were probably rightly sceptical. Overlaid onto these external influences are Hoby's own acts of intellectual and cultural interpretation, as well as his expressions of his purely subjective aesthetic pleasure and excitement. Hoby's descriptions of fountains are instances where all these strands of narrative are particularly likely to intersect and interpenetrate.

Upon his return to England, Thomas Hoby settled at Bisham in Berkshire, and he continued both to keep his diary (although in a much more rudimentary form) and to maintain his evident interest in gardens. In 1562 'were the garden and orchard planted at Bissham', and in 1563 'was the water

---

[40] Ibid., 57.

[41] *A direction for trauailers Taken out of Iustus Lipsius, and enlarged for the behoofe of the right honorable Lord, the yong Earle of Bedford, being now ready to trauell* (London, 1592), sig. B4–B4ᵛ. This is quoted and discussed by Christy Anderson, 'Learning to Read Architecture in the English Renaissance', in Lucy Gent (ed.), *Albion's Classicism: The Visual Arts in Britain, 1550–1660* (New Haven: Yale University Press, 1995), 253.

brought in lead from Puddings to the house, and the fountain placed in the garden at Bissham'.[42] No record of Hoby's own fountain survives, and it is extremely unlikely that it resembled any of the great fountains he saw in Italy that he described with such enthusiasm. But Hoby's construction of his own fountain upon his return to England does suggest another of their characteristics—their aspirational quality—that was an important part of the appearances of fountains in early modern English gardens, both real and ideal.

The travel writings of Englishmen abroad in the late sixteenth and early seventeenth centuries are (initially, at least) beguiling and apparently wonderfully informative, but they quickly become (with some notable exceptions) monotonous, as the same marvels and attractions are described with almost unaltered raptures by one writer after another. This is not necessarily an indication of a remarkable uniformity of expectation, experience, and expression among the young travellers: rather it points to one of the realities of the genre, which was that most travellers' accounts were written up retrospectively and often at many years' distance, either from memory or from brief notes, and frequently using other travellers' diaries and gazetteers as aides-mémoires (or cribs). The same was true of European travellers writing about England, and there is often blurred ground between the two groups: Paul Hentzner's journal, for example, one of the best known of such texts, draws heavily in many places on Camden's *Britannia*. Fynes Moryson's *Itinerary* (1617) is concerned largely with his travels in the 1590s, Robert Dallington's *A Survey of the great dukes state of Tuscany: In the yeare of our Lord 1596* was not published until 1605,[43] and George Sandys' *A Relation of a Iourney begun An: Dom: 1610* appeared in 1615.

Sandys' text is extremely conventional. It is particularly valuable for its discussion of fountains, however, because Sandys went on to publish the first English translation of Ovid's *Metamorphoses* (1621–32) and also because it includes an account of the same spring in Syracuse described by Thomas Hoby sixty years earlier. Sandys' classical interests and abilities are already apparent in his travelogue:

Ortygia stands at the vttermost extent, an Iland ioyned by a bridge to the rest: Wherein is the so chanted fountaine of *Arathusa*. Once a nymph of *Arcadia*, (as they fable) and beloued of the riuer *Alpheus*: turned into a spring by *Diana* for safeguard of her chastity, and conducted by her vnder seas and earth, reascended in this Iland. Followed notwithstanding by her louer.

---

[42] 'The Travels and Life of Sir Thomas Hoby', 129.
[43] Unfortunately for the readers of his translation of the *Hypnerotomachia* (1592) who have sought to argue that his translation shows evidence of his having travelled in Italy, nothing suggests that he had ever been to Italy before 1596.

Against Plemmyrium in Sicanian bay,
There lies an Ile, earst call'd Ortygia.
Hither Alpheus vnder seas (fame goes)
From Elis straid; and at thy mouth arose
Lou'd Arathuse: from whence to seas he flowes.

They so coniecturing, for that this fountaine was said to grow thicke, and sauour of garbidge, at such time as they celebrated the Olympiads: and defiled the riuer with the bloud and entrailes of the sacrifices. But *Strabo* derides the conceit, though (besides diuers more ancient authors) it be affirmed by *Seneca*, and others. The fountaine is ample, and sendeth to the adioyning sea a plentifull tribute. Before, and euen in the dayes of *Diodorus* the *Sicilian*, a number of sacred fishes were nourished herein, so said to be, for that whosoeuer did eate of them (though in time of war) were afflicted with sundry calamities.[44]

This account is obviously lengthier and more erudite than Hoby's, with its self-conscious display of learning and copious quotation of authorities. The real fountain collapses beneath the weight of citation: Sandys makes no attempt to describe it physically, let alone to personalize his description with any reference to his own observations and experiences. Elsewhere he describes the gardens of the Duke of Toledo as 'A place of surpassing delight: in which are many excellent statues, recouered from the decayes of antiquity; and euery where fountaines of fresh water, adorned with Nymphes and Satyres: where the artificiall rocks, shells, mosse and tophas, seeme, euen to excell that which they imitate'.[45] John Dixon Hunt, citing the same passage, observes that Sandys 'could be expected to recognise readily the Ovidian resonance of Italian gardens'.[46] The two descriptions (of Syracuse and Naples) are in many ways analogous. Sandys 'peoples' the spring at Syracuse with mythological figures (Arethusa, Alpheus, and Diana), while the Duke filled his gardens with Ovidian statuary. Sandys is dependent upon a literary and historical framework—upon art—to conceptualize and describe his experience of nature, while the Duke had, in his garden, used 'artificiall rocks, shells, mosse and tophas, [which] seeme, euen to excell that which they imitate'. The English writer claims authority for himself by effacing his own subjectivity and replacing it with the accounts and interpretations of classical authors, in whose company he implicitly enrols himself, so asserting himself through a rhetorical display of knowledge. The Italian noble used his garden as a theatre in which to

[44] George Sandys, *A relation of a iourney begun an: Dom: 1610 Foure bookes. Containing a description of the Turkish Empire, of AEgypt, of the Holy Land, of the remote parts of Italy, and ilands adioyning* (London, 1615), sig. X6ᵛ–Y1.

[45] Ibid., sig. Aa4ᵛ.

[46] John Dixon Hunt, *Garden and Grove: The Italian Renaissance Garden in the English Imagination 1600–1750* (rev. edn. Philadelphia: University of Pennsylvania Press, 1996), 50. Dixon Hunt includes a chapter entitled 'Ovid in the Garden', 42–58.

display his wealth and power through his manipulation of nature and art and hence his control over those who visited it. Both use fountains, one virtually metaphorical, the others literal (and, in the case of the Duke, presumably the garden at large, although Sandys's description is concerned only with what appear to be grottoes and fountains) as a measure of self-fashioning, by asserting the power that they have over the gaze of others.

Robert Dallington's and Fynes Moryson's accounts are more straightforward, and both concentrate in particular on the garden of Pratolino, which Dallington introduces thus:

> But aboue all, the great Dukes Pallace of *Pratolino* built by his brother *Francesco*, is the most admirable, not for the Pallace it selfe, or manner of the building; for there are manie can match it, if not excel it. But for the exquisite and rare inuention of Water-workes wherein it is excellent, and thought to exceede *Tiuoli* by *Rome*.[47]

The fountains are the aspect of Pratolino which determines its magnificence, displaying the wealth and good taste of its owner and the artistic skills of those whom he has been discerning enough to employ. Dallington goes on to describe the house, situated and ordered 'so as according to the winde or sunne, [the Duke] may giue his entertainment for the best ease of them he feasteth',[48] and then the giant sculpture of the Apennines which was (and is) one of the garden's most notable features:

> Out of his mouth falleth into a very faire poole, al the water that serues the worke on the other side the Pallace, among which are many sights yeelding very great content, as Noes Arke with all kinds of beasts, Hercules fighting with a Dragon, Birdes artificially singing, Organs musically playing, showres of raine plentifully downe powring, and infinite sort of such deuise, more delightsome to be seene, then pleasant to bee discoursed of.[49]

As well as showing what a prominent feature the waterworks are at Pratolino, Dallington draws attention to their aesthetic and intellectual appeal as curiosities and marvels. His conclusion is especially telling: 'To conclude, the deuise so good, the workemanship so rare, and the charge so great, as it is said constantly that it cost Duke *Francesco* three hundred thousand Crownes'.[50] In Dallington's description Francesco di Medici's garden becomes, like Sandys' description of Syracuse and the garden of the Duke of Toledo, an exercise in rhetorical self-fashioning. Its fountains (even without any mention of their symbolism or iconographic programme) are central to this: their 'deuise' and 'workemanship' correspond to *inventio* and *dispositio*, and the bottom line is

---

[47] Robert Dallington, *A suruey of the great dukes state of Tuscany In the yeare of our Lord 1596* (London, 1605), sig. C2ᵛ.
[48] Ibid., sig. C3.   [49] Ibid.   [50] Ibid.

their cost. Although Dallington makes no mention of it, one of the features of Pratolino and of the other Florentine Medici garden, Boboli, was that in contrast to, for example, the gardens of the Villa d'Este at Tivoli near Rome, there was no ready and reliable source of water. That there was water at Pratolino at all was in itself an assertion of the power and wealth of the Medici, even before its manipulation for their aesthetic and symbolic ends.

Fynes Moryson must have been travelling in Italy at roughly the same time as Robert Dallington, although his mammoth account of his travels throughout Europe, complete with exhaustive descriptions of the clothing, customs, buildings, and monuments and even currency of each country he visited, including England, did not appear in print until 1617. Moryson noted many fountains in his travels, in both garden and civic or urban settings. In Bologna in 1594, for example, he observed that 'towards the West-side of the City, is a large market place twoforked, in which is a faire conduit of water, with the Images of *Neptune*, and diuers Goddesses powring water out of their mouthes and breasts, and all made of mettall', while Pisaro 'hath a faire round Market-place, and a plesant Fountaine therein, distilling water at eight pipes'. Moryson describes fountains all over Italy: they are a standard feature of his gazetteer-like descriptions, especially of smaller towns, and on occasion, he apparently regarded a town's fountain as being its only feature of note: 'Viterbo was of old called Faliscum, and it hath 3 Cities within the Wals: but we passing suddenly through it, I obserued nothing markeable but a faire Fountaine in the Market-place'.[51]

Like Robert Dallington, Moryson devotes a lengthy passage of description to Pratolino, introducing it by alluding to the cost of the waterworks: 'the conduits whereof for water if a man well consider, he may iustly say of the gardens of *Italy*, as *Mounster* saith of the Towns of *Valesia*, that their water costs them more then their wine.' With respect to Pratolino, he also includes a useful passage of nomenclature:

I call these by the name of Fountaines, vulgarly called *Fontans*, which are buildings of stone, adorned with many carued Images distilling water, and such are placed in most parts of *Italy* in the marketplaces, open and vncouered: but in this and like Gardens, these Fountaines are wrought within little houses, which house is vulgarly called *grotta*, that is, Caue (or Den), yet are they not built vnder the earth, but aboue in the manner of a Caue.[52]

He goes on to describe the various hydraulic automata found within the grottoes, and the *giocchi d'acqua* throughout the gardens. Moryson thus

[51] Fynes Moryson, *An itinerary vvritten by Fynes Moryson Gent. First in the Latine tongue, and then translated by him into English: containing his ten yeeres trauell through the tvvelue dominions of Germany, Bohmerland, Sweitzerland, Netherland, Denmarke, Poland, Italy, Turky, France, England, Scotland, and Ireland* (London, 1617), sig. H6, I^v, M6.

[52] Ibid., sig. N4^v.

establishes the gardens of Pratolino (and, by extension, Italian gardens in general) as places of conspicuous and elaborate artifice, going beyond a simple narrative or iconographic programme and even the assertion of wealth and power through the ostentatious harnessing of scant natural resources. In the third book of the *Itinerary*, which is less a travel diary than a gazetteer and a compendium of observations on national characteristics, Moryson goes so far as to describe a devotion to fountains as being peculiarly Italian:

The Italians more willingly spend their money in building (wherein they delight to haue coole chambers, with open Tarrasses, lying vpon waters and shades, on the sides of the house where the Sunne least comes), and likewise in adorning Fountaines with shade, seates, and images, in making caues vnder the earth, and water-conduits, then in any earthly thing, their mistresse alwaies excepted.

He quickly adds of England, however, that 'the Kings Pallaces are of such magnificent building, so curious art, and such pleasure and beauty for gardens and fountaines, and are so many in number, as *England* need not enuie any other Kingdome therein'.[53] There was, therefore, a nationalistic or patriotic, as well as an aspirational element to fountains in early modern Europe. Throughout early modern Europe, fountains could be regarded as a means of asserting power and wealth through the manipulation of natural resources and a specific iconographic programme (as at Pratolino, Boboli, and the Villa d'Este, the Château d'Anet, and other continental palaces and great houses) or as a source of patriotic pride, seen in Moryson's careful statement that the gardens and fountains of the English royal palaces are such 'as England need not enuie any other Kingdome therein'.

Even Sir Thomas Hoby's installation of a presumably modest fountain in the garden of his manor house upon his return to England could itself be read as a statement of his identity as an authority upon things Italian and the surroundings in which a gentleman should live. In *The English Husbandman* (1613)[54] by the ubiquitous Gervase Markham, the analogous part played by

---

[53] Fynes Moryson, sig. Kkk3, Kkk4.

[54] There were subsequent variants, additions, and new editions in 1614, 1615, and 1635. His biographer in the *ODNB* describes him as being responsible for 'an astonishing variety of literary publications—poetry, drama, and prose . . . combined with an equally astonishing variety of non-literary works on topics such as horsemanship, veterinary medicine, husbandry, domestic economy, and even military training'. He adds that 'Markham's more literary works have never enjoyed a particularly high reputation . . . On the other hand, his factual works include a wealth of detail on many aspects of day-to-day living. For the social historian, or the re-enactor, Gervase Markham's numerous works are indispensable guides to the practicalities of Renaissance life.' Matthew Steggle, 'Markham, Gervase (1568?–1637)', *Oxford Dictionary of National Biography* (Oxford: Oxford University Press, 2004) (**www.oxforddnb.com/view/article/18065**, accessed

water features in determining the status of a garden of this more humble kind
is clearly described:

> Within this garden plot would be also either some Well, Pumpe, Conduit, Pond,
> or Cesterne for water, sith a garden, at many times of the yeere, requireth much
> watering: & this place for water you shall order and dispose according to your abillitie,
> and the nature of the soyle, as thus: if both your reputation, and your wealth be of
> the lowest account, if then your garden aford you a plaine Well, comely couered,
> or a plaine Pump, it shall be sufficient, or if for want of such springs you digge a
> fayre Pond in some conuenient part thereof, or else (which is much better) erect
> a Cesterne of leade, into which by pippes may discend all the raine-water which
> falls about any part of the house, it will serue for your purpose: but if God haue
> bestowed vpon you a greater measure of his blessings, both in wealth & account,
> if then insteade of either Well, Pumpe, Pond, or Cesterne, you erect Conduits,
> or continuall running Fountaines, composed of Antique workes, according to the
> curiositie of mans inuention, it shall be more gallant and worthy: and these Conduits
> or water-courses, you may bring in pippes of leade from other remote or more
> necessary places of water springs, standing aboue the leuell of your garden, as euery
> Artist in the profession of such workes can more amply declare vnto you, onely for
> mee let it be sufficient to let you vnderstand that euery garden would be accompanied
> with water.[55]

One could not ask for a clearer exposition of the aspirational nature of
fountains in the early modern English garden. William Lawson's *A New
Orchard and Garden* (1618) is very similar to *The English Husbandman*, and
there is in fact some material common to later editions of both works. Like
Markham, Lawson advocates the setting out of a garden as a square quartered
by paths, and like him he includes a diagram (although a more elaborate one)
which in fact shows a garden divided into six squares, on three levels with
steps in between, some planted with trees and some in knots. A fountain is
placed in the middle. His work concludes:

> What is there, of all these few that I haue reckoned, which doth not please the eye, the
> eare, the smell, and taste? And by these sences, as Organes, Pipes, and Windowes, the
> delights are carryed to refresh the gentle, generous, and noble minde. To conclude,
> what ioy may you haue, that you liuing to such an age, shall see the blessings of God
> on your labours while you liue, and leaue behind to your heires, or successors (for
> God will make heires) such a worke, that many ages after your death, shall record your

---

27 Mar. 2006). On early modern English gardening manuals, see Rebecca Bushnell, *Green Desire:
Imagining Early Modern English Gardens* (Ithaca, NY: Cornell University Press, 2003).

[55] Gervase Markham, *The English husbandman. The first part: contayning the knowledge of the
true nature of euery soyle within this kingdome: how to plow it; and the manner of the plough, and
other instruments belonging thereto. Together with the art of planting, grafting, and gardening after
our latest and rarest fashion. A worke neuer written before by any author: and now newly compiled
for the benefit of this kingdome* (London, 1613), sig. P2ᵛ–P3.

loue to your Country. And the rather, when you consider . . . to what a length of time your worke is like to last.[56]

This last statement of Lawson's has sadly been largely disproved, thanks (as Roy Strong would have it) to the depredations of Capability Brown and his ilk.[57] But his conclusion provides a useful complement to Markham's ideas about gardens, as they were particularly expressed in his remarks on fountains. Both writers were concerned, broadly speaking, with non-elite gardens,[58] which they saw as expressing the beliefs, status, personality, and aspirations of their owners. While Markham regarded the act of installing a fountain as asserting the wealth and status of the owner and even as indicating that he or she had been particularly blessed by God, Lawson treated the whole project of the garden as an expression, through physical labour and the act of creation, of Christian piety and national pride. The creation of a personal earthly paradise was its own reward.

FOUNTAINS IN MEDIEVAL LITERATURE

David Quint begins the preface to *Origins and Originality in Renaissance Literature* by quoting Ernst Curtius' statement that when new literary topoi emerge they provide ' "indications of a changed psychological state, indications which are comprehensible in no other way" '.[59] Quint's work is not concerned with fountains, but with 'the *topos* of the source, the confluent origin of the rivers of the earth', derived by Renaissance authors from Plato's *Phaedo* and Virgil's *Fourth Eclogue*, which he traces through Tasso, Spenser, and Rabelais,

---

[56] William Lawson, *A nevv orchard and garden. Or The best way for planting, grafting, and to make the ground good, for a rich orchard particularly in the north parts of England: generally for the whole kingdome, as in nature, reason, scituation, and all probability, may and doth appeare* (London, 1618), sig. I.

[57] Strong dedicates his book 'In Memory of All Those Gardens Destroyed by Capability Brown and his Successors'. In a more polemical vein, the gardening writer Christopher Stocks nominated Brown as a 'villain' in an article beginning 'Like Robert Oppenheimer, Capability Brown was a genius who unleashed a terrible new force into our world. In Oppenheimer's case it was the nuclear bomb. In the case of Capability Brown it was landscape gardening. Brown was almost single-handedly responsible for the destruction of many of the most spectacular gardens Britain has ever seen, and his malign influence remains potent to this day.' *Independent Magazine* (19 Mar. 2005), 78.

[58] A garden would, however, have to be extremely large to contain *all* the features considered 'delightsom' by Lawson; he does also refer to 'Your Gardiner', sig. H4ᵛ.

[59] David Quint, *Origin and Originality in Renaissance Literature: Versions of the Source* (New Haven: Yale University Press, 1983), p. ix; Ernst Robert Curtius, *European Literature and the Latin Middle Ages*, trans. Willard R. Trask (Princeton: Princeton University Press, 1953), 82.

among others. Any apparent similarity between Quint's work and my own is a superficial one, for he deals with rivers and oceans, and with broader issues in literary and intellectual history. I share, however, Quint's avowed intention of challenging 'Curtius' own largely ahistorical concept of the literary *topos*',[60] by emphasizing the specificity of one topos—the fountain—to a particular historical and cultural moment and place. That the fountain is also, in many respects, a transhistorical topos cannot be disputed: it is, after all, a notable feature of the *locus amoenus* as Curtius himself described it, and also a figurative detail of the discourse of governance since the days of Plutarch and of poetic creation since Horace.[61] In early modern England, however, these hitherto separate topoi of the fountain were frequently superimposed and elided into one another, meaning that the fountain trope was a point of contact and interpenetration between, for example, the discourses of governance and of poetry, between concerns over the purity of translation and the propriety of genre. Kevin Sharpe has recently observed that 'no conventions or tropes are without a history; and the changing selection, articulation and deployment of them requires, perhaps, closer attention than it has received'.[62] In Curtius' terms, the fountain is not a new topos in English Renaissance literature, but in its syncretic functionality it is revelatory of particular cultural and historical circumstances, and of the efforts of writers and artists to comprehend and interpret them. This was, in turn, reinforced by the presence of celebrated and highly prized, and mythologized, fountains in English gardens, and in the streets of English towns, which themselves displayed a particular density of signification and association in their decoration, location, history, and functionality. As Garrett Sullivan puts it, 'topography . . . [is] more than the scene set for the unfolding of human action'.[63] Just as a topos can have a physical or material referent, so a fountain in a Renaissance text is not necessarily either simply local colour or a dead metaphor, but potentially a nodal point in a complex web of associative density, both material and intertextual.

Obviously, fountains did not suddenly appear in English literature in the latter part of the sixteenth century: they can be found in many medieval and early sixteenth-century texts. Yet the fountains of medieval literature are in many respects different from those I will discuss here.[64] Writing

---

[60] Quint, *Origin and Originality*, pp. ix–x.

[61] Plutarch, *Moralia*, trans. Harold North Fowler (Cambridge, Mass.: Harvard University Press, 1969), 77 D; Horace, *Odes and Epodes*, trans. Niall Rudd (Cambridge, Mass.: Harvard University Press, 2004), 3.13.

[62] Sharpe, *Remapping Early Modern England*, 79.

[63] Garrett A. Sullivan, *The Drama of Landscape: Land, Property and Social Relations on the Early Modern Stage* (Stanford, Calif.: Stanford University Press, 1998), 198.

[64] There are some useful analogies to a discussion of fountains in medieval romance in Corinne J. Saunders, *The Forest of Medieval Romance: Avernus, Broceliande, Arden* (Cambridge:

of the relationship between real medieval and Renaissance fountains in France, Marie-Madeleine Fragonard describes 'une sorte de révolution dans l'imaginaire et la représentation . . . où plusieurs forces se relaient transformer l'usage et la représentation de l'eau' (a sort of revolution in the ways of thinking about and representing [fountains] . . . whereby a variety of forces took turns in transforming the use and the representation of water).[65] Fragonard entitles her essay 'L'Adieu aux fées' (Farewell to the fairies), thus identifying the strong association in medieval French romance and folklore between women (or fairies) and fountains.[66] But the fountains of medieval literature in general are not the plural, multivalent, monumental, and material devices which I identify in Renaissance texts. In many respects, the Fountain of Narcissus in the *Roman de la Rose* is the exception that proves the rule: it is almost the only example in medieval English literature of a fountain that is looked *into*, or even *at*. The *hortus conclusus*, the enclosed garden, can be seen as a kind of subset of the *locus amoenus*, and the Garden of Delight in the *Roman de la Rose* is probably its best-known example in medieval literature. It is, however, a more explicitly erotic space than the *locus amoenus*, partly through its invocation in the Song of Solomon 4: 12: 'A garden enclosed is my sister, my spouse; a spring shut up, a fountain sealed.' This referent is sometimes reinforced in courtly literature by the implicit recollection of the opening of Psalm 42: 'As the hart panteth after the water-brooks, so panteth my soul after thee, O God,' transferring the image of the soul's longing for God to a more worldly love object. In social reality, the enclosed garden was a private place, and therefore a potential refuge for lovers: in the medieval courts, privacy was a privileged commodity, especially for the young, and gardens were places where it was possible to find some. The garden's wall marked it off and set it apart; it became a space differentiated from other social spaces. In courtly literature, different things could happen there, and the normal rules of conduct and expectation might not necessarily apply. In *The Canterbury Tales* one finds the garden in which the two young knights see Fair Emily from their prison windows in the Knight's Tale, the erotic paradise into which January tries to tempt his young bride May, with words even borrowed from the Song of Solomon, in the Merchant's Tale, and Dorigen's garden in the Franklin's Tale. As a signifier of a particular ethical milieu and genre, the fountain of the *hortus conclusus* could perhaps be labelled the 'courtly fountain' (see Fig. 1).

D. S. Brewer, 1993), and Philippe Barrier, *Forêt légendaire: contes, légendes, coutumes, anecdotes sur les forêts de France* (Etrépilly: Christian de Bartillat, 1991).

[65] Marie-Madeleine Fragonard, 'L'Adieu aux fées', in *Sources et fontaines du Moyen Âge à l'Âge Baroque*, 3.

[66] See the discussion of the motif by Pierre Gallais, *La Fée à la fontaine et à l'arbre: un archétype du conte merveilleux et du récit courtois* (Amsterdam: Rodopi, 1992).

By comparison, when the knights of medieval romance, to use Erich Auerbach's phrase, 'set forth', they in general enter a landscape that can seem both vast and undifferentiated, which, to use an anachronistic image, resembles a rather basic map: distances and spatial relationships are unclear, and there are very few fixed points or stable landmarks. As Auerbach again puts it,

All the numerous castles and palaces, the battles and adventures, of the courtly romances . . . are things of fairyland: each time they appear before us as though sprung from the ground; their geographical relation to the known world, their sociological and economic foundations, remain unexplained . . . The world of knightly proving is a world of adventure . . . it contains nothing but the requisites of adventure.[67]

These conclusions could perhaps be modified, especially with regard to later romances. But it remains fair to say that each Arthurian knight, as he sets forth, makes his own path in both physical and narrative terms: romance cycles could be described as being made up of great webs of these narrative strands, which intersect, as forest paths do, in clearings where there are crosses or chapels or, especially, fountains. All these are nodal points where narratives begin, run together, or change direction.

The best-known fountain in Arthurian romance is the magical spring in Chrétien de Troyes's *Yvain*, written in the late twelfth century; one version of the Welsh analogue is in fact given the alternative title 'The Lady of the Fountain'. The story is a version of one of the oldest archetypes, the motif of the *rex nemorensis*, the priest of Nemi, the shrine of Diana in central Italy: this priest gains his office as the defender of the sacred tree in Diana's grove by killing his predecessor, and had in turn to be killed by his own eventual challenger. The tree—immortalized by James Frazer's *Golden Bough*, in which it appears as one of the *ur*-myths and archetypes of human civilization—is replaced by Chrétien with a fountain, thereby exemplifying the close interconnections between trees, women, and fountains in myth and folklore, as in romance. Having heard the story of a magical fountain, which raises a storm and summons a challenger when its water is poured out, the young knight Yvain leaves Arthur's court ostensibly to avenge the challenger's humiliation of his cousin Calogrenant, but in reality to prove his own valour in an adventure. He kills the challenger, marries his wife Laudine, and in turn becomes the fountain's defender. As the perilous fountain catalyses action, so it becomes the point to which the action of the romance, and its hero, must periodically return. Yvain's defeat of Laudine's first husband and his

---

[67] Erich Auerbach, *Mimesis: The Representation of Reality in Western Literature* (Princeton: Princeton University Press, 1953; repr. 2003), 130, 136. Auerbach's account of *Yvain* in *Mimesis* remains one of the best introductions to this particular romance.

assumption of the guardianship of the spring has given him a social role and
identity: he must periodically return to the fountain to be reminded of his
obligations as a knight, and the narrative in turn enters into a new phase each
time its hero raises, or responds to, the storm at the spring.

By contrast, some of Sir Thomas Malory's fountains appear just to be
fountains. They are, often literally, points of rest in the quests of Arthur's
knights, places where they pause to refresh themselves and their horses; yet
often, despite their obvious utility to the knights who stop at them, romance
fountains might as well be trees. Many of Malory's fountains, therefore,
appear to have their primary, and sometimes sole, significance grounded in
the episodic structure of romance. As the narrative paths of errant knights
intersect across the map-like surface of the romance landscape, the fountains
at which they do so accumulate significance because important things tend to
happen *at* them. They are almost never significant in themselves. As it appears
in Malory, the romance fountain is largely stripped of its potential for fantastic
and folkloric qualities, such as are sometimes found in earlier romances such
as *Yvain*.

There are many examples of such fountains: in Malory's tale of King Arthur
'the kynge saw the herte unboced and hys horse dede, he sette hym downe by
a fowntayne, and there he fell downe in grete thought'; 'Than kynge Pellynore
armed hym and mownted uppon hys horse, and rode more than a pace after
the lady that the knyght lad away. And as he rose in a foreyste he saw in
a valey a damesell sitte by a well and a wounded knyght in her armys, and
kynge Pellynor salewed hir'; 'And so they rode and cam into a depe valey
full of stonys, and thereby they sawe a fayre streme of water. Aboven thereby
was the hede of the streme, a fayre founteyne, and three damesels syttynge
thereby'.[68] To look only at such examples, and so to dismiss Malory's fountains
as boring and one-dimensional, more or less arbitrary markers in the romance
landscape, would allow a stark and easy contrast to be made with the far more
complex, intertextual, and multivalent fountains of early modern literature
that are the main subject of *England's Helicon*. But sometimes, that Malory's
knights stop at fountains, rather than at chapels, wayside crosses, or random
trees, makes a difference. Malory's more complex fountains can be considered
in a number of ways. They have particular folkloric associations, are often
strongly connected with women, and frequently introduce or occasion tests
and challenges. Malory's fountains also sometimes signal the enlargement of
his narrative in generic terms, gesturing at the possibility of different narrative
modes and ethical concerns. Such devices are drawn on especially by Spenser,

---

[68] Sir Thomas Malory, *Complete Works*, ed. Eugène Vinaver (2nd edn. Oxford: Oxford
University Press, 1971), 28, 71, 97.

but also by other early modern writers; they must certainly have shaped the interpretation of fountains in Renaissance texts by readers whose narrative and symbolic expectations and ways of reading had in turn been largely determined by medieval romance.[69]

An implausible number of Arthur's knights seem to encounter the loves of their lives at fountains in the forest, and are subsequently willing to be sent off on quests by them. In archetypal terms, this is above all because of the strong association between women and water as an element, an association familiar through the nymphs of classical literature, not least Ovid's *Metamorphoses*. In addition, according to the Aristotelian physiological model available in the Middle Ages, women are predominantly watery in their make-up, cold and moist as opposed to the heat and dryness of men. Water can additionally be seen as feminine because it is fresh and pure; it is lively and constantly changing; it sparkles and murmurs. Women are similarly supposed unstable and literally fluid, like the tides subject to the moon, to patterns of ebb and flow. Moreover, the water in a fountain, well, or pool is also contained. The fountain is both the vessel and its contents, and it therefore figures origin, a mysterious source, a point of contact with the other. The fountain from which water runs without cease suggests an absolute origin, a vast and primal interior—and anterior—space, which is both alluring and a threat. The association between women and fountains in Arthurian romance, and indeed in other literature, both medieval and post-medieval, can often be read as being straightforwardly erotic, in a way that points once again to the Song of Solomon: the sealed fountain, the enclosed garden suggest their own potential for opening and unsealing, revelation and initiation. The woman at the fountain is part of the discourse of desire, but in chivalric terms, that erotic impulse must be redirected into quest and adventure by the woman who is implicitly its object.

Women and water sources are also closely linked to the 'otherworld', the supernatural realm of fairies, dwarfs, and magic which is such a feature of early medieval romance. In Malory, the otherworld has retreated in prominence, far less to the fore than it is in Chrétien de Troyes's romances of the twelfth century, let alone in the Celtic analogues, but it is still vestigially present, perhaps above all at fountains. When Arthur lies down to rest beside a fountain, he has his first encounter with a mysterious otherworldly animal, the questing beast:

hym thoughte he herde a noyse of howundis to the som of thirty, and with that the kynge saw com towarde hym the strongest beste that ever he saw or herde of. So thys

⁶⁹ On the enduring importance of the reading of medieval romance in early modern England, see Helen Cooper, *The English Romance in Time: Transforming Motifs from Geoffrey of Monmouth to the Death of Shakespeare* (Oxford: Oxford University Press, 2004). Spenser's use of the romance tradition is especially discussed in Chapter 6.

beste wente to the welle and dranke, and the noyse was in the bestes bealy lyke unto the questing of thirty coupyl houndes, but alle the whyle the beest dranke there was no noyse in the bestes bealy. And therewith the beeste departed with a grete noyse, whereof the kynge had grete mervayle.[70]

The mysterious animal comes to drink because, in real world terms, that is what animals of whatever kind do in the forest: in folkloric terms, however, it comes to the fountain because the fountain itself is a point of access to the otherworld. Its water pours endlessly, mysteriously, from somewhere else, and when Arthur sits down beside the fountain, he enters into its experiential ambit: he '[falls] downe in grete thought', he hears and sees the strange beast, he has 'grete mervayle', and he '[falls] on sleepe'; he dreams. In another of Malory's tales, Accolon of Gaule knows immediately that he has had an encounter with the otherworld because of the close association between women and fountains:

Whan he awoke he founde hymself by a depe welles syde within half a foote, in grete perell of deth. And there com oute of that fountayne a pype of sylver, and oute of that pype ran water all on hyghe in a stone of marbil. Whan sir Accolon sawe this he blyssed hym and seyde, 'Jesu, save my lorde kynge Arthure and kynge Uryence, for thes damysels in this shippe hath betrayed us. They were fendis and no women'.[71]

To underscore the otherworldly nature of this situation, Accolon is then greeted by a dwarf 'with a grete mowthe and a flatte nose', and told that he has been sent Arthur's great sword Excalibur by Morgan le Fay.

    This association between women, fountains, and the otherworld in Arthurian romance overlaps with the function of fountains as tests or challenges. In the encounter of three knights with three women at a fountain, described at length by Malory, that Gawayne, Uwayne, and Marhaus are having an encounter with the otherworld is underscored by the fact that that there are three women—always a potent number—and that the three women are of significantly different ages. They are waiting at the fountain specifically in order to organize adventures for young knights. The fountain therefore becomes a point of initiation and of narrative and ethical origin: it is where the adventures begin and the point to which the knights must return. Participating in the adventures chosen for them by the women, the knights are educated in their social and ethical roles: their obedience to the women confirms their identities as 'arraunte knyghtes' and 'knyghtes adventures'. As the encounter with the three archetypal women at the fountain brings the young knights into contact with the otherworld, so it catalyses and initiates the next phase of their adventures and their lives. The fountain is an origin:

[70] Malory, *Works*, 28.   [71] Ibid., 84.

as the knights ride off to the west, the south, and the north, they imitate the streams or rivers which flow from the fountain of life in paradise, the four rivers of Eden described in Genesis. The fountain has become the centre of the world, and none of the knights chooses to ride back the way they have come, implicitly from the east—back to childhood and immaturity—but rather onwards.

Whereas in *Yvain*, and on occasion in Malory, fountains are the catalyst for adventures which will ultimately prove both the prowess and the virtue—after a necessary process of trials and education—of the romances' heroes, in other romances fountains are more closely involved in the testing mechanisms themselves. In Malory's Grail cycle, Sir Ector has a vision in which he sees his brother Sir Lancelot ride 'tylle that he cam unto the fayryst welle that ever he saw. And there sir Launcelot alyght and wolde have dronke of that welle; and whan he stowped to drynke of that watir the watir sanke from him. And whan sir Launcelot saw that, he turned and went thidir as he had come fro.' Nacian the hermit subsequently explains that the fountain in Ector's vision prefigures both the 'sankgraal', the Holy Grail, and Lancelot's own unworthiness to see or claim it:

And the welle whereat the watir sanke from hym whan he sholde have takyn thereoff? (And whan he saw he myght nat have hit he returned from whens he cam, for the welle betokenyth the hyghe grace of God; for the more men desyre hit to take hit, the more shall be their desire.) So whan he cam nyghe the Sankgreall he meked hym so that he hylde hym nat the man worthy to be so nyghe the holy vessell, for he had be so defoyled in dedly synne by the space of many yere . . . [72]

Near the end of the Grail romance, it is another perilous spring that affirms the perfect virtue of Lancelot's son Sir Galahad, who will succeed in the Grail quest as his father has failed. Galahad 'cam into a perelous foreyste where he founde the welle which boyled with grete wawis, as the tale tellith tofore'. ('The tale', of course, is the romance of *Yvain*.)

And as sone as sir Galahad sette hys honde thereto hit seased, so that hit brente no more, and anone the hete departed away. And cause why that hit brente, hit was a sygne of lechory that was that tyme muche used. But that hete myght nat abyde hys pure virginité. And so thys was takyn in the contrey for a miracle, and so ever afftir was hit called Galaheddis Welle.[73]

This is a rare instance of a protagonist actually interacting with a fountain in Malory's romances.

But as well as being sites where Arthurian knights come into contact with the otherworld, in the form of marvellous beasts or mysterious women,

---

[72] Ibid., 559, 562.   [73] Ibid., 600–1.

and where adventures can be found and valour tested, fountains can also be the signifiers of a shift of genre in Arthurian romance; they as it were enlarge the narrative and inflect it—sometimes very briefly—in particular ways. Fountains are often the locus of narrative hiatus or dilation, where the linear quests of knights errant are interrupted and other ways of acting or being are suggested. They are places—sometimes literally—of reflection, where questing knights, hitherto defined by their quests, experience and express some kind of interiority. In Malory's romances, knights and damsels frequently go to fountains to think, or to lament. Arthur sits by the fountain 'in grete thought', Isolde (in the romance of Trystram) 'wente hirselff unto a welle and made grete moone', and later Sir Dynadan finds another woman 'makyng grete dole' beside a well, King Mark himself overhears Sir Lameroke making 'grete langoure and dole . . . the dolefullyst complaynte of love that ever man herde',[74] and it is made clear that this is not unusual behaviour. Fountains and wells are where both knights and narratives go to think about love, and this is a construction that Arthurian romances share with other medieval genres. In Chaucer's *Troilus and Criseyde*, for example, Pandarus tells Criseyde that he has heard Troilus speaking of love as he sleeps, 'In-with the paleis gardyn, by a welle';[75] again, the *Romance of the Rose* is the pre-eminent example of this motif taken to extremes, for the lover falls in love with the rose that he sees reflected in the fountain. To look into or simply to sit beside the fountain—even in a forest setting—is to enter into the *hortus conclusus*, the space of love and lyric poetry. In medieval art and literature, a fountain is very often employed as a metonym for a *locus amoenus* or garden. The advertised presence of the fountain is sufficient for the softness of the grass, the beauty and fragrance of flowers and trees, simply to be assumed. No matter how wild the forest, the presence of the fountain can make it into a temporary garden of love.

In Sir Dynadan's description of Sir Epynogrys, 'he lay lyke a fole grennynge and wolde nat speke, and his shylde lay by hym, and his horse also stood by hym. And well I wote he was a lovear.' It is rare that the content of these lovers' laments is expounded, but it is enough that they are recorded as taking place. The fountain or well location therefore functions as a catalyst not just for adventure but also for the consideration of love and, in particular, the lamenting of the sufferings of love. Knights are given the opportunity to reveal,

---

[74] Malory, *Works*, 28, 263, 354.

[75] *The Riverside Chaucer*, ed. Larry D. Benson (Oxford: Oxford University Press, 1987), 2.509. The straightforwardness of Chaucer's fountains in comparison with those found in many Renaissance texts can be seen in Carol Falvo Heffernan, 'Wells and Streams in Three Chaucerian Gardens', *Papers on Language and Literature*, 15 (1979), 339–58. She is largely concerned with religious symbolism and the conventions of the *locus amoenus* and the earthly paradise.

in however stereotypical a fashion, another side to their character, and one that is as essential as their prowess in battle. Trystram responds to Sir Dynadan's rather sneering description of the plight of Sir Epynogrys:

'A, fayre sir', seyde sir Trystram, 'ar nat ye a lovear?'
'Mary, fye on that crauffte!' seyde sir Dynadan.
'Sir, that is yevell seyde', seyde sir Trystram, 'for a knyght may never be of proues but yf he be a lovear'.[76]

It is a cliché, but it is above all at fountains that Arthur's knights are given the opportunity to show their softer sides, to sigh and lament rather than challenge and fight. Stopping at a fountain to drink or to sleep, they must remove their helmets—sometimes they drink from them—and set down their shields. In doing so, they temporarily set aside their chivalric identities, and demonstrate instead some kind of interiority. Near the end of the tale of Trystram, a fountain provides the occasion for Sir Palomydes—who is himself secretly in love with Isolde—to lament his plight, and so indirectly to speak for the desperate situation of Trystram and Isolde themselves:

So uppon a day, in the dawnynge, sir Palomydes wente into the foreste by hymselff alone; and there he founde a well, and anone he loked into the well and in the watir he sawe his owne vysayge, how he was discolowred and defeded, a nothynge lyke as he was. 'Lorde Jesu, what may this meane?' seyde sir Palomydes. And thus he seyde to hymselff: 'A, Palomydes, Palomydes! Why arte thou thus defaded, and ever was wonte to be called one of the fayrest knyghtes of the worlde? Forsothe, I woll no more lyve this lyff, for I love that I may never gete nor recover'. And therewythall he leyde hym downe by the welle, and so began to make a ryme of La Beall Isode and of sir Trystram.[77]

Sir Palomydes' gazing at his own reflection in the fountain, seeing how his appearance has been altered by his sufferings as an unrequited lover, is the only explicit example of reflection anywhere in Malory's romances. But the principle that it encapsulates—that fountains can be places where alternative identities can be confronted and explored and where, above all, the transforming powers of love can be considered and expressed, perhaps in lyric form—is one that is implicit in many of the other fountains and wells that he describes.

There is a unique example of a medieval Arthurian romance utilizing, as a plot device, a feature that appears to have existed in a real medieval garden, which may even have been based on that romance. A celebrated episode in the romance of *Tristan and Isolde* describes one of the ways in which the lovers would communicate secretly in order to arrange their clandestine meetings.

---

[76] Malory, *Works*, 420.   [77] Ibid., 473.

In the early thirteenth-century version by Gottfried von Strassburg, Isolde's loyal companion Brangane advises Tristan:

When you see that your chance has come, take a twig of olive, cut some slivers lengthwise, and just engrave them with a 'T' on one side and an 'I' on the other, so that only your initials appear, neither more nor less. Then go into the orchard. You know the brook that flows there from the spring towards the ladies' apartments? Throw a shaving into it and let it float past the door where wretched Isolde and I come out at all times of the day to weep over our misery. When we see the shaving we shall know at once that you are by the brook... Your love-lorn friend my lady and I will always come to meet you as occasion offers.[78]

This means of communication works successfully for a little over a week, until Tristan is seen by the evil dwarf Melot and the lovers are reported to King Mark. At their next meeting it is only by good luck—they see the shadows of Mark and Melot hidden in a tree—that they are not caught. Gottfried based his version of the Tristan story upon the version of Thomas, which survives only in fragments; the brook scene is one of the passages that is missing, but it is sufficiently clear that Gottfried's source was Thomas for it to be assumed that such a scene did appear in his version also. Nothing is known about Thomas, other than Gottfried's reference to him as 'Thomas of Britain' in his Prologue; it has been plausibly suggested that Thomas was associated with the court of Henry II of England and Eleanor of Aquitaine, and that he might have been writing primarily for an English audience, sometime in the 1150s, and perhaps specifically for the King.

   Although it has been the subject of much speculation and indeed fantasy, it is broadly accepted that Henry II had a mistress called Rosamund Clifford, 'Fair Rosamund', and that he built for her at Woodstock Palace a house or bower that was known as Everswell.[79] Although it was not at the centre of a labyrinth, as legend has it, it was almost certainly named after the spring or well that was there. There are records of payments in the royal accounts for the maintenance of the fountains at Everswell from 1166 onwards and it appears in fact that there was a quite elaborate water garden. Perhaps influenced in its design by Sicilian—and so ultimately Moorish—fashions in garden design (there were close connections between the Angevin and Sicilian courts), this seems to have comprised interconnected pools, the largest surrounded by a cloister of some kind, the smallest with seats around

[78] Gottfried von Strassburg, *Tristan (with the 'Tristan' of Thomas)* (rev. edn.), ed. A. T. Hatto (London, Penguin, 2004), 231.
[79] See Howard M. Colvin, 'Royal Gardens in Medieval England', in *Medieval Gardens* (Washington, DC: Dumbarton Oaks, 1986), 17–21, and Henderson, *The Tudor House and Garden*, 74, 76.

it. The pools disappeared when Capability Brown redesigned the garden in the eighteenth century, but in the late seventeenth century the antiquarian John Aubrey had made a sketch, which clearly shows three pools connected by channels, and their proximity to the ruined buildings of Everswell, Rosamund's bower.[80]

Both garden and literary historians have suggested that Everswell might have been based upon the apparent layout of chambers, orchard, pool, and stream in the *Tristan*, which had allowed the lovers to communicate by means of the twigs floated on the waters of a stream connecting one part of a garden to another. There is an enduringly strong association in legend between water, Woodstock, and Fair Rosamund Clifford: one fourteenth-century source describes her as being bled to death in her bath at Woodstock by the jealous Queen, while later versions have her poisoned.[81] Rosamund's well or bath was still being shown to visitors to Woodstock in the late sixteenth century. In 1599 the Swiss tourist Thomas Platter was shown 'a rather large square stone basin full of water which is warm in winter and cold in summer, where the king is supposed to have bathed with his fair Rosamund'.[82] It is fitting, given my avowed concern for the intersection of real and literary, material and textual fountains in early modern literature and culture, that it is with a sixteenth-century tourist's simultaneous experience of a real feature of the English landscape and an accretion of English history, myth, and romance that I conclude this excursus into the medieval antecedents of early modern fountains, and turn once more to the question of their real and literary successors.

THE CASE FOR AN INTERDISCIPLINARY APPROACH

Recent historical scholarship has explored the changing political and cultural climate in the latter part of Elizabeth's reign, with John Guy going so far as to term the 1590s 'the second reign of Elizabeth I',[83] and many of the most

---

[80] For Aubrey's sketch, see Henderson, *The Tudor House and Garden*, 76.

[81] See T. A. Archer, 'Clifford, Rosamund (b. before 1140?, d. 1175/6)', rev. Elizabeth Hallam, *Oxford Dictionary of National Biography* (www.oxforddnb.com/view/article/5661, accessed 28 Mar. 2006).

[82] Clare Williams, *Thomas Platter's Travels in England, 1599* (London: Jonathan Cape, 1937), 117.

[83] John Guy, 'Introduction: The 1590s: The Second Reign of Elizabeth I?', in John Guy (ed.), *The Reign of Elizabeth I: Court and Culture in the Last Decade* (Cambridge: Cambridge University Press, 1995), 7. See also Wallace MacCaffrey, *Elizabeth I: War and Politics 1588–1603* (Princeton: Princeton University Press, 1992).

iconic cultural productions of Elizabeth's reign, such as *The Faerie Queene* (1590, 1596), and some of the greatest portraits, notably the 'Armada' and the 'Ditchley', date from that last decade. Some of the great houses (and their gardens) now thought of as particularly Elizabethan, such as Hardwick Hall and Holdenby, were not completed until the late 1580s or 1590s. In political terms, the 1590s were years of transition and, to some extent, hiatus, most obviously in their change of courtly 'personnel': Leicester had died in 1588, and Walsingham, Hatton, and Burghley in 1590, 1591, and 1598 respectively. Their decline was matched by the unsettling rise of Essex. Yet in cultural terms, the decade can be seen as one of assimilation and consolidation, as well as of innovation (in the theatre, for example). Even as the central motifs of the 'cult of Elizabeth' reached their fullest (some would say, most superficial) expression, perhaps forestalling the development of new cultural tropes, they frequently became denser and more nuanced. That their basic referents remained the same, the persona of Diana perhaps being the most notable, did not necessarily mean that they remained unambiguous. Ben Jonson's *The Fountaine of Selfe-Love* and Spenser's *Faerie Queene* are inseparable from the 'cult of Elizabeth' at the same time as they expose the tensions inherent in some of its most central imagery.

As the passing generation left its monuments behind, so that material record was assimilated into the literary record, which accordingly found new ways to describe and interpret it. Critics, too, must find new approaches to this material intertextuality. Louis Montrose has coined the useful phrase 'the Elizabethan political imaginary' to describe 'the collective repertoire of representational forms and figures—mythological, rhetorical, narrative, iconic—in which the beliefs and practices of Tudor political culture were pervasively articulated',[84] and he includes houses and gardens, as well as literary texts, pageants, and images in his discussion. Patricia Fumerton's work has made it virtually axiomatic that portrait miniatures cannot be interpreted and appreciated as simple images, but that they must be apprehended as material objects and ornaments, markers of status and relationship, and in the context of the social and spatial configurations of elite early modern households.[85] Clark Hulse has written persuasively of the 'curious willingness of Elizabethan painters . . . to treat the picture as a writing surface',[86] and gardens and fountains too could be the sites for inscriptions, mottoes, and even whole

---

[84] Louis Montrose, 'Spenser and the Elizabethan Political Imaginary', *English Literary History*, 69 (2002), 907.

[85] Patricia Fumerton, *Cultural Aesthetics: Renaissance Literature and the Practice of Social Ornament* (Chicago: University of Chicago Press, 1991).

[86] Clark Hulse, *The Rule of Art: Literature and Painting in the Renaissance* (Chicago: University of Chicago Press, 1990), 133.

poems.[87] Elizabeth Goldring's exploration of the picture collection of Robert Dudley, Earl of Leicester, has similarly revealed that full-size portraits too could play a significant part in the 'Elizabethan political imaginary', not only in their symbolic content but also in the ways in which they were displayed, when, where, and to whom.[88] Christy Anderson has written specifically about 'Learning to Read Architecture in the English Renaissance',[89] and writing of the decorative programme at Theobalds, James Sutton takes it for granted that

Elizabethan readers . . . were more active than contemporary readers, as demonstrated by marginal commentary surviving in documents: handwritten quibbles, arguments, even corrections of the text are often found. William Cecil, a well-trained humanist scholar, would have read in this manner, and he surely encouraged Robert in active reading too. These ideas are clearly significant to any attempt to read the Cecils' own cultural productions.

Sutton makes no distinction in this respect between 'texts, houses, [and] interiors',[90] and his noting of annotating practices among early modern readers draws attention to the material status of the text, the book as object. These are the plural, associative strategies of interpretation that must be applied to early modern gardens and their fountains, and to their counterparts in early modern texts.

Part I, 'Sources and Reflections', discusses the *Hypnerotomachia Poliphili* (1499) and Sidney's *New Arcadia* (1582–4). The *Hypnerotomachia Poliphili*, one of the most beautiful illustrated books of the Renaissance, was published in Venice in 1499. A collectors' trophy for centuries, it has attracted little serious literary criticism, despite its fame and influence (not least on garden design). Chapter 1, 'Some Fair Book: The *Hypnerotomachia* in England' gives an account of the text's history, culminating in its partial translation into English in 1592, which was dedicated to the Earl of Essex and to the memory of Sir Philip Sidney. Chapter 2, 'Reading Fountains in the *Hypnerotomachia*', discusses the romance itself. It shows how the amazing fountains encountered

[87] See Anderson, 'Learning to Read Architecture', 251 and, for a more theorized account, John Dixon Hunt, *Greater Perfections: The Practice of Garden Theory* (London: Thames and Hudson, 2000), 119–25 and Michael Charlesworth, 'Movement, Intersubjectivity, and Mercantile Morality at Stourhead', in Conan (ed.), *Landscape Design and the Experience of Motion* 263–85 (although this is an eighteenth-century example). The poems in the gardens at Nonsuch are discussed in Chapter 12.

[88] Elizabeth Goldring, 'Portraits of Queen Elizabeth I and the Earl of Leicester for Kenilworth Castle', *Burlington Magazine*, 147 (2005), 654–60, and 'Portraiture, Patronage and the Progresses: Robert Dudley, Earl of Leicester and the Kenilworth Festivities of 1575', in Jayne Archer, Elizabeth Goldring, and Sarah Knight (eds.), *The Progresses, Pageants and Entertainments of Queen Elizabeth I* (Oxford: Oxford University Press, 2007), 163–88.

[89] In *Albion's Classicism*, 239–86.

[90] James M. Sutton, 'The Decorative Program at Elizabethan Theobalds: Educating an Heir and Promoting a Dynasty', *Studies in the Decorative Arts* (Fall/Winter 1999–2000), 38.

by Poliphilus, the hero, are central to the romance's structure and ethos, simultaneously punctuating the narrative and joining its various strands of allegory. The *Hypnerotomachia* is therefore itself a paradigm of the ways in which fountains can structure landscape, narrative, and ethical or aesthetic programmes. Chapter 3, 'The Fountains of Venus and Adonis: Revelation and Reflection', focuses first on the romance's climactic Fountain of Venus, and then on its central Fountain of Adonis, demonstrating that this latter is the structural device whereby the *Hypnerotomachia*'s two books are reflected on to each other. It suggests that here the fountain's surface becomes a metaphor for fiction, art, love, and imagination. Chapter 4, 'The Fountain of Aeneas: Sidney Rewrites the *Hypnerotomachia*', shows that Philip Sidney adapted this Fountain of Adonis in crucial ways in an important passage near the beginning of his *New Arcadia* (*c*.1582–4): I argue that this short episode records Sidney's historical opposition to Elizabeth's proposed marriage with the Duke of Anjou, as well as exploring his own ideas about fiction, love, and art. This is the first demonstration of the *Hypnerotomachia*'s influence on English literature, but it is likely that Sidney was also influenced by his experience of English gardens, and notably by their use of reflection to make moral or ideological points.

Part II, 'Living Waters', focuses on Spenser's *The Faerie Queene* (1590). Chapter 5, '*Ad Fontes*: Elizabeth and the English Bible', opens with the appearance of the English Bible in the climactic pageant of Elizabeth I's coronation entry in 1559, when she was presented with the book at the Little Conduit in Cheapside. The moment became a defining one in the Queen's self-presentation and cultural memory, and is here located within a wider use of images of fountains in Protestant Humanist discussions of biblical translation and church practice. Chapter 6, 'The Christian Knight: Redcrosse Learns to Read', suggests that in writing Book 1 of *The Faerie Queene* Spenser was particularly influenced by the fountain imagery in Erasmus' *Enchiridion*. It traces Redcrosse's journey through the 'landscape of the narrative', from his disastrous encounter with the ghastly parodic fountain Errour, past his nadir when he is seduced by the evil Duessa beside a fountain in a glade, to his triumph at the Well of Life at the Book's end. Chapter 7, 'The Well of Life: All Things Made New', considers the Well of Life in more detail, locating it in relation to Protestant ideas about the sacraments, and in particular Calvinist ideas about the Word of God. But the chapter also locates Spenser's well more literally in the English landscape, by considering it in terms of the transformation of medieval holy wells into antiquarian or 'medical' sites and through an investigation of fountain imagery in devotional objects. Chapter 8, 'Fountains Seen and Unseen', discusses the ways in which fountains appear in Books 2 and 3 of *The Faerie Queene*. For Book 2 ends with an elaborate fountain in the Bowre of Bliss whereby Spenser addresses questions of excess, eroticism, the morality of art, and the pleasures of looking (similarly, at Kenilworth an elaborate Ovidian fountain inflamed the passions of onlookers), and Book 3 suggestively reworks three Ovidian fountain metamorphoses, to raise questions about the nature of looking, reading, fiction, and love.

Part III, 'Poisoned Springs', has as its focus Ben Jonson's play *The Fountaine of Selfe-Love* (1600), now better known as *Cynthia's Revels*. Chapter 9, 'The Public Fountain: Elizabethan Politics and the Humanist Tradition', discusses the fountain as an image for government, which dates back to Plutarch and was much elaborated by Renaissance humanists, and continues to explore the association between Elizabeth I and fountains, discussing a portrait medal and the embroidered decoration of her clothes. Chapter 10, 'A Visual Metaphor: Staging the Fountain', discusses the staging of Jonson's play. It examines the evidence of contemporary staging practices, and suggests that a large 'prop' fountain appeared on stage, as both scenery and a visual and material metaphor for the play's concerns. Chapter 11, 'The Fountain of Salmacis: Self-Love and Satire', discusses the play itself, which concerns the craze among a group of decadent courtiers for the waters of a magic fountain: they are members of 'Cynthia's' court, a thinly disguised version of Elizabeth's. Jonson specifically draws the image of the court as a corrupting fountain from the *Policraticus* of John of Salisbury, a twelfth-century political treatise. Chapter 12, 'Diana's Justice: Essex, Nonsuch, and Hampton Court', discusses the relationship between Jonson's play and the Earl of Essex. It argues that, as well as being a satire on court frivolities, Jonson's play used his audience's knowledge of some of the great fountains in royal gardens to make a coded plea for clemency towards the Earl of Essex, the disgraced Actaeon to Elizabeth's Diana. A brief conclusion considers the case for the ways of reading texts, images, objects, and landscapes that the previous chapters have explored, advocating a *modus legendi* that is active, participatory, and concertedly interdisciplinary. It suggests that early modern texts should be treated not merely as being complemented by, but as coextensive with, other cultural productions, arguing for a labour of imagination that seeks less to recreate 'authentic' historical experiences than to reanimate the lively and interconnected intellectual, cultural, and aesthetic principles in which they were grounded.

Part I

Sources and Reflections:
The *Hypnerotomachia Poliphili* (1499)
and Sidney's *New Arcadia* (1582–1584)

1

'Some Fair Book': The *Hypnerotomachia Poliphili* in England

By 1581, Philip Sidney had finished the first version of his 'idle work', the *Arcadia*. At the time he was himself experiencing a period of distance from the court and its concerns, if not quite the alienation and virtual exile that used to be attributed to this period in his life, which lasted until about 1583, the year in which he married Frances Walsingham and was finally knighted. Sidney spent much of this time at Wilton in Wiltshire, the country residence of his beloved sister Mary Sidney, Countess of Pembroke. It was and is a famous estate. Although Wilton was extensively rebuilt and its gardens and park elaborately remodelled in the 1630s, it was even in Sidney's time (like Penshurst, its perhaps more famous counterpart in Kent) a place where poetry and landscape, in their broadest senses, combined to mutual effect. Even before its subsequent and celebrated remodelling by Inigo Jones and Isaac de Caus, Wilton had a garden which, as will be seen, appears to have borne traces of a literary influence that can be linked to Sidney's own reading and interests. In turn, his knowledge and experience of the great estates of the day—not just Wilton and Penshurst, but Cecil's Theobalds and Burghley House, Leicester's Kenilworth, the royal palaces, as well as the various palaces and houses that he had visited in Europe—must have informed his revisions of the *Arcadia*, where notable details of gardens and architecture appear.

Wilton's library records for the relevant period are lost, but at any rate it is almost certain that Sidney had no particular book in mind when, in the early 1580s, he composed his eleventh sonnet in *Astrophil and Stella*:

> In truth, O Love, with what a boyish kind
> Thou dost proceed in thy most serious ways:
> That when the heaven to thee his best displays
> Yet of that best thou leav'st the best behind.
> For like a child, that some fair book doth find,
> With gilded leaves or coloured vellum plays,
> Or at the most, on some fine picture stays,
> But never heeds the fruit of writer's mind:

So when thou saw'st, in nature's cabinet,
Stella, thou straight look'st babies in her eyes,
In her cheek's pit thou did'st thy pit-fold set,
And in her breast bo-peep or couching lies,
Playing and shining in each outward part:
But, fool, seek'st not to get into her heart.[1]

Despite the imagery of children's games, any 'fair book' called to mind by Sidney is unlikely to have been one aimed specifically at children, a genre almost unknown in the sixteenth century. Katherine Duncan-Jones has suggested that he could in fact have been thinking of the Sidney Psalter, the fifteenth-century illuminated manuscript of the Psalms (now at Trinity College, Cambridge) in which the Sidneys recorded their family history.[2] But the images that Sidney uses—of the reader drawn to pictures at the expense, at least initially, of words; of the nature of reflection, as Stella's eyes become both mirror and window—are those that engage with the wider context of the nature of both literature and the visual (and material) arts, and the relationship between them, questions that are known to have preoccupied Sidney at this time. It remains tantalizing to speculate, however, that Sidney could have had a particular book in mind, and that hypothetical book, its fountains, its concern with reflection and the nature of fiction, love, and art, and some ways in which it might be read (not least by Sidney), is the subject of the first four chapters of this book.

My hypothetical 'fair book' is the *Hypnerotomachia Poliphili*, architectural fantasy, philological nightmare, 'impossible, erudite, silly romance'.[3] Michael Leslie notes, in his contribution to a volume of essays devoted to the work, that 'the *Hypnerotomachia* is universally recognized as a "book" rather than simply as a "text", enjoying a status as a physical object, a word and image combination, that still has to be argued for in connection with many other works';[4] in an analogous vein, Lucy Gent describes the *Hypnerotomachia* as occupying 'a kind of hinterland between a classical realist past, already being investigated by early archaeologists, and the printed page'.[5] In the context of

---

[1] Sonnet 11 from *Astrophil and Stella*, in Philip Sidney, *The Major Works*, ed. Katherine Duncan-Jones (Oxford: Oxford University Press, 1989), 157.

[2] Katherine Duncan-Jones, *Sir Philip Sidney, Courtier Poet* (London: Hamish Hamilton, 1991), 15–16.

[3] William M. Ivins, Jr., 'Artistic Aspects of Fifteenth-Century Printing', *Papers of the Bibliographic Society of America*, 26 (1932), 41. Ivins' paper had been delivered to the Chicago meeting of the Society in December 1930.

[4] Michael Leslie, 'The *Hypnerotomachia* and the Elizabethan Landscape Entertainments', *Word & Image*, 14 (1998), 130. Leslie goes on to consider the vexed question of the *Hypnerotomachia*'s early modern English reception, and is careful to make no claims as to its direct influence upon the entertainments that he discusses.

[5] Gent, 'Introduction', in *Albion's Classicism*, 13.

this book and its project, the *Hypnerotomachia* has a metatextual status; it is both text and object and as such, its existence leaves traces and tantalizing gaps; it functions as a kind of metaphor for the lost gardens and lost fountains of early modern England on its own terms, but also in relation to the other texts that are the subjects of this book. Sidney knew and adapted it, but his copy is lost; it appears to have influenced the gardens at Wilton, but they too have disappeared in the form in which Sidney knew them. It has often been suggested that Edmund Spenser, whose *Faerie Queene* is the subject of Part II, must have read the *Hypnerotomachia*, but there is no evidence of his having access to a copy, and apparent traces of its influence in the *Faerie Queene* are too insubstantial to be persuasive; similarly, the gardens that Spenser himself may have known, such as that at Kenilworth, have long been lost.[6] Ben Jonson's *The Fountaine of Selfe-Love, or Cynthias Revels* is the subject of Part III, and his copy of the *Hypnerotomachia* in fact survives in the British Library, but it has proved equally difficult to identify any positive traces of its influence upon his writings.[7] Most copies of the *Hypnerotomachia* are infuriatingly short of annotations or marks of ownership: Jonson's copy in the British Library has both so copiously as to be almost illegible, but not in Jonson's hand.[8] The 'golden world' that the *Hypnerotomachia* sets forth

[6] The appearance of an essay on the *Hypnerotomachia* in the *Spenser Encyclopedia* is therefore perhaps misleading, although it does suggest a few possible echoes in *The Faerie Queene*: the arithmological stanza in 2.9.22, and the Neoplatonic tendencies of the description of Belphoebe in 2.3.21–31. The first three books of *The Faerie Queene* of course pre-date the publication of Dallington's 1592 translation. Lucy Gent, '*Hypnerotomachia Poliphili*', in A. C. Hamilton (ed.), *The Spenser Encyclopedia* (Toronto: University of Toronto Press, 1990), 385–6; see also Michael Leslie, 'Edmund Spenser: Art and *The Faerie Queene* (Chatterton Lecture on Poetry)', *Proceedings of the British Academy*, 76 (1990), 79, 81, 87, and *passim*. Kenilworth is discussed in detail in Chapter 8.

[7] A. W. Johnson makes an honourable and sustained attempt in his *Ben Jonson: Poetry and Architecture* (Oxford: Oxford University Press, 1994), but it is ultimately not convincing for, as Leslie points out, 'everything about Renaissance architecture that is contained in the *Hypnerotomachia* and that also appears in Ben Jonson's works is much more readily available in the common architectural texts of the period', and, in any case, such possible allusions as Johnson points to are too faint or subtle, for 'it is highly unlikely that [Jonson] would use such a recondite, learned, and rare text as the *Hypnerotomachia* without ensuring that everyone knew that he had absorbed it as part of his self-education in the classics and European literature. Jonson is simply not the man to make a sly or shy allusion.' Leslie, 'The *Hypnerotomachia* and the Elizabethan Landscape Entertainments', 132.

[8] In his catalogue of Jonson's library in *Studies in Philology*, 71/5 (1974), David McPherson notes the following: 'Rejected by *H&S* (i.e. Herford and Simpson) I.262 as a forgery, but probably genuine. Both motto and signature (normal form) (i.e. "tanquam Explorator" and "Sum Ben: Ionsonij.") are printed rather than written in script and are larger than normal, it is true. But Jonson seems to have written larger on big folio title pages. If this is a forgery, we should probably reject several other books . . . This volume is heavily underlined with pencil, but the occasional annotations, which are usually translating Italian into Latin, are not in Jonson's hand (e.g., Sig. M4)', 38. McPherson's description of the copy as 'heavily underlined' with 'occasional

'outdoes any world the historian can offer; it gives the human imagination what it wants, an impossible object of desire; and it is inseparable from the fact that it is lost';[9] like the fountains of early modern England, and the great gardens in which they were set, the *Hypnerotomachia* at once figures presence and absence, and its place in the literary, cultural, and artistic record of the Renaissance in England is important, yet shifting, fragmented, and indistinct.

This book about real and literary fountains in early modern England began with Sidney and will end with Essex; Sidney will be returned to in Chapter 4, and Spenser and Jonson in Parts II and III, but the subject of its first three chapters is the *Hypnerotomachia*, that quintessentially Renaissance text, and its amazing fountains. The *Hypnerotomachia*'s woodcuts have long been plundered to illustrate works of garden history, their leafy arbours, elaborate topiary, and exotic fountains put forward as evidence of fashions in garden design in both England and continental Europe. But it remains a book that has been much noted and little read. To begin this study of fountains in early modern English literature and culture with the *Hypnerotomachia* therefore has a multiple purpose: to discuss Colonna's romance itself and some ways in which it might work (and in particular the function of the fountains which are such a feature of its illustrations and narrative), and also to explore the very particular use Philip Sidney made of one of those fountains, and to what end, in his *New Arcadia*. But it also sets out to explore (in some small degree) the relationship between the textual, the visual, the material, and the experiential in one Renaissance text (that is also a fabulous object and, more, a veritable garden of earthly—and unearthly—delights) and therefore to suggest how such relationships might more generally be apprehended and delineated in and among early modern texts, images, objects, spaces, and experiences.

The *Hypnerotomachia* is a (if not the) paradigm for the syncretic potentiality of Renaissance fountains, real and imagined, and the way in which they can structure both landscapes and texts. The capacity of the fountains in the romance to absorb multiple layers of significance means that they function

---

annotations' gives a rather misleading impression of its actual state. On page after page, the margins are scrawled over in smudged grey pencil in a huge, cursive Italic script. One of the two other recorded owners is easy to identify: Thomas Bourne, who bought the book for 9s. 6d. in 1641 and recorded this on the flyleaf; he may have been the Thomas Bourne who matriculated at St John's College, Cambridge, in 1624. The other name on the flyleaf is possibly 'Heydon'; as there are a number of astrological, astronomical, and alchemical symbols on the flyleaf, it suggests that this is Christopher Heydon (1561–1623), the soldier, traveller, and astrologer. See below.

   [9] Gent, 'Introduction', in *Albion's Classicism*, 13.

both as liminal points of revelation and as nodes of syncretism, where different strands of narrative intersect. One of the associations of fountains established in the *Hypnerotomachia* is their informability, their capacity for syncretism *per se*, and their creation or facilitation of narrative openness and intertextuality. Colonna's romance is an important starting point for any discussion of fountains in English Renaissance literature. It makes a difference to the ways of thinking about and experiencing landscape, and gardens in particular, just as the knowledge and experience of real landscapes and gardens (and fountains) in the early modern period can shape ways of reading texts in which such settings are often vital. The arrival and influence of the *Hypnerotomachia* in England in the 1580s and 1590s is therefore a vital development in early modern literature and culture, a key Renaissance moment.

The *Hypnerotomachia* is a famous and valuable book, but it is not particularly rare. It has always been expensive and, as William Ivins noted in 1930, 'with the possible exception of the *Nuremburg chronicle*, which was too big to be read or used, it is today the commonest of fifteenth-century books';[10] it has been, for most of its history, more a collector's trophy than essential reading. Copies abound, the majority in pristine condition, whether immaculately restored or unread: Pozzi and Ciapponi collate fourteen copies in their table of variants, but include none in the United Kingdom (there are four in the British Library alone) and only one in the United States; neither do they include holdings in Florence and Rome.[11] One of the three superb copies of the 1499 folio in the Fitzwilliam Museum in Cambridge, for example, is bound in blue morocco and has its initial capitals beautifully illuminated and gilded;[12] another copy of the 1561 French edition in the Cambridge University Library is pristine, save that every naked nymph has been tinted a delicate pink.[13] Given the erotic nature of the romance and many of its illustrations, it is unsurprising that there appears to have been something of a frisson in the possession of a copy, even one of the many where the most explicit illustration, of the sacrifice to Priapus, has been censored with a crude black box.

When Aldus Manutius published the first edition in 1499, which numbered some 600 copies, it appears not to have been particularly popular, for it took half a century for the edition to sell out. It was, however, influential and in many ways seminal, especially given that the press had only acquired its first Roman type in 1495: not quite the first illustrated book to appear from the Aldine press, but by far the most elaborate, it was typographically innovative, with its own new font ('Poliphilus', still in use today), its characteristic 'goblet'

---

[10] Ivins, 'Artistic Aspects of Fifteenth-Century Printing', 40.

[11] *Hypnerotomachia Poliphili*, ed. Giovanni Pozzi and Lucia A. Ciapponi (Padua: Editrice Antenore, 1964). Henceforth *Hypnerotomachia* (1964).

[12] Marlay Bequest, 1912.   [13] Cambridge University Library SSS.40.23.

shapes at the end of chapters, and, in its illustrations, Greek, Hebrew, and even Arabic scripts (the first printed examples of the latter). It included elaborate imprese and pseudo-hieroglyphics, one of which, the dolphin and anchor, became the insignia of the Aldine press. Although the identity of the author was not at first known, by the early sixteenth century decoding of the acrostic formed by the initial letters of the first thirty-eight chapters had revealed that 'POLIAM FRATER FRANCISCVS COLVMNA PERAMAVIT' ('Brother Francesco Colonna loved Polia greatly'), and a MS note to this effect is not infrequently found in copies of the text.[14] Colonna was a Dominican monk who was born in Treviso and educated in Padua, but spent most of his life at the monastery of St John and St Paul in Venice, where he died in 1527 (apparently at the age of 94). Although other authors have been suggested, most notably and recently Leon Battista Alberti,[15] there seems no real reason to doubt this traditional attribution.

The second Aldine edition was published in 1545, and in 1546 a French translation was published by Jacques Kerver in Paris. As with Dallington's later effort, to describe the *Songe de Poliphile*[16] as a translation is misleading, although for different reasons: Jean Martin's version is shorter than the original by about a third, compressing many of the long descriptive passages. The woodcuts in the *Songe* are redrawn from the Aldine originals, although mostly based upon them, but they are far more elaborate and detailed, and some new illustrations are included. A second French edition followed in 1561, and a third in 1600, with the addition of an alchemical preface by Béroalde. It is not unlikely that it was as the *Songe de Poliphile* that the *Hypnerotomachia* first came to England, perhaps via the Low Countries, and, as will be seen, this seems to have been the version known to Sidney. It has been shown, for example, that Jan Van Der Noot (1538/9–1596/1601) drew heavily on the *Songe*, virtually copying part of its plot as well as several of its illustrations, in his Christian epic *Das Buch Extasis*.[17] This was published in Cologne in 1576,

---

[14] For example, in Cambridge University Library Inc.3.B.3.134 [1830].

[15] See, for example, Liane Le Faivre's *Leon Battista Alberti's Hypnerotomachia Poliphili: Re-cognizing the Architectural Body in the Early Italian Renaissance* (Cambridge, Mass.: MIT Press, 1997) and Roswitha Stewering's *Architektur und Natur in der 'Hypnerotomachia Poliphili' (Manutius 1499) und die Zuschreibung des Werkes an Niccolo Lelio Cosmico* (Hamburg: Lit, 1996) for two of the recent cases made for different authors. Earlier attributions included Eliseo da Treviso, and a second Francesco Colonna.

[16] To differentiate between the three versions, *Hypnerotomachia* is here used generically or to refer to the Italian text; although the French and English texts are properly titled *Hypnerotomachie, ou Discours du Songe de Poliphile* and *Hypnerotomachia: The Strife of Love in a Dreame*, they are referred to by their subtitles, as is conventional.

[17] Van Der Noot is best known via Edmund Spenser's translation of his sonnets in the *Theatre for Worldlings* (1569). See C. A. Zaalberg, *Das Buch Extasis van Jan Van Der Noot* (Assen: Van Gorcum, 1954).

with French and Dutch versions following in 1579. It seems, however, that Van Der Noot's composition of *Das Buch* post-dated his period of residence in England (1567–*c*.1570).

Even before its apparent arrival in England, there is a telling instance of a speaking loss or lack regarding the *Hypnerotomachia* and its reception. It should be perhaps the earliest English example of knowledge of the *Hypnerotomachia*, but it in fact suggests an ignorance of it, which allows a closer identification of when exactly it might have been that the *Hypnerotomachia* was first being read in England, and by whom. It is to be found in Sir Thomas Hoby's translation of Castiglione's *The Book of the Courtier*, which was first published in 1561; Hoby himself records, however, that the third Book (where the reference is found) was translated in 1552. In a discussion of the proper conduct of the lover, one of the participants states that

in times past I have knowen some that in writinge and speaking to women vsed euermore the woordes of *Poliphilus*, and ruffled so in their subtill pointes of Rhetoricke, that the women were out of conceite with their owne selues, and reckened themselues most ignoraunt, and an houre seemed a thousand yeere to them, to ende that talke and to be rid of them. (Ll2ᵛ)

Hoby's margin note, beginning at line 2 of the quotation above and therefore most probably providing a gloss on '*Poliphilus*', adds, 'Men that professe to be louinge in woordes'. But this is surely not the proper import of the name of the protagonist of the *Hypnerotomachia*, nor, indeed, of the context. Castiglione must mean men who talk like Colonna's Poliphilus: that is, who are (as the examples in this and the chapters following will show) hyperbolic, long-winded, pleonastic, and neologistic to the point where an hour spent in their company 'seemed a thousand yeere'. This is the sense in which a speaker in the Venetian senate was shouted down with cries of 'Poliphilian words!' Hoby seems to read it as meaning men who are, colloquially speaking, 'all talk'. If this inference is correct, then it suggests that either Hoby himself, Italophile though he was, was unaware of the precise associations of 'Poliphilus', or that he decided that the allusion would be meaningless to his English audience and so attempted to redefine it more generally, probably along etymological lines. Either way, it suggests that 'Poliphilus' and his eponymous text did not enjoy widespread currency in mid-sixteenth-century England. In the context of a discussion of fountains, this seems a particular shame for Hoby, given that, as has already been seen, he was very interested in fountains, describing many that he had seen during his travels in Italy and evidently delighting in their technicalities as much as in their beauty.[18]

---

[18] See the discussion of Hoby in the Introduction.

In 1592, six years after Sidney's death, this most famous 'picture' book of
the Renaissance finally appeared in an English translation, nearly a century
after it had first been published. Its translator signed himself R.D., and is
generally assumed to be Robert Dallington.[19] To describe *The Strife of Love
in a Dreame* (as Dallington's perhaps painfully literal subtitle had it) as the
Hypnerotomachia's English translation is misleading, for Dallington's quarto
peters out after translating only roughly the first two-fifths of the admittedly
mammoth original; a complete English translation did not appear until 1999.[20]
Educated at Benet College (later Corpus Christi), Cambridge, Dallington was
at first a Norfolk schoolmaster,[21] but he clearly had aspirations to court circles:
he went on to write accounts of his travels in France and Italy (discussed
in the Introduction), became a Gentleman of the Privy Chamber to Henry,
Prince of Wales, and eventually succeeded Francis Beaumont as Master of
Charterhouse. Like so many other writers of the last decade of the sixteenth
century, he addressed his dedicatory epistle to Robert Devereux, Earl of Essex:
but the book itself was dedicated 'To the Thrise Honovrable and Ever Lyving
Vertues of Syr *Phillip Sydney* Knight; and to the right honorable and others
whatsoever, who living loved him, and being dead give him his dve' (A1ᵛ).
Neither of these dedications is surprising: 1592 by no means marked the end
of the outpourings of memorial works dedicated to Sidney, though he had
been dead six years, and Essex, widely acknowledged (not least by himself) as
Sidney's true heir, was to receive more literary dedications in the decade leading
up to his death than anyone but Queen Elizabeth herself. Dallington was, as
it were, climbing on both bandwagons: he was to repeat his endorsement
of Essex in more practical, if even more risky, terms when he joined the
Essex rebellion in February 1601, for which he was briefly imprisoned and
fined £100. (The Essex rebellion, and the connection between Ben Jonson's
play and the Earl, is discussed in Chapter 12.) Dallington's dedications of his
translation to both Sidney and Essex may have been utterly conventional, but
his memorialization of Sidney in this context repays further attention, for in
translating the *Hypnerotomachia* he was bringing to an English audience a
work whose influence upon Sidney, and upon early modern literature and
culture in general, has never been fully explored.

---

[19] See C. S. Knighton, 'Dallington, Sir Robert (1561–1636 × 8)', *Oxford Dictionary of Nation-
al Biography* (www.oxforddnb.com/view/article/7042, accessed 3 Mar. 2006), and also Karl
Josef Höltgen, 'Sir Robert Dallington (1561–1637): Author, Traveler, and Pioneer of Taste',
Huntington Library Quarterly, 47 (1984), 147–77.

[20] Francesco Colonna, *Hypnerotomachia Poliphili*, trans. Joscelyn Godwin (London: Thames
and Hudson, 1999). All quotations, unless otherwise stated, are taken from this translation, and
have been checked against the Italian original.

[21] His patrons were the Buttes family, who had houses at Thornage and Great Ryburgh.

As well as being incomplete, Dallington's 1592 English translation appeared as a quarto, rather than in the more expensive folio format. Not surprisingly, like the *Songe* it has redrawn illustrations, but omits many, and those included are far less sophisticated than the originals. Only seven copies (some of them fragmentary) survive, which could suggest that it was popular, and its publication may have been complex: it appeared under three separate imprints, although apparently only two editions, all in 1592; it seems never to have been reprinted.[22] By 1599, it had enjoyed enough popular success (or notoriety) to be the butt of a joke by Thomas Nashe, when in the Epistle Dedicatory to his *Lenten Stuffe*, he said of his book 'Hugge it, ingle it, kisse it, and cull it now thou has it, & renounce eating of greene beefe and garlike, till Martlemas, if it be not the next stile to *The Strife of Loue in a Dreame*, or, the *Lamentable burning of Teuerton*'.[23] This latter concerned an event in April 1598, and any imputed connection between the two works is mystifying: it is a short, unpolished, moralized account, the style of which has nothing in common with *The Strife of Loue in a Dreame*. Some topical joke may have been intended, perhaps simply in the disjunction between the two texts, or else in their common and short-lived popularity, or else Nashe was simply being deliberately and ironically obscure.

Nashe's particular note of the 'stile' of *The Strife of Love in a Dreame* draws attention to one of the reasons why the *Hypnerotomachia* has been so little read. Colonna's original is, as Ivins described it, 'written in a jargon that is almost macaronic',[24] which its most recent translator points out 'must have been almost as difficult for sixteenth-century readers as it is today'.[25] (Godwin's translation does not attempt to reproduce this feature of the original.) It is a hybrid somewhere between Latin and Italian, stuffed with neologisms (many of them Greek in origin) and prolix and contorted in its syntax. The *Songe*'s translation greatly modified this feature of the text, but Dallington attempted to reproduce it in English, to bewildering and often comic effect. Nashe parodied this style and diction elsewhere in *Lenten Stuffe*, telling his dedicatee 'Lustie Humfrey' that his words in the Epistle Dedicatory were meant to 'notifie to your diminutiue excelsitude, and compendiate greatnesse, what my zeale is towardes you', and 'his Readers, hee cares not what they be': 'Let me speake to you about my huge woords which I vse in this booke'.[26] Nashe's use of 'huge woords' was deliberately bathetic in the disjunction between it and his subject matter, for the subject of the piece was his stay in Yarmouth after the trouble caused by his involvement in *The Isle of Dogs* (1597), and it included

---

[22] STC 5577, 5578, 5578.2.   [23] Sig. A3. The Teverton pamphlet is STC 24093.
[24] Ivins, 'Artistic Aspects of Fifteenth-Century Printing', 41.
[25] *Hypnerotomachia* (1999), p. x.   [26] Sig. A2, A4ᵛ.

his 'new Play neuer played before, of the praise of the RED HERRING'. But in undertaking such a laborious task as the translation of Colonna's romance, and however unsuccessfully, Dallington was surely responding to a climate of interest in the *Hypnerotomachia*, and not only in the work itself, but in art and architecture, antiquity and philology, gardens, Greek literature and culture, and romance. Given this environment, it is not surprising that he undertook his work in Sidney's name, for it was a culture in which Sidney had participated, and which he himself had helped to shape.

The critical history of the *Hypnerotomachia*, like that of its early reception, is uneven. In his preface to a facsimile of the *Hypnerotomachia*, Peter Dronke comments:

Though so much has been achieved in the understanding of Francesco and his work, there is still . . . a dearth of *literary* understanding. Within what genre and tradition was Francesco writing? What were his artistic intentions? How far did he succeed in realizing these intentions? How possible is it to perceive coherence in Francesco's design?[27]

There have been few full-length studies of the romance, and those that have appeared have been written to very particular agendas, notably Linda Fierz-David's *The Dream of Poliphilo* (1950) and Emanuela Kretzulesco-Quaranta's *Les Jardins du Songe 'Poliphile' et la mystique de la Renaissance* (1976).[28] Karen Pinkus notes

the overwhelming number of attempts to read the text within some broad interpretive spectrum or frame: Jungian, alchemical,[29] humanist-archeological, as a giant rebus occulting the narrative of an actual erotic encounter, and so on. Alternately, scholars will extract a single figure . . . in support of an iconographical motif study; this second reading ignores the question of a structural narrative logic that ultimately grants significance to the particular images.

---

[27] Peter Dronke, 'Introduction', in *Hypnerotomachia Poliphili (Venetiis, Aldo Manuzio, 1499)* (Zaragoza: Ediciones del Pórtico, 1981), 10.

[28] Linda Fierz-David, *The Dream of Poliphilo*, trans. Mary Hottinger (New York: Pantheon, 1950); Emanuela Kretzulesco-Quaranta, *Les Jardins du Songe 'Poliphile' et la mystique de la Renaissance* (Rome: Editrice Magma, 1976). In addition to the essays in the special volume devoted to the *Hypnerotomachia, Word & Image* (1998), two of the best recent accounts of the *Hypnerotomachia* are by Rosemary Trippe, 'The *Hypnerotomachia Poliphili*, Image, Text, and Vernacular Poetics', *Renaissance Quarterly*, 55 (2002), 1222–58, and chapter 10, 'A Special License' (together with appendix 1), in Patricia Fortini Brown, *Venice & Antiquity: The Venetian Sense of the Past* (New Haven: Yale University Press, 1996).

[29] Fierz-David's study is both Jungian and alchemical. Karen Pinkus dismisses both Jung and Fierz-David, saying that they 'impose a pre-established frame onto Colonna's text which they read completely ahistorically'. Karen Pinkus, 'The Moving Force in Colonna's *Hypnerotomachia Poliphili*', in Rhoda Schnur (ed.), *Conventus Neo-Latini Hafniensis: Eighth International Congress of Neo-Latin Studies* (Copenhagen: Medieval and Renaissance Texts and Studies, 1992), 831.

It is precisely this last area that the following two chapters investigate, arguing that the *Hypnerotomachia* is indeed highly structured and coherent on a number of interconnecting levels, and that its fountains in particular allow it to combine and invoke different narrative conventions, traditions, and topoi. Fountains in the *Hypnerotomachia* are used as structural devices, delimiting the various sections of the romance and providing essential points of reference and contact between its two books. They also invoke particular narrative conventions, and enable connections to be made between the different narratives operating within the romance, allowing Poliphilus' search for Polia to be seen as an allegory of human life and in spiritual or sacramental terms. Gilles Polizzi, one of the most prolific commentators on the French translation of the *Hypnerotomachia*, comments that the romance 's'inscrit . . . dans une tradition exégétique qui a accoutumé les lecteurs à distinguer, dans un texte, plusieurs niveaux de sens' (is written . . . within an exegetical tradition whereby readers were used to discerning, in one text, several layers of meaning).[30] The fountains stimulate and facilitate this way of reading.

Almost no traces of the illustrations of *The Strife of Love in a Dreame* (or indeed those of the Italian or French versions) survive in the visual arts of the period in England: although Anthony Wells-Cole notes 'the copying of a triumphal arch for the title page of Samuel Daniel's *Complaynt of Rosamund* (1592)',[31] even this is not an instance of copying so much as recycling: the printer, Simon Waterson, simply reused for the title page of the Daniel the woodcut showing the entrance to the pyramid in *The Strife of Love in a Dreame*,[32] inserting the title into the blank space of the archway. Yet at the same time as his specific copy of the book fails to elucidate how or when Ben Jonson might have read the *Hypnerotomachia*, the traces that it retains of an earlier owner do provide tangible evidence of its reception and influence in early modern England—and it is evidence that is at once textual, visual, and material, and that was once materially present and is now lost. If I am right in my reading of a faded, cropped autograph on the flyleaf as 'Heydon',[33] then this same copy of the *Hypnerotomachia* points instead to the first known instance of its influence on English art and architecture, a very few years after Sidney (as Chapter 4 will show) adapted it in his *Arcadia*. In 1593 Christopher Heydon, soldier, traveller, and astrologer, erected a massive monument to his

---

[30] Gilles Polizzi, 'L'Esthétique de l'énigme: le spectacle et le sens dans le *Songe de Poliphile*', *Rivista di letterature moderne e comparate*, NS 41/.3 (1988), 210.

[31] Anthony Wells-Cole, *Art and Decoration in Elizabethan and Jacobean England: The Influence of Continental Prints, 1558–1625* (New Haven: Yale University Press, 1997), 22.

[32] Sig. G4.

[33] I am very grateful to Angus Vine for taking the time to compare the flyleaf autograph with known examples of Heydon's signature; he confirmed my identification.

first wife Mirabel in the church of St Margaret in Saxlingham, Norfolk. It was in the form of 'an Egyptian pyramid of marble and stone, supported by pillars, and reaching almost to the top of the chancel . . . which takes up almost the entire building'; it was, in addition, 'covered with symbolic hieroglyphs'.[34] Perhaps inevitably, the tomb was dismantled in 1789, and only fragments of it remain, but it was clearly drawn directly from the *Hypnerotomachia*. Heydon was known to have travelled widely in Europe in the early 1580s, after receiving his Cambridge BA in 1579; it is worth noting that his time at Peterhouse coincided with the period spent at Corpus Christi (only a few moments' walk away) by another young man with strong north Norfolk connections, and who, like him, went on to be closely associated with the Earl of Essex: Robert Dallington. This short excursus into reception history aptly demonstrates the interconnectedness of the literary, the visual, and the material in early modern England that this book as a whole explores, at the same time as it demonstrates why the *Hypnerotomachia*, and its fountains, should be its point of origin.

[34] See Bernard Capp, 'Heydon, Sir Christopher (1561–1623)', *Oxford Dictionary of National Biography* (www.oxforddnb.com/view/article/13166, accessed 2 Mar. 2006), and Nikolaus Pevsner and Bill Wilson, *Norfolk 1: Norwich and North-East (The Buildings of England)* (New Haven: Yale University Press, 2002), 656. There is a detailed description of the tomb by Francis Blomefield, *An Essay Towards a Topographical History of the County of Norfolk* (London: William Miller, 1807), vi. 508–10. The Norfolk antiquary Tom Martin drew the monument in about 1740; his sketches and descriptions survive in Rye MS 17, vol. 3, fos. 184 ff. in the Norfolk Record Office in Norwich.

2

Reading Fountains in the *Hypnerotomachia*

Before discussing Sidney and the *Hypnerotomachia*, and the *Hypnerotomachia* in general, it would seem wise to give a brief summary of its action. In this chapter and the next the romance will be discussed in the order in which it unfolds, for it is so long and convoluted that any more thematic approach risks getting completely lost.

After a night of lovesick insomnia, tormented by desire for his beloved Polia, Poliphilus falls asleep and dreams that he is in a wood. There, he falls asleep again, and dreams that he is first in a forest, where, as he is terribly thirsty, he is about to drink from a spring when he is distracted by beautiful music. He goes in search of the source of the music, and finds a valley full of amazing architectural fragments—broken columns, a winged horse, a colossus, an elephant with an obelisk growing out of it. At the end of the valley is a vast pyramid with an elaborate carved entrance, through which he is chased by a dragon, emerging (via a dark tunnel) into a beautiful country. There he finally quenches his thirst at the Fountain of the Sleeping Nymph, and meets the nymphs of the five senses. He bathes with them in the octagonal bath-house, where he is squirted by the trickster fountain. The nymphs take him to the palace of Queen Eleuterylida ('free will'), where he has an audience with the queen, participates in an exotic banquet, watches a chess ballet, and sees many other marvels. He leaves the palace to go with two other nymphs, Logistica ('reason') and Thelemia ('will' or 'desire'), to the portals of the realm of Queen Telosia ('goal', 'final end'). On the journey he sees more marvels and, at the portals, he meets the various guardians of the three doors (labelled Theodoxia, 'glory of God', Cosmodoxia, 'glory of the world', and Erototrophos, 'mother of love'), and chooses this last door dedicated to Venus. Passing through it he finds himself in another pleasant country. There he meets a woman who, it transpires, is Polia, his beloved. Together they witness a triumphal procession depicting the loves of Jove (Europa, Leda, Danae, and Semele), another of Vertumnus and Pomona, and see a sacrifice to Priapus. Then, they go to the Temple of Venus, beside the sea, to participate in a ritual in which the burning torch that Polia carries will be immersed in a sacred well. After this and other rituals, Poliphilus and Polia voyage in Cupid's boat to Venus' island of Cytherea, at the centre of which is the Fountain of Venus. At the climax of the ceremonies there, Venus is revealed bathing in her fountain. Following this, at the end of the first book, the lovers and various attendant nymphs go to the Fountain of Adonis, beside which they sit and hear Polia tell the history of the lovers' relationship. This forms the second book of the romance. Polia's story describes how Poliphilus first fell in love with her, her initial rejection of him and of all love, and the eventual softening of her resolve, and includes the verbatim quotation of the lengthy love-letters sent to her by Poliphilus. The lovers are united at the end, but at the very last, her story concluded, Polia vanishes, and Poliphilus awakes alone.

The *Hypnerotomachia Poliphili*, or 'The dream-love-conflict of Poliphilus', is divided into two books. Although the romance's dream-vision frame encompasses both its books, they are of vastly disparate lengths and quite different in tone and aesthetic. Book 2 is less than a quarter of the length of Book 1, and may have been written first, then incorporated into the frame of the larger work; it includes the date '1467' as its (possibly fictive) date of completion (F3), and describes Polia as having come of age in 1462 (A3^v). As Joscelyn Godwin, the translator of the first complete English edition, points out, as well as being shorter, the second book 'has no descriptions of works of art or architecture. Apart from its realistic illustrations, its interest is psychological rather than aesthetic, as it relates the thorny history of Poliphilo and Polia's love',[1] while in their introduction to the Italian critical edition of the *Hypnerotomachia* Giovanni Pozzi and Lucia Ciapponi observe that 'le due sezioni riflettono sicuramente due esperienze letterarie distinte' (the two parts definitely reflect two distinct literary experiences), but add that they are 'malamente riunite con un accorgimento narrativo dei più banali' (badly joined together by an extremely banal narrative device).[2] In fact this is far from being the case, for the join between the two books is both subtle and vital, as the discussion of the romance in this chapter and the one following it will show. Book 1 is fantastic and dream-like, while Book 2 is in many respects more realistic and conventional, but the two are intimately connected on a number of levels and the spectacular fountains which are such a feature of the landscape (and illustrations) of Book 1 are crucial to this.[3] To take just one example, Book 2 'explains' why the main impulse driving Poliphilus, and hence the romance, in its first few chapters is a simple, physical one: thirst.

[1] *Hypnerotomachia Poliphili* (1999), pp. xii–xiii.
[2] *Hypnerotomachia* (1964), 2.8. All translations from Italian are my own.
[3] For a previous, brief account of some of the *Hypnerotomachia*'s fountains, see Comito, 'Beauty Bare', 18–22, 42–3, 50–1.

The romance's conventional dream-vision opening is shaped by Poliphilus' physical needs and desires, for sleep and water, as well as for Polia, and also by his curiosity about the environment in which he finds himself. Poliphilus first describes his thirst in the second chapter: 'Verye thirstie I was . . . and withall so extreamely set on heate, as the fresh ayre seemed to doe me more hurt then good' (B3ᵛ).[4] Almost immediately he finds a spring and kneels to drink from his cupped hands. But

it fell so out, that I had no sooner taken water into the palme of my hand, offering the same to my open mouth, ready to receiue it: I heard a doricall songe, wherewith I was as greatly delighted, as if I had heard the Thracian *Thamiras* . . . The sweetnes whereof so greatly delighted me, as thereby I was rauished of my remembrance, and my vnderstanding so taken from me, as I let fall my desired water. (B4)

Poliphilus' thirst is replaced by his desire to find the source of the music: 'And then euen as a birde, which through the sweetnes of the call forgetteth to remember the Fowlers deceit, so I letting slip that which nature stood in need of, hastened my selfe back with all speed towarde that attractiue melodie' (B4). But what has in fact happened is that the two have been elided: Poliphilus' thirst becomes his determination to locate the source of the beautiful antique song. It is no accident, surely, that the stream which he does find has its *source* so clearly described ('a pleasant spring or head of water . . . with a great vayne boyling vp, about the which did growe diuers sweet hearbes and water flowers, and from the same did flowe a cleare and chrystalline current streame', B3ᵛ) just before Poliphilus is distracted by wanting to locate the origin of the music. Several critics have commented that Poliphilus is really in love with antiquity, or that Polia is a personification of antiquity.[5] But that Poliphilus' desire for Polia coexists with his love of antiquity does not necessarily mean that the two objects of his desire are one and the same. At this stage, however, both Poliphilus' passions are represented by his physical thirst, and it is therefore not surprising that in Book 1, he goes on to encounter nine fountains, many of them symbolically and architecturally elaborate, and several of them unmistakably erotic. In the order in which Poliphilus comes to them, these are the spring from which he fails to drink, the sleeping nymph,

---

[4] Quotations are taken from the 1592 Dallington translation as far as possible (that is, until it concludes approximately two-fifths of the way through the romance). They have been checked against both the Italian text and the Godwin translation; on occasion the latter has been given, as being less oblique than the Dallington. Page references for all quotations from the *Hypnerotomachia* are given in the main body of the text.

[5] See Fierz-David, *The Dream of Poliphilo, passim*, Roswitha Stewering, 'The Relationship between World, Landscape and Polia in the *Hypnerotomachia Poliphili*', *Word & Image*, 14 (1998), 2–10, and Nathaniel Wallace, 'Architextual Poetics: The *Hypnerotomachia* and the Rise of the European Emblem', *Emblematica*, 8/1 (1994), 1–27.

the *puer mingens*, the courtyard fountain at the palace of Queen Eleuterylida, the two fountains on wheels at her banquet, the well in the Temple of Venus Physizoa, the Fountain of Venus, and the Fountain of Adonis. There are also others mentioned in passing, notably in the gardens of the palace of the Queen and in the gardens of Cytherea, but these are the main ones which are particularized and with which Poliphilus interacts. As this chapter in particular will show, these fountains are structurally, ethically, and aesthetically crucial to the romance.

To return to the *Hypnerotomachia*'s beginning, Poliphilus' fruitless search for the source of the music makes him even more thirsty and exhausted, and he lies down under a tree, 'taking into my hands halfe aliue, as my last refuge, the moyst and bedewed leaues, preserued in the coole shadow of the greene Oke: putting the same to my pale and drye lippes, with a greedy desire in licking of them to satisfie my distempred mouth with theyr moisture' (B4^v-C1). He falls asleep (in his dream), and begins a new dream, in which he finds himself in a far more pleasant environment. He sees in the distance a complex pyramid structure, blocking the end of the valley, the exploration of which occupies him for some time. It is this pyramid, illustrated on sig. B1^v of the 1499 Aldine edition and on sig. C4 of Dallington's 1592 translation, that was the visual source for the tomb of Mirabel Heydon in Saxlingham church, discussed in the previous chapter. While Poliphilus explores the pyramid and its environs, his thirst appears to have been forgotten, but the connection between his love of the monuments of antiquity and of Polia is made more explicit:

when I applyed my sences to consider, and addressed my eyes with diligent obseruation, curiouslie to ouerlooke euerie perticular part of this sweete composed obiect, and most rare and goodly imagerie and virgin like bodyes, without cracke or flaw, with a long drawne breath, and somewhat opening my mouth, I set a deepe sighe. In so much as my amorous and sounding breathing . . . gaue an accho [*sic*], and did put me in minde of my Angelike and extreame desired *Polia*. (D2^v)

Despite this thought of his beloved, Poliphilus' relentless passion for description continues, and it is not for some time that he is again moved to think of Polia, once more by the pleasure with which he regards the ancient monuments. Just as Poliphilus turns to leave the pyramid's porch, which he has been examining, he is confronted by a dragon and forced to flee back through the dark, winding passages of the pyramid. He emerges on its other side into a 'fayre and plentifull countrie' (I3^v) (Fig. 2).

In this new environment, Poliphilus encounters other fine edifices, but the first significant building he sees turns out to be a fountain: 'I found a building eight square, with a rare and wonderfull fountaine: which was not altogither amisse. For as yet I had not quenched and slaked my thirst' (K1ᵛ). Poliphilus' thirst has been transferred unabated from his first dream to his second, but it has until this point been elided with his desire to examine and understand his new environment. This new fountain is the catalyst for the redifferentiation of the two. It is in the form of a sleeping nymph[6] watched by three satyrs, with water flowing from her breasts. After Poliphilus describes the scene in his customary detail, he admits: 'I could not say whether the temptation to drink came more from the burning thirst of that whole day and the one before, or from the beauty of the source, whose chill indicated that the stone was lying' (73). There is, again, that elision of thirst, desire, and the love and admiration of beautifully crafted things that has given an underlying momentum to the romance until this point. As Alberto Pérez-Gomez puts it, the *Hypnerotomachia* demonstrates that

architectural meaning is not something intellectual, a 'formal' question of proportional relationships or abstract aesthetic values, but rather originates in the erotic impulse itself, in the need to quench our physical thirst: the existential condition to which humanity can only be reconciled within the realm of poiesis (the making of culture, that is, art and architecture) and its metaphoric imagination.[7]

It is surprising that Pérez-Gomez does not remark on the crucial way in which the narrative' fountains articulate this principle. Poliphilus' drinking from the fountain marks the end of what is the first major section of the romance. He is about to encounter the five nymphs who will be his companions for the next stage. His refreshment and revival as he drinks from the breast of the fountain nymph parallels his revival in Book 2 when Polia exposes her breasts to him (421), an incident which seems gratuitous in its own context. Both incidents mark points of transition in the romance, and they are related by the carefully constructed nexus of thirst and desire.

One of the functions of the fountains in Book 1 is clearly their literalization of the motif of desire as thirst, and its quenching, which can be seen as having been 'projected back' into Book 1 from Book 2.[8] But they also have further narrative functions, marking key moments of epiphany, transition, or transformation in Poliphilus' journey. In particular they provide a link between the setting and the different strands or possible readings of the romance, and construct and contribute to the 'sacramental narrative' of the *Hypnerotomachia*, whereby, as Poliphilus journeys from birth to maturity, he is simultaneously initiated into

[6] See Elisabeth B. MacDougall, 'The Sleeping Nymph: Origins of a Humanist Fountain Type', *Art Bulletin*, 57 (1975), 357–65.
[7] Alberto Pérez-Gomez, 'The *Hypnerotomachia Poliphili* by Francesco Colonna: The Erotic Nature of Architectural Meaning', in Vaughan Hart and Peter Hicks (eds.), *Paper Palaces: The Rise of the Renaissance Architectural Treatise* (New Haven: Yale University Press, 1998), 92–3.
[8] This connection is explored in more detail in Chapter 3.

pagan, or at the very least secular, versions of the appropriate sacraments of the Church. Poliphilus' thirst may give the narrative its initial momentum, but he manages to drink from the second fountain he encounters, that of the sleeping nymph, and so, temporarily at least, to slake it. This is preceded by his lengthy exploration of the ruined antiquities around the pyramid, and then his terrifying flight from the dragon through its labyrinthine passages, until he emerges safe into the realm of Queen Eleuterylida. This episode is obviously a (re)birth: Poliphilus finally escapes through 'a narrow funnel-shaped tube' (65); Queen Eleuterylida's country, into which he emerges, is literally that of 'Free-will' (a synonym for 'human life'); and his first action is to suckle at the breast of a statue.

In addition, the pyramid itself can, with the benefit of hindsight, be seen as fulfilling many of the characteristics of the fountain type, so reinforcing the romance's punctuation by fountains at key moments. There are a number of reasons for suggesting this interpretation, unlikely though it may seem. First, it is clearly identified as sacred to Venus, with a Greek inscription on the portal which translates as 'To the blessed Mother, the Goddess Venus and to her Son, Amor, Bacchus and Demeter have given of their own substances' (51). Many of the other fountains in the romance are explicitly associated with Venus, and Poliphilus himself says that 'reason perswaded mee to suppose, that with in might bee the Aultar of *Venus* for hir misticall Sacrifices and sacred flames, or the representation of hir Godhead, or the *Aphrodise* of hir selfe and hir little Archer' (H2ᵛ). When he reaches what is presumably the sanctuary, he sees three golden statues, which would correspond to Venus, Ceres, and Bacchus, the three gods who are much later revealed together in the Fountain of Venus at the climax of the romance. Furthermore, the forecourt of the pyramid is full of ruins including 'Great lauers condites, and other infinite fragments of notable woorkmanship' (C2). The pyramid is guarded by a dragon, a common feature of both Renaissance and classical fountains: Sir James Frazer appended a note to his Loeb translation of Apollodorus 3.4 (the story of Cadmus) that it is 'a common superstition that springs are guarded by dragons or serpents'. The fountain that Poliphilus will later encounter in the courtyard of Queen Eleuterylida's palace includes dragons, and indeed among the elaborate decorations on the pyramid's portal, mosaics tell the story of Europa and her brothers who 'valiauntly kylled the skalie fierce Dragon that kepte the fayre Fountayne' (H3ᵛ). The pyramid is clearly not a fountain *per se*, but it has important fountain elements in its composition and significance; it participates in and contributes to the symbolic economy which they help to structure in the romance. In particular, it prefigures the Fountain of Venus, adding to the romance's circularity, and reinforces the strong liminal associations of fountains in the text. Perhaps a dry fountain, or one that he cannot fully appreciate and understand, is most appropriate to Poliphilus at this stage in his life and journey, representing his as yet unawakened sensibilities.

Once he has passed the limen of the pyramid of Venus, been born into the realm of free will and suckled at the breast of ΠΑΝΤΑ ΤΟΚΑ ΔΙ ('the mother of all', Venus), Poliphilus meets the nymphs of the five senses, Aphea ('touch'), Osfressia ('smell'), Orassia ('sight'), Achoe ('hearing'), and Geussia ('taste'). He is sensually educated by them, as well as learning about their country, as he bathes with them. His drenching by the ΓΕΛΟΙΑΣΤΟΣ ('trickster') fountain corresponds to baptism (Fig. 3), especially coming as it does after Poliphilus has been closely questioned by the nymphs and has named himself. This device consists of a urinating boy (one of the most common fountain types of the Renaissance, known as the *puer mingens* or *putto pissatore*), held up by two nymphs, set into one of the interior walls of the bath-house: when Poliphilus goes to fill a jug from the stream of cold water, he activates a mechanism hidden in a trick step, which causes the jet to change direction and squirt him in the face. Such water jokes were well known in Elizabethan gardens and, far from being merely frivolous diversions, they sometimes, like the fountain which here drenches Poliphilus, had an underlying moral import; one such, at Kenilworth, is discussed in Chapter 8, and another, at Nonsuch, in Chapter 12. Similar 'antike boyes' could be found on the fountain in Spenser's Bowre of Bliss, as well as on the great fountain at Hampton Court, and they can still be seen on the fountain at the centre of the Great Court in Trinity College, Cambridge.[9] The baptismal interpretation of this particular water joke in the *Hypnerotomachia*, suggested by the centrality of the figure of the child, is strengthened by the octagonal bath-house, a shape frequently used for baptismal fonts and baptisteries, and by the way in which Poliphilus is afterwards 'anointed'. The unguent, which Poliphilus assumes is a liniment for his aching muscles, instead has an aphrodisiac effect not noted in chrism: it is a sacrament of Venus, as Poliphilus is initiated into the realm of both free will and sensual pleasure.

Another feature of the *Hypnerotomachia* introduced by the pyramid and the ruins that surround it (the elephant, the colossus, and the winged horse), and which reaches its fullest expression in the Fountain of the Sleeping Nymph, is its exploration of scopophilia, or voyeurism, the erotic pleasure of looking, for Poliphilus derives pleasure, above all, from looking at beautiful things. In the figure of the leering satyr, at the Fountain of the Sleeping Nymph, both Poliphilus and the reader are implicated, as the nymph's naked

---

[9] This fountain, and 'antike boyes' on English fountains in general, is discussed by Henderson, *The Tudor House and Garden*, 187–8.

body is displayed simultaneously to the satyr, Poliphilus, and the reader; the erotic pleasure of the gaze is henceforth implied in every other woodcut and lovingly detailed description. One of the illustrations added to the *Songe* depicts the interior of the bath-house, a section of the wall cut away to reveal the five naked nymphs. Poliphilus is seated in the foreground looking in, and the reader is invited to share his privileged perspective. The fountains of the romance are particularly good examples of this celebratory voyeurism because of their materialization of the connection between thirst and desire, between physical need, material and sensory experience, and visual pleasure. Helena Szépe investigates the scopophilia in the romance, discussing the sleeping nymph and suggesting that 'the visual emphasis of the book stems in part from the premise of the text as a discourse of desire'. In the instance of the sleeping nymph fountain, the reader's action in turning the page even mirrors that of the satyr as he draws aside the curtain to reveal the nymph's naked body. Szépe makes the shrewd observation that 'Desire is ultimately displaced onto the body of the book as a beautiful object, and collector's prize'.[10] The reader cannot but be aware of the status of this text as an object, of its physical existence as a book, and its illustrations are less lively than they are concrete. Their representation of architectural fragments, of elaborately carved and constructed edifices (and even, in the French version, of diagrams of their proportions), is solidly material; that which looks like a classical scene set in a landscape is frequently a bas relief (or, in the case of the sleeping nymph, for example, a fountain) extracted from its immediate surroundings or context and enlarged, and accordingly the illustrations depicting 'real' events in the narrative themselves take on something of a sculptural quality. This is particularly true of the later scenes of the triumphal processions, where first the scenes illustrating the sides of the chariots are enlarged as separate illustrations, telling, for example, the story of Europa or of Semele, and then the triumph as a whole being depicted on much the same scale. The events witnessed by Poliphilus and Polia (and the reader) thus take on the quality of a sculptural frieze, unfolding in space and, more, in matter, as much as in time. Again, the physicality of the book reinforces this aspect of the text, for the narrative can only progress through the physical participation of the reader in turning pages, as a frieze can only be appreciated as one walks along its length—or a garden as one wanders in it.

In some instances, this emphasis on the material is developed further for both protagonist and perhaps reader: although Poliphilus undoubtedly takes

---

[10] Helena Katalin Szépe, 'Desire in the Printed Dream of Poliphilo', *Art History*, 19/3 (1996), 370–1, 381.

visual pleasure in the *puer mingens*, knowing how it works in a technical sense also pleases him intellectually: 'I founde out the concauitie, and perceiued that any heauy weight, being put vpon the moueable stepping, that it would rise vp like the Keye and Iacke of a Virginall, and lift vp the Boyes pricke, and finding out the deuise and curious workemanship thereof, I was greatly contented' (M3). Thomas Hoby was similarly delighted by the 'devices' of the fountains he saw in Italy, and visitors to English Renaissance gardens were also charmed and fascinated by the ingenuity of water jokes and inventive fountains such as those at Nonsuch, Theobalds, and Kenilworth.[11] At other points in the *Hypnerotomachia*, the reader's intellectual curiosity is fed with diagrams and geometrical formulae as well as pictures, and with typographical *tours de force*. The compulsion of desire, its visual character, and its tendency to displacement and transferral (Poliphilus' desire for Polia becomes the desire for antiquity and for water; the reader desires simultaneously to read, to look, and to possess) are therefore crucial links between reader and protagonist, propelling Poliphilus through his dream landscape and the reader through the book. To read the *Hypnerotomachia*, and to consider the way in which the fountains in particular compel the attention of the reader as much as they at once stimulate and assuage Poliphilus' desire, is to see how the book is like a garden, which is not so much read as experienced. In the vast dream garden-landscape of the *Hypnerotomachia*, buildings, statues, inscriptions, and fountains supply meaning and structure to both the narrative which unfolds within it and the experience of reading that narrative. There is a parallel here with the way in which, in Elizabethan portraits (both full-size and miniature), mottoes (or even poems), symbols, and settings, both realistic and fantastical, at once invest a portrait with meaning on its own terms as a discrete entity, and suggest a process of apprehension, or particular strategy of interpretation whereby it might be viewed, read, or understood.[12] The *Hypnerotomachia* is far from being the only text to operate thus, and early modern gardens 'worked' in much the same way.

When Poliphilus and the five nymphs arrive at the palace of Queen Eleuterylida, the first notable feature commented upon by him is an amazingly opulent fountain (N3ᵛ, 90), made of gold and semi-precious stones, and surmounted by golden statues of the Three Graces bearing cornucopiae (Fig. 4). This fountain again has a liminal function, signalling that Poliphilus is entering even more deeply into an environment of artifice, opulence, and sensual, especially visual, pleasure: it heralds the extraordinary aesthetic opulence that

---

[11] See the discussion of Hoby in the Introduction, and of Theobalds, Kenilworth, and Nonsuch in Chapters 4, 8, and 12 respectively.

[12] See the discussion of inscriptions in the Introduction, and also the particular discussion of the portrait of Sir George Delves in Chapter 11.

Poliphilus will find at the palace. The entire episode functions almost entirely as a self-indulgent piece of *amplificatio* to the main business of the plot, which is ostensibly Poliphilus' quest for Polia. Poliphilus' visit to the court of Queen Eleuterylida is the most medieval passage of the romance, and the nature of the romance as a quasi-medieval quest (especially in its French translation) is one of Gilles Polizzi's preoccupations. Particularly at the beginning of Book 1, he sees Poliphilus as negotiating the typical terrain encountered by the quest hero: 'une "forêt obscure", une "rivière ténébreuse", puis un "val périlleux" ' (a 'dark forest', a 'gloomy stream', then a 'perilous valley').[13] He notes that Poliphilus' quest, 'de la "forêt obscure" à Cythère, du désordre à l'ordre... agence sous une forme nouvelle une topique conventionnelle empruntée aux récits de quête médiévaux' (from the 'dark forest' to Cytherea, from disorder to order... presents in a new form a conventional topic borrowed from the tales of medieval quests), which leads in turn to 'un compromis entre l'espace narratif linéaire des romans médiévaux et une représentation "moderne" projetée dans une topographie cohérente' (a compromise between the linear narrative space of medieval romances and a 'modern' spectacle realized in a coherent topography).[14] Fountains are, of course, a feature of many medieval romances, and it has been suggested that some of the details of the feast are drawn from accounts of the banquets of the medieval dukes of Burgundy; certainly one of the few surviving medieval table fountains comes from that court.[15] Although completely unchivalric, Book 1 of the *Hypnerotomachia* does in many respects resemble the quests of medieval French romance, not least in its linear structure and the way in which guidance is given to the protagonist by women. It is therefore unsurprising that the French translator added a few more medievalizing touches, such as a comparison between the Queen's palace and a 'royaume de Faerie'. Comparison with the *Roman de la Rose*, however, a text with which it engages at several key points, shows that the *Hypnerotomachia*'s ethos—and its fountains—are decidedly un-medieval: it remains a quintessentially Renaissance text.[16] Again, its illustrations are important here: they are largely sculptural in effect as opposed to simply pictorial, and the narrative's action, like the experience of reading it, is sensual and participatory.

Poliphilus' stay at the court of Queen Eleuterylida marks another transition in his quest for Polia and also in his 'life'. Having arrived there in the company

---

[13] Gilles Polizzi, 'Le *Poliphile* ou l'*Idée* du jardin: pour une analyse littéraire de l'esthétique colonienne', *Word & Image*, 14/1–2 (1998), 66.

[14] Ibid. 65.   [15] See Miller, *French Renaissance Fountains*.

[16] See my discussion of some aspects of this comparison in 'Sacred and Profane Love: Four Fountains in the *Hypnerotomachia* (1499) and the *Roman de la Rose*', *Word & Image*, 22 (2006), 1–13.

of the nymphs of the five senses, he leaves with Logistica and Thelemia, Reason and Desire. His encounter with the *puer mingens* corresponded to baptism in the romance's 'sacramental narrative', and this particular narrative strand continues at the court of Queen Eleuterylida: after the banquet, attendant nymphs bring in a tree of coral, planted in a hill of emeralds, with flowers made of precious stones and 'real' apples, which Poliphilus and some of the others are offered and eat. As if this were not an obvious enough Eucharistic allegory, a large wheeled fountain then appears, sprinkling (aspersing, censing) the company with 'a perfume such as my senses had never known before' (116) (Fig. 5). More nymphs bring 'a great cuppe of golde, and her highnesse affably saluting vs, drunke Nectar, and afterwardes euerie one of vs after other, with reuerent, mutual, and solemne honours done, did drinke a most pleasaunt farewell' (R2). This 'communion' marks Poliphilus' attainment of reason as much as his departure with Logistica and Thelemia does. The palace fountains are the last that Poliphilus encounters before meeting Polia, but on the journey to the portals of Queen Telosia, Logistica takes him up a tower that overlooks a water garden made as a labyrinth. This is clearly an allegory of human life, divided by seven towers into seven cycles, each of seven revolutions. (The water labyrinth is another illustration added to the *Songe* that does not appear in the *Hypnerotomachia*, although perhaps unsuccessfully.) A voyage through the labyrinth becomes increasingly dangerous and difficult, and the towers bear Greek slogans such as 'ΔΟΖΑ ΚΟΣΜΙΚΗΩΣΠΟΜΦΟΛΥΣ' (Worldly glory is like a bubble) and 'ΘΕΟΝΛΥΚΟΣΔΥΣ ΑΔΓΗΤΟΣ' (The wolf of the gods is hard-hearted). The labyrinth is inhabited by an invisible dragon and in the final tower is a judge, 'balancing euery ones actions, and helping whom hee will helpe' (T1). Its appearance at this point draws attention to one of Poliphilus' 'narratives' particularly aptly, as he has now reached 'maturity'.

After passing through the Erototrophos ('mother of love') gate at the portals of Queen Telosia (having rejected Theodoxia, 'glory of God', and Cosmodoxia, 'glory of the world'), and finding himself in a pleasant countryside filled with lovers, Poliphilus meets the nymph whom he goes on to realize is Polia. When he first encounters her, she is carrying 'in her snowe white left arme, close to her body, a kindled and burning Torch' (X4^v). It is shortly after this that Dallington's translation ends, following the triumph of Pomona and Vertumnus, but omitting the sacrifice to Priapus. At the end of *The Strife of Love in a Dreame* the lovers go to 'an olde decaied temple' by the sea (Cc2^v), but it is only mentioned in passing: an ending is cobbled together without them being definitely united, let alone consummating their love, and without Poliphilus ever awaking. Having continued to hold on to the burning torch for the next seventy-five pages (in the 1499 folio), Polia finally utilizes it in the first part of the rituals at the Temple of Venus Physizoa, beside the sea.

While simple, physical thirst has disappeared as a motivation for Poliphilus, the 'pagan' rituals which take place at the temple, and other subsequent ceremonies, continue to revolve around water. They are initially centred around a well or cistern, and involve Poliphilus, Polia, the priestess, and seven acolytes. The doorway into the temple is labelled ΚΥΛΟΠΗΡΑ, which is a sanctuary of Venus on Mount Hermettus; in Ben Jonson's copy of the 1545 folio in the British Library, it has been glossed 'a certaine fountaine whear woemen dranke at to conceaue wth childe' (n6^v). The well is located in the centre of the main part of the temple, and it is fed by an ingenious catchment system with rainwater from the roof. The nine women and Poliphilus assemble at 'the fateful mouth of the mysterious well' (214), with the acolytes bringing various ritual implements. The cover is unlocked, and consecrated salt water is poured in by the priestess. Finally, the purpose of the torch becomes clear:

Thereupon [the priestess] caused the burning torch to be inverted with its flame in the middle of the opening, and questioning the nymph [Polia] she said: 'Daughter, what is your wish and desire?' The nymph replied: 'Holy Priestess, I ask grace for him, that together we may attain the amorous kingdom of the divine Mother, and drink of that sacred fountain'. Likewise she said to me: 'And you, my son, what do you ask?' I replied humbly, 'Most sacred lady, I not only beg the efficacious grace of the supernal Mother, but above all, that she whom I believe to be my most desired Polia should keep me no longer vacillating in such amorous torment'. The divine Priestess said to me: 'Son, take now this torch, lit by her pure hand, and holding it thus, say thrice after me: "As the water extinguishes this burning torch, so let the fire of love be rekindled in her cold and stony heart"'. I said this with the holy ritual and the proper words, just as the Hierophant had told me. When it was finished, all the virgin priestesses, expert in their venerable ministry, responded 'So be it'. The last time, she had me immerse the torch reverently in the cold cistern. (216)

Why a burning torch should be associated with Polia and extinguished by Poliphilus is not immediately apparent. Earlier she has explained to him 'I must take this torch, lit by your love, to the sacred temple, and, as you will see, offer and extinguish it there' (179). After the ceremony, she tells him that

your ardent and excessive desire and your constant and persistent love have altogether stolen me away from the college of chastity, and forced me to extinguish my torch... Look: I feel the fire of fervent love spreading and tingling throughout my whole being... Here I am with my profuse tears to quench your burning heart. (217–18)

The torch has therefore been a symbol both of Poliphilus' love for Polia, which he has symbolically shared with her in the water, and the Vestal torch of chastity which Polia has now relinquished. It is also obviously phallic, and the more erotic aspects of the romance's fountains will be discussed in the next chapter, in the context of the Fountain of Venus.[17] The union of fire and water, which will be the metaphorical end of Book 2, is here accomplished in 'pagan' ritual (Fig. 6).

The rest of the rituals take place in an inner 'chapel', and involve the immolation of doves and swans, the writing of arcane characters in their ashes and blood, and the conjuring of a miraculous rose-bush and vision of Cupid. At the climax of the ritual, Poliphilus, Polia, and the priestess eat the fruit of the marvellous bush. The 'pagan' rituals undertaken by Polia and Poliphilus in the Temple of Venus Physizoa reflect the interplay between fire and water in the romance. But they too are part of the romance's 'sacramental programme' (and hence of its allegory of human life), and they are discussed in these terms by Peter Dronke. According to him, the description of the ceremony 'is coloured both by antiquarian lore about the rites performed by Roman vestal virgins (which Francesco culled largely from explications of rare words in Paulus Diaconus) and by transpositions from the Christian liturgy, in particular that of Easter Saturday'.[18] In the rite of the Easter Saturday Vigil, as it was practised in Venice in the time of Colonna, both fire (the Paschal candle) and water (the baptismal waters of the font) are blessed. 'The blessing of the font begins with the renowned psalm-image where water epitomizes the quenching of desire: "As the hart longs for the water-brooks, so my soul longs for you"'.[19] This *Sicut cervus* motif can be seen as operating throughout the romance. The (unlit) end of the Paschal candle is plunged into the font three times, symbolizing the blessing and vivifying of the water by the power of the Holy Spirit. Dronke describes Colonna's version thus:

In the profane counterpart to this ritual created by Francesco Colonna, there is similarly fire and water, the torch and the font. Here too, before the fire descends into the water and kindles the water with its loving power, comes a prayer which the priestess instructs Poliphilo to say three times . . . After each utterance of this prayer, as of those that follow, the participants respond 'Amen' (Cusì fia). When, the third time, Poliphilo plunges the lit torch into the font, its vivifying force is made manifest in the heroine.[20]

Other liturgical features not commented upon by Dronke are also present. For example, the pouring of salt water into the well recalls the making of holy

---

[17] Rosemary Trippe considers the torch as phallus in some detail, pointing out that in the illustration of Poliphilus' initial reunion with Polia beside the jasmine pergola (i7 in the Aldine editions) the way in which Poliphilus holds a bunched-together handful of his gown expresses his sexual arousal, mirroring the erect nature of Polia's torch in the same illustration. See Trippe, 'The *Hypnerotomachia Poliphili*, Image, Text, and Vernacular Poetics', *passim*, and especially 1243–8.

[18] Dronke, 'Introduction', *Hypnerotomachia Poliphili*, 41.

[19] Ibid. 58. Psalm 42: 1–2.   [20] Dronke, 'Introduction', 59.

water, and the question-and-answer formula used by the priestess suggests
that used with a candidate for baptism.

As the blessing of the candle and water in the *Sancto Sabato* rite is followed
by the sacrifice of the first Mass of Easter, so in this 'pagan' reinvention of
the ritual there is a sacrifice, of birds sacred to Venus, and a 'communion', as
the participants eat the rose-bush's fruit (233). That the eating of the fruit is
'Eucharistic' is emphasized by Poliphilus' comment that 'By this apparition I
guessed that a divine being was present, and suspected that the holy Mother
herself was *concealed in this species*' (233). This is glossed clearly by Pozzi:

The figure of the rosebush conceals the divinity of Venus. This is evidence of the
transposition of the real presence in the sacrament of the Eucharist. This confirms
the use of the term 'species' which is the technical term by which theology designates
the bread and the wine after consecration. The spiritual eating of the fruit imitates the
communion rite which usually accompanies Christian matrimony.[21]

Pozzi regards the ritual as a marriage. But the Easter Vigil elements of the
ceremony suggest that it is also meant to recall both the baptism of new converts
and the taking of holy orders, which would be as fitting an interpretation,
as during the ceremony Polia is rebaptized and changes her votive allegiance
from Diana to Venus.

As the lovers leave the temple together, Poliphilus describes his heart as
'infused with an inner sweetness and its hurtful fires quenched in celestial
dew' (235), an image that recalls his desperate attempt to quench his thirst
with the dew-covered leaves at the beginning of the romance (19), as well as
anticipating much of the imagery used to characterize the lovers' relationship
in Book 2. A point of equilibrium has been reached, in that ice has been
melted and burning pain cooled: both the romance and the relationship can
now move towards their final stage at the Fountain of Venus. Poliphilus
contemplates his beloved's beauty in a description that, as Roswitha Stewering
observes, blends seamlessly into his description of the idyllic landscape. In
particular, he comments:

I was stupefied, anxious, tense and curious, wondering with astonishment how and
why that crimson fluid turns pure milk-white when one presses the precious flesh
of the rounded wrist, and for a little while does not return. No less did I wonder by
what artifice Madame Nature had formed this lovely body, and flooded it with all the
perfume of Arabia. (239)

---

[21] '*in quella specie occultato*: sotto la figura dell'albero delle rose era occultata la divinità
di Venere. È evidente la trasposizione della presenza reale nel sacramento dell'Eucarestia. Lo
conferma l'uso del termine "specie" che è la parola tecnica con cui la teologia designa il pane e il
vino dopo la consacrazione. Nella manducazione dei frutti è imitato il rito della comunione, il
quale ordinariamente accompagna il matrimonio cristiano', sig. p1n.

Polia has already told Poliphilus 'I feel the fire of fervent love spreading and tingling throughout my whole being' (218) at the end of the ceremony just concluded, and both of these anticipate Polia's description, in Book 2, of her feeling when Poliphilus revives in her arms. Stewering points out that Poliphilus' description of Polia 'combines the delightful countryside with the figure of Polia by using . . . an anthropo-physiological device . . . relating Polia's blood circulation to its macrocosmic equivalent. The human blood circulation was thought to be a network of veins fed by an inner lake of blood'.[22] This is a particularly subtle example of the way in which Polia is constructed as a fountain in the romance, a device that will be considered at more length in the next chapter, as well as being yet another instance of the way in which fountains provide it with metaphorical and hence structural coherence.

After this preparatory ceremony at the Temple of Venus Physizoa, the next major event in Book 1 of the *Hypnerotomachia* is the reception of Polia and Poliphilus at the Fountain of Venus, for which they must travel to the island of Cytherea. This is the climax of all the various strands of the narrative, and in particular of the lovers' now completely integrated spiritual and erotic journeys. Between these two episodes, however, are four enormous passages of amplification. The first is Poliphilus' exploration of the Polyandrion, a collection of funerary monuments around a ruined temple formerly frequented by spurned and unhappy lovers (242–73). He is dispatched there by Polia because he 'was tempted, in this solitary place, to the Herculean audacity of violently possessing the divine nymph': 'She came to my rescue as my only saviour and said to me gently: "Poliphilo, my best-beloved, I am well aware that you are extremely fond of looking at the works of antiquity . . . Take your pleasure in looking at these"' (240, 242). So this is what Poliphilus does, happily examining and interpreting the ruins, until, in a neat piece of symmetry, he is prompted by a mosaic depicting the rape of Proserpina to fear that Polia could also have been snatched away in his absence (272). He rushes back to her in a mad panic, and falls exhausted into her arms.

When Cupid arrives in his barque, the lovers begin their voyage to Cytherea (274–91). There are descriptions of the boat, Cupid's wings, the banner reading 'Amor Vincit Omnia', and the conditions of the sea (and the myriad sea gods and nymphs that accompany the boat), but especially of the six nymphs who row and sail the boat, every aspect of whom is lingeringly described by Poliphilus. He also dwells again on his desire for the consummation of his relationship with Polia. Poliphilus' exploration of the Polyandrion and his account of the voyage in Cupid's barque furnish opportunities for the display of Colonna's virtuoso antiquarianism, but they also return desire to the forefront

22 Stewering, 'The Relationship between World, Landscape and Polia', 6.

of the romance. The voyage's description emphasizes the romance's languidly erotic atmosphere, and the strongly visual character of that eroticism, but despite Poliphilus' desire for consummation and the narrative's increasing erotic tension, the passages of description are concerned with deferral as much as with arousal and anticipation, a process in which the reader is also involved.

A third passage of description, of the island of Cytherea, particularly demonstrates this, and it is masterfully controlled and manipulated; Roswitha Stewering additionally describes it as an example of the narrative's oscillations between 'the perspective of experience' and 'the dream perspective', the latter of which is 'inconsistent with temporal logic'.[23] As the island is circular, it follows that the subsections into which it is divided get smaller the closer one gets to the centre, and hence that progress through them towards the centre should become progressively faster. Colonna works against this by making the descriptions of the island more and more detailed. Even more disconcertingly for the reader, when the description of the island finally ends outside the 'theatre', in the middle of which is the Fountain of Venus, it is revealed that the account has not been an 'eyewitness' one, but rather a 'bird's-eye view' before Poliphilus and Polia have even disembarked. After the party step ashore there are yet more lengthy descriptions to come: of the costumes worn by the Cytherean nymphs (Colonna has a particular fetish for footwear), of Cupid's triumphal procession, and, finally, of the 'theatre', which is a coliseum-like structure made of semi-precious stones and metals, decorated all over with carvings and mosaics. 'In the middle of this arena, at the very centre, was the sacred and delicious fountain of the divine Mother and mistress of Amor himself, most artistically made' (353). Even with the fountain having finally been glimpsed, the deferral continues: 'But before I speak of the sacred fount, I will first describe the unheard-of disposition and the wonderful interior of the theatre' (353). But finally, a full five pages later, the lovers are presented by Psyche 'before the sacrosanct Cytherean fount' (357). This is the fountain towards which all the other fountains of the romance thus far have led; it at once fulfils and overgoes the plural potentialities of the fountain figure. Laden with spiritual, mythological, Platonic, and erotic symbolism, as the following chapter explores, it epitomizes all that fountains can do and be in Renaissance texts.

[23] Roswitha Stewering, 'Architectural Representations in the *Hypnerotomachia Poliphili* (Aldus Manutius, 1499)', *Journal of the Society of Architectural Historians*, 59 (2000), 14. Stewering also notes that the Fountain of Venus is later described in a similar way, the features of its interior being described before its concealing veil is torn; see Chapter 3.

3

The Fountains of Venus and Adonis: Revelation and Reflection

The first book of the *Hypnerotomachia Poliphili*, and indeed the romance as a whole, reaches its climax at the Fountain of Venus.[1] This fountain is at the centre of an amphitheatre, itself at the centre of Venus' island of Cytherea. It is a heptagonal structure, with pillars of sapphire, emerald, and turquoise, an unidentified yellow stone, jasper, topaz, and beryl; there are carvings of hermaphrodite, male, and female children, and astrological symbols; its cupola is a transparent crystal, surmounted with a carbuncle the size of an ostrich egg (359–60). Unusually, the fountain is not illustrated and, as Martine Furno has pointed out, this is only one of the many ways in which it is 'quite different from those [fountains] previously described in the story . . . it evokes the structure of a baptistery'.[2] As such, it recalls the other initiations of the text, notably Poliphilus' encounter with the *puer mingens* fountain near the beginning of Book 1, and the first ritual which he and Polia underwent in the earlier Temple of Venus. The inscription on the base reads ΩΣΝΕΡ ΣΠΙΝΘΗΡ ΚΗΛΗΘΜΟΣ (seduction is like a spark),[3] and between the two pillars forming the entrance is a luxurious curtain embroidered 'ΥΜΗΝ' (Hymen). The symbolism of the passage is basic; it is analogous to the description of the consummation/rape at the end of the *Roman de la Rose*, although it is perhaps less crude:

While Polia and I knelt there on bended knee, the divine lord Cupid gave the golden arrow to the nymph Synesia ('union') and made a courteous sign that she should offer it to Polia, and that she, with this fearful arrow, should tear and rend the noble curtain. But Polia was distressed by the order to tear and damage it, and although she was subject to this divine command, she seemed uneasy with it and hesitated to

---

[1] There is a translation of the passage describing the fountain, together with a commentary identifying some of its architectural sources, by Martine Furno, 'Imaginary Architecture and Antiquity: The Fountain of Venus in Francesco Colonna's *Hypnerotomachia Poliphili*', in Alina Payne, Ann Kuttner, and Rebekah Smick (eds.), *Antiquity and its Interpreters* (Cambridge: Cambridge University Press, 2000), 70–82.

[2] Ibid., 77.   [3] Furno translates this as 'the charm is like a sparkle'; ibid. 76.

obey. The Lord (Cupid), smiling, straightway enjoined the nymph Synesia to give the arrow to the nymph Philedia ('voluptuousness'), and she then presented it to me. And I completed the penetration that the honey-sweet and wholesome Polia dared not do, avid as I was to behold the most holy Mother. No sooner had I taken the divine instrument than I was surrounded by a sourceless flame, and with urgent emotion I violently struck the little curtain. As it parted, I saw Polia look almost saddened, and the emerald column made a din as if it were breaking in pieces. And behold! I saw clearly the divine form of her venerable majesty as she issued from the springing fountain, the delicious source of every beauty. No sooner had the unexpected sight met my eyes than both of us were filled with extreme sweetness, and invaded by the novel pleasure that we had desired daily. (361)

The Fountain of Venus is, unambiguously, a material metaphor for sexual consummation and erotic ecstasy. It does indeed recall the *Romance of the Rose*, but it does a great deal more besides.[4] In the context of the romance as a whole, it reinforces and epitomizes the polymorphousness (and the polysemy) of pleasure: textual, visual, material, sensual, and sexual. Although Plato's account of desire and its fulfilment in the *Phaedrus*[5] is undoubtedly important to the episode, in the Fountain of Venus Colonna eschews Plato's elevated, relatively abstract (if sensuous) images of the feathered wings of the soul to present his readers with a metaphor that is gloriously, spectacularly, and unapologetically material, gorgeous to look at, thoroughly sensual to apprehend, and eagerly solicitous of the reader's imaginative and erotic participation.

Venus stands up to her waist in the basin full of foamy and fragrant water, and Poliphilus' description of the goddess initially dwells on her hair:

how beautiful was her golden hair, delicately arranged on her milk-white forehead and trained into little curls, with errant and restless tips which the curling prevented from straightening! . . . The lovely hair, finer than the most tenuous gold thread, hung down upon the pure water. (362)

This both anticipates the description of Polia drying her hair in the sun when Poliphilus fell in love with her, in Book 2, where it is described as 'like threads of gold' (386), and also recalls the first description of the nymph who, in Book 1, turns out to be Polia, whose hair is again described as 'fili d'oro' (gold thread) (145; i5). The attribute is a conventional topos of the blazon of female beauty, but it is given enough emphasis in the description of Venus to encourage her identification with Polia. (It is also strongly reminiscent of

---

[4] See my comparative discussion of the fountains in the *Hypnerotomachia* and the *Romance of the Rose* in 'Sacred and Profane Love'.

[5] Plato, *Phaedrus*, trans. Robin Waterfield (Oxford: Oxford University Press, 2002), 251 A–E and 255 C–D. These passages are further discussed below.

the great Botticelli portrayal of the Venus Anadyomene, *The Birth of Venus*, c.1485.) The terms of the identification of Polia with Venus as goddess perhaps recall a specific passage from the *Phaedrus*, which Colonna apparently draws on a number of times in his descriptions of the ecstasies of love:

> But when someone who has only recently been initiated . . . sees a marvellous face or a bodily form which is a good reflection of beauty, at first he shivers and is gripped by something like the fear he felt then, and the sight also moves him to revere his beloved as if [he] were a god.[6]

Before beginning to describe Venus' naked body, the interior of the fountain, and the goddess's attendants, Poliphilus has similarly commented: 'I began to experience a justifiable fear, thinking of what Aristeo's son [Actaeon] saw in the valley of Gargaphia' (361–2). This recollection of the *Phaedrus* and the reference to Actaeon appositely emphasize the place in the narrative of the erotic pleasure of looking and its possible ramifications. Revealing and looking at the naked body of the goddess Venus, Poliphilus is also revealing and 'possessing' the body of his beloved Polia; his pleasure in her is at once reverent and ecstatic, a cathartic experience of spiritual and sexual bliss. Here it is Venus, not Diana, who is the object of the gaze; there will be no negative repercussions for this act of voyeurism. The revelation of Venus, the sight of her naked body, symbolizes the sexual union of the lovers. The goddess addresses the lovers from the middle of the fountain, where she is surrounded by flowering plants and fluttering doves, and attended by the Three Graces.[7] A fourth nymph is also in attendance, as are Ceres and Bacchus, who dispense perfume into the fountain. Venus assents to the lovers' supplications, unites them eternally, and gives them each four attendant nymphs to foster and enhance their relationship.[8]

In the next part of the ritual, Cupid quickly fires an arrow into Poliphilus' heart, draws it out, fires it again into Polia's and then draws it out once more and places it in the fountain:

> I immediately began to feel the honey-sweet burning of a fierce flame inside myself, in my very viscera, which spread like the Lernaean Hydra and possessed my whole being, set me trembling with amorous ardour . . . My mind was so shaken and weakened that it could not understand whether I was undergoing a change like that of Hermaphroditus and Salmacis, when they embraced in the cool and lively fountain

---

[6] Plato, *Phaedrus*, 251 A, p. 34.

[7] The Graces are named as Eurydomene ('giver'), Eurymone ('returner'), and Eurymeduse ('ruler'), and the fourth nymph as Peristeria ('dove-like').

[8] Poliphilus is given Enosina ('oneness'), Monori ('unity'), Phrontida ('reflection'), and Critoa ('choice'), and Polia Adiacorista ('inseparable'), Pistinia ('faith'), Sophrosyne ('wisdom'), and Edosia ('modesty').

and found themselves transformed into the single form of their promiscuous union. I felt no more nor less than the unhappy Biblis, when she felt her tears turning into the liquid spring. (366)

Poliphilus' choice of Ovidian referents is, of course, especially appropriate here, and his experience of sexual ecstasy is presented in terms which are not only 'fountain-based', but which draw on two of the most transgressive of the narratives in the *Metamorphoses*, concerned with female sexual aggression and incest respectively. Here, the possibility of transgression is itself, like the limits of identity and human experience and the very boundaries of the human body, transcended. Once again, there is here a strong recollection of *Phaedrus* 251, in the description of the ecstasy of love as one of mingled pleasure and pain; it is of particular note, perhaps, that in Platonic terms it is the sight of the beloved's beauty which is the cause of both desire and ecstasy, pain and pleasure, and also that both beauty and desire are depicted in flowing, liquid terms.[9] Like Plato, Colonna elides the visual, the material, the sensual, the erotic, and the spiritual.

There are clear similarities between this ceremony and the earlier one in the Temple of Venus on the seashore, in which Poliphilus and Polia participated before their voyage to Cytherea, which can be seen as a more ritualized preparatory version. There are also, again, obvious Christian analogies, not least because as her final act Venus sprinkles the lovers with salt water from an oyster shell. She delivers a private homily to the lovers, at which point Mars strides in, throws off his armour and joins her in the fountain. The nymphs and the lovers depart, making their way to the Fountain of Adonis and the end of Book 1. Eric MacPhail describes the aspersion of the lovers by Venus at the end of the ceremony as 'a pagan version of baptism'.[10] This is surely not the primary significance of the episode: the aspersion is clearly a final blessing concluding a ceremony approximating marriage. Venus' various pronouncements confirm this:

---

[9] 'When [the soul] gazes on the young man's beauty, and receives the particles emanating from it as they approach and flow in—which, of course, is why we call it desire—it is watered and heated, and it recovers from its pain and is glad . . . The sight of him opens the irrigation channels of desire . . .'. Waterfield notes in his commentary that 'Plato is hazarding an extremely fanciful etymology, according to which *himeros* ("desire") is derived from the *i* in the Greek word for "approach", *mere* ("particles"), and *rhein* ("flow").' Plato, *Phaedrus*, 251 c, 251 e, p. 35; 251 c n., p. 93. Theresa Krier discusses this motif in the context of classical and Renaissance theories of sight, in relation to Spenser and Milton, and in particular to the vision of the Hermaphrodite at the end of Book 3 of Spenser's *Faerie Queene*, in *Gazing on Secret Sights: Spenser, Classical Imitation, and the Decorums of Vision* (Ithaca, NY: Cornell University Press, 1990). This episode is considered at length in Chapter 8.

[10] Eric MacPhail, 'Prophecy and Memory in the Renaissance Dream Vision', in Earl Miner et al. (eds.), *The Force of Vision II: Visions in History; Visions of the Other* (Tokyo: International Comparative Literature Association, 1991), 195.

both of you, loving each other equally, shall serve my amorous fires with full consent, and enjoy blessed and glorious bliss under my safe protection . . . [Polia] shall live attached by equal decree to her lover Poliphilo in a Herculean knot . . . If she wavers, may he support her; in worry and care, may she receive blessings; and for her pleasure, may he bind her in the tightest embrace. (365)

She also presents the lovers with rings. More important than the quasi-liturgical aspects of this ceremony, however, is its sanctification of sexual initiation and union. It is the culmination of the romance's simultaneous glorification of visual, intellectual, spiritual, and sexual pleasure, a profane vision of the living fountain, the living god desired and thirsted for by the psalmist in Psalm 42.[11] If overt sacramental parallels are sought, the earlier temple ceremony is one of betrothal, in which the lovers declare their intent and are enrolled as followers of Venus, a compact sealed by their participation in the 'Eucharist'. The ceremony at the Fountain of Venus is the marriage proper and in particular its consummation, where the symbolic 'communion' of Venus in 'species' is replaced by her 'unveiled' 'real presence', and the pleasures experienced by Poliphilus at the earlier rites are surpassed by those of total ecstasy. Of this conflation of sexual and religious initiation, which is indebted to the epiphanic vision of Isis in Book 11 of Apuleius' *Metamorphoses* as well as to the *Romance of the Rose*[12] and to Plato's *Phaedrus*, Polizzi comments: 'il n'y a pas à choisir entre deux interprétations distinctes, car les deux se confondent dans la même image' (there is no need to choose between these two distinct interpretations, because both are united in the same image).[13] As Leonard Barkan observes in his discussion of Ronsard's *Amour* 20, 'Water . . . suggests in the context of the Narcissus myth the barrier that the speaker must cross so as actually to enter the reality of the pagan dream world. To plunge into the fountain is to enter that reality and to experience the sexual act at once'.[14] Similarly discussing Ronsard (in this case 'Le Baing de Calirée'), Hélène Casanova-Robin makes the same observation: 'Le bain se fait métonymie de la relation charnelle, associé au plaisir de tous les sens' (The bath becomes a metonym for the sexual act, associated with pleasure for all the senses).[15] The same could be said of the fountains of the *Hypnerotomachia*: the hymeneal veil of the Fountain of Venus is also the surface of its water, the body of the goddess, and the body of Poliphilus' beloved Polia. But the vision of the goddess is no mere reflection or shadow, and Poliphilus is a triumphant Narcissus, whose polymorphous fantasies of

---

[11] This psalm is revisited in the context of Spenser's *Faerie Queene* in Chapter 8.
[12] See 'Sacred and Profane Love'.   [13] Polizzi, 'L'Esthétique de l'énigme', 228.
[14] Leonard Barkan, *The Gods Made Flesh: Metamorphosis and the Pursuit of Paganism* (New Haven: Yale University Press, 1986), 221.
[15] Casanova-Robin, *Diane et Actéon*, 221.

sensuality are materialized as he finally both reveals and enters into the waters
of the fountain.

The romance thus reaches its climax at the *Fountain* of Venus for several
reasons. First, fountains throughout the romance have often been eroticized
in their imagery and associations. They epitomize that elision of erotic and
visual pleasure, of desire and thirst and hence Poliphilus' solipsistic and
self-referential relationship with aesthetic objects (he values them as much
for their pleasurable effect upon him as for any notion of their intrin-
sic worth) that is one of the *Hypnerotomachia*'s most distinctive features.
All the fountains of the romance have been spectacular to look at, soliciting the gaze of both Poliphilus and the reader in terms more or less
erotic. More, they have invited Poliphilus to touch, to drink, and to wonder; they have delighted his senses, his eyes, and his mind, and aroused
his desires. It is therefore unsurprising that Polia herself is identified as
a fountain, in ways that will shortly be explored in greater detail, and so
with Venus, specifically the sea-born Venus Anadyomene in which aspect
the goddess appears in her fountain. Of all the various exotic, erotic, and
anthropomorphic fountains encountered in the *Hypnerotomachia*, the Fountain of Venus is the true 'living fountain'. When the goddess is revealed,
she stands

> naked in the middle of the transparent and limpid waters of the basin, which reached
> up to her ample and divine waist, reflecting the Cytherean body without making it
> seem larger, smaller, doubled or refracted; it was visible simple and whole, as perfect
> as it was in itself . . . The divine body appeared luminous and transparent, displaying
> its majesty and venerable aspect with exceptional clarity and blazing like a precious
> and coruscating carbuncle in the rays of the sun; for it was made from a miraculous
> compound which humans have never conceived of. (362)

Again, 'the part of her body that was above the water shone no more nor less
than the splendid rays of the sun in polished crystal' (363). The Fountain of
Venus functions as a reinvention of various Christian tropes: of the chaste
woman, especially the Virgin Mary, as a sealed fountain, and of Christ as a
well of living water.[16] But the Trinity in which Venus appears is completed by
Ceres and Bacchus, and she is not the spring of life but 'the delicious source of
every beauty': seeing her indeed confers salvation, but through the experience
of sexual ecstasy. In the climax of Colonna's romance, worldly, erotic love
is claimed as divine and transcendent. Venus is not merely *in* the fountain:
she *is* the fountain. So, whereas in Book 2 Polia becomes aware of her love
for Poliphilus as 'a sudden new feeling that caused the blood that had been

---

[16] Song of Solomon 4: 12 and John 4: 14.

blocked up by sorrow and excessive fear to course through my veins' (422),[17] at the climax of Book 1 sexual ecstasy is represented as this revelatory vision of a divine and living fountain. The presence of a real fountain actualizes the romance's Ovidian strand, and Polia's frequent use of Ovidian comparisons in Book 2 is transferred to Poliphilus in their moment of union, as he identifies with Actaeon, Hermaphroditus and Salmacis, and Biblis (366), all themselves strongly associated with transformation at, by, or into fountains. He is also a Narcissus figure, who triumphantly succeeds in his embrace of the fountain.[18] The Fountain of Venus is, like the other fountains of the *Hypnerotomachia*, liminal, as its hymeneal curtain makes clear; it is also climactic. As such, it elides the many associations of fountains in the romance. That it is not illustrated initially seems odd, or even disappointing for, as the illustrations of the previous chapter have shown, fountains are the subject of some of the *Hypnerotomachia*'s most beautiful woodcuts; they are such a notable feature of the book as a visual and material object that even the *Strife* (which omits many of the illustrations overall) includes all those of fountains. Roswitha Stewering has suggested that the Fountain of Venus remains unillustrated because of 'the artist's desire to avoid strong reactions among readers, who, given the highly erotic text, were already confronted with material that could easily have elicited unwelcome attention from the Inquisition',[19] but given the explicit nature of many of the other woodcuts (notably the Fountain of the Sleeping Nymph and the Sacrifice to Priapus, both of which were indeed sometimes censored) this seems unlikely. It is, instead, perhaps a deliberate and daring omission. The reader is invited to imagine, to reinvent for him- or herself, the precise details—visual, material, and experiential—of his or her own personal erotic epiphany, within the exotic and suggestive frame that Colonna creates.[20]

Book 1 ends at the Fountain of Adonis (Fig. 7) on the Island of Cytherea, and all of Book 2 (with the exception of Poliphilus' awakening on the last page) is therefore set beside, or framed by, that fountain, although this is easily forgotten as Polia's story, the telling of which occupies the bulk of Book 2, unfolds. The Fountain of Adonis is the most significant feature of the *Hypnerotomachia* that is imitated almost wholesale by Philip Sidney, in ways to be explored more fully in the course of the next chapter, and it is with

---

[17] Again, compare the *Phaedrus*: 'The sight of [the beloved] opens the irrigation channels of desire and frees the former blockage; it finds relief and an end to the stinging pain . . .'. Plato, *Phaedrus*, 251 E, p. 35.

[18] The question of Narcissus' embrace is discussed in more detail in Chapter 4.

[19] Stewering goes on to suggest that such an illustration would 'contaminate' the 'visual logic' of the romance's architecture, which she outlines in her essay 'Architectural Representations', 15–16 and *passim*.

[20] See my further discussion of this aspect of the Fountain of Venus in 'Sacred and Profane Love'.

this imitation and adaptation that the *Hypnerotomachia* apparently arrives in England. The Fountain of Adonis has several qualities that set it apart from the other fountains, and indeed the other illustrations, in the romance. It is, for example, the only object illustrated in the text in the round, from three different angles, and in perspective, in comparison with the other fountains, statues, and other sculptural figures in the book, the illustrations of which often have the quality of bas reliefs. Even more unusually, the Fountain of Adonis is also depicted as being totally integrated into its surroundings: it has a naturalistic garden setting, with water cascading out into a pool, and then into channels which irrigate the garden. The fountain is straightforward and realistic in its appearance, being formed from a simple box tomb, with a statue of a seated Venus, nursing Cupid, on top. Its sides are ornamented with reliefs showing the death of Adonis, and the statue of Venus cunningly makes use of the various coloured veins in the stone (372–3).[21] Colonna's Adonis fountain is very simple compared with all the other fountains hitherto encountered by Poliphilus. It has no moving parts, no great variety of precious metals and gemstones, and no hidden, mysterious devices. It resembles in some ways a common form of fountain in Renaissance Italy, which 'recycled' parts of antique sarcophagi: a fountain of this type is depicted in Titian's *Sacred and Profane Love*.[22] Perhaps most significant, however, are the interactions of the romance's characters with the Fountain of Adonis. First of all, Poliphilus, Polia, and the nymphs kiss the extended foot of the statue of Venus, and the nymphs describe to the lovers the annual rituals centred on the fountain, commemorating the death of Adonis. They then all dance around it. Finally, in the scene shown in the last illustration of Book 1, they simply turn their backs on it, sitting at the far end of the pool to listen to Polia's story (Fig. 8).

It is no accident, therefore, that the *Hypnerotomachia*'s most realistic fountain is used as the pivot for the romance's change of books, and hence of narrative mode and aesthetic. The Fountain of Adonis is introduced as yet another locus of arcane ritual, but it is quickly 'neutralized' into a topos not of pagan rite, classical allusion, or even of love *per se*, but of narrative convention. The tradition it invokes is that of Boccaccio's *Decameron*: it is a beautiful fountain beside which stories are told. Compare the description of the *locus amoenus* from Day Three of the *Decameron*, which becomes the setting for the storytelling on subsequent days:

a lawn of exceedingly fine grass, of so deep a green as to almost seem black, dotted all over with possibly a thousand different kinds of gaily-coloured flowers, and surrounded by a line of flourishing, bright green orange- and lemon-trees . . . In the middle of this

---

[21] The fountain is described and discussed in more detail in Chapter 4.
[22] See Edgar Wind, *Pagan Mysteries in the Renaissance* (Harmondsworth: Penguin, 1967), 142.

lawn there stood a fountain of pure white marble, covered with marvellous bas-reliefs. From a figure standing on a column in the centre of the fountain, a jet of water, whether natural or artificial I know not, but sufficiently powerful to drive a mill with ease, gushed high into the sky before cascading downwards and falling with a delectable plash into the crystal-clear pool below. [23]

Indeed, there are strong similarities between the scene as it is illustrated in the *Hypnerotomachia* and the frontispiece of the De Gregori edition of the *Decameron*, published in Venice in 1492.[24] Such a fountain is hence particularly appropriate for story-telling by women,[25] if the *Decameron*, where female characters predominate, is being specifically invoked here,[26] and the story told by Polia is conventional in its telling, socially realistic (set in a real city that has been threatened by plague, as in the *Decameron*), and peopled with real characters who share ordinary relationships, such as Polia's nurse and her fickle best friend: exactly the sort of story one would expect to hear from a young woman in this setting.

This join between the two books of the *Hypnerotomachia* at the Fountain of Adonis is discussed again with reference to Sidney's *New Arcadia* in the next chapter. The story that is told beside that fountain, Polia's account of her relationship with Poliphilus, forms the *Hypnerotomachia*'s second book and, although it is indeed the sort of story that is narrated beside a fountain, in fact it involves not a single 'real' fountain, in stark contrast to Book 1. There is, instead, a very strong strand of imagery related to fountains throughout: whereas in Book 1 metaphors—of thirst as desire, of sexual ecstasy—are made material as spectacular fountains, in Book 2 they remain metaphors. This establishes a network of associations which is fed back into Book 1 on a number of levels, providing narrative impetus and significantly contributing to the aesthetic, narrative, and structural cohesion of the romance as a whole. It is generally believed that Book 2 was written first: to understand the relationship between the two as being one in which a city becomes a vast, dreamlike garden landscape and (frequently quite conventional) metaphors are made material gives an insight not only into the possible process of composition,

---

[23] Giovanni Boccaccio, *The Decameron*, trans. G. H. McWilliam (Harmondsworth: Penguin, 1995), 190.

[24] See the discussion of gardens in the *Decameron* by Raffaella Fabiani Giannetto, 'Writing the Garden in the Age of Humanism: Petrarch and Boccaccio', *Studies in the History of Gardens and Designed Landscapes*, 23 (2003), 244 ff.; the 1492 frontispiece is illustrated, p. 250.

[25] Although Polia's story, including her autobiography and family history, is in fact 'dreamed' by Poliphilus, it is substantially different from Book 1. Attributing it to Polia is a convenient way of differentiating it.

[26] A. Kent Hieatt and Anne Lake Prescott describe Book 2 as 'Boccaccian', although they do not link their choice of this adjective specifically to the fountain setting. See 'Contemporizing Antiquity: The *Hypnerotomachia* and its Afterlife in France', *Word & Image*, 8/4 (1992), 304.

but also into ways of reading such metaphors in general and, even more, of apprehending and interpreting similar things and experiences in the 'real' world, and not least in real gardens.

Polia begins her story conventionally, asserting her own unworthiness as a narrator by saying that her story 'may resemble the frightful squawk of the cormorant who once was Aesachus, rather than the sweet song of the plaintive Philomela' (381). There may be a joke here at the expense of Poliphilus and his linguistic excesses, as well as a foreshadowing of the romance's end: Aesachus fell in love with Hesperia when he 'beheld [her] drying her flowing hair in the sun'.[27] This is the situation in which Poliphilus has become infatuated with Polia (386), and the nightingale's song wakes Poliphilus at his dream's end. Polia apostrophizes the listening nymphs and the Fountain of Adonis beside which they are all sitting. Then, however, she expresses further doubts about her ability to tell her story at all: 'Do not wonder if you see me trembling all over, and my pious eyes turning to rivers of tears, for my tranquil mind is shaken by the thought of lacerated Dirce, mourning Biblis, envied Galathea, fleeing Arethusa and dolorous Egeria' (382). These are all women associated with metamorphosis into springs and streams: Dirce was torn to pieces by a bull and gave her name to a Theban stream,[28] Biblis became a fountain when her brother Caunus rejected her, and Acis, Galatea's lover, was killed by the cyclops and became a river god.[29] Arethusa was changed by Diana into a stream that she might escape the river god Alpheus and Egeria, mourning her husband Numa, was also turned by her into a spring.[30] As if these pointed comparisons were not enough, Polia continues:

What will-power, what exertion, what resolution are required of the untutored tongue for such a story! For my race was unfortunate from the start, considering that some members of it were transformed by just and divine vengeance into surging springs and running rivers . . . How could I tell of such a ruinous and thwarted destiny without heavy sighs, a troubled voice, and words marred by sobbing? How, without flooding my dry cheeks with tears? (382)

Polia thus explicitly locates herself at the intersection of two traditions of metamorphosis into sources of water, the mythological and the historical, at the same time as she warns her audience of the likelihood of her bursting into tears. She both establishes topoi upon which her story will continually draw, and begins to construct herself as a human fountain. Polia gives the history of her family, the Lelli, various members of which were transformed into fountains, streams, springs, and rivers because they allowed Murgania,

[27] Ovid, *Metamorphoses*, 11.752 ff.
[28] Apuleius, *The Golden Ass*, trans. E. J. Kenny (London: Penguin, 1998), 6.27.
[29] Ovid, *Metamorphoses*, 9.454 ff. and 663–5, 13.882–97.   [30] Ibid. 5.572 ff., 15.547–51.

one of the daughters, to be worshipped in opposition to Venus. She then describes how Poliphilus fell in love with her when he saw her drying her hair. In this, the last paragraph of Book 2's opening chapter, the opposition is introduced which will metaphorically comment on the development of the relationship as Book 2 progresses and is then translated, and transformed, back into Book 1.

On seeing Polia sunning herself, Poliphilus 'suddenly [takes] fire with immeasurable and increasing love'; he 'burn[s] with longing'; he feels 'first and novel fires in his breast' (386). Polia, on the other hand, comments that 'Many a time, when looking at my clear image in the mirror, I wondered whether the fate of Narcissus would be mine also, when I saw myself clearly in the mirror—as is obvious to you now from my looks' (386). (She does at least go on to add: 'And lest I appear to be boasting, let me recall the following adage: If lying and falsehood is a vice, it is no less to conceal the truth', 386.) Poliphilus, smitten, returns daily to gaze up at Polia's window, but 'if he did catch the slightest glimpse of me, as rarely happened, he could perceive no more sign or hint of love than in a flint-stone. And if my frigid heart was not averse to him, it was made from a substance very far from susceptible to amorous fires' (387). Poliphilus is fire: Polia is water, stone, and ice. This is, of course, an utterly conventional Petrarchan conceit, found in any number of sonnets throughout the Italian, French, and English Renaissance, and not least in Sidney's *Astrophil and Stella*. But Colonna's sustained and inventive handling of it, and the way in which it is integrated on a number of levels, and above all into the physical settings and the very materiality of his characters and their experiences, in such a long and elaborate narrative, is quite remarkable. In the order in which the two books of the *Hypnerotomachia* are to be read, Book 1 prepares the reader for the centrality, and the vitality, of the capacity of material objects to function as externalized intellectual, emotional, and sensual devices; in so doing, it reanimates conventional Petrarchan and Platonic tropes. For Colonna, love, desire, and ultimately sexual ecstasy are intellectual and spiritual experiences because they are physical and sensual, and not in spite of it.

Further examples of the metaphors of stone, ice, and fire abound. Sick with the plague, Polia vows herself, if she recovers, to the goddess Diana, and 'the most beautiful portion of [her] flowering girlhood and [her] charming youth [was to be] used up in chilly continence . . . [her] sterile breast was washed and scrubbed absolutely clean of love' (388–9). After Polia's ceremony of consecration in Diana's temple, Poliphilus finds her there alone: 'No sooner did I see him before me than I felt polluted; my confused heart froze like the diamond which fire cannot melt, and became hard and rigid as the porphyry stone' (390). As he gazes on her, he grows pale and bursts into tears, explaining that 'I am consumed with fire in your absence, my radiant sun Polia. I melt like liquefying wax, but now, in your solar presence, I am taken with a freezing fit' (391). Rebuffed, but undeterred, he returns again the next day and, after several more pages of outpourings, falls to the ground 'as one dead' (396), prompting Polia to compare herself with exemplars of cruelty, including Anaxarete, whose hard-heartedness drove her lover Iphis to suicide and who was changed into a stone.[31] But at the same time 'there was not the slightest vestige of pity in [her], for [her] determined will was imprisoned in [her] cruel and stony breast as surely as the stone in that sacred tomb [i.e. Adonis's] and just as if [she] had drunk of the river of the Citoni' (397); this stream turned those who drank from it into stone.[32] At this point in the story, as Polia is telling it, Poliphilus really seems to die: Polia drags his lifeless body into a corner of the temple and runs away. She is still, however, unmoved, commenting that her 'icy breast [is still] frozen harder than the crystal of the northern Alps' and that, in a telling image, 'Love could in no way cleave to [her heart] or even approach it . . . just as wax, although malleable, will not stick to wet stone' (399).

On her way home from the temple, however, Polia is transported by a whirlwind into a forest to see the torture and execution of two women by Cupid, for having disobeyed his laws. The sight, naturally, terrifies her, and for the first time she 'began to weep bitterly, shedding floods of tears, stifling [her] frequent sighs and soft groans . . . turned [her] tearful eyes down to [her] chaste and shining breast, eyes that [she] believed to be henceforth transformed into dewy tears . . . [her] face was streaked with many rivulets of tears' (403, 404). Once re-transported to her home, she sleeps, but has a terrible dream in which two executioners drag her from her bed. She wakes, soaked with tears, and is comforted by her nurse, who offers help to remove from her heart 'this hardened mass of ice which time and habit had caused to grow' (409). The nurse tells Polia Boccaccian cautionary tales—'the inescapable anger of the gods sooner or later takes its infallible vengeance. This is what Apollo brought on Castalia for her refusal' (416)[33]—and sends her to see the high priestess in the Temple of Venus. Instead, Polia returns to Poliphilus' body at the Temple of Diana, and throws herself upon him. But she 'had already made [her] eyes into lakes of tears whose steady drips soaked both him and [herself] . . . when [she] placed [her] hand on his cold chest and felt therein a tiny, stifled pulse beating' (421). Poliphilus revives in Polia's arms (although the precise final antidote is not exactly courtly: 'I uncovered my—or rather his—white

---

[31] Ovid, *Metamorphoses*, 14.698 ff. The myth of Anaxarete is drawn on by Spenser in Book 2 of *The Faerie Queene*, in the Fountain of the Chaste Nymph; this is discussed in Chapter 8.
[32] Ibid. 15.313–14.   [33] Castalia was transformed into the eponymous spring.

and apple-shaped breasts and showed them to him with a tender expression and seductive eyes; and in no time at all he regained consciousness', 421). This passage both anticipates, in chronological terms, and recalls, in terms of narrative, Poliphilus' revival by the waters which flow from the breast of the Sleeping Nymph. At his first words to her Polia herself is also transformed: 'I felt my heart ripped through the middle by a kind of amorous sweetness, pity and extreme joy—a sudden new feeling that caused the blood that had been blocked up by sorrow and fear to course through my veins, overwhelming and astonishing me' (422). Polia, hitherto a frozen fountain, has thawed, and once again it is the *Phaedrus* which is invoked, where the sight of the beloved 'opens the irrigation channels of desire and frees the former blockage', conferring ecstasy.[34] The lovers kiss, and are speedily evicted from the temple by Diana's priestesses. Polia returns home to sit in her chamber and contemplate her new way of life: 'For love of him I henceforth renounced all hardness and put aside all austerity; I gently tamed my wild and disagreeable soul, and transformed my frigid breast into a furnace of burning love . . . my coldness into fervid heat' (425). She sees a vision of Venus and Cupid chasing away Diana's chariot of ice with a fiery torch—here a rare example in Book 2 of a metaphor made visible, if not material—and goes to repent of her past conduct to the high priestess in the Temple of Venus, where Poliphilus is waiting.

At the Temple of Venus, the equivalent in Book 2 to Book 1's Temple of Venus, in which the lovers' rites of betrothal took place, Poliphilus petitions the priestess to make Polia look kindly upon him and to unite them, 'for I have no little hope that the ministry of those alluring eyes in the midst of my overflowing heart will turn my incredible suffering into voluptuous pleasure, and dampen a little my wanton and ardent fires' (430). Polia protests that she is already utterly besotted with Poliphilus, they kiss, and the high priestess approves their union, asking Poliphilus to tell her the story of how he fell in love with Polia. He does so—at length, although not repeating what Polia has previously narrated. (This is all still ostensibly within the frame of Polia's narration: she is presumably quoting verbatim.) He describes the effect upon him of seeing her at the consecration ceremony: 'I reckoned her fair and honest presence to be my best helper, like heavenly dew and an assuaging remedy, for my inflammable and fragile heart' (438). He quotes the first letter that he sent to Polia, full of images of burning, but admits that his 'words were as wasted as if [he] had addressed them to a marble statue' (446); his second letter protested that 'you appear ever more unyielding, and colder than frozen ice[.] Your bosom is chillier than the springs of Derce and Nome' (447). Only the knowledge of her beauties and virtues has kept him 'bedewed and moistened

---

[34] Plato, *Phaedrus*, 251 E, discussed above.

in the midst of [his] fervour; otherwise [his] heart would turn to coal' (448). These letters having been unsuccessful, he sent a third letter, equally without effect: she was still 'frozen more stiffly than the Arcadian Styx' (454). This is the point at which Poliphilus 'died', rejected by Polia as he confronted her in the temple. He describes how his soul made a journey to the heavens for an audience with Venus and Cupid, and how Cupid showed a simulacrum of Polia to Venus and then transfixed her heart with a flaming arrow (as at the Fountain of Venus in Book 1). As a final (and probably intentionally bathetic) touch to yet another eulogy of Polia's beauty, Poliphilus adds that 'To my burning fever, she was as timely, healing, efficacious and speedy medicine, far more acceptable than the puddle of muddy water seemed to Lucius when the bag stuffed with tow caught fire' (459).[35] Poliphilus finally revives in Polia's arms. The story ends with the priestess uniting them, and Polia's narration at the Fountain of Adonis also finishes.

The nymphs once again dance around the fountain, then take their leave. Polia and Poliphilus declare their love again, embrace again, but Polia dissolves into a fragrant mist and vanishes. 'This was the point, O gentle readers, at which, alas, I awoke', begins the final chapter. Book 2 of the *Hypnerotomachia* therefore tells the story of the union of fire and icy stone; of the cooling, but not dampening, of the painful fires of the lover's infatuation and the warming and thawing of a 'frozen fountain'. Poliphilus is refreshed with heavenly dew, while Polia learns to weep and to enjoy the new sensation of her own warm blood in her veins. It is not only a Boccaccian, but a Petrarchan and Platonic narrative. These processes are set against a background of Ovidian metamorphosis into sources of water and its particular connection with love and sexuality, so invoking the erotic associations of fountains throughout the romance, not least in its first book. The way in which fountains assert this possibility of coexistent layers of meaning is itself part of their meaning and function in the romance; at the same time, they promote and epitomize the celebration of the material, and the sensual, the visual and the experiential. They are more than visible symbols, or metaphors made material, although they are both those things: they assert the potency and the value of the visual, the material, and the sensual of themselves. These things, in Colonna's romance, are true and real and transcendent at the same time as they point towards, and suggest ways of accessing, the true, the real and the transcendent.

The Fountain of Venus epitomizes the symbolic polysemy of the fountain, while the Fountain of Adonis appropriates and reinvents its syncretic possibilities for narratological and structural ends. The latter's identification with Adonis recalls the context of Ovidian metamorphosis within which the

---

[35] Apuleius, *The Golden Ass*, 7.19–20.

romance operates, while its associated arcane rituals suggest the 'pagan' and antiquarian ethos of the text. As a typical romance (or even Boccaccian) *locus amoenus* it invokes new and particular narrative conventions. Most crucially, however, the Fountain of Adonis is the structural mechanism whereby the romance turns back upon itself, for in Book 2 the pervasive fountain imagery is substituted for the 'real' fountains of Book 1, while the Petrarchan discourse of fire, heat, stone, ice, and water of the second book explains why Poliphilus' primary motivation at the beginning of Book 1 is thirst. In many instances the relevant episodes and images actually map on to each other, for (as should now be obvious) the two books of the *Hypnerotomachia* tell the same story, but from different perspectives and in different narrative modes: both have as their climax the piercing of the lovers' hearts, in the presence of Venus, with Cupid's flaming arrow. This structure has in fact been anticipated by another fountain in Book 1, that of the Three Graces in the courtyard of the palace of Queen Eleuterylida.[36] As the Fountain of Adonis marks the mid point of the romance as a whole, this earlier fountain introduces the middle section of Book 1. A diagram included by Gilles Polizzi in one of his essays on the *Songe* demonstrates that the Fountain of the Three Graces has its elements described completely counter-intuitively, in an order that goes neither with, nor against, the flow of the water, but rather in a figure-of-eight, from middle to bottom to middle to top and back to the middle again.[37] This suggests an analogy with the structural function of the Fountain of Adonis, through the limen of which the romance as a whole doubles back on itself.

With the union of Poliphilus and Polia at the Fountain of Venus, the multiple threads of the romance are drawn together; at, and through, the Fountain of Adonis, the romance itself is transformed. This final fountain is the mirror in which the first and second books are reflected on to each other. As it completes Book 1's narrative as an allegory of life, the Fountain of Adonis is also strongly associated with death and memorial, as much as with the discussion and celebration of love. It commemorates the death of Adonis and suggests the deaths of both Poliphilus and Polia, for Polia vanishes from beside the fountain at the romance's end, and her epitaph is on its final page. It is where the 'death' of Poliphilus is described, and where the dream finally ends, and this association with death again invokes Narcissus, who also dies beside a fountain, in love with a reflection, an image or fiction of love. In the *Roman de la Rose* the story of Narcissus' fate is inscribed on the rim of the fountain beside which he died, much as the carvings on Colonna's Adonis fountain also tell the story of his death. The Fountain of Adonis may be the most 'realistic' fountain

---

[36] This fountain is discussed in Chapter 2.
[37] Polizzi, 'Le *Poliphile* ou l'*Idée* du jardin', 67, 70–1.

of the whole romance, yet it, too, is polysemous and manifoldly liminal. This fountain at the centre of the *Hypnerotomachia*'s final *locus amoenus* has a function which is at once both reflexive and transformative, epitomizing a principle in which all the fountains of the text to some extent participate. It suggests ways of seeing and ways of reading that colour what follows it, and also that which has come before; it invites the reader to participate in these, and to revel in the erotic pleasures not only of seeing, but of gazing; of touching and possessing; of reading and imagining. Like the veil of the Fountain of Venus, the surface of water, and the page itself, the Fountain of Adonis is a blank, endlessly informable space, a place to think about love, art, and imagination; a place where, through these last, desire can be realized, and death can be transcended. It resonates, tympanum-like, yet permeably, with its accumulation of multivalent significances, between Book 1 and Book 2, Cytherea and Treviso, 'dream' and 'reality'.

4

The Fountain of Aeneas: Sidney Rewrites
the *Hypnerotomachia*

One of Philip Sidney's most striking additions to his revised *Arcadia* is his description of a not dissimilar setting to the *Hypnerotomachia*'s Fountain of Adonis, and his adaptation of Colonna's fountain acts as a sophisticated and suggestive frame to the subsequent action and concerns of his romance in ways that have hitherto not been elucidated. Sidney's borrowing from the *Hypnerotomachia* is the first discernible instance of its literary influence in Elizabethan England, some ten years before there is any trace of its influence on art or architecture and indeed before its partial translation into English by Robert Dallington, *The Strife of Love in a Dreame* (1592), appropriately enough dedicated to Sidney's memory.[1] Sidney's description of the fountain forms part of the house, garden, and picture gallery of Kalander, the benevolent nobleman with whom the disguised Musidorus stays after his rescue from shipwreck on the Arcadian coast. The passage has become a *locus classicus* for discussions of *ekphrasis* and the relationship between Renaissance literature and the visual arts, and an understanding of both the importance of fountains in the *Hypnerotomachia*, and the nature and function of the Fountain of Adonis in particular, has important and suggestive implications for how this passage in the revised *Arcadia*, and indeed the *Arcadia* in general, might be read:

But Palladius [the name initially assumed by Musidorus] having gotten his health, and only staying there to be in place where he might hear answer of the ships set forth, Kalander one afternoon led him abroad to a well-arrayed ground he had behind his house, which he thought to show him before his going as the place himself more than in any other delighted. The backside of the house was neither field, garden nor orchard, or rather it was both field, garden and orchard; for as soon as the descending of the stairs had delivered them down, they came into a place cunningly set with trees of the most taste-pleasing fruits; but scarcely they had taken that into their consideration

---

[1] See the discussion of Robert Dallington, and of the tomb of Mirabel Heydon (1593), in Chapter 1.

but that they were suddenly swept into a delicate green; of each side of the green a thicket, and behind the thickets again new beds of flowers, which being under the trees, the trees were to them a pavilion and they to the trees a mosaical floor, so that it seemed that Art therein would needs be delightful by counterfeiting his enemy Error and making order in confusion.

In the midst of all the place was a fair pond whose shaking crystal was a perfect mirror to all the other beauties, so that it bare show of two gardens; one in deed, the other in shadows. And in one of the thickets was a fine marble fountain made thus: a naked Venus made of white marble, wherein the graver had used such cunning, that the natural blue veins of the marble were framed in fit places to set forth the beautiful veins of her body. At her breast she had her babe Aeneas, who seemed, having begun to suck, to leave that to look upon her fair eyes which smiled at the babe's folly, meanwhile the breast running.[2]

This description of the fountain is clearly drawn both from the illustration of the Fountain of Adonis in the *Hypnerotomachia* and from the text which accompanies it (Fig. 9):

On the flat top of this tomb was a sculpture of the divine Mother, sitting with her child, astonishingly executed in tricoloured sardonyx. She was seated on an antique chair which did not exceed the vein of sard, whereas the entire Cytherean body was made with incredible artifice and skill out of the milky vein of onyx. She was almost undressed, for only a veil made from a red vein was left to conceal the secrets of nature, covering part of one hip; then the rest of it fell to the floor, wandered up by the left breast, then turned aside, circled the shoulders and hung down to the water, imitating with wonderful skill the outlines of the sacred members. The statue indicated motherly love by showing her embracing and nursing Cupid; and the cheeks of both of them, together with her right nipple, were pleasingly coloured by the reddish vein. Oh, it was a beautiful work, miraculous to look upon, wanting only the breath of life! Her curly hair was parted around the forehead and passed over the smooth temples to the top of the head, where it was tied with a complicated knot; then the free portion descended like tendrils as far as the seat. The sculptor had hollowed out the locks of the hair with supreme skill by means of a drill, keeping them only within the translucent vein of sard, outdoing the ring of fortunate Polycrates which Augustus enclosed in a golden horn and dedicated in the Temple of Concord. The left foot was drawn back against the chair, and the right one extended to the edge or limit of the surface . . . (373–4)

It can be noted, although it is not especially germane to my discussion here, that certain details in Sidney's account more closely parallel the French *Songe* than the Italian text of the original *Hypnerotomachia*. For example, the specific description of the infant Aeneas and his mother Venus smiling at each other in the *Arcadia* recalls the *Songe*: 'Elle tenoit son fils entre ses braz, qui tetoit la mammelle gauche, regardant sa mere, & elle lui, si

---

[2] *The Countess of Pembroke's Arcadia*, ed. Maurice Evans (London: Penguin, 1977), 73–4.

gracieusement q*ue* chacu*n* y prenoit grant plaisir' (she held her son in her arms, and he suckled at her left breast, looking at his mother, and she at him, so gracefully that they each took great pleasure in it) (Y4ᵛ),[3] but there is no equivalent in the Italian original. Sidney's description of the sculptor's skill in making use of the natural coloration of the stone is also much closer to the French than to the Italian: 'Les ioues de la deesse & de l'enfant, ensemble le petit tetin, estoie*nt* vn peu colorez de vermeil, à l'occasio*n* d'vne veine de la pierre qui s'estoit trouuée à propos' (the cheeks of the goddess and her child, together with her nipple, were rosily tinted, thanks to a convenient vein in the stone) (Y4ᵛ). As with other passages, such as the description of the Cytherean nymphs in the *Songe* that I have elsewhere identified as a probable source for Sidney's initial description of Cleophila/Zelmane,[4] the version in the *Songe* is simply more compact. And, as with the description of the nymphs, the vivid passage describing the Fountain of Adonis is closely associated with a strong visual image. It is not inconceivable that Sidney's attention was initially drawn by the illustration of the fountain and thence into the immediately surrounding text for further details (that of the use of the different coloured veins in the stone to add verisimilitude to Venus' body, for example).

To return to the sonnet from *Astrophil and Stella* with which the first chapter of this discussion of the *Hypnerotomachia* and Sidney's *Arcadia* began, it is here, in his adaptation of Colonna's Fountain of Adonis, that Sidney does indeed move beyond the 'fine picture', to consider and to '[heed] the fruit of writer's mind'. If Sidney was indeed a particularly visual reader of the *Hypnerotomachia*, his reading of the text directed (at least at first) by its illustrations rather than its narrative, there is an analogue here with Colonna's Poliphilus himself, whose attention (and desire) is so readily drawn to the visual and the material, the sensual and the experiential. Indeed, these are qualities implicitly shared by Pyrocles, one of the heroes of Sidney's *Arcadia*, who falls in love with a woman when he sees her portrait, in the picture gallery set in Kalander's garden, near the spectacular fountain and its beautiful reflecting pool. But, however he first read it, Sidney goes on to adapt Colonna's scenario in a sophisticated and knowing way that goes beyond mere borrowing for its own sake. In so doing he reveals a profound understanding of how the Fountain of Adonis works within the broader context of the *Hypnerotomachia*, as well as on its own terms. Through this adaptation of not only text and image, but the structural device that they combine to form, he frames his own

---

[3] There is no English translation of the *Songe*, although a critical edition has been published: *Francesco Colonna, Le Songe de Poliphile*, ed. Gilles Polizzi (Paris: Imprimerie Nationale, 1994).

[4] 'Sidney's Zelmane and the *Songe de Poliphile*', *Sidney Journal*, 21 (2003), 67–75.

romance with a potent image for the operation, and the morality, of fiction, love, art, and imagination.

Sidney's debt here to the *Hypnerotomachia*, although not specifically to the *Songe*, has been noted by others, in particular Lucy Gent in her introduction to a facsimile edition of *The Strife of Love in a Dreame*.[5] Yet there are also important differences between Sidney's Venus fountain and Colonna's. Most obviously and significantly, Sidney's Venus nurses Aeneas, whereas her prototype in the *Hypnerotomachia* is depicted with her other son, Cupid. As Katherine Duncan-Jones has noted, 'Venus suckling Aeneas does not seem to be at all a usual subject, either in literature or in visual artefacts. Perhaps the invention here is Sidney's'.[6] The invention is certainly Sidney's, but it is surely meant to resonate specifically with its source, without knowledge of which much of the moral force of the substitution is lost. In the context of a discussion of the *Hypnerotomachia*, Sidney, and Kalander's garden, it is striking to note that there was in the centre of the main court at Theobalds, the great country house of William Cecil, Lord Burghley, a large fountain depicting Venus and Cupid. If this fountain was also known to Sidney—the dates are not impossible—then this too adds another dimension to the fountain in Kalander's Arcadian garden. Cupid, capricious, unmanageable, eternally a child, is replaced with the infant Aeneas, who will become a model of piety, a nation builder, and an epic hero. This substitution has many potential significances. It has implications for the genre in which Sidney is writing: unlike the more conventional romance of the *Old Arcadia*, the *New Arcadia* is determinedly mixed in its genre, with aspects far more characteristic of epic. Aeneas is the greatest epic hero and his story is that of the fall and rise of nations. It is more overtly political and concerned with the nature of good government. In particular, by his abandonment of Dido Aeneas overcomes excessive, improper, and impolitic love, putting imperial destiny and duty before passion, and it is the political implications of this particular aspect of Sidney's substitution that I will explore here, through the medium (an appropriate one, given the broader context of the Kalander passage) of portraiture.

That Sidney was interested in, and influenced by, the visual arts is well known. In criticism of the *Arcadia*, the 'Ermine' portrait, now at Hatfield House, is often cited in reference to the impresa of Clitophon, champion of Queen Helen of Corinth in Book 1 of the *New Arcadia*: comprising an ermine and the motto 'Rather dead than spotted', it is placed on Queen Helen's

---

    [5] Francesco Colonna, *Hypnerotomachia: The Strife of Love in a Dreame*, trans. R.D., ed. Lucy Gent (New York, 1973), p. vii.

    [6] Katherine Duncan-Jones, 'Sidney and Titian', in John Carey and Helen Peters (eds.), *English Renaissance Studies Presented to Dame Helen Gardner in Honour of her Seventieth Birthday* (Oxford: Clarendon Press, 1980), 6.

portrait. Although this particular portrait is dated 1585, and so most likely post-dates Sidney's revisions of the *Arcadia*, Roy Strong has also identified an ermine in Zuccaro's portrait sketch of Elizabeth of May 1575, one of a pair completed for Robert Dudley, Earl of Leicester, in the context of Elizabeth's visit to Kenilworth in the same year,[7] and therefore probably known to Sidney. Likewise, still another of the great Elizabethan portraits usefully contextualizes Sidney's substitution of Aeneas for Cupid in Kalander's Venus fountain. This is the 'Sieve' portrait, painted in two versions, in series dated by Strong to *c.*1579 and *c.*1580–3. The greatest of these, the 'Siena', includes as part of its elaborate background Elizabeth's familiar column, symbol of constancy, here decorated with cameo-like lozenges depicting scenes from the story of Dido and Aeneas. Strong has argued persuasively that the portrait was painted in about 1580 for Sir Christopher Hatton, who appears in the background. The jasper column and the motto below it, and the sieve emblem itself, are all drawn from Petrarch's 'Triumph of Chastity', and Strong suggests that the portrait casts Elizabeth as Aeneas, one who must reject passion and forge England's imperial destiny; the globe in the mid-ground of the picture is turned to the Americas.[8] But equally, Elizabeth could also be identified (although less flatteringly) with Dido, whose other name, Elissa, had been played on by Spenser in the April Eclogue of the *Shepheardes Calender* in 1579, betrayed and abandoned by her lover, having been distracted from her own business of rule.

Like Sidney, Sir Christopher Hatton was a fierce opponent of Elizabeth's proposed marriage with the Duke of Anjou, and this particular historical narrative can surely be seen in the 'Sieve' portrait, through its emphasis on Elizabeth's chastity, the implicit connection between this and England's imperial successes, and the misfortunes of Dido and Aeneas. Can the prominent place accorded Aeneas in Kalander's garden of love, contrary to Sidney's source, also be read as recalling and recording (albeit at a prudent historical distance) this particular anti-marriage context, especially given Sidney's own letter to the Queen on the subject in 1579? As Blair Worden has pointed out,

[T]he *Old Arcadia* was written at a time of deep divisions within the Elizabethan regime, which were intensified by the marriage negotiations between the queen and Anjou. The anxiety roused in Sidney by those negotiations, which were held from 1578 to 1581, did not die with them. The influence of them, and of the meditations they induced in him, persisted into the *New Arcadia*.[9]

---

[7] On the great fountain at Kenilworth, also erected on the occasion of Elizabeth's 1575 progress, see Chapter 8.

[8] See Strong's discussion in *Gloriana: The Portraits of Queen Elizabeth I* (London: Thames and Hudson, 1987; repr. 2003), 100–7.

[9] Blair Worden, *The Sound of Virtue: Philip Sidney's* Arcadia *and Elizabethan Politics* (New Haven: Yale University Press, 1996), 15–16.

The Venus–Cupid fountain at Theobalds not only provides a close material analogue or even source for Sidney's Aeneas fountain (although one that by no means diminishes the importance of the *Hypnerotomachia* as a primary textual and visual source, especially since the exact date of the Theobalds fountain remains uncertain) but it also, in Sidney's substitution of Aeneas for Cupid, has a potential resonance within the historical context of the French marriage. Burghley was in many respects a supporter of the proposed marriage with Anjou: Sidney's pointed transformation of a fountain erected by Cecil, possibly celebrating his monarch in her aspect as 'Venus-Virgo', could glance reprovingly at this also.[10]

Aeneas appears several times in Sidney's *Defence*, as the best possible example of the exemplary value of literature:

But if anything be already said in the defence of sweet poetry, all concurreth to the maintaining the heroical, which is not only a kind, but the best and most accomplished kind of poetry. For as the image of each action stirreth and instructeth the mind, so the lofty image of such worthies [as Achilles, Cyrus, Aeneas, Turnus, Tydeus, and Rinaldo] most inflameth the mind with desire to be worthy, and informs with counsel how to be worthy. Only let Aeneas be worn in the tablet of your memory—how he governeth himself in the ruin of his country, in the preserving his old father, and carrying away his religious ceremonies; in obeying God's commandment to leave Dido, though not only all passionate kindness but even the human consideration of virtuous gratefulness would have craved other of him; how in storms, how in sports, how in war, how in peace, how a fugitive, how victorious, how besieged, how besieging, how to strangers, how to allies, how to enemies, how to his own; lastly, how in his inward self, and how in his outward government—and I think in a mind not prejudiced with a prejudicating humour he will be found in excellency fruitful, yea even as Horace saith, *melius Chrysippo et Crantore*.[11]

As Gavin Alexander points out in his note on this passage, ' "Tables" or "tablets" were also boards on which portraits were painted; the image is thus closely related to the thread of visual metaphors centred on the "speaking picture". Sidney's list alludes to all the central matter of the *Aeneid*'.[12] Sidney's image of the 'tablet' of the memory here recalls the strongly material textuality of the *Hypnerotomachia*, the way in which it is at once text-as-story, landscape-as-experience, book-as-object. The tablet or table is a surface which

[10] There is also perhaps a recollection of Venus' own substitution of Cupid for Aeneas's own son Ascanius in order to ensnare Dido in *Aeneid* 1.657 ff. I am grateful to Gavin Alexander for this suggestion.

[11] 'Better than Chrysippus and Crantor'. Gavin Alexander (ed.), *Sidney's 'The Defence of Poesy' and Selected Renaissance Literary Criticism* (London: Penguin, 2004), 29–30.

[12] Ibid. 339 n. 148. Sidney's phrase is perhaps recalled by Hamlet. See *Hamlet*, ed. Ann Thompson and Neil Taylor, The Arden Shakespeare: Third Series (London: Thomson Learning, 2006), 1.5.98, 107.

can be inscribed with writing or painted with an image; in either case, it at once materializes an idea, that idea's importance, and the metaphor which expresses both of these. It neatly anticipates the pictorial nature of the description of Kalander's garden in the *Arcadia*, and of course the picture gallery itself, which is part of the garden both physically or spatially and in terms of the ways in which the garden and the gallery, and their description, are experienced, and not simply seen, by both reader and protagonist.

The figure of Aeneas and its associations in Sidney's other writings (and implicitly in the *Arcadia*) give garden and gallery, and the ensuing action of the romance, a particular moral colour. The qualities Sidney attributes to him are those desirable in any exemplary ruler, not least in Elizabeth, and in any epic hero: the appearance of Aeneas so near the beginning of the *Arcadia*, albeit as a baby, transformed into a fountain in a garden of love that has been taken straight out of a romance, must surely be interpreted with reference to Sidney's treatment of him in the *Defence* as well as in the historical (and even art historical) context suggested above. Katherine Duncan-Jones has noted, furthermore, that a work dedicated to Sidney *c.*1585 explicitly compared him to Aeneas: this was Abraham Fraunce's manuscript compilation of a summary of Ramist logic and a series of imprese. The binding was illustrated with a picture of Aeneas, 'a dominating figure on the departing sailing ship', clearly meant to be identified with Sidney, and Duncan-Jones suggests that 'Fraunce was bidding Sidney farewell as he went off on some expedition which he himself would have liked to join, and this may be the expected mission to the Netherlands'.[13] Aeneas here is the man of action that Sidney apparently so longed to be.

But the prominence accorded Aeneas in both the *Defence* and at this point in the *New Arcadia* can also be read in terms of Sidney's development as outlined by Roger Kuin, when he suggested that '[i]n the *Defence* we see him setting his thoughts in order for his new role; the *Old Arcadia* and the sonnets are very much marks of *otium*, while in the revision he is making serious progress toward an alternative to a courtier-text'.[14] Kuin's 'new role' for Sidney is that of the '*Fürstendiener*', defined by him as 'middle-aged scholar-diplomats in the service of mostly minor and Protestant princes', a role promoted and fostered in Sidney's case by Hubert Languet. Although this is perhaps too neat a characterization of both the *New Arcadia* and Sidney himself, it does draw attention obliquely to a final and hitherto unexplored aspect of Sidney's transformation of Colonna: that in the *Hypnerotomachia*,

---

[13] Fraunce's book is now Bodleian Library MS Rawl. D. 345; Duncan-Jones, *Courtier Poet*, 155.

[14] Roger Kuin, 'Sir Philip Sidney: The Courtier and the Text', *English Literary Renaissance*, 19 (1989), 269.

the Fountain of Adonis is also his tomb. In the *Metamorphoses*[15] (although to a far lesser degree than in Shakespeare's *Venus and Adonis*, for example), Adonis is characterized as silent and submissive, obedient to the whims of the powerful Venus. (Embedded in Ovid's Adonis narrative there is also the story of Atalanta, a powerful woman undone by marriage; her picture appears in Kalander's gallery.) Adonis dies in the pursuit of the hunt, perhaps the most characteristic activity of the Elizabethan courtier's *otium*, and his fatal wounding by the boar makes literal his symbolic emasculation at the hands of the goddess. Given the subsequent manner of Sidney's death (and, indeed, its re-imagination in Ovidian terms in Spenser's *Astrophel*), this all seems a little too good to be true. But to recognize the possibility that Sidney's reinvention of Colonna's Fountain of Venus and Cupid as a fountain of Venus and Aeneas yet retains some ghost or palimpsest of Adonis's tomb surely strengthens Kuin's suggestion of Sidney's turning his back on, or at least radically reinventing, both the 'courtier-text' and the role of the courtier itself. Whatever the finer nuances of the device, it remains a satisfyingly rich and suggestive adaptation of Colonna's original at this key expository and catalytic point in the *New Arcadia*'s narrative. As with the Fountain of Adonis in the *Hypnerotomachia*, a garden with a fountain is the appropriate setting for storytelling and for love: Kalander is about to relate the story of Basilius' misguided government, and Musidorus is about to see the portrait of Philoclea and hear a description of Pamela. It frames the ensuing action, and the work as a whole, in a very particular ethical and aesthetic way, and one that is very much of its historical moment.

Despite my attempts here to complicate it, Sidney's substitution of Aeneas for Cupid in his reworking of Colonna's Fountain of Adonis remains on one level relatively straightforward in its referents and potential significations: it is firmly material (or concrete) in its historicity and its generic and ethical associations. But as with Colonna's Adonis fountain in the wider context of the *Hypnerotomachia* as a whole, Sidney's treatment of the place and the play of water in the garden of Kalander goes beyond the material, raising suggestive questions about the nature of art and of fiction. It is perhaps not going too far to suggest that Sidney recognized some of the ways in which the Adonis fountain functions in the *Hypnerotomachia*, and in particular the importance of its reflective qualities. Perhaps adjacent to Kalander's Venus fountain (although the text is a little unclear) there is a reflecting pool: 'In the midst of all the place was a fair pond whose shaking crystal was a fair mirror to all the other beauties, so that it bare show of two gardens; one in deed, the other in shadows.' As Norman Farmer has pointed out, the reflective

---

[15] Ovid, *Metamorphoses*, 10.519 f.

qualities of the pool are also closely modelled on a fountain in the garden of Clitophon in Achilles Tatius' romance: 'In the midst of the flowers a fountain was spurting, and a square conduit for its stream had been traced around it by human hand. The water served as a mirror for the flowers, so that the grove seemed to be doubled, part real and part reflection'.[16] But the relationship here between Sidney's 'two gardens', the real one and its reflection in the surface of the pool, is also the same as that between the two books of the *Hypnerotomachia*, where Book 1 'shadows' the more literal Book 2, implicitly raising the question as to which is the more 'real', the world of Petrarchan and Platonic metaphors or one in which those metaphors are made flesh, as spectacular sights and sensual lived experiences.[17] In the *Arcadia*, which hinges on disguise and transformation and the ways in which the adoption of a fictitious identity can allow the simultaneous concealment and revelation of truth (Pyrocles/Zelmane's lyric 'Transform'd in show, but more transform'd in mind' being but the most succinct example of this), the reflective pool with which Sidney begins his exposition and frames the two princes' falling in love is a potent image for the transforming power of fiction—and of love. Like the Venus fountain itself, it seems to draw on the *Hypnerotomachia*, but it could also have a secondary source, the identity of which will be returned to at the end of this chapter.

If the Venus and Aeneas fountain has a specifically didactic or ethical function, then it is also possible to see the reflective pool as part of this same programme, in a way that may demonstrate Sidney's knowledge of current fashions in garden design. At least two early modern English gardens used reflective pools as part of their design schemes, to didactic as well as aesthetic effect, and perhaps in direct invocation of the long established genre of the 'speculum' or 'mirror', anthologies of moral, spiritual, or political exempla. Two of the best-known examples of this genre available to Sidney were the *Mirror for Magistrates*, which appeared first in 1559 and went through numerous editions in the sixteenth and seventeenth centuries (Sidney refers

---

[16] Achilles Tatius, *Leucippe and Clitophon*, trans. Tim Whitmarsh (Oxford: Oxford University Press, 2001), 1.15, p. 16. Although Farmer dismisses outright any possibility of Sidney's having been influenced by the *Hypnerotomachia*, a footnote makes clear that he had consulted only *The Strife of Love in a Dreame*, attempting to draw a comparison between Sidney's Aeneas fountain and the Fountain of the Sleeping Nymph. The *Strife* ends long before the Fountain of Adonis is reached. Ironically, Farmer goes on to illustrate his discussion elsewhere with an illustration of Semele from one of the triumphs in the *Hypnerotomachia*. His discussion of the Aeneas fountain, and in particular of the figure of Venus, is useful, however. Norman K. Farmer, *Poets and the Visual Arts in Renaissance England* (Austin: University of Texas Press, 1984), 6 and Chapter 1, *passim*.

[17] One is reminded, too, of the 'golden' world of poetry and its opposition to the real 'brazen' world invoked in Sidney's *Defence*.

to it in his *Defence of Poetry*), and the *Miroir de l'âme pécheresse* (1531) of
Marguerite d'Angoulême, Queen of Navarre, translated by Princess Elizabeth
as a New Year's gift to Katherine Parr in 1544 as *The Mirror or Glass of the
Sinful Soul*. The first of several continental editions of Elizabeth's translation
appeared in 1548; London editions followed in 1568 and in the 1590s. Conduct
manuals of the period also used 'mirror' or 'glass' in their titles, for example
Philip Stubbes's *A crystal glass for Christian women* (1591) and Barnabe
Rich's *My lady's looking glass* (1616), and in 1578 Margaret Tyler published a
translation of a Spanish romance under the title *The mirror of princely deeds
and knighthood*.

In 1561, William Cecil had acquired from Venice statues, most probably
busts, of the twelve Caesars. By 1598 when Paul Hentzner visited, these statues
(or perhaps another similar set, for there were also busts of the Caesars in
the house) had been erected in the summerhouse at Theobalds. Theobalds
had a complex iconographic programme encompassing both garden and
house which, it has been suggested, was at least partly directed towards the
education in governance of Burghley's second and favourite son, Robert
Cecil.[18] In the house, scenes from English history appeared in murals, while
decorative genealogical tables displayed, county by county, the descents of
the great families of England. In the summerhouse, located on the south
side of the enormous 'great garden', the ceiling was also painted with what
the Bohemian tourist Baron Waldstein described, when he visited Theobalds
in 1600, as 'appropriate episodes from history'. That this was classical as
opposed to English history is suggested by the terms of the Parliamentary
Survey, where it was described as 'excellently well painted, all ye seeling over
with naked men & woomen'.[19] This summerhouse appears to have been on
two levels, the circular room with the painted ceiling being the upper storey,
while below there was an ornamental pool. The busts of the twelve Caesars
overlooked this pool, and were presumably reflected in it. There was a similar
arrangement at Raglan Castle in Gwent, seat of the earls of Worcester. It
was probably Edward Somerset (1553–1628), fourth earl, who succeeded in

[18] For the summerhouse at Theobalds, see Paula Henderson, 'The Architecture of the Tudor
Garden', *Garden History*, 27 (1999), 64–7, as well as her discussion 'A Shared Passion: the
Cecils and their Gardens' in Pauline Croft (ed.), *Patronage, Culture and Power: The Early Cecils,
1558–1612* (New Haven: Yale University Press, 2002), 99–120. For Theobalds in general, see
Malcolm Airs, 'Pomp or Glory: The Influence of Theobalds', in the same volume (pp. 3–19);
John Summerson, 'The Building of Theobalds, 1564–1585', *Archaeologia*, 97 (1959), 107–26;
Martin Andrews, 'Theobalds Palace: The Gardens and Park', *Garden History*, 21 (1993), 129–49;
James M. Sutton, 'The Decorative Program at Elizabethan Theobalds' and *Materializing Space at
an Early Modern Prodigy House: The Cecils at Theobalds, 1564–1607* (Aldershot: Ashgate, 2004).
[19] Quoted by Henderson, 'A Shared Passion', 104. See also Henderson's discussion of
Theobalds in *The Tudor House and Garden*.

1589, who installed statues of Roman emperors in specially constructed niches overlooking the moat. Although the statues have disappeared, the curved wall with its niches remains, some of which still show traces of their patterned shellwork decoration, and the original effect, mirrored in the moat, must have been striking.[20]

Given the moral and didactic connotations of the 'mirror' as a literary genre, there is surely an educational or exemplary intention in the provision of pools to reflect classical exemplars of governance, especially at Theobalds, with its broadly educational programme in the house and the garden's iconography and decorative schemes, and in particular the specific architectural context of the summerhouse, with its ceiling of 'appropriate episodes from history'. (In a perhaps deliberate contrast, the pictures in Kalander's summerhouse are mostly 'traditional moral emblems expressing all the varied passions of love with which his story is to deal'.[21]) Reflective pools in gardens can therefore be read as on one level materializing a literary genre. There is of course no way of knowing when the statues of the emperors were thus set up in the Theobalds summerhouse, and hence whether Sidney might have seen or at least been aware of their configuration. That by 1587 William Harrison could include Theobalds in his list of famous English gardens suggests that most of the garden's elaborate design and decoration was in place by that year, but this could simply be politic flattery on Harrison's part; most of the rebuilding work in the house itself, however, is known to have been completed by the mid-1580s. James Sutton suggests a completion date of *c*.1573 for the great middle court, roughly the same for various of the five loggias, 1578 for the outer gate, and *c*.1585 for the fountain or 'conduit court', where the great fountain of Venus and Cupid was located.[22]

In both its sculptural content and the closely related reflecting pool, Sidney's Fountain of Aeneas in Kalander's garden can therefore be located at the intersection of Sidney's reading of the *Hypnerotomachia* (or the *Songe de Poliphile*) and his knowledge and experience of the great gardens being created by his peers and contemporaries in England. While there are various early seventeenth-century accounts of the fountains at Wilton which seem to have pre-dated Isaac de Caus's elaborate works there in the 1630s (there are, for example, close analogues to fountains known to have been at Wilton in the *Urania* of Mary Wroth, Sidney's niece, which pre-dates de Caus)[23]

[20] On Raglan, see Elizabeth H. Whittle, 'The Renaissance Gardens of Raglan Castle', *Garden History*, 17 (1989), 83–94.

[21] *The Countess of Pembroke's Arcadia*, 849.

[22] 'The Decorative Program at Elizabethan Theobalds', 35.

[23] The most notable of these is 'a Fountaine made in the fashion of an Emperiall Crowne with a Globe on the toppe, out of the which like a full shower of raine the water came so plentifully,

no description survives of any fountain that could have been based on one in the *Hypnerotomachia*. But it is tantalizing to note that in 1623 John Taylor ('the Water Poet') found at Wilton, and recorded in his *A New Discouery by Sea, with a Wherry, from London to Salisbury*, 'Walkes, hedges, and Arbours, of all manner of most delicate fruit Trees, planting and placing them in such admirable Artlike fashions, resembling both diuine and morrall remembrances, as three Arbours standing in a Triangle, hauing each a recourse to a greater Arbour in the midst, resembleth three in one, and one in three' (C2ᵛ). His phrase 'admirable Artlike fashions, resembling both diuine and morrall remembrances' could equally be applied to the complex designs and arcane symbolism of the gardens of the *Hypnerotomachia*, and in fact both the Italian and French editions of the *Hypnerotomachia* illustrate the curious construction of an obelisk, cube, and sphere which is explained as an emblem of the Trinity: but only the *Songe*'s illustration (H2) locates it in the midst of a leafy, possibly triangular arbour. There is, of course, no way of knowing if these arbours even dated from the 1580s, let alone whether they had anything to do with Sidney's reading of the *Hypnerotomachia*. But, like the identification of Astrophil's 'fair book' with the *Hypnerotomachia*, it is an attractive hypothesis, and one that is a neat and suggestive counterpart to Sidney's almost literal confluence of borrowed fountains, real and literary, in his garden of Kalander; that there could have been, in a garden he knew so well, a device borrowed from the pages of one of the Renaissance's greatest romances.

There remains, finally, a third and even perhaps more suggestive element to Sidney's fountain, one which might further illuminate his perennial concern with the nature of art and literature and their relationship one to another, as well as suggesting something of Sidney's own anxieties about his status and identity as a writer. This returns, albeit indirectly, to the text with which this discussion of the *Hypnerotomachia* began, Sidney's *Astrophil and Stella*, and it ought not to be forgotten that Sidney's composition of his sonnet sequence overlapped with that of his *Defence*, and no doubt his contemplation of the revision of his *Arcadia*.[24] Lucy Gent has argued persuasively for Sidney's

---

and showringly, as it resembled such plenty, so finely was it counterfeited, and the trees grewe so, as who hadde stood in the wood would not suddenly have knowne whether it rayned or no', *The First Part of the Countess of Mongomerie's Urania*, ed. Josephine A. Roberts (Binghamton, NY: Renaissance English Text Society, 1995), 424. The first part of the *Urania* was published in 1621, and so apparently pre-dated de Caus's work at Wilton, although there are very similar fountains illustrated in de Caus's *Le Jardin de Wilton* (*c*.1645). Wroth knew Wilton well; it also appears that she may have known the *Hypnerotomachia*.

[24] It could also be noted that Sidney was among the first poet-lovers, if not the first such, to name himself as well as his beloved and, like Colonna's hero, he is literally named as the lover of his mistress. The first point is made by, among others, Alan Sinfield, 'Sidney and Astrophil', *Studies in English Literature*, 20 (1980), 27.

knowledge of Alberti's treatise *On Painting*, for example in his use of the details of painters' techniques in rendering lustrous surfaces through the skilful deployment of black and white paint in sonnet seven ('When Nature made her chief worke, Stella's eyes, | In colour black, why wrapt she beames so bright? | Would she in beamy black, like painter wise, | Frame daintiest lustre, mixt of shades and light?'), and his apparent understanding of chiaroscuro in the Third Eclogues, where the crooks of Philoclea's knees are contrasted with the fairness of her skin, 'Like cunning Painter shadowing white'.[25] Various of Alberti's writings were in the library of John Dee, and therefore potentially available to Sidney; he may well have had his own copy of one of the many continental editions.

It is, however, with a less technical aspect of Alberti's treatise that this chapter and the discussion of the *Hypnerotomachia*, as well as of Sidney's garden of Kalander, concludes; one that is suggestive not only in the context of the *Arcadia* but in that of Sidney's writing, and his ideas and anxieties about literature, in general. At the beginning of Book 2 of his treatise, Alberti embarks upon an apology for painting, asserting its pre-eminence among the arts:

Is it not true that painting is the mistress of all the arts or their principal ornament? . . . Indeed, hardly any art, except the very meanest, can be found that does not somehow pertain to painting. So I would venture to assert that whatever beauty there is in things has been derived from painting. Painting was honoured by our ancestors with this special distinction that, whereas all other artists were called craftsmen, the painter alone was not counted among their number. Consequently I used to tell my friends that the inventor of painting, according to the poets, was Narcissus, who was turned into a flower; for, as painting is the flower of all the arts, so the tale of Narcissus fits our purpose perfectly. What is painting but the act of embracing, by means of art, the surface of the pool?[26]

As Mary Pardo puts it, 'the "embrace of art" is also a pun on tactile, and more properly carnal knowledge'.[27] In these terms, Alberti's image of art's embrace of the surface of the pool is strongly reminiscent of Colonna's fountains in the *Hypnerotomachia*, both the climactic Fountain of Venus and the reflective, transforming matrix of the Fountain of Adonis, in the ways in which they have been discussed here and in the previous chapter, although indeed the reverse might well be true: although *On Painting* was

[25] See Leon Battista Alberti, *On Painting*, trans. Cecil Grayson, ed. Martin Kemp (London: Penguin, 1991), Book 2, p. 81 f., and Lucy Gent, *Picture and Poetry 1560–1620* (Leamington Spa: James Hall, 1981), 26–7.

[26] Alberti, Book 2, p. 61.

[27] Mary Pardo, 'Artifice and Seduction in Titian', in James Grantham Turner (ed.), *Sexuality and Gender in Early Modern Europe* (Cambridge: Cambridge University Press, 1993), 81.

not printed until 1540,[28] Colonna's borrowing from Alberti's writings (which circulated widely in manuscript), and notably from his *On the Art of Building*, is demonstrable. In both of the *Hypnerotomachia*'s climactic fountains, Venus' as well as Adonis', the reflecting surface of the water becomes the visual, material, and experiential point of access to an eroticized landscape of the imagination. The reflective qualities of the Fountain of Adonis and of Sidney's reinvention of it as the Fountain of Aeneas enlarge their respective romances in spatial as well as narrative terms, at the same time as their surfaces are blank spaces, even pages—they are, quite literally, *lacunae*—that connote not loss, but potentiality.[29]

Narcissus' embrace of the surface of the pool is a potent image not only for painting, but for poetry and fiction also, and Alberti's formulation is thus an image that also seems to lurk behind Sidney's vivid and pictorial evocation of the 'fair pond, whose shaking crystal was a perfect mirror to all the other beauties, so that it bare show of two gardens; one in deed, the other in shadows'. Linda Gregerson has suggested that Edmund Spenser, like Sidney (and like Colonna), thought 'in specular terms. The figure of the mirror in *The Faerie Queene*, like the mirror the capacious poem constitutes, is a variable and supple thing . . . The best of mirrors, so Spenser repeatedly proposes, gives back an oblique and permeable likeness, so that its realm is one of opportunity rather than entrapment'.[30] Spenser's mirrors and indeed his fountains and his epic poem itself, subject of the next four chapters, would have been impossible without Sidney's. No mirror can be perfect, and to seek to embrace the reflected garden may be to destroy it, and in so doing to risk one's own destruction; Sidney was less daring and confident in this regard than was Colonna, and he solicits a similarly wary circumspection from his reader. Narcissus is a far from unambivalent figure, and the spectre of self-love and of ultimately sterile self-regard in love haunts not only the *Arcadia* but others of Sidney's works: Astrophil must look in his heart and write, but while Stella is his object and his muse, he must not be distracted by his own reflection in Stella's eyes. The shadow of Narcissus, like Adonis' palimpsestic ghost, in turn haunts Kalander's garden, and *Arcadia* itself: he is a figure implicit in the *Arcadia*'s wider economy of disguise, transformation, imitation, and counterfeit, Astrophil's anxieties about love and poetry, and indeed in the *Defence*'s concern with both these issues and those assessing the morality of art.

---

[28] The Latin text was printed in Basel in 1540, and an Italian translation (although not Alberti's own) in Venice in 1547.

[29] Linda Gregerson describes Kalander's garden as 'the garden of allegory' and the pool as 'a veil that simultaneously conceals and reveals'. *The Reformation of the Subject*, 116, 117.

[30] Ibid. 20.

Book 1 of the *Hypnerotomachia* dares to imagine Narcissus' successful embrace; to borrow Leonard Barkan's phrase, it is indeed concerned with 'the gods made flesh'. In passing, Julia Kristeva described the *Hypnerotomachia* as 'the apotheosis of the sacred's slide toward voluptuousness'[31]—yet the exact reverse is as, if not more, true. The *Hypnerotomachia*'s pervasive profanity—and also its nature as a quintessentially Renaissance text—arises not from the way in which it parodies Christian ceremonies, but from its suggestion that such an embrace is possible; that the naked goddess can, without fear, be seen in all her transcendent glory, and that there is no power greater than that of the human artistic and erotic imagination. Sidney is more circumspect, but knowingly so. He gestures at the world of reflection, of perfect mimesis and perfect beauty, but circumscribes it both aesthetically and generically. Adonis is dead and Aeneas has replaced Cupid; as the twelve Caesars were mirrored in the summerhouse's pool at Theobalds, so love must be tempered with the demands of politics and romance with epic aspiration. In borrowing, and transforming, the *Hypnerotomachia*'s Fountain of Adonis, Sidney both acknowledges the power of art and fiction, of love and imagination, and seeks in Kalander's garden, as in the *New Arcadia*, to channel it to more moral ends.

[31] Julia Kristeva, *Desire in Language: A Semiotic Approach to Literature and Art*, ed. Leon S. Roudiez, trans. Thomas Gora, Alice Jardine, and Leon S. Roudiez (Oxford: Basil Blackwell, 1982), 253.

Part II

Living Waters:
Spenser's *The Faerie Queene* (1590)

5

Ad Fontes: Elizabeth and the English Bible

On 14 January 1559, the 25-year-old Elizabeth Tudor made her coronation entry into the city of London.[1] Accompanied by her courtiers, she processed along a route that had become familiar on such occasions, from the Tower of London to Westminster, encountering elaborate tableaux on specially erected stages, listening to speeches composed for the occasion, graciously acknowledging the enthusiastic responses of the crowd, and, finally, being formally welcomed on behalf of the Mayor and Aldermen. The twelve companies of the city lined the streets, 'apparelled with manye ryche furres, and their liuery whodes vppon their shoulders in comely and semely maner, hauing before the*m* sondry persones well apparelled in silkes & chaines of golde . . . beside a number of riche hanginges, aswell of Tapistrie, Arras, clothes of golde, siluer, veluet, damaske, Sattin, and other silkes plentifullye hanged'.[2] As the author of the main account of the festivities put it, 'so that if a man shoulde say well, he could not better tearme the citie of London that time, than a stage wherin was shewed the wonderfull spectacle, of a noble hearted princesse toward her most louing people, & the peoples exceding comfort in beholding so worthy a soueraigne'.[3] The climax of the pageantry was the presentation of the city's gift to the Queen. '[T]he right worshipfull maister Ranulph Cholmeley Recorder of the citie' made a speech professing the city's loyalty, and presented her with 'a purse of crimeson sattin richely wrought with gold, wherin the citie gaue vnto the Quenes maiestie a thousand markes in gold'.[4] The Queen accepted the gift graciously and answered the Recorder in terms which made clear the reciprocal nature of her relationship with the city:

I thanke my lord maior, his brethren, & you all. And wheras your request is that I should continue your good ladie & quene, be ye ensured, that I wil be as good vnto

---

[1] See my longer discussion of Elizabeth's coronation entry in 'Location as Metaphor: *Veritas Temporis Filia* (1559) and its Afterlife', in Archer, Goldring, and Knight (eds.), *The Progresses, Pageants and Entertainments of Queen Elizabeth I*, 65–85. There is a useful discussion by Steven Mullaney, *The Place of the Stage: License, Play, and Power in Renaissance England* (Ann Arbor: University of Michigan Press, 1988), 11 ff.

[2] *The passage of our most drad Soueraigne Lady Quene Elyzabeth through the citie of London to westminster the daye before her coronacion Anno 1558* [i.e. 1559] (London, 1559), sig. C2ᵛ.

[3] Ibid., sig. A2ᵛ.   [4] Ibid., sig. C3.

you, as euer quene was to her people. No wille in me can lacke, neither doe I trust shall ther lacke any power. And perswade your selues, that for the safetie and quietnes of you all, I will not spare, if nede be to spend my blood, God thanke you all.[5]

This presentation and a number of the tableaux were staged in Cheapside, in between the Cross and the end of Paul's Churchyard; Cheapside had been the usual location for such pageantry, both royal and civic, since at least the reign of Henry VI.

Before the presentation of the city's monetary gift, however, the Queen had been distracted by the pageant which was to follow it: 'Sone after that her grace passed the crosse [in Cheap] she had espyed the pageant erected at the little conduit in cheape, and incontinent required to know what it might signify'.[6] When, finally, the Queen was allowed to approach this pageant, she would have seen that its staging consisted of two hills,

The one of them being on the North syde of the same pageaunt, was made cragged, barreyn, and stonye, in the whiche was erected one tree, artificiallye made, all withered and deadde, with braunches accordinglye . . . The other hylle on the South syde was made fayre, freshe, grene, and beawtifull, the grounde thereof full of flowres and beawtie, and on the same was erected also one tree very freshe and fayre.[7]

Beside each tree was an appropriately dressed 'personage', and the first hill was labelled (in English and Latin) '*Ruinosa Respublica*' and the second '*Respublica bene instituta*'. Each tree displayed further 'tables', which gave the various reasons for their respective states:

Causes of a ruinous common weale are these. *Want of the feare of god. Disobedience to rulers. Blindnes of guides. Briberie in maiestrats. Rebellion in subiectes. Ciuill disagrement. Flattring of princes. Vnmercifulnes in rulers. Vnthankfulnes in subiects.* Causes of a florishing common weale. *Feare of god. A wise prince. Learned rulers. Obedience to officers. Obedient subiectes. Louers of the common weale. Vertue rewarded. Vice chastened.*[8]

Between these two hills

was made artificiallye one hollowe place or caue, with doore and locke enclosed, oute of the whiche, a lyttle before the Queenes hyghnes commynge thither, issued one personage whose name was Tyme, apparaylled as an olde man with a Sythe in his hande, hauynge wynges artificiallye made, leadinge a personage of lesser stature than himselfe, whiche was fynely and well apparaylled, all cladde in whyte silke, and directlye ouer her head was set her name and tytle in latin and Englyshe, *Temporis filia,* the daughter of Tyme. Which two so appoynted, went forwarde, toward the South

---

[5] *The passage of our most drad Soueraigne Lady Quene Elyzabeth through the citie of London to westminster the daye before her coronacion Anno 1558* [i.e. 1559] (London, 1559), sig. C3ᵛ.
[6] Ibid., sig. C2ᵛ.   [7] Ibid., sig. C3ᵛ, C4.   [8] Ibid., sig. D1–D1ᵛ.

syde of the pageant. And on her brest was written her propre name, which was *Veritas*. Trueth who helde a booke in her hande vpon the which was writen, *verbum veritatis*, the woorde of trueth.[9]

The book was an English Bible. It was let down 'by a silken lace'[10] and passed by Sir John Parrat, one of the attendant gentlemen, to the Queen.

This pageant was at the ideological heart of the Queen's civic welcome and, in itself and in combination with the other tableaux, it expressed particular hopes for Elizabeth's reign on the part of the city. It made pointed reference to the reign of Elizabeth's immediate predecessor, her half-sister Mary; Mary herself had used 'Veritas Temporis Filia' as a motto, and its close association here with Elizabeth could therefore be read as a deliberate and explicit rejection of Mary's reign and its principles. Beyond its particular details, the pageant of *Veritas temporis filia* at the Little Conduit made fundamental points about the nature of good government and the proper ordering of relationships in a flourishing commonwealth. After explaining the characters of the tableau, a child orator pointed its moral, and applied it directly to the Queen:

> . . . Now since y^t Time again his daughter truth hath brought,
> We trust O worthy quene, thou wilt this truth embrace
> And since thou vnderstandste the good estate and nought
> We trust welth thou wilt plant, and barrennes displace.
>
> But for to heale the sore, and cure that is not seene,
> Which thing y^t boke of truth doth teache in writing playn:
> She doth present to thee the same, O worthy Quene,
> For that, that wordes do flye, but wryting doth remayn.[11]

Using terminology that would soon become widely familiar through the Elizabethan homilies on obedience, the descriptions of the ruined and the flourishing commonwealths affixed to the two trees made clear the absolute interdependence of spiritual and temporal order, and the mutual obligations of ruler and subjects in pursuing them. Elizabeth was presented with a didactic and even-handed prescription for government, warning her that the commonweal could be destroyed by '*Blindnes of guides*' and '*Vnmercifulnes in rulers*' as much as by '*Rebellion in subjectes*' and '*Vnthankfulnes in subiects*'.[12]

Like the relationship between city and prince, gestured at in the gift of the gold-filled purse which immediately preceded this particular pageant, the ideal relationship between monarch and subjects was a reciprocal one of mutual obligation, grounded in truth, the Word, and the fear of God. Its symbolic centre was not the device of the two hills, not yet even the revelation of Time

---

[9] Ibid., sig. C4–C4^v. [10] Ibid., sig. C2^v.
[11] Ibid., sig. C4^v; these are the last two stanzas of four. [12] Ibid., sig. D1.

and his daughter Truth. Rather it was the gift of the English Bible, a gift which breached the notional fourth wall of the pageant's symbolic staging and drew the Queen into its action.

The metaphor which underpinned both this principle of transformation and, specifically, the pageant of *Veritas Temporis Filia* and the gift of the English Bible was that of the fountain. As this chapter goes on to show, the fountain was perhaps the most common and potent metaphor for the Scriptures in the sixteenth and early seventeenth centuries; it is for this reason, above all, that Spenser uses it to structure the first book of *The Faerie Queene*, in so doing establishing a programme for the two following books of the 1590 version of the poem. In Elizabeth Tudor's coronation entry and the pageant of Truth the Daughter of Time, the fountain metaphor was present not overtly in its text or staging, but implicitly in its location, at the Little Conduit, and in its spiritual and ideological agenda. Less than a decade after the coronation, a Flemish artist struck a portrait medal of the Queen, its reverse portraying Faith as a woman at a fountain and its motto 'The Divine Fountain of the Realm'. When the scene of the coronation pageant was reimagined by George Peele in his mayoral pageant *Descensus Astraeae* in 1591, and by Thomas Heywood in the first part of *If You Know Not Me, You Know Nobody* in 1606, the fountain became explicit. Peele staged it—his pageant car was dominated by a fountain—and Heywood employed it as the central image of his Elizabeth's final speech, in which she declares of the English Bible:

> This is true foode for rich men and for poore,
> Who drinkes of this is certaine ne're to perish
> This will the soule with heauenly vertue cherish,
> Lay hand vppon this Anchor euery soule,
> Your names shalbe in an eternall scrowle;
> Who builds on this dwel's in a happy state,
> This is the fountaine cleere imaculate,
> That happy yssue that shall vs succeed,
> And in our populous Kingdome this booke read.[13]

But for the pageant's writer or writers and their audience—and for the Queen—the metaphor could remain implicit. The English Bible was to be the refreshing fountain for the Queen and, through her, for her realm and its people.

---

[13] Sig. F3ᵛ–F4. For Peele's *Descensus Astraeae*, see Chapter 10. For Heywood's *If You Know Not Me*, see 'Location as Metaphor: *Veritas Temporis Filia*'; it is also discussed by Jonathan Gil Harris, 'This Is Not a Pipe: Water Supply, Incontinent Sources, and the Leaky Body Politic', in Richard Burt and John Michael Archer (eds.), *Enclosure Acts: Sexuality, Property and Culture in Early Modern England* (Ithaca, NY: Cornell University Press, 1994), 203–28. For the van Herwijk medal, see Chapter 9.

There is of course no way of knowing whether the young Edmund Spenser was present in the streets of London—perhaps even in Cheapside, perhaps even in sight of this climactic pageant of *Veritas Temporis Filia*—on that January day in 1559. He had been born (perhaps in Smithfield) in about 1552,[14] an area of London about half a mile from St Paul's. The sole record of his early life in London names him as one of the beneficiaries of the charity of wealthy London lawyer, Alexander Nowell, who left each of thirty-one London schoolboys one shilling and a gown to wear in his funeral procession, in February 1569.[15] Spenser was evidently then in his final year of school, for the next surviving trace of his whereabouts is his matriculation at Pembroke Hall,[16] Cambridge, in May of the same year. Spenser's possible presence at Elizabeth's coronation entry must remain unknowable, but he was all the same connected to it in an important and appropriately literary way, albeit an indirect one. The main account of the coronation entry, printed in 1559 by Richard Tottel as *The Quenes Maiesties Passage*, is generally believed to have been written by Richard Mulcaster (and it has been suggested, in default of other evidence of authorship, that he was also the author of some or all of the pageants and speeches), the man responsible for Spenser's schooling.

Richard Mulcaster (1531/2–1611) became in 1561 the first headmaster of the Merchant Taylors' School, as a scholar of which the young Edmund Spenser received his gown and shilling dole in 1569.[17] He remained its headmaster until 1586, when he resigned because of a dispute over pay, and under his headship, Merchant Taylors' had become one of the largest schools in England, educating a mixture of fee-paying students and poor scholars, of whom, it seems, Spenser was one. Surviving details of the curriculum reveal the excellent grounding that he would have received in Latin and Greek, and even possibly some Hebrew. It has been suggested that Spenser remained close to his former teacher, possibly naming his children Sylvanus and Katherine after Mulcaster's son Silvan and daughter (and wife), and that he paid specific tribute to him as the 'good olde shephearde, *Wrenock*', who 'made me by arte more cunning in the same'.[18] Like his pupil, Mulcaster was interested

[14] This date is largely derived from the assumption that he was 16 or 17 when he matriculated in Cambridge.
[15] Andrew Hadfield, 'Spenser, Edmund (1552?–1599)', *Oxford Dictionary of National Biography* (www.oxforddnb.com/view/article/26145, accessed 14 Mar. 2006).
[16] Now Pembroke College.
[17] The school established by the Merchant Taylors was located on a site known as the Manor of the Rose, near the church of St Lawrence Pountney. The church was not rebuilt after the Great Fire, although Laurence Pountney Hill and Lane survive in the maze of streets to the east of Cannon Street Station.
[18] *The Shepheardes Calender*, 'December', lines 41–2, in *The Shorter Poems*, ed. Richard A. McCabe (London: Penguin, 1999). For Mulcaster's biography, see www.oxforddnb.com/view/article/19509?docPos=2. 'Mast. Wrenock' is an anagram of 'Mownckaster'.

in language, and the English language in particular. His second educational treatise, *The First Part of the Elementarie* (1582), discussed spelling reform, among other things, and, although he published some verse in Latin, he wrote in his 'Peroration' to the *Elementarie* that 'I loue *Rome*, but *London* better, I fauor *Italie*, but *England* more, I honor the *Latin*, but I worship the *English*' (Hh[v]). In the course of his pamphlet war with Thomas Nashe, Spenser's friend Gabriel Harvey included Mulcaster among those 'whose seuerall writings the siluer file of the workeman recommendeth to the plausible interreinement of the daintiest Censure',[19] and he quoted extensively from Mulcaster's first educational treatise, the *Positions . . . which are necessarie for the training vp of children* (1581) in the margins of his other books. It is especially pertinent to note, in the context of this discussion of Spenser, London, and the English Bible, that it was probably Mulcaster who introduced Spenser to Jan Van Der Noot, thus expediting his first foray into print (Van Der Noot was the cousin of Mulcaster's good friend Emanuel Van Meteren), that translations of *The Seven Psalms*, Ecclesiastes, and the *Canticum canticorum* are included in the list of Spenser's own 'lost works', and that no fewer than seven eventual translators of the 1611 Authorized Version, out of a total of forty-seven, studied at Merchant Taylors' under Mulcaster.[20]

Edmund Spenser was, therefore, born a Londoner. He was shaped, intellectually and spiritually, by his time at Merchant Taylors' School and Cambridge. As much recent work has emphasized, the bulk of his formative experiences, politically, professionally, and personally, took place in Ireland. But upon the loss of his Irish possessions, it was to London that he returned, and it was in London that, only a short while after that return, he died. Spenser has become familiar as a great poet of the natural environment, of rivers, hills, forests, and the sea; the human interventions within these landscapes that he depicts, such as the Cave of Mammon, the Houses of Pride, Holiness, Alma, and Busirane, and the Bowre of Bliss, are heavily allegorical, great set-pieces that seem to exist both within and on a different plane from their pastoral, littoral, or forest environs. Yet Spenser was not a child of the countryside, but had himself grown up at the very heart of a 'built environment' that was, in its own way, every bit as densely symbolic and even numinous as the gardens, caves, and castles that he would create. Overtly at its times of pageantry, and

---

[19] *Pierces supererogation or A new prayse of the old asse* (London, 1593), sig. Bb. Mulcaster's editor suggests that Harvey's enthusiasm for Mulcaster may in part have been occasioned by Nashe's dislike of his writings, *Positions Concerning the Training Up of Children*, ed. William Barker (Toronto: Toronto University Press, 1994), p. xxxv.

[20] These included Thomas Dove (later Bishop of Peterborough) and Lancelot Andrewes (later Bishop, successively, of Chichester, Ely, and Winchester, and Dean of the Chapel Royal), both of whom were contemporaries of Spenser's not only at school, but also at Pembroke.

residually thereafter, London was a city of gods, saints, prophets, and ancient heroes, a city of which Spenser never ceased to be a citizen. In his *Prothalamion* and *The Faerie Queene*, and in many others of his poems, it was a city that, like his mentor Mulcaster, and his contemporaries and successors like John Stow, William Camden, John Norden, and Ben Jonson, he both imaginatively inhabited and wrote.

Elizabeth Tudor's coronation entry, as recorded and perhaps written by Richard Mulcaster, had exemplified this vision of London. The city streets were transformed to welcome the young Queen, their monuments decorated with hangings, paint, and gilding, and they were filled not only by the city officials, the courtiers, and the citizens, but figures from history, myth, and the Bible: Elizabeth's father and grandparents, and even her mother, Anne Boleyn; Deborah and the Beatitudes; 'Gotmagot the Albione, and Corineus the Briton, two gya*n*tes bigge in stature furnished accordingly',[21] and of course Time and his daughter Truth. Yet in the climactic pageant of *Veritas Temporis Filia*, Elizabeth herself was accorded transformative powers. Through her agency as a wise and benevolent ruler, she was to revive the barren commonwealth. Above all, through her mediation of the Word of God, the English Bible, to her people, while at the same time drawing restorative strength and succour from it herself, she was to bring in a new age: 'Tyme, quod she, and Tyme hath brought me hether . . . she thanked the citie for that gyft, and sayde that she woulde oftentymes read ouer that booke . . . be ye ensured, that I wil be as good vnto you, as euer quene was to her people. No wille in me can lacke, neither doe I trust shall ther lacke any power'.[22]

The Little Conduit, the setting and the unifying metaphor for this climactic and defining moment, retained its own independent valency even as it made visible these crucial principles of Protestant monarchy. Like the other London conduits (several of which had also been used as the basis for pageant stages, and all of which had been decorated for the occasion) it was a site of civic and community importance, and even identity, for Londoners. The conduits, as they were recorded by the antiquarian John Stow and as they appeared and were utilized in pageantry, were a vital point of contact not only between past and present London, but between real and ideal London. Their description prompted the invocation of an idealized citizenry, past and present, a physical and historical quasi-archaeological layering. As is particularly apparent in his descriptions of festivals such as Elizabeth's coronation entry in his *Survay* and *Annales*, John Stow's London was in many ways a nostalgic, idealized city. It was particularly nostalgic in its depiction of harmonious, altruistic

---

[21] *The passage of our most drad Soueraigne Lady Quene Elyzabeth*, sig. E1.
[22] Ibid., sig. C2^v, C3^v.

communities. The conduits, their construction and maintenance, and even buckets to enable the poor to earn money as water-carriers, were frequent objects of benefaction in citizens' wills, and thus they became points in the city topography where the benevolent intentions of past citizens were absorbed into and made manifest in the landscape; where altruism was transformed into a local, unostentatious, functional materiality. Stow devoted his second chapter[23] to 'the Auncient and Present Riuers, Brooks, Boorns, Pooles, wels, and Conduites of fresh water, seruing the Citie',[24] and near the end of the *Survay* remarked, 'Neyther may I omit that none other place is so plentifully watered with springs, as *London* is'.[25] His work was thus, roughly, framed by his emphasis of a feature of London's topography and history that has now become completely unfamiliar, its local water supply.

But, for all Stow's praise of London as a well-irrigated city, a recurrent feature of his history of the city's water supply was that it was constantly under pressure from London's ever-expanding population, which simultaneously increased demand and diminished the supply available from traditional sources through encroachment and pollution.[26] Stow's narrative has been read as one of loss and decay, *fin de siècle* nostalgia for a city that perhaps never was. But the *Survay* itself functions as a record of continuity and, in its mixture of history and chorography, of a spatial and monumental simultaneity. Nothing is ever lost:[27] in Stow's record, as in Elizabeth Tudor's coronation entry and, indeed, in London itself and in Spenser's *Faerie Queene* (as Chapter 7 in particular explores), the legendary, distant, and recent pasts coexisted with the present. The layers of antiquarian detail recovered and set down by Stow re-attached themselves to the places and events that he described all the more prominently in his act of doing so. When he wrote of Elizabeth's coronation entry, forty years before the publication of the *Survay*, that distant event became current

---

[23] In fact a translation of William fitz Stephen's twelfth-century account.

[24] Sig. B5ᵛ.   [25] Sig. Gg4.

[26] Even William fitz Stephen's account, quoted verbatim by Stow, recorded this situation in the twelfth century. Fitz Stephen noted that '[a]unciently vntill the Conquerors time, and 200 yeres after' (sig. B5ᵛ), London's water supply needs were met by the Thames and three other rivers and three wells ('to wit *Holly* well, *Clements* well, and *Clarkes* well') as well as other local wells and springs. But Stow added that 'Holywel is much decayed and marred with filthinesse, purposely layd there, for the heightthening of the ground, for garden plots'; although '*Clements* Well' and '*Clarkes wel*' remained serviceable 'the other smaller wels that stood neare vnto *Clarkes wel*, to wit *Skinners wel*, *Fagges well*, *Todwell*, *Lodes well*, and *Redwell*, are all decayed and so filled vp. that their places are now hardly discerned' (sig. B7ᵛ).

[27] 'No space ever vanishes utterly, leaving no trace. Even the sites of Troy, Susa or Leptis Magna still enshrine the superimposed spaces of the succession of cities that have occupied them. Were it otherwise, there would be no "interpenetration", whether of spaces, rhythms or polarities,' Henri Lefebvre, *The Production of Space*, trans. Donald Nicholson-Smith (Oxford: Basil Blackwell, 1991), 164.

once more; it was reanimated by the thickly allusive descriptions of the streets and sites, such as the conduits, where it was enacted and, in turn, became part of them once more.

The attention that Stow paid to the conduits reached beyond the specificity of historical London and asserted London's identity as the equal or superior to the two other great types of the city, Rome and Jerusalem. Introducing his account of the New River,[28] Stow's continuator (in the *Annales*) observed that 'The sacred Scriptures, and all other auncient Historians, make great mention of Welles, and Riuers, and of their names, and scituation: the Annales of Rome, and the Chronicles of other Citties, make due memory of their Aquataries'.[29] This identification of London with Rome, and its capacity for transformation into the New Jerusalem, were frequently encountered in the pageants making up medieval and early modern coronation entries into the city.[30] It was essential to London's identity as a great city, a new Rome in temporal power and civic virtue and a New Jerusalem in righteousness, that it be well irrigated.

This immanent, multivalent London retains an important and eloquent presence in *The Faerie Queene*, and particularly in the first three books. In Book 3 (and 4) it appears as Troynovant, the New Troy, heir to the values and status of both Troy and Rome, that city's first successor in the *translatio imperii*; in Book 2 it is Cleopolis, the city of fame, the history of the foundation of which is read by Guyon in Eumnestes' chamber in the Castle of Alma. London as Cleopolis has already been introduced in Book 1 as the location of Gloriana's court (1.7.46) and, more significantly, it is used as a basis of comparison by Redcrosse when the hermit shows him the vision of the New Jerusalem from the Mount of Contemplation:

> Faire knight (quoth he) *Hierusalem* that is,
> The new *Hierusalem*, that God has built
> For those to dwell in, that are chosen his,

---

[28] The New River was a private project undertaken by the engineer and goldsmith Hugh Middleton to bring water from the springs of Chadwell and Amwell to London. It took five years to complete and was officially opened in 1613 by the Lord Mayor, Middleton's brother Thomas, with verses written by Thomas Middleton the playwright. A detailed account of its construction and opening is given in Munday's continuation of Stow (1618), in a special insert (*–*2^v) between fos. 20 and 21.

[29] 1631, sig. Iii6^v.

[30] Gordon Kipling notes that 'from the first appearance of a single pageant in 1377 during Richard II's coronation entry to Edward VI's coronation triumph of 1547, each London royal entry included at least one pageant representation of the New Jerusalem'. These usually took the form of 'celestial castles' from which angels descended and heavenly music was heard, which were frequently erected on the conduits. Gordon Kipling, ' "He That Saw It Would Not Believe It": Anne Boleyn's Royal Entry into London', in Alexandra F. Johnston and Wim Hüsken (eds.), *Civic Ritual and Drama* (Amsterdam: Rodopi, 1997), 52.

His chosen people purg'd from sinful guilt,
With pretious blood, which cruelly was spilt
On cursed tree, of that vnspotted lam,
That for the sinnes of al the world was kilt:
Now are they Saints all in that Citty sam,
More dear vnto their God, then younglings to their dam.

Till now, then said the knight, I weened well,
That great *Cleopolis*, where I haue beene,
In which that fairest *Fary Queene* doth dwell,
The fairest Citty was, that might be seene;
And that bright towre all built of christall clene,
Panthea, seemd the brightest thing, that was:
But now by proofe all otherwise I weene;
For this great Citty that does far surpas,
And this bright Angels towre quite dims that tower of glas.

Most trew, then said the holy aged man;
Yet is *Cleopolis* for earthly frame,
The fairest peece, that eie beholden can:
And well beseemes all knights of noble name,
That couett in th'immortall booke of fame
To be eternized, that same to haunt,
And doen their seruice to that soueraigne Dame,
That glory does to them for guerdon graunt:
For she is heuenly borne, and heauen may iustly vaunt.

(1.10.57–9)

Here, and in its subsequent representations as Troynovant, London is implicitly both Cleopolis and the New Jerusalem itself, the city of God's chosen people. More significantly, in the context of my discussion of Spenser's *Faerie Queene* and its fountains here and in the following three chapters, the connection that was made between the English Bible, the Queen, and the city in 1559 is one that resonates both specifically and analogically with Spenser's poem and its concerns. Just as, in the pageant of *Veritas Temporis Filia*, the conduit location acted as the implicit unifying metaphor for the didactic political and religious agenda of Mulcaster and the city (and court) authorities who had commissioned and organized the festivities, so Spenser—perhaps even influenced by his knowledge of those events—uses versions of fountains, as images as well as locations, to explore and articulate similar ideas about literature and language, religion and politics, art and morality, and about the nature and meaning of landscape. The remainder of this chapter, and the three following, will explore some of the ways in which he does so.

The motif of the fountain is a central one in discussions of the Christian (and especially the Protestant Humanist) imperative to right reading. The first homily in the 1547 *Certayne Sermons* (more commonly known as the *Book of Homilies*) is 'A fruitful exhortation, to the readyng and knowledge of holy scripture', which opens thus:

Vnto a Christian man, there can be nothyng, either more necessarie, or profitable, then the knowledge of holy scripture: forasmuche as in it, is conteyned Gods true worde, settyng furth his glorie, and also mannes duetie. And there is no truth, nor doctrine, necessary for our iustificacion, and euerlastyng saluacion, but that is (or maie be) drawen out of that fountain, and welle of truth. Therfore as many as be desirous, to entre into the right and perfect waie vnto God, must applie their myndes, to knowe holy scripture, without the which, they can neither sufficiently knowe God and his will, neither their office and duetie, And as drynke is pleasaunt to them, that be drie, and meat to them that be hungery, so is the readyng, hearyng, searchyng, and studiyng of holy scripture... Let vs diligently search for the welle of life, in the bokes of the new and old Testament, and not ronne to the stinkyng podelles of mennes tradicions, deuised by mannes imaginacion, for our iustificacion and saluacion.[31]

The first Elizabethan edition of the *Homilies* appeared not long after the new Queen's coronation, and it was published—and read—in ever-expanding editions throughout her reign. The straightforward metaphorical identification of the Bible as a life-giving fountain, encountered here, accords perfectly with the symbolism of the Well of Life in canto 11 of Book 1 of *The Faerie Queene*: yet, as this discussion will show, fountains in Spenser are only very rarely so unambiguous. As the next chapter in particular explores, Spenser's fountains tend to operate as sites of overt syncretism and intertextuality, taxing the interpretative resources of the reader and frequently, as in Redcrosse's case, misleading the protagonist. In Book 1, they furnish the landscape of the narrative with catalytic (or catastrophic) landmarks, which shape both Redcrosse's quest and the reading of it.

The concern with accurate and 'true' sources in a textual sense is of course a central humanist one, conceptualized as the return, literally, *ad fontes*. For example, Erasmus used the conventional image of the fountain to defend his return to the Greek in two of the prefatory letters to his translation of the New Testament:

By clearing obstacles away I have opened up a field in which those who wish hereafter to expound the Holy Scriptures can share their sport more readily or meet in conflict with less waste of time. Those who have a feeling for the old theology have a powerful support to help their efforts towards the goal. Again, he who says with the man in the parable 'The new wine is better', and neglects the old through his interest in our more recent vintage of theology—he too has the means of indulging his preference with

---

[31] Sig. A3ᵛ, A4.

greater certainty and confidence. And even supposing he gains nothing from this, at least he will lose nothing from his own store if these advantages accrue to those who would rather draw their knowledge of Scripture from the purest springs than from such streams and pools as may be handy, so often poured from one of them into another, not to say fouled by the muddy feet of swine and asses.[32]

I perceived that the teaching which is our salvation was to be had in a purer and more lively form if sought at the fountain-head and drawn from the actual sources than from pools and runnels. And so I have revised the whole New Testament (as they call it) against the standard of the Greek original.[33]

For Erasmus, the 'streams and pools as may be handy' stand for the Vulgate and the effects of the 'muddy feet of swine and asses' the accretions of scribal interpolation and tortuous scholastic explication and elaboration. A similar (and perhaps even derivative) use of Erasmus' fountain metaphor is found in the dedication (to Queen Elizabeth) of *A defense of the sincere and true translation of the Holy Scriptures into the English tongve* (1583) by William Fulke (1538–89), which had as its occasion the appearance of the Rheims-Douai New Testament: 'They [Catholics] also at the last are become Translators of the New Testament into English. In which, that I speake nothing of their insincere purpose, in leauing the pure fountaine of the originall veritie, to follow the crooked streame of their barbarous vulgar Latin translation'.[34] More polemical Protestant Humanists made, using the same metaphors, a connection between the textual corruptions of the Vulgate and the perceived doctrinal corruptions of the Catholic Church. The 'stinkyng podelles of mennes tradicions, deuised by mannes imaginacion' invoked in the *Homilies* similarly refer to such textual and exegetical elaborations, as well as to the traditions of Roman Catholic worship and doctrine. Framing such concern with accurate interpretation is Erasmus' with the integrity and accuracy of the sources themselves, for proper reading (and church practice) are impossible if texts themselves are corrupt. As the next chapter shows, a like concern can be seen at the beginning of Spenser's narrative, where a distorted version of the beginning of the Bible prompts first misreading and then a susceptibility to being misled.

Two Old Testament texts are central to the expression of this motif in Protestant polemics and apologetics and, as will be seen, they are similarly important to Book 1 of Spenser's *Faerie Queene*. These are Genesis 26: 15: 'For all the wells which his father's servants had digged in the days of Abraham

---

[32] 'To the Reader', Desiderius Erasmus, *The Correspondence of Erasmus: Letters 298 to 445, 1514 to 1516*, trans. R. A. B. Mynors and D. F. S. Thomson (Toronto: University of Toronto Press, 1976), 203.
[33] 'To Leo X', ibid. 222.
[34] Sig. A2. The passage is quoted from the second edition of 1617.

his father, the Philistines had stopped them and filled them with earth' and Jeremiah 2: 13: 'For my people have committed two evils; they have forsaken me the fountain of living waters, and hewed them out cisterns, broken cisterns, that can hold no water.' As is apparent from the examples already quoted, these two texts were favourites of those writing in support of vernacular translations of the Bible and the Reformation in general. In Bishop John Jewel's *An Apologie or answere in defence of the Churche of Englande*,[35] a systematic account of the doctrine and practices of the English Church, both are expanded and applied to the perceived corruption of the Catholic Church:

Thei haue stopped vp saith [Jeremiah], al the vaines of cleere springing water, and haue digged vp for the people deceiuable and puddlelike pyttes full of myre and filth, whiche neither haue nor are able to hold pure water.

But wherefore I pray you haue they them selfe, the citizens and dwellers of Rome remoued, and come downe from those seauen hilles, whervpon Rome sometime stood, to dwel rather in the plaine called Mars his field. They wil say peraduenture, by cause the conductes of water, wher with out menne cannot commodiouslye liue, haue now failed and ar dried vp in those hilles. Well then, lett them giue vs lyke leaue in seeking the water of eternal lyfe, that they giue them selfes in seekyng the water of the well, for the water verely fayled amongest them.... Euen so these menne haue broken in peeces al the pypes and conduites, they haue stopped vp al the springs, & choked vp the fountaine of liuyng water with durte and myre. And as Caligula many yeres past locked fast vp al the storehouses of corne in Rome, & thereby brought a generall derth and famyne amongest the people, euen to these men by damming vp all the fountaines of Goddes word, haue brought the people into a peetiful thirst.[36]

By contrast, Jewel says of the Church of England that

we haue searched out of ye holy Bible whiche we are sure cannot deceiue, one sure fourme of Religion, and haue retorned againe vnto the Primatiue Churche of the auncient Fathers and Apostles, that is to say, to the first ground and beginning of thinges, as vnto the very foundations & head springes of Christes church.[37]

In Jewel's *Apologie*, as in other Protestant writings, the springs simply 'stopped and ... filled with earth' in Genesis have become (quite logically) polluted pools; the broken cisterns of Jeremiah become broken pipes, frustrating the transmission of the word of God to the people.

---

[35] The *Apologia ecclesiae anglicanae* was first published in 1562, and an English translation appeared the same year. Quotations are taken from the better-known translation by Ann Bacon, which was published in 1564 and many times thereafter. Jewel's work was one of the most controversial and influential texts of the period; by the 1570s Archbishop Parker was recommending that a copy be kept in every parish church in England.

[36] Sig. L2ᵛ–L3, L6ᵛ–L8. Erasmus uses the same texts in the Epistle Dedicatory to the *Enchiridion*.

[37] Sig. Q3–Q3ᵛ

Not least in its portrayal of versions of the New Jerusalem, it has long been recognized that the Book of Revelation is an important influence and structural analogue for Book 1 of *The Faerie Queene*.[38] Yet, perhaps because Revelation is such an obvious source, and also because its employment is particularly easy to interpret if Spenser is primarily seen as the poet of English Protestant nationalism, the importance of other biblical texts—such as those from Genesis and Jeremiah just quoted—and also paratexts (such as commentaries and exegeses) in reading *The Faerie Queene* has often been overlooked. It is all too easy to establish a Revelatory checklist of, for example, the Woman Clothed with the Sun, the Water and the Tree of Life, the Beast with Seven Heads, and the Whore of Babylon, and to leave it at that. Here, I will focus more on those passages and motifs typologically related to Revelation in both the Old and the New Testaments.[39] Simply identifying the possible biblical referents of Spenser's language and imagery, as Naseeb Shaheen has done in the useful but at times frustratingly narrow and terse *Biblical References in The Faerie Queene*,[40] only begins the process of setting *The Faerie Queene* (at least partially) in its contemporary religious intertext. It is fatuous but perhaps necessary to observe that Spenser and his contemporary readership knew the Bible far better than modern readers can ever hope to. Mostly untroubled by philological questions over authorship and dating (although not, as has already been seen, by the issues raised by vernacular translation), Spenser also lived in an environment (at school and in Cambridge, for example) with a far more intensive and wide-ranging lectionary than that now familiar. Spenser's Bible was a hugely complex nexus of interconnecting texts, operating frequently at a minutely detailed level, which yet remained an organic whole. Carol Kaske has suggested that it was the approach needed to read this Bible that Spenser wanted his readers to bring to *The Faerie Queene*:

I propose that Spenser—who, like all good Protestants, must have spent considerable time in meditating on the Scriptures—developed themes in pieces scattered throughout a work and related them with hook-words. Consequently, in reading *The Faerie Queene*... I submit that we should pay attention to the signifiers, collate those passages that contain the same hook-word, and compile a mental concordance. Because the Bible was perceived as requiring this kind of reading, and because every Protestant

---

[38] See, for example, Josephine Waters Bennett, *The Evolution of the Faerie Queene* (Chicago: University of Chicago Press, 1942), and also John Erskine Hankins, 'Spenser and the Revelation of St. John', *PMLA* 60 (1945), 364–81.

[39] In Chapter 7 I will suggest that the Gospel of John is also particularly important: in Spenser's time Revelation and the Gospel, together with the three Johannine Epistles, were generally assumed to have the same author.

[40] Naseeb Shaheen, *Biblical References in The Faerie Queene* (Memphis: Memphis State University Press, 1976).

was required to read the Bible, Spenser could count on readers to read his work in the same way, provided he dropped enough hints.[41]

Kaske's assessment of Spenser's readership is perhaps overly optimistic, if the evidence left by early readers such as John Dixon and even Ben Jonson is anything to go by, and her understanding of the early modern holdings of Cambridge college libraries is sadly misguided, although that is less of an issue here.[42] Similarly, to read *The Faerie Queene* (let alone the whole Bible) in this way is, for modern readers, an immense and perhaps unrecoverable task. But by way of a 'test case', I suggest that, as is frequently the case in the Bible, the fountain is one of these important religious signifiers in *The Faerie Queene*. As has already been seen, it is also an image that transcends the boundaries of the scriptural text to become an important symbol in exegesis, commentary, and polemic.

One possible point of entry into this proposed way of reading is the huge volume of commentary on the Book of Revelation found in Elizabethan England. Josephine Waters Bennett pointed to this as evidence of the importance of Revelation to the English Protestant *Zeitgeist* from the 1570s onwards. She did not, however, explore the question as to whether these works themselves might be useful in constructing an approach to reading *The Faerie Queene*, or as possible sources for its imagery. Biblical intertextuality encompasses frequently polemical exegesis and commentary. In John Bale's *The Image of Both Churches*,[43] as in others of its ilk, each verse is glossed with its other biblical referents as well as commented upon, a simple way in to a broader and more intertextual (or, as Kaske suggests, 'concordantial') approach to reading the Bible in *The Faerie Queene*. Thus in Bale's work, for example, Revelation 7: 17 appears in this way:

And shall leade them vnto fountaynes of lyuinge water. He shal brynge them vnto the fountaynes of the lyunge waters, and make them such well springes as shall flowe vp

[41] Carol V. Kaske, *Spenser and Biblical Poetics* (Ithaca, NY: Cornell University Press, 1999), 21.
[42] Kaske assumes that colleges listed as owning a book by H. M. Adams, *Catalogue of Books Printed on the Continent of Europe, 1501–1600, in Cambridge Libraries* (Cambridge: Cambridge University Press, 1967), 'presumably owned it in Spenser's time'. Kaske, *Spenser and Biblical Poetics*, 5.
[43] Bale's work was first published in 1545, being reprinted several times by 1580. I quote the 1548 edition. Florence Sandler has pointed out that 'it is generally supposed that Spenser has presented in the Legend of Holiness the "Image of Both Churches" familiar to Elizabethan readers through the works of Bale and Foxe', but she does not go into more specific detail regarding Bale's particular influence on Spenser. Florence Sandler, 'The Faerie Queene: An Elizabethan Apocalypse', in C. A. Patrides and Joseph Wittreich (eds.), *The Apocalypse in English Renaissance Thought and Literature: Patterns, Antecedents, and Repercussions* (Manchester: Manchester University Press, 1984), 160. Bale's influence on Spenser is, however, discussed by John N. King, *Spenser's Poetry and the Reformation Tradition* (Princeton: Princeton University Press, 1990).

into the lyfe euerlastynge. His doctryne must do it and none other, for none other, for none cometh to the father but by hym. Psal. 53. John. 4. Eccli. 2. John. 14. Apoc. 21. John. 16.[44]

Again, this approach allows one to go beyond a 'check-list' interpretation of Book 1's religio-historical allegory: the equation Duessa = Whore of Babylon = Papacy is a beginning, not an end; one must read both backwards and forwards. Kaske observes that Spenser 'is no Bunyan; his Bible is still encrusted with patristic and medieval traditions derived from the Apocrypha and pseudepigrapha and from commentaries, devotions, homilies, idealistic literature, the liturgy and religious art'.[45] To this might be added the religio-political environment, textual, material, and even urban, that as writer, civil servant, and Protestant, in an intellectual and ideological milieu shaped by London, Cambridge, and Ireland, Spenser would have been unable to ignore. To take account of all this and the frightening diversity it accords an already dense text is a task well beyond the scope of this discussion, if not an impossibility. The next chapter in particular seeks to make it more manageable by bringing the focus back once again to fountains, setting those encountered in Book 1 alongside their biblical analogues (and other literary sources) in their proper exegetical, typological, and polemical contexts, in order to show the complexity and logic—and significance—of an important aspect of the structure and themes of Book 1.

If one reads Book 1 of *The Faerie Queene* as a series of wanderings from (water) source to source, the structural analogue of the wanderings of the children of Israel is an obvious one. In *The Great Code*, Northrop Frye reads the Bible in terms of humanity's relationship with water (on various symbolic levels) when he describes the Bible as having

a narrative structure that is roughly U-shaped, the apostasy being followed by a descent into disaster and bondage, which in turn is followed by repentance, then by a rise through deliverance to a point more or less on the level from which the descent began . . . The entire Bible, viewed as a 'divine comedy', is contained within a U-shaped story of this sort, one in which man, as explained, loses the tree and water of life at the beginning of Genesis and gets them back at the end of Revelation.[46]

He could have been describing Redcrosse's narrative trajectory. Spenser's Faeryland is not an arid desert, although (following Revelation and, indeed, the Pentateuch) it is on occasion characterized as a wilderness; but then neither was Spenser's England. Yet the day before her coronation, Elizabeth Tudor stood in Cheapside and was invited—even compelled—to transform

---

[44] Sig. O2.   [45] Kaske, *Spenser and Biblical Poetics*, 13.

[46] Northrop Frye, *The Great Code: The Bible and Literature* (London: Routledge and Kegan Paul, 1982), 169.

the barren commonwealth, to act herself as a conduit for the refreshing springs of the Word of God, in a pageant apparently devised and scripted by the man who was to be responsible for Spenser's education. The biblical narrative of the search for fresh springs remained appropriate to an ideological milieu which sought its spiritual refreshment from what was perceived as the 'true', Protestant, vernacular, naturalized fountain of God's word rather than the corrupt and polluting puddle of Catholicism, and the preface to John Bale's *Image of Both Churches* had similarly envisaged the Reformed Church as fleeing into a wilderness: 'Into the desert sendeth the Lorde hys church, whan ye filthy sprite by his spightfull spiritualte speweth out hys execrable waters'.[47] Spenser says of Una, abandoned by Redcrosse, 'Yet she most faithfull Ladie all this while | Forsaken, wofull, solitarie mayd | Farre from all peoples prease, as in exile, | In wildernesse and wastfull deserts strayd' (1.3.3). The source for both is Revelation 12: 6, 14. Like *The Faerie Queene*, Bale's world (and Mulcaster's, and Spenser's) was not one in which all fountains or sources were unambiguously good, but rather one which called for discretion, discrimination, fortitude, and careful reading.

In 1601, two years after Spenser's death and two years before his own ascent to the throne of England, James VI had proposed to the general assembly of the Church in Scotland the need for a new translation of the Bible. Little came of his proposal at this time, but when it was reiterated at the Hampton Court conference in 1604, the outcome was very different, for the most lasting legacy of that meeting was the 'King James Bible', more properly the Authorized Version. One of the King's motivations was his dislike of the Geneva translation in particular, specifically on account of its copious marginal glosses, some of which he described as 'partial, untrue, seditious, and savouring of treason'.[48] The translators were eventually instructed: 'No marginal notes at all to be affixed, but only for the explanation of the Hebrew and Greek words which cannot without some circumlocution so briefly and fitly be expressed in the text'.[49] The Authorized Version is a deeply conservative text, closely based on earlier translations and even, in its Latinate vocabulary, on the Vulgate.

Yet the committee of translators, a significant number of whom were likely to have been well known to Spenser in his formative years (and theirs), prefaced their translation with an epistle 'The Translators to the Reader' that was as saturated in the familiar humanist imagery of the *fontes* as anything written by Erasmus, Jewel, Bale, or, indeed, Spenser himself. It describes Jerome as having translated the Old Testament 'out of the very fountains themselves', previous

[47] Sig. A5ᵛ.
[48] *The Bible: Authorized King James Version with Apocrypha* (Oxford: Oxford University Press, 1997), p. xxvi.
[49] Ibid., p. xxvii.

Latin texts having been 'not out of the *Hebrew* fountain . . . but out of the *Greek* stream; therefore the *Greek* being not altogether clear, the *Latin* derived from it must needs be muddy'; the reader is reassured that the translators too have worked from 'the *Hebrew* text of the Old Testament, the Greek of the New. These are the two golden pipes, or rather conduits, where-through the olive branches empty themselves into the gold'.[50] And, in terms that are as Spenserian as much as they are what must now be called biblical, the Scriptures are called

not only an armour, but also a whole armoury of weapons . . . not a herb, but a tree, or rather a whole paradise of trees of life . . . a shower of heavenly bread . . . a whole cellar full of oil vessels . . . In a word, it is a panary of wholesome food against fenowed traditions;[51] a physician's shop (as St *Basil* calls it) of preservatives against poisoned heresies; a pandect of profitable laws against rebellious spirits; a treasury of most costly jewels against beggarly rudiments; finally, a fountain of most pure water springing up into everlasting life.

The translators go on to assert:

Translation it is that openeth the window, to let in the light; that breaketh the shell, that we may eat the kernel; that putteth aside the curtain, that we may look into the most holy place; that removeth the cover of the well, that we may come by the water; even as *Jacob* rolled away the stone from the mouth of the well, by which means the flocks of *Laban* were watered. Indeed without translation into the vulgar tongue, the unlearned are but like children at *Jacob*'s well (which was deep) without a bucket or something to draw with . . .

Almost the preface's last image is that of the fountain, one familiar in both early humanist scholarship and Protestant polemic, and one which underpins Book 1 of Spenser's *Faerie Queene*: 'Ye are brought unto fountains of living water which ye digged not; do not cast earth into them, with the Philistines, neither prefer broken pits before them . . .'[52]

This chapter began with the gift of the English Bible to Elizabeth Tudor the day before her coronation in January 1559, a gift which relied on its location at the Little Conduit in Cheapside to materialize its underlying metaphor and ideology: that Elizabeth herself was to be a fountain, mediating the Word of God to her people and bringing refreshment and prosperity to the commonwealth. In the first half of the seventeenth century, following the appearance of the Authorized Version of the Bible, a peculiarly English fashion for embroidered book-bindings[53] once again materialized these metaphors

[50] *The Bible: Authorized King James Version with Apocrypha*, pp. lviii, lxvi.
[51] A panary is a storehouse for bread; 'fenowed' is a variant of 'finewed', 'mouldy'.
[52] *The Bible*, pp. lvi, lvii, lxix.
[53] See Cyril Davenport, 'Embroidered Bindings of Bibles in the Possession of the British and Foreign Bible Society', *Burlington Magazine*, 4 (1904), 267–80.

of spiritual refreshment in the Word. A Bible and Prayer Book now in the Metropolitan Museum of Art in New York has on its cover a vivid illustration of the Garden of Eden, its central fountain of life worked in silver thread,[54] while a Prayer Book and Psalter dating from the 1630s in the Victoria and Albert Museum has a brightly embroidered cover, with medallions of the four Evangelists in its corners and an elaborately architectural fountain of life in its centre.[55] In early modern English social and spiritual life and practice, the figure of the fountain had a presence that was potent and lively, connecting the coronation of a Protestant Queen with the mundane water-fetching of her people in the streets of the New Jerusalem, the humanist manifesto 'ad fontes' with Protestant apologetics, a royal Bible with the pious material accoutrements of private devotions. It is no wonder, then, that Spenser's fountains are so far from being dead metaphors, nor yet that they are also so visual, so material and experiential in their referents and intertextuality.

[54] See the illustration in Thomasina Beck, *Gardening with Silk and Gold: A History of Gardens in Embroidery* (London: David and Charles, 1997), 46. The Prayerbook was printed in 1607.

[55] The Victoria and Albert example (Museum Number T.6–1988) was probably the work of professionals in the Broderers' Company; the books were printed in 1633 and 1634 respectively.

6

The Christian Knight: Redcrosse Learns to Read

The Faerie Queene has often been characterized as unfinished, open, and 'endlesse', particularly in recent criticism, and the poem as a whole is certainly labyrinthine, allusive, and ostentatiously intertextual. Yet its first Book is in many respects a highly 'finished', discrete literary unit and, moreover, it is a Book that is vitally concerned with beginnings and endings, origins and sources and, especially, the poet's own negotiations of their congruences and confluences. In this chapter and the one following it, I will suggest that in Book 1 of *The Faerie Queene* Spenser employs various kinds of fountains to explore not only ideas about sources, but also Protestant Humanist reading practices, questions of genre, the relationship between landscape, narrative, and nation, and his own inheritances, responsibilities, and anxieties as an English poet. Some of what I will show and argue here is necessarily synthetic, juxtaposing some long-established strands of Spenser criticism. My focus on the fountains, however, is a fresh one, and reveals that in Spenser's usage this figure is far from being either merely topographical set dressing or a dead metaphor. Rather, it is a syncretic device around which his narratives and ethical concerns frequently coalesce.

This chapter explores the fountains of Book 1 of *The Faerie Queene* in relation to three influences, in which concerns with sources and genre tend to overlap. The first (and largest) is religious writing. As in the previous chapter, this includes the Bible but also other religious writings that could have been among Spenser's influences, mainly about the reading of Scripture. Chief among these is Erasmus' *Enchiridion* (1533), which furnishes a number of suggestive parallels with Spenser's own account of the Christian knight; I will also continue to refer to John Bale's *The Image of Both Churches* (1548). The second is the literary conventions, expectations, and values of the courtly romance. The third is the classical tradition, but more the Ovidian than the epic (about which much has already been written in relation to *The Faerie*

Queene).[1] If Errour is seen as a parodic fountain, as I will shortly suggest, then Redcrosse journeys from the antithesis of the fountain in canto 1 to the true fountain, the Well of Life, in canto 11, which is the subject of the next chapter. He meets his downfall beside the fountain with Duessa in canto 7, while the narrative is shaped by a number of other 'watery' features along the way. Both landscape and quest are palimpsestic and intertextual, with structures and motifs drawn from many interpenetrating (and sometimes conflicting) sources and traditions. Negotiating them therefore solicits a unifying interpretative strategy (which could perhaps be termed Protestant Humanist); reading Redcrosse's journey through its fountains helps to access and understand it.

In Book 1 the difficulties of Redcrosse's quest and the obstacles that he faces are often brought about by his shortcomings as a reader or interpreter of signs. Redcrosse 'misreads' characters but, more crucially, he misreads genre. This means that he spends the first half of the Book in a story that is not rightfully his own. Whatever the relationship of Spenser's 'Letter to Raleigh' to the main body of the poem, it is reasonable to assume that included in Spenser's avowed intent of 'fashion[ing] a gentleman or noble person in vertuous and gentle discipline' might be some prescription of the proper way to read, of what should be read, and of how the reader should situate a text in relation to both its literary antecedence and its contemporary intertexts. In Redcrosse's case, learning to read properly is part of his task as a Christian knight. Redcrosse's initial deficiencies as a reader can be seen as a caution to the reader of the poem, as well as denoting Spenser's own anxieties over the aesthetic, generic, and ethical position of his project.

At the beginning of Book 1 of *The Faerie Queene*, Redcrosse's incipient apostasy is not so much ideological as generic, for when Redcrosse and Una take shelter in what they later identify as the 'wandring wood', they enter fully into the world of romance.[2] In some respects, the opening of the Book has already established them as its denizens, or at least its aspirants. Redcrosse is bound 'Vpon a great aduenture' and longs 'To proue his puissance in battell braue', and although Una's mount is initially introduced as the Christ-like 'lowly Asse more white then snow' by the end of the stanza this has become 'her palfrey slow', stock mount of the romance lady. Without the benefit

---

[1] A full-length account of the Ovidian, as opposed to the Virgilian, nature of Spenser's poem is given by Syrithe Pugh, *Spenser and Ovid* (Aldershot: Ashgate, 2005).

[2] See Patricia Parker, *Inescapable Romance: Studies in the Poetics of a Mode* (Princeton: Princeton University Press, 1979), 64–5. That they shelter from a storm also recalls, of course, the fateful encounter between Dido and Aeneas during the hunt in Book 4 of the *Aeneid*.

of hindsight, which renders more significant seemingly minor details,[3] the opening of Book 1 is that of a romance, as the knight and his lady set forth. While the object of his quest (the dragon fight) is clearly announced (although its particular occasion is only set out in the 'Letter to Raleigh'), Redcrosse is in reality looking for adventure, in general, along the way, and as soon as possible. Despite his 'divine' mission and the 'bloudie Crosse' on his armour, Redcrosse wants to be a knight errant, and the landscape is shaped to his romantic desires; in Syrithe Pugh's useful formulation, 'Spenser makes the Wandring Wood an extended metaphor of digressive romance poetry in the poem', and the entry into the wood is 'an ostentatiously "romance" moment'.[4] The imperative to shelter in the woods is partly a generic convention, but Redcrosse and his companions also go into the woods because the knight is seeking an initiatory adventure. To labour the point, it is because Redcrosse mistakenly wants to be a romance hero, a knight *errant*, that he enters the 'wandring wood' (Lat. *errare*, to wander) and hence that he encounters *Errour*.[5]

When knight errant Redcrosse fights and kills Errour he is, in terms of the genre in which he has enrolled himself, merely killing the romance monster which he has sought, and perhaps even summoned.[6] Redcrosse is still the *miles Christi* in his theological essentials, as the efficacy of Una's exhortation 'Add faith vnto your force' shows. But the combat confirms the misguided nature of his choices in the story so far. He is in fact ill prepared for the fight and only 'lifts his game' at the last because he is 'fearefull more of shame | Then of the certeine perill he stood in'. 'Errours endlesse traine' has more usually been interpreted as sin and theological controversy, as have the vile creatures in her filthy vomit, but the serpent's coils can also be seen as the repetitive, never-ending cycles of romance.[7] The monster's inky offspring, although they

---

[3] For example, the cross on Redcrosse's breastplate would not be out of place in a romance setting: what is odd, however, is the way in which his arms are described in the first stanza as battered but never before borne by him.

[4] Pugh, *Spenser and Ovid*, 44, 45.

[5] Patrick Cullen comments on the wood's intertextuality: 'Wandering Wood is the *selva oscura* of pilgrimage literature . . . It is also a figure for the garden in which the first Adam was tempted and the wilderness in which the second Adam overcame the error to which the first Adam had succumbed.' *Infernal Triad: The Flesh, the World, and the Devil in Spenser and Milton* (Princeton: Princeton University Press, 1974), 25. Hamilton notes the Errour/*errare* connection but does not link this with Redcrosse's adoption of the persona of the knight *errant*. Lawrence F. Rhu, 'Romancing the Word: Pre-Texts and Contexts for the Errour Episode', *Spenser Studies*, 11 (1994), 101–9, usefully examines Errour in the light of Tasso's narrative theory, and touches indirectly on this idea.

[6] 'To triumph over Errour is merely to triumph over the error of being in the woods in the first place,' Cullen, *Infernal Triad*, 32.

[7] See Pugh, *Spenser and Ovid*, 53.

'him encombred sore, but could not hurt at all' have nevertheless corrupted the knight in a generic or textual way. Errour is accordingly constructed as a parodic fountain, a polluted and poisonous source structurally and thematically—and theologically—opposed to the Well of Life, whose subtle and pernicious influence throughout the Book is exacerbated, not ended, by her death at Redcrosse's hand. Redcrosse dooms himself, through his combat with Errour, to spend the rest of the Book's first half as the protagonist of a romance. He rescues a damsel in distress and has several pointless combats with random 'paynim' knights. But the traditional romance structure, based around a linear series of more or less random conquests that can continue indefinitely (such as is enthusiastically pursued by Redcrosse in the first half of the Book), is shown to be at best ill suited to the mission of the Christian knight. At worst it is fatally flawed.

As Donald Cheney observes, 'what seems to be involved here ultimately is Spenser's evaluation of the chivalric milieu within which his action is set'.[8] In *The Scholemaster*, published posthumously in 1570, Roger Ascham had (quite conventionally) referred to 'papistry' as a 'standyng poole' which had formerly 'couered and ouerflowed all England',[9] and he had furthermore made an explicit connection between the spiritual state of the English nation and the reading of 'certaine bookes of Cheualrie', singling out especially '*Morte Arthure*: the whole pleasure of which booke standeth in two speciall poyntes, in open mans slaughter, and bold bawdrye'. Even worse than Malory, Ascham continued, was the fashion for romances translated from the Italian, which placed the youth of England in even worse moral danger than the days 'when Papistrie ouerflowed all'.[10] In Book 1, Spenser shows the plight of such a young man, both ill equipped to read the Scriptures and swayed by the dangerous allurements of romance, at the same time as he reinvents that genre to more moral ends; the Book in some respects functions as 'a fictionalized defence of poetry'.[11] But Redcrosse cannot liberate Eden and transform the unredeemed world in which he wanders through his own isolated agency as an errant knight. He can only seek to learn to read properly, to see clearly, and so transcend his physical environment and his fleshly self. Like the streets of London at times of pageant and in histories and gazetteers, and in which Spenser grew up, the landscape in which Redcrosse wanders is in fact palimpsestic in its textuality. It is not exclusively epic or romantic or biblical; it is neither England nor Faeryland, but both and more besides. It combines layer upon layer of

---

[8] Donald Cheney, *Spenser's Image of Nature: Wild Man and Shepherd in The Faerie Queene* (New Haven: Yale University Press, 1966), 40.
[9] Sig. I3.   [10] Ibid., sig. I3ᵛ.
[11] King, *Spenser's Poetry and the Reformation Tradition*, 184. King notes the passage in Ascham, 201.

revealed meaning accessible to those who can read it properly, so leading them to the transcendent reality of Eden, the New Jerusalem, and the end of time.[12] Fake damsels in distress and stock-in-trade paynim knights are merely generic distractions. The logical outcome of his chosen romance narrative is his 'dalliance' with Duessa in canto 7, although it is a debased and uncourtly scene; it is, however, the very lowest point of his seemingly forgotten quest as the *miles Christi*. This is the downward trajectory he chooses and confirms in his initiatory combat with Errour, which introduces (or even unleashes) the perils of multivalence, multiplicity, and deception that he must thereafter overcome. Redcrosse becomes a traditional and superficially quite successful knight errant, but as a misguided and unsuccessful Protestant Humanist reader he travels further and further from the true end of his quest as the knight of holiness.

Although an article by Robin Headlam Wells[13] discusses Spenser's debt to Erasmus' *Enchiridion Militis Christiani*, it concentrates almost exclusively on the theological parallels or similarities between the two works. There appears to have been no critical investigation of the possible influence of (or even direct borrowing from) Erasmus' text in Spenser's depiction of his own *miles Christi*.[14] The *Enchiridion* was translated into English as *The Manuell of the Christen Knyght*, possibly by William Tyndale, in 1533; the many subsequent editions of the English translation gave it the more literal title *The hansome weapon of a Christian knight*. Miles Coverdale published an abridged English translation in Antwerp in 1545, which the title page described as '*Very profitable and necessary to be rede of all trew Christen men*', and the Latin text went through huge numbers of editions all over continental Europe throughout the sixteenth century. There is an obvious connection between Erasmus' text and Spenser's, both in their shared consideration of the figure of the Christian knight and the similar intentions of their projects. Erasmus framed his work as a guide or 'how to' handbook, while Spenser announces his intention of 'fashioning' a virtuous gentleman. Any definite connection between the two texts cannot be proved—albeit the enormous popularity of the *Enchiridion* surely makes it more than likely—but their juxtaposition is

---

[12] My reading of landscape as palimpsestic has been influenced by the analogous discussion of romance and epic modes in Patrick J. Cook, *Milton, Spenser and the Epic Tradition* (Aldershot: Scolar Press, 1996). See also Wayne Erickson, *Mapping the Faerie Queene: Quest Structures and the World of the Poem* (New York: Garland Publishing, 1996).

[13] Robin Headlam Wells, 'Spenser's Christian Knight: Erasmian Theology in *The Faerie Queene*, Book I', *Anglia*, 97 (1979), 350–66.

[14] Florence Sandler goes so far as to say that 'if there is one book which more than any other could have provided Spenser with the inspiration for the Legend of Holiness, it is the *Enchiridion Militis Christiani*', 'The Faerie Queene: An Elizabethan Apocalypse', 151, but she does not pursue the point.

useful, with Erasmus' work shedding some light on the complicated nexuses being deciphered here between fountains, Scripture, reading, baptism, and the proper narrative shape of the Christian's journey in the world.

Much of Erasmus' handbook is devoted to instructing the would-be knight in how he should prepare his mind for his Christian mission by the careful reading of the Bible, and he does so in terms that are particularly relevant to this reading of Book 1. In the *Enchiridion* (as in the translation prefaces quoted in the previous chapter), Erasmus uses the conventional metaphor of a fountain to refer to the Scriptures: 'all the trewe fountayne and vayne of Christes philosophy is hydde in the gospell and the epystels of the apostles . . . the pure fountayne of the gospell and the epystels and moste approued interpretours'.[15] Significantly, he goes on to figure the process of interpretation and discovery of spiritual nourishment and truth—the finding out of such spiritual fountains—as a labour specifically opposed to the labours of the world and human concerns:

Oh how infortunate were we if Christe had not lefte some sparkes of his doctryne vnto vs/& as it were lyuely and euerlastynge vaynes of his godly mynde . . . Let vs seke these vaynes vntyll we fynde fresshe water whiche springeth in to euerlastyng lyfe. We delue and dygge ye grounde meruaylously depe for to plucke out rychesse/whiche nourissheth vyce: And shall we not labour than the ryche erthe of Christe to get out that thing whiche is our soules helthe? . . . Christ is a stone/but this stone hath sparkes of celestyall fyre/and vaynes of lyuely water.[16]

The Christian knight in both Erasmus and Spenser is armed with the armour of Ephesians 6, but Erasmus makes clear that he also has other resources for his mission: 'who so euer wyl take vpon hym to fyght agaynst the hole hoost of vices/of the which seuen be counted as chefe captaynes/must prouyde hym of two specyall wepons. Prayer & knowledge/otherwyse called lernynge'.[17] It is knowledge, and also the process of learning itself, that will be so important to Redcrosse's journey and his failures in the first half of the Book. As Florence Sandler puts it, 'One of the effects of Spenser's writing an Erasmian Legend of Holiness is that actual, not simply imputed, holiness is seen as something to be learned and attained'.[18] Spenser's intention is educational.

As has already been suggested, it is Errour's intervention in the narrative that most catastrophically misshapes Redcrosse's trajectory in the Book's first half. She appears thus, when mistakenly sought out by Redcrosse:

> his glistring armor made
> A litle glooming light, much like a shade,

[15] 'Epistle Dedicatory', sig. A7–A7ᵛ.   [16] 'Epistle Dedicatory', sig. A8ᵛ.
[17] Sig. B2.   [18] Sandler, '*The Faerie Queene*: An Elizabethan Apocalypse', 153.

By which he saw the vgly monster plaine,
Halfe like a serpent horribly displaide,
But th'other halfe did womans shape retaine,
Most lothsome, filthie, foule, and full of vile disdaine.

And as she lay vpon the durtie ground,
Her huge long taile her den all ouerspred,
Yet was in knots and many boughtes vpwound,
Pointed with mortall sting. Of her there bred
A thousand yong ones, which she dayly fed,
Sucking vpon her poisnous dugs, eachone
Of sundrie shapes, yet all ill fauored:
Soone as that vncouth light vpon them shone,
Into her mouth they crept, and suddain all were gone.

Their dam vpstart, out of her den effraide,
And rushed forth, hurling her hideous taile
About her cursed head, whose folds displaid
Were stretcht now forth at length without entraile.
She lookt about, and seeing one in mayle
Armed to point, sought backe to turne againe;
For light she hated as the deadly bale,
Ay wont in desert darknesse to remaine,
Where plaine none might her see, nor she see any plaine. (1.1.14–16)

Here the subtle shift in versification from the mostly end-stopped lines of
stanza 14 to the prominent enjambements of stanzas 15 and 16, describing the
deformities of Errour's offspring and the coiling length of her tail, reinforces the
polluting nature of the monster herself; a similar device marks the description
of her vomit a few stanzas later. Errour's threat is such that she cannot be
contained within Spenser's carefully controlled stanzaic form: she overflows
its bounds. As well as functioning as a parodic fountain structurally opposed
to the Well of Life in the pattern of the book as a whole, Errour also directly
recalls, and parodies once again, the figure of Truth in the 1558 coronation
pageant, emerging 'as a perverse Veritas from her cave of disfame'.[19] She
represents both a corrupted parody of the true source and (specifically textual)
apostasy from that source, as in the Protestant glosses on Genesis 26: 15 and
Jeremiah 2: 13 discussed in the previous chapter. In biblical terms, her lair
is at the heart of a parodic Eden, in an originary wood; again in terms of
the coronation pageant, she can be found amongst the trees of a deceptively
flourishing commonwealth, in which she takes the place not only of Veritas,
but of the conduit, the English Bible, and the Queen herself. In their naming

---

[19] King, *Spenser's Poetry and the Reformation Tradition*, 13.

of the trees, Redcrosse and Una imitate Adam and Eve. Compare Genesis 3: 8, with the Geneva glosses:

Afterward they heard the voyce of the Lord God walking in the garden in the coole of the day, and the man and his wife hid themselues from the presence of the Lord God among the trees of the garden. *The sinfull conscience fleeth Gods presence Signifying, that when men forsake Gods woorde, which is the fountaine of life, they reiect God himselfe, and so fall to their owne inuentions, and uaine confidence, and procure to themselues destruction, Iona. 2.8. Zacha. 10.2.*

It seems not unlikely that Spenser was drawing on these glosses as much as the text in his account of Redcrosse and Una's catastrophic entry into the wood. Errour is the hybrid serpent of the garden, recalling the artistic tradition of representing the Edenic serpent as half-woman, half-serpent (or lizard), although it has to be said that she lacks the traditional allure of the first tempter. (Spenser would have seen one such image in a window in the north range of the chapel of King's College in Cambridge: the scene of Adam and Eve tempted by the serpent appears above that of the Annunciation and the Nativity. Such a corrective structure is akin to Spenser's own.) Some aspects of Errour's description additionally recall Erasmus' evocation of the Edenic serpent in his own first chapter:

the slypper serpent the fyrst breker of peace/father of vnquietnes/otherwhiles hydde in the grene grasse/lurkynge in his caues/wrapped togyder in a hondred rounde rolle ceaseth not to watche and lye in a wayte bynethe in the hele of our woman/whome he ones poysoned. By the woman is vnder stande the carnall parte of a man/otherwise called sensualite.[20]

The suggestion that it is 'the carnall parte of a man/otherwise called sensualite' that is particularly susceptible to the wiles of the serpent is especially pertinent to Errour's effect on Redcrosse, for his desire to be a romance hero can be seen as carnal or worldly.

The temptations that Errour offers are therefore more subtle than, although perhaps not unrelated to, the temptation offered to Eve (particularly if that is interpreted as the sin of *curiositas*, not *cupiditas*). She is, though, more overtly revolting:

> Therewith she spewd out of her filthie maw
> A floud of poyson horrible and blacke,
> Full of great lumpes of flesh and gobbets raw,
> Which stunck so vildly, that it forst him slacke
> His grasping hold, and from her turne him backe:
> Her vomit full of bookes and papers was,

[20] Sig. A2–A2ᵛ.

With loathly frogs and toades, which eyes did lacke,
And creeping sought way in the weedy gras:
Her filthie parbreake all the place defiled has.
(1.1.20)

Errour's disgusting effluents parody the waters of Eden described in Genesis 2: 10–11, 13–14 and in Una's description of her parents' kingdom to Arthur in 7.43, 'which *Phison* and *Euphrates* floweth by, | And *Gehons* golden waues doe wash continually'. She is, in all senses, the antithesis of the fountain (or well) of life. This is an antithesis that can be seen in the implied opposition between the dragon (who caused the fleeing of the Woman Clothed with the Sun) and the living water in Revelation. While her hybrid form recalls the Edenic serpent, it at the same time draws elements from the dragons of Revelation, particularly in the detail of her vomiting. Two important texts from Revelation in this respect are 12: 15: 'And the serpent cast out of his mouth water after the woman as it had ben a fludde, that he myght cause her to be caryed away of the fludde' and 16: 13: 'And I sawe three vncleane spirites like frogges, come out of the mouth of ye dragon, & out of the mouth of the beast, & out of the mouth of the false prophete.'

John Bale's glossing in *The Image of Both Churches* of these two verses from Revelation seems also to have influenced Spenser's portrayal of Errour. Some of what Bale extrapolates from the first ('And the serpent cast out of his mouth water after the woman, like a flood, that he might cause her to be caried away of the flood', 12: 15) is as follows:

A doctrine of hypocresie, errours and lyes, hath alwayes passed from the Synagoge of sathan. None other frutes hath gone from them, than waueryng supersticions, Idolatry, and Heythen ceremonies. These hath flowed forth like a great riuer . . . Thys stynkynge water dyd the Serpent vomet oute by hys rauenouse Antichristes, which are his insaciable mouth, to stoppe the passage of the woman. Suche is alwayes the mischeuouse nature of the deuill and hys angels. Vengeable assaultes haue they, & innumerable craftes to deceyue the innocent not knowynge them. Oure fyrste mother Eua was thus trapped in the begynnynge, and so had bene drouned wyth Adam her husbande, had they not hadde fayth in ye promised sede. And innumerable multitude had bene and are yet to this daye swallowed vp of this flood & without great difficulte none escapeth it. Excedynge is the compasse, stodye, and practyse of this false generacion. Euermore poure they out their poyson, they dispute their matters with errours and lyes, with counsels & customes, hauing vpon their syde ye darkened powers . . . But the lyuinge waters of the Lorde sauoreth not in their mouthes, their own broken cisternes doth please them best. Better is to a swyne a fylte puddle, than a swete ronninge waters. No where will he drinke, but wher he maye wallowe his carkas. No doctryne please to them, vnlesse it maintayneth their synne.[21]

21 Sig. F4ᵛ–5ᵛ.

The second ('And I sawe three vncleane spirits like frogs come out of the mouth of that dragon, and out of the mouth of that beast, and out of the mouth of that false prophet', 16: 13) he glosses thus:

Idolatrye was that yll sprete, whyche fyrst went out from the serpent, and hathe contynued euer sens in the worlde vnder ye coloure of good woorkes, as pylgrimage, deuocion, and laboure. Erroure in abhominable fylthynesse was the sprete which came from the beastlye Antechrist defilyng the whole christianitie with innumerable supersticions vnder the coloure of chast lyunge, in priesthode, sacrifices, and ceremonyes. Hipocresie was the foule sprete whiche issewed from the false preachers, poisoning the catholique fayth with false doctrine vnder the coloure of religion, pretendynge abstinence, prayer, and clennesse.[22]

Both these passages from Bale demonstrate the intertextual (or concordantial) approach to exegesis that he employs, referring as they do to Genesis and Jeremiah, combining (like Jewel) all the referents into a general image of filth and pollution, applied to Catholic ritual and theology. The juxtaposition of Genesis and Apocalypse, found in Spenser and reinforced by Bale (in, for example, his linking of the perceived corruption of the Catholic Church with the Fall), draws the reader's attention to the eventual symmetry and circularity of the Book, and to the corrective nature of Redcrosse's final dragon combat. Bale's glossing of the texts from Revelation associates the figure of a vomiting dragon with hypocrisy, falsehood, disputatiousness, and Catholic practice in general, and his commentary also demonstrates a concern with the corruption of texts and the neglect or abandonment of the true sources. Apparently drawing on these or like sources, both primary and secondary, it is with a strikingly similar image of pollution and corruption, textual, doctrinal, spiritual, and moral, that Spenser begins *The Faerie Queene*.

Yet the description of Errour also draws on other, non-biblical texts, and in so doing raises further questions about sources, creation, reading, and writing. In the Proem to Book 1 Spenser introduces, in his imitation of the (putative) opening lines of the *Aeneid*, his concern with (and perhaps anxieties about) literary sources and landmarks and his own perceived position relative to them and to their demands. Poetry itself is shown to be a process of negotiation and navigation which, in *The Faerie Queene*, is enacted in an unstable and thickly intertextual landscape: just how critical and finely balanced is that process is shown in Redcrosse's combat with Errour. The monster's own literary sources are various, and many are well documented. Her description is in the main drawn from Hesiod's account of Echidna:

And in a hollow cave she [the nymph Callirhoë] bare another monster, irresistible, in no wise like either to mortal men or to the undying gods, even the goddess fierce

---

[22] Sig. P8.

Echidna who is half a nymph with glancing eyes and fair cheeks, and half again a huge snake, great and awful, with speckled skin, eating raw flesh beneath the secret parts of the holy earth.[23]

There are, however, other more subtle and suggestive classical sources or influences. For example, that canto 1.21 follows *Metamorphoses* 1.416–37 is a critical commonplace (the passage describes the generation of creatures from the mud left after the flood through the action of the sun) and the description of the specific origin of the Python, which follows it immediately, could also be significant as an influence upon Spenser's own creation of Errour:

Thee also she [earth] then bore, thou huge Python, thou snake unknown before, who wast a terror to new-created men; so huge a space of mountain-side didst thou fill. This monster the god of the bow destroyed with lethal arms never before used except against does and wild she-goats, crushing him with countless darts, well-nigh emptying his quiver, till the creature's poisonous blood flowed from the black wounds.[24]

The Python is associated with Apollo (he killed it to establish his shrine at Delphi) and hence with the triumph of poetry and creativity.[25] Yet in its spontaneous birth out of mud and sun, the Python's creation is non-authorial, and it is therefore a threatening chthonic image of alternative artistic or literary inspiration and production.[26]

Errour's classical precursors, therefore, add a dimension of horrific and depraved maternity to the monster's depiction as a parodic or infernal source. As Maureen Quilligan puts it, 'Errour is a parodic, perverted version of the good-mother figure, to be revealed in canto 10 of the first book of *The Faerie Queene* in the nursing portrait of Charissa'.[27] The Python, although male

---

[23] Hesiod, *Theogony*, in *The Homeric Hymns and Homerica*, trans. Hugh G. Evelyn-White (Cambridge, Mass.: Harvard University Press, 1967), 295 f.

[24] Ovid, *Metamorphoses*, 1.438–44.

[25] Errour does not herself guard a spring, but she is analogous to other classical serpent figures that do, and Redcrosse is hence a version of Cadmus, an archetypal dragon-slayer. His character is also, of course, closely indebted to the St George legends, a source I have not discussed here. Syrithe Pugh notes both the Nile passage and its proximity to the Python, but does not explicitly explore the connection between the Python and Errour. *Spenser and Ovid*, 51–2.

[26] Like Errour, the Ovidian monster is also linked with misinformation, for Apollo only went to Delphi because he was directed there by the nymph Telphusa. She failed to warn him about the Python because she did not want his shrine established at her own spring. By way of punishment, the angry god buried the nymph and her spring under a pile of stones: her waters became poisonous and later caused the death of Tiresias the seer.

[27] *Milton's Spenser: The Politics of Reading* (Ithaca, NY: Cornell University Press, 1983), 90. See also Joanne Craig, ' "All Flesh Doth Frailtie Breed": Mothers and Children in *The Faerie Queene*', *Texas Studies in Literature and Language*, 42 (2000), 16–32; Caroline McManus, 'The "Carefull Nourse": Female Piety in Spenser's Legend of Holiness', *Huntingdon Library Quarterly*, 60 (1999), 381–406; Elizabeth A. Spiller, 'Poetic Parthenogenesis and Spenser's Idea of Creation in *The Faerie Queene*', *Studies in English Literature*, 40 (2000), 63–79. The parody of Charissa is

in the *Metamorphoses*, is threatening simply in its spontaneous generation from slime, which is a loaded word throughout *The Faerie Queene*: compare the description of Orgoglio as 'this monstrous masse of earthly slyme', 1.7.9, and the stipulation in 3.6.3 that Belphoebe was born 'Pure and vnspotted from all loathly crime, | That is ingenerate in fleshly slime'. It is a type of disordered, unauthored creation. In other sources, however, the Python is explicitly female, and acts as foster mother to another monster, Typhon. Another version of the death of the Python notes this:

> But near by was a sweet flowing spring, and there with his strong bow the lord, the son of Zeus, killed the bloated, great she-dragon, a fierce monster wont to do great mischief to men upon earth, to men themselves and to their thin-shanked sheep; for she was a very bloody plague. She . . . brought up fell, cruel Typhon to be a plague to men.[28]

Typhon was himself a son of Gaia/earth, and in turn fathered various monsters on Echidna, different sources naming Orthus, Cerberus, the Hydra, and the Chimaera. With reference to Spenser's Errour, it is perhaps significant that Echidna's offspring are all many-headed. Thus Redcrosse kills Errour (by decapitating her) but still continues to err,[29] as the cutting off of one hydra-head only leads to the growth of others.[30] It is surely significant also that as Errour's classical antecedents both Typhon and the Python are engendered from earth, and from earth out of control: it is Redcrosse's own earthly nature that he must, in part, master, in his quest to become St George of England.

The 'bookes and papers' vomited by Errour have been linked with controversialist pamphlets and with the scholastic tradition. In an important article, John M. Steadman suggests that '[a]s a personification of learned error, Spenser's monster may have been influenced by Renaissance interpretations of similar serpentine hybrids as symbols of human erudition and rhetorical

also noted by Zailig Pollock, 'The Dragon, the Lady and the Dragon Lady in Book I of *The Faerie Queene*', *English Studies in Canada*, 7 (1981), 270–81. See also J. D. Pheifer, 'Errour and Echidna in *The Faerie Queene*: A Study in Literary Tradition', in John Scattergood (ed.), *Literature and Learning in Medieval and Renaissance England: Essays Presented to Fitzroy Pyle* (Blackrock: Irish Academic Press, 1984), 127–74. Pheifer in particular discusses Echidna and the tradition of the cannibalistic generation of vipers as a source for Errour and her children.

[28] Hesiod, 'Homeric Hymn to Pythian Apollo', in *The Homeric Hymns*, 300–6.

[29] The motif of infernal maternity is invoked again in 1.12.10, where the townsfolk fear even after the (male) dragon's death that 'in his wombe might lurke some hidden nest | Of many Dragonets, his fruitfull seed'. This link is noted in King, *Spenser's Poetry and the Reformation Tradition*, 224.

[30] S. K. Heninger notes that Orgoglio is probably based in part upon descriptions of Typhon in Hesiod's *Theogony*. Errour, a version of the Python and of Echidna, can therefore be seen as beginning the process that leads Redcrosse to Orgoglio, a version of Typhon, foster son of one and lover of the other. 'The Orgoglio Episode in *The Faerie Queene*', *English Literary History*, 26 (1959), 183–6.

subtlety'.[31] Steadman discerns in Errour the use, in emblems, of Echidna and the Chimaera as figures of rhetoric and erudition, in combination with the labyrinth, a figure of philosophy (itself elaborated by Calvin in the *Institutes* into an image of 'oversubtle theological speculation').[32] Elsewhere in the *Institutes*, an image closely reminiscent of Errour and her children is used of the philosophical speculation that leads to polytheism and idolatry:

Hence that immense flood of error with which the whole world is overflowed . . . Like water gushing forth from an immense and copious spring, immense crowds of gods have issued from the human mind, every man giving himself full license, and devising some peculiar form of divinity, to meet his own views. It is unnecessary here to attempt a catalogue of the superstitions with which the world was overspread. (1.5.12)

This model of creation too is threatening in its disorder and uncertain authorial status; it is a fountain that threatens to engulf rather than nourish and refresh. I do not intend here to give a systematic account of Calvin's theological influence on Spenser, but I will return to possible echoes of Calvin's writings and thought elsewhere in Book 1 in the next chapter.

The vomited papers also emphasize Errour's nature as a figure of threatening material textuality. While Errour's vomit, her 'streame of cole black bloud', and her children's 'bowels gushing forth' make her a parodic fountain, they also make her a parody of the printing press.[33] Errour can perhaps even be seen as a hideous invocation and parody of the imitative poet's touchstone, Horace's ode to the *Fons Bandusiae*:

> O fons Bandusiae splendidior vitro
> dulci digne mero non sine floribus,
> cras donaberis haedo,
>   cui frons turgida cornibus
> primis et venerem et proelia destinat;
> frustra: nam gelidos inficiet tibi
> rubro sanguine rivos
>   lascivi suboles gregis.

O spring of Bandusia, more glittering than glass, who deserve sweet wine, yes, and flowers as well, tomorrow you will be presented with a kid, whose forehead is swollen with budding horns, marking him out for love and warfare—all in vain; for the offspring of the lustful herd will stain your cool springs with his red blood.[34]

---

[31] John M. Steadman, 'Spenser's *Errour* and the Renaissance Allegorical Tradition', *Neuphilologische Mitteilungen*, 62 (1961), 23.

[32] Ibid. 24–7, 30. This aspect of her significance anticipates the sophistry of Archimago, to be discussed below, as well as reflecting some of Bale's glosses.

[33] See the discussion by Rhu, 'Romancing the Word', 101–9.

[34] Horace, *Odes and Epodes*, trans. Niall Rudd (Cambridge, Mass.: Harvard University Press, 2004), *Odes*, 3.13, 1–8.

Even in images, such as this, that express their very origins, language and poetry encompass their own vulnerability to corruption. In *The Shepheardes Calender*, two of the woodcuts (*April* and *December*) depict Colin beside a fountain, while *June* begins with an invocation of the bird who 'to the waters fall their tunes attemper right', and Cuddie calls on 'Thou pleasant spring... whose streames my tricklinge teares did ofte augment' in *August*.[35] Patrick Cheney has gone so far as to describe this trope as a 'Spenserian signature', noted in *The Return from Parnassus*;[36] that it is such a notable feature of Spenser's self-proclaimed apprentice-piece in poetry reinforces his identification of fountains in *The Faerie Queene* with the very origins of poetry. In the figure of Errour, drawn from so many textual and cultural traditions, Spenser depicts the anxiety of being a Protestant poet (and reader) in an epic (and hence classical) context, and perhaps of publication. If Errour's poisoned 'parbreake' figures the process of going into print, and hence a corrupt and corrupting poetry, then Spenser is right to be apprehensive, as he implicates himself in the perpetuation of the very process that he exposes. Spenser's most explicit expression of apprehension about the role of the poet is found in 5.9.25–6, and is therefore technically outside the scope of my discussion here. But it is surely significant that the same metaphor is used there, where the poet 'BON FONS' is transformed into '*Malfont* ... Eyther for th'euill, which he did therein, | Or that he likened was to a welhed | Of euill words, and wicked sclaunders by him shed'. Through the image of the fountain or well, the bad, corrupting poet is implicitly opposed to Spenser's model and frequent source, 'Dan *Chaucer*, well of English vndefyled' (4.2.32), 'That old *Dan Geffrey* (in whose gentle spright | The pure well head of Poesie did dwell' (7.7.9), the 'Good Poet' of 6.3.1. This particular nexus of associations, anxieties, and moral judgements about writing, reading, and sources also begins with Errour.

Redcrosse's combat with Errour leads directly to the narrative's next catastrophe, his deception by the evil Archimago when he and Una subsequently take shelter for the night in the false hermitage.[37] It is entirely consistent with Spenser's apparent anxiety about the corruptible nature of water that, once Redcrosse and Una are asleep (sleep itself being described as 'sweet slombring deaw', 1.1.36), Archimago conjures watery simulacra to disturb, deceive, and so separate the couple. The likeness of Una is 'fram'd of liquid ayre'. Hamilton glosses this as 'bright'; both senses (this and the more familiar modern one

---

[35] Edmund Spenser, *The Shorter Poems*, ed. McCabe, *June*, 8; *August*, 155–6.

[36] 'The waters fall he tun'd for fame', quoted by Cheney, *Marlowe's Counterfeit Profession: Ovid, Spenser, Counter-Nationhood* (Toronto: University of Toronto Press, 1997), 74.

[37] The 'sacred fountaine' outside the hermitage is discussed at length in Chapter 7; following Hamilton, Cheney interprets it as the Ovidian fountain of *Amores* 3.1.3; *Marlowe's Counterfeit Profession*, 74.

of 'fluid') were, however, current,[38] and the creation of the likeness of Una (and then the Squire) from moist air is in keeping with the imagery used elsewhere of dreams (in stanzas 40–2) and of the first simulacrum's effect on Redcrosse: 'his manly hart did melt away, | Bathed in wanton blis and wicked ioy' (1.47).[39] If 'watery' rather than 'bright' is the primary sense of 'liquid', then there is an obvious analogue in 3.8.5–9, when the witch makes false Florimell out of 'purest snow in massy mould congeald' (8.6) and animates the simulacrum with 'A wicked Spright' (8.8). In Book 1, after (and even because of) Redcrosse's fight with Errour, water is associated not with truth but deception.[40] Because of Errour's subtle and invidious pollutions, after her spectacular demise even a 'Christall streame' and a 'sacred fountaine' are ignored without a second glance, while cunning and corrupt (but eloquent) versions of scriptural truth and spirituality are welcomed. 'Sweet slombring deaw' leaves Una and Redcrosse 'drownd in deadly sleepe' and a watery fake, parodying the numinous associations of 'dew' elsewhere in *The Faerie Queene*, deceives the impulsive hero into running away, and so acts as the catalyst for the narrative's next phase.

The nadir of Redcrosse's narrative journey comes at his encounter with Duessa by the fountain in canto 7. Although richly intertextual in classical and romance terms the scene also has many important biblical referents. The pleasance where Redcrosse disarms and rests is a *locus amoenus* typical of the romance tradition:[41]

> Hee feedes vpon the cooling shade, and bayes
> His sweatie forehead in the breathing wind,
> Which through the trembling leaues full gently playes
> Wherein the chearefull birds of sundry kind
> Doe chaunt sweet musick, to delight his mynd. (1.7.3)

[38] The latter was perhaps more so, as the *OED* cites 1590 *FQ* 3 as the first occurrence of the latter.

[39] Elsewhere Spenser uses the image of dew to describe other, more numinous, acts of creation, for example, that of Belphoebe (and Amoret) in 3.6.3: 'Her berth was of the wombe of Morning dew'. The false Una is 'borne without her dew' (1.1.46), which Hamilton compares to *Amoretti* 74.6: 'from mothers womb deriu'd by dew descent'. I will suggest in Chapter 7 that this false 'dew' is ultimately fulfilled typologically in the balm that flows from the Tree of Life in canto 11.

[40] An exception is Fradubio's account in canto 2 of how he saw Duessa revealed when she was bathing. Redcrosse, however, fails to heed the warning and does not himself recognize Duessa/Fidessa: his sight has been corrupted. The situation described here is a version of the Diana–Actaeon encounter (one of at least three in *The Faerie Queene*, all somewhat unconventional), and Fradubio's punishment is therefore appropriately metamorphic.

[41] Redcrosse should be wary, given what he encountered on the previous occasion he rested in a similar spot: Fradubio and Fraelissa's wretched prison. It was, after all, there that he was warned of 'one *Duessa* a false sorceresse, | That many *errant* knights hath bought to wretchednesse' (1.2.34), second emphasis mine.

The rendezvous beside a fountain is familiar in courtly literature, and the posture of disdain and reproach initially adopted by Duessa is one typical of the courtly mistress. Her anger, whether genuine or feigned (of Duessa, one suspects the latter), does not last long, however, and the pair are soon reconciled. The pleasance becomes a version of the even more private *hortus conclusus*: 'the ioyous shade, | Which shielded them against the boyling heat, | And with greene boughes decking a gloomy glade, | About the fountaine like a girlond made' (7.4); a perfect place for lovers. Here, the three run-on lines which end the first half of the canto's third stanza perhaps mirror the long narrative divagation that has brought Redcrosse to this place; the resulting emphasis on 'mind' at the caesura is surely ironic (what has he been thinking?) and the return to strongly end-stopped lines in the next stanza emphasizes his entrapment in the world of romance; he can go no further. The 'gloomy glade', however, recalls the situation of Errour's den, as well as the grove of Fradubio and Fraelissa (1.2.28–45) and the place where Redcrosse has earlier come across the pagan Sansloy (1.6.40);[42] as Syrithe Pugh puts it, Errour's den has in fact been 'programmatic' for *The Faerie Queene*, and it has become a location repeatedly recalled and revisited throughout the poem.[43] A true courtly knight, however, let alone a Christian one, would surely never consummate his relationship with his lady in this fashion. The true courtly relationship between lover and mistress is chaste, even if the literature seems mainly concerned with transgressors, and thus romance, as a genre, is concerned with endless deferrals and complications, both narrative and interpersonal. Redcrosse is 'carelesse of his health, *and of his fame*' (7.7) as both the *miles Christi* and the knight errant in his breaching of generic conventions in this way. Having set out as *miles Christi* and then enthusiastically adopted the persona of the knight errant, he has debased and forsaken even that, for without an endlessly unattainable mistress as his prize and incentive, he can go no further. His romance career must come to an abrupt end.

While it is overlaid with particular romance associations and functionality, more prominent in the depiction of the fountain in canto 7 and its effects is its pseudo-Ovidian origin. Spenser invents an aetiology behind the effects of the fountain, which he borrows from the myth of Salmacis and Hermaphroditus.[44]

---

[42] This first is noted by Douglas Brooks-Davies, *Spenser's Faerie Queene: A Critical Commentary on Books I and II* (Manchester: Manchester University Press, 1977), 69, and the latter by Darryl J. Gless, *Interpretation and Theology in Spenser* (Cambridge: Cambridge University Press, 1994), 115.

[43] Pugh, *Spenser and Ovid*, 54. Pugh also notes the connection between Fradubio and Fraelissa and canto 7, which she discusses in a section titled 'Fradubio and Fraelissa: Redcrosse's Failure as an Intertextual Reader', 69 ff.

[44] Ovid, *Metamorphoses*, 4.306–88.

For Redcrosse, as for Hermaphroditus, an encounter with a sexually aggressive woman (although Redcrosse is a more willing partner than his Ovidian counterpart) leads to emasculation and loss of identity in the matrix of the fountain. He is enfeebled, and he lays aside his eponymous armour; he is 'Disarmd, disgraste, and inwardly dismayde' (7.11), the heavy punctuation reinforcing his exhaustion and creating an analogous experience for the reader, anticipated in the earlier description of the fountain's waters as 'dull and slow' (7.5). Yet Spenser's explanation that the nymph of the fountain was punished by Diana for having 'sat downe to rest in middest of the race' invokes a biblical injunction: 'Know ye not that they which run in a race run all, but one receiveth the prize?' (1 Corinthians 9: 24). There are even closer analogues in the marginal notes of the Geneva Bible, in which the metaphor of life as a race occurs frequently (more so than in the text itself). The gloss on 1 Thessalonians 1: 6 ('And ye became followeres of vs, and of the Lorde, and receiued the worde in much affliction, with ioy of the holy Ghost') is particularly pertinent: '*An other reason, because euen to that day, they embraced the Gospel with great cheerfulnes, in so much that they were an example to all their neighbours: so it should be more shame to them to faint in the mid race.*' Redcrosse's arms and initial eagerness for his mission suggest that he is one such. As Hamilton notes, stanzas 12 and 13 of canto 7, where Orgoglio attacks Redcrosse, are Book 1's exact middle. This fountain, therefore, affords a neat example of Spenser's blending of classical and biblical sources, here to make a point about both the Christian mission and the interpretative task of the reader: what is to be the fate of readers who, like Redcrosse, relax the vigilance of their reading? When, beside that fountain, Redcrosse lays aside his Ephesian armour, another passage from Erasmus' *Enchiridion* is therefore particularly apt:

In these worldly warres a man may be often tymes at rest/as in the depe of the wynter/or in tyme of truce: but we as longe as we kepe warre in this body/may departe from our harneys & wepons no season/no not as the saying is one fynger brede. We must euer stande afore the tentes & make watche/for our aduersary is neuer ydle: but whan he is most calme & styll/whan he fayneth to flee or to make truce/euen than most of al he ymagineth gyle: & thou hast neuer more nede to kepe watche than whan he maketh countenaunce or semblaunce of peace. Thou hast neuer lesse nede to feare than whan he assaulteth the with open warre. Therfore let thy fyrst care be that thy mynde be not vnarmed.[45]

What underlies the entire first half of Book 1 after Redcrosse's apparently successful defeat of Errour is that the knight's mind is unarmed: he has failed to demonstrate the combined receptiveness to learning and mental vigilance

---

[45] Sig. B1ᵛ.

necessary for success in his mission. A second passage from the *Enchiridion* explains the emaciated state that Redcrosse will be reduced to in Orgoglio's dungeon and why he will be thus reduced, with an implicit reproach, for as a Christian knight he should have been better prepared (and known better in the first place):

> It is no meruayle that the comen people be seruants to the lawe and princyples of this worlde/as they whiche are vnlerned/neyther haue wysdome more than they borow of other mennes heeds: it is more to be meruayled that they whiche are as chefe of Christes relygyon/in the same captyuyte perysshe for hunger/and wydder away for thurst. why perysshe they for hunger? Bycause they haue not lerned of Christ to breake barly loues/they only lycke rounde aboute the rough & sharpe codde or huske/they sucke out no mary or swete lycoure. And whye wydder they so awaye for thurst? for bycause they haue not lerned of Moyses to fette water out of the spyrituall rocke of stone/neyther haue drunke of the ryuers of the water of lyfe whiche floweth/issueth/or springeth out of the bely of Christ: and that was spoken verely of the spyrit/not of the flesshe.[46]

There may even be, in canto 7, a play on the title of the *Enchiridion* itself. In stanza 11 Redcrosse feebly attempts to 'weeld his bootlesse single blade': an enchiridion is both a manual and a small dagger. Without his 'breastplate of righteousness' and 'shield of faith' Redcrosse is left only with 'the sword of the Spirit, which is the word of God'. But because he does not know how to read the Scriptures properly and so is incapable of interpreting visual and textual signs in their light, it remains just a sword, and is of no use when he is faced with the dire consequences of his own unthinking carnal nature.[47]

A second biblical source for the episode is the important Old Testament series of encounters between men and women at wells: Abraham and Hagar, Isaac and Rebecca, Jacob and Rachel. In the New Testament, these are typologically fulfilled and transformed in the meeting between Christ and the Samaritan woman in John 4, and it is this which is particularly invoked in canto 7. Redcrosse's disastrous version of one of the most important moments in the Gospels is in fact anticipated earlier in the Book by Una's encounter with Corceca and Abessa. Daughter Abessa figures the unthinking adherence to tradition initially espoused by the Samaritan woman when she tells Christ that 'our fathers worshipped on this mountain' (4: 20):[48] perhaps significantly,

---

[46] Sig. L4[v].

[47] See the discussion of this by King, *Spenser's Poetry and the Reformation Tradition*, 195–7, and Gless, *Interpretation and Theology in Spenser*, 122.

[48] See the extended discussion of the episode in these terms, with particular reference to Hagar as a type of the Samaritan woman and so of Abessa, by Kathryn Walls, 'Abessa and the Lion: *The Faerie Queene* 1.3.1–12', *Spenser Studies*, 5 (1984), 3–30. The conventional interpretation of this encounter, with Abessa/the Samaritan woman standing for Torah, Synagogue, or the Old Law, is both outlined and modified by Gless, *Interpretation and Theology in Spenser*, 85–6.

the only evidence of a water source is Abessa's water pot. Yet whereas the Samaritan drops her water pot in her haste to bring the news of Christ to her people (John 4: 28–9), Abessa drops hers 'in order to retreat more quickly into the familiarity and seeming safety of her mother's cottage. The Samaritan is what Abessa might have become'.[49] This suggests that her well may no longer exist, or that the water she carries was drawn long ago and borne untasted thereafter. In recalling both the Samaritan woman and Hagar (who carries 'the jug of the insipid law which she so passionately loves'),[50] Spenser employs the Protestant commonplace of attacking Catholicism as 'a reversion to the legalism and ceremonial of Judaism';[51] the subsequent characterization of Abessa's mother Corceca as a parody of extreme Catholic piety bears this out (1.3.13–14). Like Christ, Redcrosse is resting because he is tired ('Iesus then wearied in the iourney, sate thus on the well', 4: 6). But the water that he drinks from the spring is far more negative in its effects than the water of Jacob's Well. That water is deficient only because it will satisfy bodily thirst alone, and that only temporarily: while Christ offers the Samaritan woman 'a well of water springing up into everlasting life' (4: 14), Duessa's fountain is enervating and deadly, the antithesis of the living water.[52]

Duessa becomes the fountain, and Redcrosse's drinking stands for his fornication. Duessa is therefore the antithesis of the chaste-woman-as-sealed-fountain type of the Song of Solomon. She is perhaps even the wicked woman described in Ecclesiasticus 26: 12: 'As one that goeth by the way, and is thirsty, so shall she open her mouth, and drinke of euery next water: by euery hedge shall she sit downe, & open her quiuer against euery arrowe.' In a famous essay, John W. Shroeder interprets the effects of Redcrosse's dalliance with Duessa (described in 1.7.6) in terms of pseudo-Aristotelian physiology as

a literal statement of the aftermath of coition. Red Crosse's major symptoms are two: faintness and chill. These are precisely the two *sequelae* of ejaculation given in the *Problemata*... The knight is enfeebled as the result of his first act of venery with Duessa, the drink he takes of the fountain is the metaphor for that act, his enfeeblement displays both the classic symptoms.

He notes also, in line with the passage from Ecclesiasticus just quoted, that 'the female pudend, considered as an object of sexual desire, is a fountain,

---

[49] Walls, 'Abessa and the Lion', 15.

[50] Desiderius Erasmus, *Paraphrases on Romans and Galatians*, ed. Robert D. Sider, trans. John B. Payne, Albert Rabil, and Warren S. Smith (Toronto: University of Toronto Press, 1984), Galatians 4: 30.

[51] Walls, 'Abessa and the Lion', 10.

[52] There is perhaps another subtle parallel with John 4 in that Redcrosse is oblivious to Duessa's duplicity and in particular to her promiscuity. Christ, however, knows that the Samaritan woman has been married many times (4: 17–18).

pool, spring or river, from which a man drinks to ease his thirst or in which he bathes to allay his body's heat, is metaphorically commonplace'.[53] Most of all, however, the elision of Duessa with the fountain in canto 7 reflects Protestant commentary on the Whore of Babylon, which typically conflates physical and spiritual fornication.[54] In Van Der Noot's *A Theatre for Voluptuous Worldlings* (1569), to which the schoolboy Spenser (perhaps through the contacts of his schoolmaster Richard Mulcaster) contributed sonnets, for example, the Whore of Babylon is described as 'the mother and fountaine both of spiritual and carnall whordom and abhomination'.[55] In *The Image of Both Churches*, John Bale is even more explicit:

Her verye name agreynge to her frutes, is this. Great Babylon, in mischefe farre aboue the cytye of the Chaldeanes, and muchmore full of confusyon. For she is the orignall mother, the cause, the beginninge, the rote, the springe, and the fountayne of all spyrytuall fornicacions, and in a maner of all flashlye abhoominacions also done vpon the earth. This is to the faithfull sort, as a written name of her, euident, clere open and manifest. But to the vnfaithfull it is onlye as a mysterye hydde, darke, obscure, and neglect.[56]

Bale and Van Der Noot, like other writers, use 'fountain' to mean 'source'. But Spenser's use of the trope as both location and controlling image demonstrates that it was far from being a dead metaphor. It is surely no accident that it is the scene in which the Duessa-fountain is Redcrosse's downfall that leads directly to Duessa's most explicit identification as the Whore, as she is dressed by Orgoglio in 'gold and purple pale' and mounted on the seven-headed beast (1.7.16 f; Revelation 17). In Bale's terms, Redcrosse has become the archetype of the unfaithful Christian because he has failed to read Duessa's name. In fact, he should have done so as early as 1.2.13, when he first meets Duessa, 'clad in scarlot red, | Purfled with gold and pearle of rich assay', and wins her from Sansfoy. But Redcrosse is at this point newly and deeply involved in his quest to be the romantic knight errant, and he sees 'Fidessa' only as a potential cause and trophy; as John N. King puts it, 'Redcrosse's failure to recognise this seductress, whose character represents a fusion of an Arthurian

---

[53] John W. Shroeder, 'Spenser's Erotic Drama: The Orgoglio Episode', *English Literary History*, 29 (1962), 145, 148.

[54] See D. Douglas Waters, *Duessa as Theological Satire* (Columbia: University of Missouri Press, 1970), *passim*.

[55] Sig. K4.

[56] Sig. R4ᵛ. Compare also Bale's gloss regarding the children of Jezebel, Revelation 2: 23: 'And as touchinge here supersticiouse chyldren, which from their begynnynge hath euermore sucked owt of her venemouse brestes all poyson and vngodlynesse, forsakinge, yea and abhorringe the swete veyne of ye liuinge waters, then wil I slee with death & condemnacion euerlastinge prepared for ye deuil & his angels' (E6). This text and its gloss are also relevant to the depiction of Errour and her children.

witch similar to Morgan le Fay with the great harlot of Revelation, intensifies a sense of the moral failure of romance'.[57] The scene elides the 'standing poole' of Catholicism with the very texts that Roger Ascham condemned: Redcrosse has failed utterly as a reader.

For Erasmus in the *Enchiridion*, to be baptized is to be at once enrolled as Christ's soldier and to embark upon a process of interpretation, of learning to read the Scriptures. He emphasizes that Christian knighthood is a baptismal covenant:

> For who so euer is at one with vyces hath broken truce made bytwene him & god in tyme of baptym . . . Oh thou chrysten man remembrest thou not whan thou were professed & consecrate with the holy mysteryes of ye fountayne of lyfe/how thou boundest thy selfe to be a faythfull sowdyour vnto thy captayne Chryst/to whome thou owest thy lyfe twyse/both bycause he gaue it the/& also bycause he restored it agayne to the.[58]

In the service of baptism itself, the child is signed with the cross 'in token that hereafter he shall not be ashamed to confess the faith of Christ crucified, and manfully to fight under his banner against sin, the world and the devil, and to continue Christ's faithful soldier unto his life's end'. Baptism (even in the Prayer Book) is an initiation into a community united by its textuality, one way of proving membership of which is 'to hear sermons. And . . . [to] learn the Creed, the Lord's Prayer, and the Ten Commandments in the English Tongue.' The child's godparents are exhorted by the minister to be responsible for this. Erasmus himself enjoins the Christian knight to the careful study and interpretation of Scripture, and uses a particularly apt image in so doing:

> ofte mencion is made in scripture of welles fountaynes & ryuers/by whiche is signified nothyng else but that we ought to enquyre & serche diligently for the mysteryes hydde in scripture. What signyfyeth water hydde in ye vaynes of the erth but mystery couered or hyd in the litterall sence. What meaneth the same conueyed abrode but mystery opened & expouned. which beyng spred & dilated bothe wyde & brode/to the edyfying of ye hearers/what cause is there why it myght not be called a ryuer. Wherfore yf thou dedycate thy selfe holly to the study of scripture & exercyse thy mynde day and nyght in ye lawe of god/no feare shall trouble the/neyther by day nor night: but thou shalte agaynst all assawltes of thyne ennemyes be armed & exercysed also.[59]

If only Redcrosse had prepared himself in this way! He would, as has been seen elsewhere, have recognized Duessa; he would have been aware of the imperative to read fountains. Several critics (notably Patrick Cullen) have influentially observed that Redcrosse is called upon in the course of the Book

---

[57] King, *Spenser's Poetry and the Reformation Tradition*, 202.   [58] Sig. A3–A3ᵛ.
[59] Sig. B4ᵛ–B5. Although I have not quoted it until this point, this text has underpinned my reading and argument.

to resist and fight against the powers of the world, the flesh, and the devil.[60] It is in these encounters, therefore, that he revisits his responsibilities as a baptized *miles Christi*, and it should not be at all surprising that they all involve versions of the fountain of baptism and of the Word that must be correctly interpreted, negotiated, and revealed.

Redcrosse's two main encounters with versions of fountains in Book 1 of *The Faerie Queene* operate within an intertextual and syncretic framework and ethos. In the first half of the book, he embarks upon a process of apostasy that is at once generic, textual, and spiritual. He forsakes his proper Christian mission to pursue the more glamorous quest of the knight errant; at the same time he abandons his Christian moral principles and his chastity. This pattern of the rejection of the pure for the corrupt, the true for the false, the transcendent for the worldly and mundane, is that of the texts from Jeremiah and Genesis, explored in the previous chapter, and of the wanton destruction depicted in Revelation. Redcrosse lusts not so much after false gods as after corrupted and unreliable sources, polluted and poisonous fountains, anathema to the good Protestant reader. It is in his final encounter with a fountain, the Well of Life, that he will be, in the terms of Erasmus' *Enchiridion* which so notably underpin Book 1, finally reborn as a reader and as *miles Christi*, which are one and the same.

---

[60] Or sin, the world, and the devil as per the wording in the baptism service: this makes more obvious their principal identifications with Errour, Duessa, and the dragon.

7

The Well of Life: All Things Made New

Some two hundred years before Spenser's composition of *The Faerie Queene*, Piers Plowman and his companions met a pilgrim. Langland's pilgrim is

> Apparailled as a paynym in pilgrymes wise.
> He bar a burdoune ybounde with a brood liste
> In a withwynde wise ywounden aboute.
> A bolle and a bagge he bar by his syde.
> An hundred of ampulles on his hat seten,
> Signes of Syse and shelles of Galice,
> And many a crouch on his cloke, and keyes of Rome,
> And the vernicle bifore, for men shoulde knowe
> And se bi hise signes whom he sought hadde. (516–24)[1]

The 'shelles of Galice', the scallop shells of the Santiago de Compostela pilgrimage, are still familiar today, but the 'hundred of ampulles [that] on his hat seten' are perhaps less so. *Ampullae* were a subset of the pilgrim badges, usually made of stamped tin, lead, or pewter, that were the standard souvenir of pilgrimage sites all over Europe and the Holy Land; each shrine had its own particular badges.[2] As the name suggests, *ampullae* were not simply badges but little bottles, which were filled by pilgrims with water from wells or springs at the place of pilgrimage, and then sewn onto the clothing (most commonly, as in *Piers Plowman*, the hat) using the conveniently placed handles or lugs of the bottle, as sign, souvenir, and talisman. Thus medieval English pilgrims did not just visit holy wells (or the wells and springs that were secondary attractions at other pilgrimage sites) to experience their

---

[1] *burdoune* = staff, *brood liste* = strip of cloth, *bolle* = bowl, *ampulles* = phials, *seten* = sat, *Syse* = Assisi, *crouch* = cross-ornament. William Langland, *The Vision of Piers Plowman: A Critical Edition of the B-Text Based on Trinity College Cambridge MS B.15.17* (2nd edn.), ed. A. V. C. Schmidt (London: Everyman, 1995), Passus V, ll. 516–24, p. 89.

[2] Brian Spencer, *Pilgrim Souvenirs and Secular Badges*, Museum of London: Medieval Finds from Excavations in London 7 (London: Stationery Office, 1998), 3. Because pilgrim badges were frequently left as propitiatory offerings at river crossings by medieval travellers, they are one of the commonest finds for amateur 'mudlarks': there are more than 1,000 examples in the collections of the Museum of London.

miraculous spiritual benefits *in situ*, but very often carried away their water in a manner even more formalized (and fetishized) than a Lourdes pilgrim might today (Fig. 10).[3]

The wells at Walsingham were typical of the wells and springs to be found at many of the great pilgrimage sites of medieval England. The first written record of the wells there dates from the late fourteenth century, in the account of a Marian miracle whereby a boy fell into the well and apparently drowned, only to revive and live on to become sub-prior,[4] but *ampullae* from Walsingham survive from as early as the late thirteenth century.[5] In one of his best-known colloquies, Erasmus' had included a satirical description of visits to the shrines at Walsingham and Canterbury. Erasmus' description has been much quoted as evidence of the credulousness of pre-Reformation English popular culture (and of Erasmus' own reforming enthusiasm):

OGYGIUS I haue bene on pylgremage at saynt Iames in Compostella, & at my retourne I dyd more relygyously vysyte our lady of Walsyngam in England, a very holy pylgremage, but I dyd rather vysyte her. For I was ther before within this thre yere . . . Before that chapell there was a litle howsse, whiche he sayd ones in wynter tyme whan yt there was litle rowme to couer the reliques, that it was sodenly broght & sett in that place. Under that house there was a couple of pittes, bothe fulle of water to the brynkys, and thay say that ye sprynge of thos pittes is dedicate to our lady, that water is very colde, and medycynable for the hede ake and that hart-burnynge.

MENEDEMUS If that cold water wyll hele the paynes in the hede and stomake, than wyll oyle putowte fyre from hensforthe.

OGYGIUS It is a myrakle that I tell, good syr, orels what maruayle shuld it be, yt cowld water shuld slake thurste?

MENEDEMUS This may well be one parte of your tale.

OGYGIUS Thay say that the fowntayne dyd sodenly sprynge owte of the erthe at the commaundement of our lady . . .[6]

---

[3] Marina Warner, *Alone of All her Sex: The Myth and Cult of the Virgin Mary* (London: Weidenfeld and Nicolson, 1976; repr. Vintage, 2000), 311.

[4] J. C. Dickinson, *The Shrine of Our Lady at Walsingham* (Cambridge: Cambridge University Press, 1956), 136.

[5] Examples of Walsingham *ampullae* found in London include some in the shape of a church, decorated with scenes of the Virgin and Child and the Coronation of the Virgin, while fourteenth-and fifteenth-century Walsingham *ampullae* were mainly decorated with a crowned 'W'. Spencer, *Pilgrim Souvenirs*, 144–7.

[6] *A dialoge or communication of two persons deuysyd and set forthe in the laten tonge, by the noble and famose clarke. Desiderius Erasmus' intituled [the] pylgremage of pure deuotyon. Newly translatyd into Englishe* (London?, 1540), A1ᵛ, B4-B4ᵛ. Dickinson commented, somewhat bitterly, that '[a]s a critic Erasmus' was neither well informed nor friendly. His own sensitive nature had clearly suffered from the foolish attempt to make him take the religious habit as a young boy, and, like many distinguished foreigners in Cambridge since, he found the English climate and diet inconducive to real peace of mind.' Dickinson, *Walsingham*, 54.

The implicit contrast in Erasmus' satire between the miraculous and the medical or scientific is one to which I will return, for by the time Spenser was writing, it was one that had become virtually redundant. In the Reformed landscape of Elizabethan England, healing springs and wells had been effectively reinvented by medicine and science, yet they remained vital signs of God's grace and favour towards the English people.

Two hat badges of a very different kind from those affected by Langland's pilgrim are on display at the British Museum. Made from enamelled gold and dating from about 1540, they depict Christ and the Woman of Samaria at the Well (John 4); the larger, less than 2.5 inches in diameter, includes the inscription, engraved on the well itself, 'OF A TREWTHE THOW ART THE TREW MESSIAS' (Fig. 11). They have been identified as the product of a London workshop, which has been subsequently linked to some fifteen other surviving objects *c.*1520–60.[7] Religious subjects for hat badges in the Renaissance were far from being unusual, although classical subjects were also popular, but two aspects of these hat badges set them apart: they are the only surviving instance of hat badges depicting the same biblical scene, and the larger is the only one to combine such a biblical scene with an English inscription. The English text, 'Of a trewthe thow art the trew Messias', is not directly biblical in origin, but appears to combine in paraphrase the woman's comment, 'Sir, I see that thou art a prophet' (4: 19), 'I know that Messias cometh, which is called Christ' (4: 25), and 'Is not this the Christ?' (4: 29) with the reported reaction of the Samaritans: 'this is indeed the Christ, the Saviour of the world' (4: 42). Its inscription on the well is particularly suggestive: the text is elided visually with the well, and so with the 'well of water springing up into everlasting life' (4: 14), which is Christ himself and the Word itself; and the Word is in English. There is an anticipation here of *Veritas Temporis Filia* and the English Bible.

I begin my discussion of Spenser's Well of Life at the end of Book 1 of *The Faerie Queene* with these examples because they demonstrate (and in appropriately material and experiential terms) the first stages of the cultural and ideological shifts in the English landscape upon which Spenser's well—and his other fountains—draws, and in which it participates. In this chapter, I will suggest that Spenser's well can be located within what Alexandra Walsham, in her discussion of 'the post-Reformation history of holy wells', has called

a tale not of an iconoclastic stripping of altars and shrines, but of adaptation and accommodation—on the part of both Protestant authorities and the populace. Nor is

---

[7] It has also been suggested that Holbein may have been involved in the design; drawings by him for other hat badges depicting biblical subjects survive. On the hat badges, see the articles by Hugh Tait in the *British Museum Quarterly*, 20 (1955), 37–8 and *The Connoisseur*, 154 (1963), 147–53.

it a story of the onwards march of secular science and medicine . . . [but] a prolonged period of religious and cultural transition. Holy wells and healing springs may have as much to tell us about how England became a Protestant nation as a Christian one.[8]

Book 1 of Spenser's *Faerie Queene* is set in a landscape that, like early modern London, is palimpsestic, a landscape in which (to pursue the analogy) fountains and other water sources might be seen as wormholes, interpenetrating the layers both of the narrative and the environment in which it unfolds, and compelling the careful attention of the reader. Spenser's Well of Life is a holy well and a healing spring but, like the well on the Tudor hat badge, it is also the Living Water and the Word of God; it combines in its action the *ampullae's* pre-Reformation thaumaturgy of sacred water, reinflected not only sacramentally but textually, the providentialist Protestant medical culture increasingly growing up around wells and baths in the second half of the sixteenth century, and a nationalistic investment in the natural wonders of the English landscape.

In the 1570s and 1580s, at the same time as England was experiencing a resurgence of interest in the Book of Revelation and Spenser was beginning to write *The Faerie Queene*, there was a terrific vogue for 'taking the waters' or 'going to the bath'.[9] The Queen herself visited Bath for nearly a week in the summer of 1574, and in 1577 demanded that Burghley send her a barrel of Buxton water;[10] Mary, Queen of Scots, visited Buxton no fewer than nine times during the period of her captivity, and met with both Burghley and Leicester there, and Leicester himself also frequented the baths at Newnham Regis (King's Newnham), which were some ten miles from Kenilworth: his last letter before his death mentioned his hope for a cure 'at the bath'.[11]

The relative importance of the Irish context here is vexed. It is, of course, now widely recognized that the Irish landscape in general had a profound influence upon *The Faerie Queene*, most notably in Book 6 and the *Mutabilitie Cantos*. Yet whether Irish holy wells in particular might have influenced Spenser's conception of his fountains, and especially the Well of Life, is a different matter. Although huge numbers of holy wells are now known of in Ireland, with many still existing today, whether they were a comparable feature of sixteenth-century popular religious practices is uncertain. There

---

[8] Alexandra Walsham, 'Reforming the Waters: Holy Wells and Healing Springs in Protestant England', in Diana Wood (ed.), *Life and Thought in the Northern Church c.1100–c.1700: Essays in Honour of Claire Cross* (Woodbridge: Boydell Press, 1999), 255.

[9] See Phyllis Hembry, *The English Spa, 1560–1815: A Social History* (London: Athlone Press, 1990), 2 and *passim*.

[10] When it arrived on 8 August, 'angered by rumours that she needed the water for her sore legs, she pettishly spurned it as having lost some virtue in transit', ibid. 24.

[11] There were other short-lived sites, notably at Newton, near St Neots, in Huntingdonshire, one at Clifton, near Bristol, and even one at Ratcliff, in London. Ibid. 13–17.

are in fact only disparate records of such wells prior to the late seventeenth century and, in particular, there is almost no evidence in the period for the 'Celtic origins' hypothesis, whereby a pre-Christian origin is claimed for sites now at the centre of Catholic devotions. Spenser does not mention them in the *Vewe*; neither do they appear in Giraldus Cambrensis, nor in many sixteenth-century accounts of devotional practices, such as those by the Jesuits David Woolfe and William Good (1560s). Barnaby Rich includes a chapter '*Of the superstitious conceit that is holden of the Irish, about certaine Wels*' in his *New Description of Ireland* (1610), observing that 'there is no infirmity, but it might be cured at sundry sanctified and holy wels, whereof there are great plenty in *Ireland*' and concluding that

I might speake of diuers other Wels, for I think there is neyther *Apostle* nor *Patriarch*, that neuer came neere vnto Ireland, and yet there be Welles, Fountaines, and other holy places, that be attributed vnto them. But if I should speake of the wonders and myracles, which they say are wrought there, it would make a more admirable history then that of sir *Iohn Mandevile*: It woulde vndoo all the Physitians in *England* and *Ireland*. For at those holy Wels, and at many other of those sanctified places, the blinde are made to see, the Lame are made to goe, the Cripple is restored to his limbes, or what disease soeuer, neuer so strange, neuer so inueterate, which is not there cured.[12]

The details Rich gives of the wells around Dublin are curiously imprecise, however, and pertain more to the general customs of fairs than to the 'rounding' and other practices later associated with Irish wells. There is some evidence from both the colonial and Catholic authorities that from the last decade of the sixteenth century and beyond, gatherings at holy wells were becoming more widespread and popular with, for example, a proclamation made in 1590, 'inhibiting the resort to the well near Rathefernam upon paine of death'.[13] But as James Rattue has usefully pointed out, '[t]he Celtocentrism

[12] Sigs. I2, I3ᵛ.

[13] Robert Steele, *A Bibliography of Royal Proclamations of the Tudor and Stuart Sovereigns* (Oxford: Oxford University Press, 1910), vol. ii, part 1, p. 12, no. 137. In the seventeenth century there was 'a more careful monitoring of the sort of sacred places associated with [Irish] saints. Most commonly these were holy wells. References to such wells, for example, feature prominently in synodal decrees . . . Decisions were taken whereby Catholic secular clergy were given the right to arbitrate on which wells were holy and which superstitious. Bishops were instructed to stop gatherings at unapproved wells and not to authorise any new ones. In extreme cases this might involve proprietorial rights being established as when a well was improved and a wall erected around it by the parish priest who clearly approved of it. For those wells and holy places which were approved the celebrations had to be in line with the devotional and civilized standards expected of Tridentine Catholicism and not follow the traditional practices of pilgrimage, which were seen as profane, riotous affairs,' Raymond Gillespie, *Devoted People: Belief and Religion in Early Modern Ireland* (Manchester: Manchester University Press, 1997), 159. Discussion of Irish holy wells can additionally be found in Michael Carroll, *Irish Pilgrimage: Holy Wells and Popular*

of well-research has left a peculiarly English experience out of the picture',[14] and it is partly for that reason that it is the baths at Buxton in Derbyshire that I want briefly to discuss here, as a historical and social illustration of this transformation of the English landscape in which Spenser locates his Well of Life.

Buxton's mineral springs had been known to the Romans, who named the settlement Aquae Arnemetae, but they were rediscovered in the mid-fifteenth century, and Buxton is one of the few wells for which there is definite evidence of suppression at the Reformation: 'In August 1538 Thomas Cromwell's commissioner Sir William Bassett "lokkyd upp and sealyd the bathys" at the shrine of St Anne of Buxton "that non schall enter to wasche [in] them", and "dyd take away cruchys, schertes, and schetes . . . being thynges thatt dyd alure and intyse the ygnorantt pepull" '.[15] The main source for the history of the bath at Buxton is the treatise published by the physician John Jones in 1572, *The Benefit of the auncient Bathes of Buckstones*, the occasion of which was the refounding of the baths by George Talbot, the Earl of Shrewsbury (sometime keeper of Mary, Queen of Scots, and husband of Bess of Hardwick), who undertook major building work there in the early 1570s:

Ioyning to the cheefe springe, betwene the riuer, and the Bathe, is a very goodly house, foure square, foure stories hye, so well compacte, with houses of office, beneathe and aboue, & round about, with a great chambre, and other goodly lodgings, to the number of. 30: that it is and wilbee a bewty to behold: and very notable for the honorable and worshipfull, that shal neede to repaire thither: as also for other. Yea, the porest shal haue lodgings, & beds hard by, for their vses only. The baths also so brauely beutified with seats round about: defended from the ambient ayre: and chimneys for fyre, to ayre your garmintes in the Bathes syde, and other necessaries: most decent.[16]

Jones' concerns, like Shrewsbury's in his building projects, were practical and medical. His manual is full of advice as to rest, diet, and exercise, so as to maximize the benefits of the mineral baths. Yet he did not overlook more spiritual concerns, concluding his treatise with 'The Prayer vsually to be sayd before Bathing'.[17] The springs at Buxton were to be approached with due reverence and humility, bearing in mind that sickness and affliction might well be God's punishment for sin. As the physician and divine William Turner had written of Bath in the 1560s, 'If God hath smitten you any disease, before ye go to any bath, for ye healing of it, call to youre remembraunce, how oft and

---

Catholic Devotion (Baltimore: Johns Hopkins University Press, 1999), and James Rattue, *The Living Stream: Holy Wells in Historical Context* (Woodbridge: Boydell, 1995).

[14] Rattue, *The Living Stream*, 7.   [15] Walsham, 'Reforming the Waters', 232.

[16] Sig. A2ᵛ. An illustration of Shrewsbury's building is inserted between this and the next page.

[17] Sig. G1–G1ᵛ.

wher in ye haue displeased God'.[18] Such virtue as the waters may possess is a sign of God's blessing and bounty. Jones's dedication to Shrewsbury asserts that 'God, and nature, dyd nothing in vaine', and that 'greate and hidden benefytes' (like medicinal baths) are 'preordinate by prouidence diuine', and many other examples of this are evinced.[19]

To take the waters was an act of intellectual, as much as spiritual faith, and also of patriotism:[20] Jones followed his dedication to Shrewsbury with two commendatory poems, the second of which specifically endorsed Buxton for patriotic reasons:

> Though forein soyle in worthy gifts doth maruelously abound,
> yet England may be bold to bost, wherin the like are found.
> How many vse to bathes abrode far hence with cost to range,
> wherby they may their lothsome lims to helthfull members change
> But such (onlesse they more desire for wil then helth to rome)
> they may haue help with charges lesse and soner, here at home,
> At Buckstones bathes whose vertues here, is lernedly displayd.
> Therfore disdaine not this to read that hath the same bewrayd.[21]

These are sentiments that Spenser would seem to share with regard to his project of an English epic. Yet Buxton, despite its acclamation (together with the other English spas) as the patriotic choice for those English people seeking to take the waters, was periodically tainted with accusations of being a centre for recusancy. This was partly, no doubt, because of its associations with Mary, Queen of Scots, noted in Philemon Holland's translation of Camden's *Britannia* (1610):[22]

[Buxton was] begunne againe to bee resorted unto, by concurse of the greatest gentlemen and of the nobility. At which time that most unfortunate Lady, Mary

---

[18] *A Booke of the natures and properties, as well of the bathes in England as of other bathes in Germanye and Italye, very necessarye for all suche persons that can not be healed without the helpe of natural bathes, lately ouersene and enlarged by William Turner Doctor in Physick* (1568), sig. D2^v.

[19] Jones, *Benefit*, sig. ‡2.

[20] William Turner defended his decision to write about Bath thus: 'Wherefore seynge that I intende to write of the vertues and properties of diuerse bathes that are in far countrees, I thynke that it were mete before I wryte of any Foren bath, for sparing of greate laboure and sauinge of much money, to shewe fyrste the vertues of oure oune bathes. For if they be able to helpe mennis diseases: what shall men nede to go into farre countrees to seke that remedy there, whyche they maye haue at home?', *Booke of the natures and properties*, sig. B1.

[21] ‡4. The poem is by Thomas Lupton, known only by his literary compositions, of which this is the earliest. His *ODNB* biographer notes that he expressed similarly nationalistic sentiments in his commendatory poem for Barnaby Rich's *Alarm to England* (1578). It is likely that Spenser would have known Rich, given the Irish experiences and concerns that they shared; it is therefore not impossible either that Spenser might have known Lupton.

[22] Although not in the 1586 Latin original. The account presumably dates from around the time of the improvements made by Shrewsbury.

Queene of *Scots* bad farewell unto *Buxton* with this *Distichon*, by a little change of *Caesars* verses concerning *Feltria*, in this wise.

> Buxtona *quae calidae celebrabere nominee lymphae,*
> *Forte mihi post hac non adeunda, vale.*
> *Buxton,* that of great name shalt be, for hote and holsome baine,
> Farewell, for I perhaps shall not thee ever see againe.[23]

Buxton also drew the attention of Elizabeth's most notorious agent in the pursuit (and torture) of recusants, Richard Topcliffe, himself a native of Derbyshire. In 1578 Topcliffe wrote to Shrewsbury that

I was so happy laytly, emongs other good graces, that her Majesty did tell me of sundry lewde Popishe beasts that have resorted to Buxtons from these cuntries in the sowthe [where Elizabeth was on progress] synce my Lord did cume from thence: Her Highnes dowbtethe not but yow regard them well enough; emongs whom there is a detestable Popish Preest, one Dyrham, or Durande, as I remember at the bathe, or lurking in those partts after the Ladyes . . . unworthy be they to receve any fruite of God's good blessinge under your Lordship's rewle (as that bathe is) who will not serve God; and shall in that infected place poysone others with Papistrie, and disobedience of her Majesty's lawes.[24]

The Privy Council were periodically concerned about the visits of Catholic priests, and other recusants, to Buxton and the surrounding area throughout the last quarter of the century; this reached a crisis during the Babington Plot of 1586, as Anthony Babington himself had a house in the area, near Matlock, which was to be used as a base, and it was known that other conspirators had arranged to meet at Buxton itself.[25] Yet the suggestion is not that such groups of recusants were drawn to the baths because of their continued status as sites of Catholic pilgrimage, but rather that going to the baths could be an acceptable cover for journeys of other kinds[26] and, by 1587, William Harrison could in general, contrast the wells and springs of England, 'which I impute

---

[23] William Camden, *Britain, or a Chorographicall Description*, trans. Philemon Holland (London, 1610), sig. Aaa.

[24] John Nichols (ed.), *The Progresses and Public Processions of Queen Elizabeth* (London, 1823), ii, 217–18. Helen Hackett discusses Topcliffe's letter, and goes so far as to suggest that ' "going to Buxton" may have been a contemporary euphemism for going to try and see Mary Queen of Scots'. *Virgin Mother, Maiden Queen: Elizabeth I and the Cult of the Virgin Mary* (London: Macmillan, 1996), 4.

[25] Hembry, *The English Spa*, 24.

[26] The exception to this is Holywell, St Winifred's Well in Flintshire, Wales, which appears to have survived the Reformation virtually intact, and to have maintained a continuous tradition of pilgrimage from the Middle Ages until the present day. Holywell was in the late sixteenth century a centre for both pilgrimage and recusant activity, most notably in 1605, when a large number of those involved in the Gunpowder Plot, their families, and Jesuit associates met at Holywell not long before the plot was set in motion. The best account of Holywell in the post-Reformation era is that given by Alexandra Walsham, 'Holywell: Contesting Sacred Space

wholly to the blessing of God, who hath ordained nothing amongst us in this our temperate region but that which is good, wholesome, and most commodious for our nation', with

divers wells which have wrought many miracles in time of superstition . . . but as their virtues are now found out to be but baits to draw men and women unto them, either for gain unto the places where they were or satisfaction of the lewd disposition of such as hunted after other game.

As Almighty God hath in most plentiful manner bestowed infinite and those very notable benefits upon this isle of Britain, whereby it is not a little enriched, so in hot and natural baths (whereof we have divers in sundry places) it manifestly appeareth that He hath not forgotten England. [27]

A similarly patriotic sentiment opens Walter Baley's account of the baths at Newnham Regis, much patronized by Leicester:

The benefits no doubt are great and manifold which almightie God of his large bountie & exceeding goodnes of late yeeres hath plentifully bestowed vppon this little soile of England, since the prosperous reigne of our most gratious Souereigne, wherein the Gospell hath sincerely and freely beene preached . . . Infinite more tokens may particularly be recited, by the which men may iustly gather arguments of Gods well pleased mind with the gouernment of our most gratious Queene; amongst the which the bathes and medicinall waters of late yeeres discouered in sundrie parts of England, are not of least moment.[28]

The connection that Baley makes here between the way in which God's bounty has been made manifest in the physical landscape of England and the propagation of Scripture is a telling one. As Spenser was writing *The Faerie Queene*, healing waters were becoming a sign of God's favour towards the English nation, and an endorsement of Protestantism and the Protestant Queen. Yet they, and their literary avatars—like the landscape of which they were a feature—retained traces of their past.

in Post-Reformation Wales', in Will Coster and Andrew Spicer (eds.), *Sacred Space in Early Modern Europe* (Cambridge: Cambridge University Press, 2005), 211–36. Walsham describes Holywell in the early modern period as 'an emblem of vibrant Tridentine Catholicism . . . a powerful weapon in [missionary priests'] campaign to combat and convert heretics, rouse lapsed Catholics out of their spiritual lethargy . . . a focal point of anti-Protestantism and a nexus with an heroic if spurious past'. I am very grateful to Alex Walsham for allowing me to see a copy of this essay prior to its publication.

[27] William Harrison, *The Description of England*, ed. Georges Edelen (Ithaca, NY: Cornell University Press, 1968), 272, 274, 284.

[28] *A Briefe Discours of certain Bathes or medicinall Waters in the Countie of Wareicke neere vnto a village called Newnham Regis* (London, 1587), sig. A2, A2ᵛ. That Spenser may have known Baley is not impossible; Baley was in the service of the Earl of Leicester and, although Regius Professor at Oxford, he mainly lived in London.

It is to some of these avatars in *The Faerie Queene*, and in particular to the Well of Life, that I now turn. In terms of the ways in which I have been discussing the 'fountains' of Book 1, it is in some respects odd that the Well of Life in canto 11 has attracted so much critical attention and even controversy. For while the earlier fountains (and fountain analogues) of the Book function as nodes of syncretism, drawing on scriptural, exegetical, classical, and romance sources to focus, in their multivalence, issues of interpretation and moral and generic choice, the Well of Life is the ultimate type, the final *telos*, the unifying signifier:

> It fortuned (as fayre it then befell,)
> Behind his backe vnweeting, where he stood,
> Of auncient time there was a springing well,
> From which fast trickled forth a siluer flood,
> Full of great vertues, and for med'cine good.
> Whylome, before that cursed Dragon got
> That happy land, and all with innocent blood
> Defyld those sacred waues, it rightly hot
> *The well of life*, ne yet his vertues had forgot.
>
> For vnto life the dead it could restore,
> And guilt of sinfull crimes cleane wash away,
> Those that with sicknesse were infected sore,
> It could recure, and aged long decay
> Renew, as one were borne that very day.
> Both *Silo* this, and *Iordan* did excell,
> And th'English *Bath*, and eke the german *Spau*,
> Ne can *Cephise*, nor *Hebrus* match this well:
> Into the same the knight backe ouerthrowen, fell. (1.11.29–30)

In his catalogue of other numinous or otherwise well-known springs, all of which the Well of Life overgoes, Spenser implicitly rejects the multiplicity and multivalence hitherto associated with fountains in the Book even as he builds on it. The *Cephise* (Cephisus) is mentioned several times in the *Metamorphoses*, notably at 1.369, when Pyrrha and Deucalion ritually cleanse themselves in its waters before consulting Themis as to how the world should be repeopled after the flood.[29] *Cephise* is therefore associated with both cleansing and creation[30] but in a pagan rather than a Christian context. *Hebrus* invokes

[29] Cephisus the river god was also the father, by his rape of the nymph Liriope, of Narcissus (*Metamorphoses*, 3.342–6). The river could therefore be associated with violent, self-regarding, and ultimately sterile creation, as well as with pagan (and therefore imperfect) cleansing. With reference to the Pyrrha/Deucalion passage, it is perhaps significant that the river's waters are described as 'nondum liquidas'—'not yet clear'.

[30] The Ovidian context is not far distant from the passage describing the 'birth' of the Python: it is less than fifty lines after.

the perils of specifically poetic creation, for it was down the Hebrus that Orpheus' severed head floated after he had been dismembered by the Thracian women: 'The poet's limbs lay scattered all around; but his head and lyre, O Hebrus, thou didst receive, and (a marvel!) while they floated in midstream the lyre gave forth some mournful notes, mournfully the lifeless tongue murmured, mournfully the banks replied'.[31] Worldly concerns—such as those of romance, for example—or at least the ills of the sinful flesh are dismissed with the references to 'th'English *Bath*, and eke the german *Spau*': the Living Well will 'excell' and replace those too. This Well will supersede even the other Gospel waters of *Silo* (Siloam, John 9: 7) and the *Iordan* (Matthew 3: 16).

With reference to the tropes of romance in particular, in his discussion of the dependence of the Legend of Holiness on the Middle English romance of Bevis of Southampton, Andrew King points out that the Well of Life specifically remakes the well into which Bevis falls during his own combat with a dragon. That well has been given healing powers because it has been bathed in by a virgin; it 'belongs to medieval popular religion—faith which sees a sanctity or magical efficacy in physical objects themselves, rather than perceiving the object as merely representational of an abstract quality which can only be arrived at through faith, grace and prayer'.[32] In terms of the way in which this chapter began, Bevis of Southampton's well could be typified by the *ampullae*. But the Well of Life is the 'well of water, springing vp into euerlasting life' promised by Christ to the Samaritan woman in John 4: 14, and again in Revelation 21: 6: 'I wil giue to him yt is a thirst, of the wel of the water of life freely.' Even in the Well of Life, Spenser is remaking romance.

The Well of Life, of John and Revelation, in Spenser's account not only excels but makes redundant all of these types of spiritual cleansing and renewal, the mundane remedies for carnal frailties, and poetic and human creation. For the 'wel of the water of life' in Revelation is itself introduced thus:

And he that sate vpon the throne, sayd, Behold, I make all things newe: and he sayde vnto me, Write, for these wordes are faithfull and true. And he said vnto me, It is done, I am Alpha & Omega, the beginning and the ende. I will giue to him yt is a thirst, of the wel of the water of life freely. (21: 5–6)

In invoking this text, Spenser draws attention to the singularity and unity of the end of Redcrosse's quest, which sweeps away not only the narrative divagations but the intertextual strategies and diversions of the story so far. In his depiction of the Well, Spenser also responds to (and participates in) the metamorphosis of the English landscape from one in which people went on pilgrimage, for

---

[31] Ovid, *Metamorphoses*, 11.50–3.

[32] Andrew King, *The Faerie Queene and Middle English Romance: The Matter of Just Memory* (Oxford: Clarendon Press, 2000), 141.

their souls' health, to holy wells, to one where, more often than not, those very same sites were resorted to for the good of the body (with additional layers of antiquarian interest and national pride for good measure). Yet, as Alexandra Walsham puts it, 'it is necessary . . . to resist the temptation to speak of secularisation. In the guise of healing springs Protestantism preserved, even if it redefined, the concept of a sacralised landscape'.[33] Spenser's fountains, as the previous chapters have shown, can be sites of tension and contestation, at the same time as they promise cleansing and refreshment: as he was writing *The Faerie Queene*, so were the wells and springs of England. The Well of Life is the true fountain both in and outside of the text, at once a corrective to and a replacement for all the debased, parodic, misunderstood, or unrevealed versions that have preceded it.

One such is found in the Book's first canto when, soon after his defeat of Errour, Redcrosse, and Una meet Archimago and join him at his hermitage for the night:

> A litle lowly Hermitage it was,
> Downe in a dale, hard by a forests side,
> Far from resort of people, that did pas
> In traueill to and froe: a litle wyde
> There was an holy chappell edifyde,
> Wherein the Hermite dewly wont to say
> His holy thinges each morne and euentyde:
> Thereby a christall streame did gently play,
> Which from a sacred fountaine welled forth alway. (1.1.34)

This reference to a 'sacred' fountain has puzzled many critics, as it seems closely reminiscent of the Well of Life in the way in which it is described, and therefore difficult to reconcile with the hypocrisy, corruption, and mischief-making of Archimago. Yet in the context of the reading I have been pursuing, it does seem appropriate to look for a theological or spiritual significance for the fountain, given its close association with Archimago and his hermitage. Hamilton notes that the latter is a false hermitage, parodying the true hermitage (and hermit) in canto 10. Archimago's manner of speech ('He told of Saintes and Popes, and euermore | He strowd an *Aue-Mary* after and before', 1.1.35) makes it clear that this is the abode of a Catholic hermit. Such a sacred fountain—a holy well—is merely an expectable ingredient of the set-up, as at Walsingham and countless other shrines and sites of pilgrimage. In terms of the Protestant exegesis and commentary discussed above, however, it is also significant that the 'fountaine' is *outside* both hermitage and chapel. The allegory suggests that the Catholic Church has plenty of 'pleasing words' but no longer engages

---

[33] Walsham, 'Holywell', 236.

with the pure word of God at its source. Instead, it relies on the accretions of ritual (the hermit says 'His holy things each morne and euentyde'), tradition (Archimago's 'Saintes and Popes'—and, presumably, the spiritual efficacy of visiting holy hermits and sacred wells), and sophistical blandishments (Archimago 'well could file his tongue as smooth as glas').[34] Because of his encounter with Errour, Redcrosse is susceptible to the blandishments of false or misleading words and language, at the same time as he is incidentally seduced by the whole 'package' of cultic practices (hermit, holy well); the device of the fountain here makes the two inseparable and even interchangeable. He thus prefers and accepts uncritically Archimago's mediated version of Christian history, rather than seeking it for himself at source.

To return here briefly to John Bale's commentary on Revelation, discussed at length in the previous chapter, it can be seen that Archimago's sacred fountain can stand specifically for the corruption of the Scriptures. Of Revelation 8: 10, Bale writes:

Thys starre fel into the thyrd part of the ryuers, whych are the scriptures peruerted, and into the fountaynes of waters, which are Goods awne uery wordes depraued. These haue the false doctours, yea pernicious heretykes infected with theyr erroures, corrupted with theyr lyes, and with theyr false interpretacions made them bitter and vnsauery . . . These *with* their bitter heresyes and theyr noysome doctryne destroyed the pyttes of Abraham, they trobled the text, thei mixed the trueth *with* falshede, they poysoned the waters, thei toke awaye the louesomenesse of theim, they left them vnpure and vnperfyght (not that they can be so of theim selues, but of theyr false workynge) they made them vnplesaunt, vnprofitable, yea and most perelouse vnto many.[35]

Archimago is a 'false doctour', troubling the text. Spiritual and scriptural truth can never be of itself 'vnpure and vnperfyght', but it can be dishonestly mediated, 'peruerted', and 'depraued'. The Word of God cannot be destroyed, but it can be polluted, corrupted, and hidden, or—as Redcrosse's unquestioning acceptance of Archimago's version of things, while the 'sacred fountaine' stands by, suggests—simply left unrecognized and ignored: in Douglas Waters' neat formulation, it stands 'for the word of God carefully preserved and (from a Protestant angle) "reserved" by the papists'.[36] In a comment that could be applied not only to Redcrosse's stay at the false hermitage but to the Book as a whole, John King identifies his problem as an

inability to grasp the fundamental relationship between *res* and *signa*. By taking words and things as univocal phenomena, he ignores the symbolic or theological dimension

[34] Compare John Bale's vilification of Catholic lies and hypocrisy, quoted in Chapter 6.
[35] Sig. P2–P2ᵛ.
[36] Douglas Waters, 'Errour's Den and Archimago's Hermitage: Symbolic Lust and Symbolic Witchcraft', *English Literary History*, 33 (1966), 287.

by which they may point to concealed spiritual meanings; more importantly, he cannot judge the corresponding power of words and deeds to deceive and confuse . . . Not until he learns that spiritual experience transcends the deceptive world of outward appearances does he finally learn to speak and read.[37]

In his incipient apostasy, Redcrosse therefore reads the first holy well that he encounters (if he reads it at all) as a spiritual end in itself, and not as a dense and compelling theological signifier, one which points (like the healing baths of late sixteenth-century England) through, and beyond, the cultic and thaumaturgic, to the textual and the ideological.

The way in which this false fountain in canto 1 will eventually be corrected by the Well of Life in canto 11 is anticipated by a further pair of related images, the golden cups borne in turn by Duessa and Fidelia. Duessa's cup appears in canto 8, when she is finally revealed as Orgoglio's mistress and as the Whore of Babylon; it materializes when Arthur's Squire joins his lord in the fight against Orgoglio and the seven-headed beast:

> Then tooke the angrie witch her golden cup,
> Which still she bore, replete with magick artes;
> Death and despeyre did many thereof sup,
> And secret poyson through their inner parts,
> Th'eternall bale of heauie wounded harts;
> Which after charmes and some enchauntments said,
> She lightly sprinkled on his weaker partes;
> Therewith his sturdie corage soone was quayd,
> And all his sences were with suddein dread dismayd. (1.8.14)

Like the miracle-working water from holy wells, the contents of Duessa's cup are sprinkled; their effects, however, enervate, rather than heal. The referent in Revelation[38] retrospectively reinforces Duessa's identification with the fountain, via Redcrosse's fornication, in the previous canto, and Hamilton

---

[37] King, *Spenser's Poetry and the Reformation Tradition*, 212–13; see also David Norbrook, *Poetry and Politics in the English Renaissance* (London: Routledge and Kegan Paul, 1984), 111.

[38] 'And the woman was arayed in purple & skarlet, and gilded with golde, and precious stones, and pearles, and had a cup of gold in her hand, ful of abominations, and filthines of her fornication . . . For all nations haue drunken of the wine of the wrath of her fornication, and the kings of the earth haue committed fornication with her,' 17: 4, 18: 3. Bale glosses her cup thus: 'More ouer in her hande which is her exterioure ministracion, she hath a golden cuppe, full of abhominacions and fythynesse of her execrable whoredom. This cuppe is the false relygyon that she daylye mynistreth, besides the chalice whom her merchauntes most damnablye abuseth. And it containeth al doctrine of deuils, all beastly errours and lies, al deceithful poure, all glittering workes of hipocrites, all craftye wisdome of the fleshe, and subtile practyses of mans witte, besydes philosopye, logick, rhetorick, and sophistrye. Yea, al prodigiouse kyndes of Idolatry, fornicacyon, sodometrye, & wickednesse. Outwardlye it semeth golde, pretending the glorye of God, the holye name of Christ, the sacred scriptures of the Byble, perpetuall vyrginite of lyfe, and all are but counterfet colours and shaddowes of hipocrisy in ye outwarde letter and name.

notes that the effects of the contents of the cup, 'sprinkled' upon the Squire, are similarly enervating.[39] Spenser was to employ this image of the poisoned cup again in his discussion of the religious history of Ireland in the *Vewe*:

The generall faulte Comethe not of anie late abuse either in the people or theire priestes who Cane teache no better then they knowe nor shew no more lighte then they haue sene but in the firste Institucion and plantinge of religion in all that realme . . . what other Coulde they learne then suche trashe as was taughte them And drinke of that Cupp of fornicacion with which the purple Harlott had then made all nacions drunken . . . since they drunke not from the pure springe of life but onelye tasted of suche trobled waters as weare broughte vnto them the druggs thereof haue bred greate Contagion in theire Soules the which dailye encreasinge And beinge still Augmented with theire owne lewde lives and filthie Conuersacion hathe now bred in them the generall disease that Cannot but onelye with verye strong purgacions be Clensed and Carryed awaie . . .[40]

This is reminiscent of Topcliffe's splenetic condemnation of Buxton as an 'infected place'. In 1597 John Dixon, the poem's first known reader, similarly glossed the cup as being 'filled with false doctrine and blasphemies'.[41] But with the revelation of Arthur's adamantine shield, Duessa's cup itself becomes ineffectual. She throws it to the ground (1.8.25) and tries to run away. At the House of Holinesse, however, Fidelia offers a further alternative: 'And in her right hand bore a cup of gold, | With wine and water fild vp to the hight, | In which a Serpent did himselfe enfold' (1.10.13). As Hamilton notes, this cup holds 'the healing blood and baptismal water that issued from the side of the crucified Christ; see John 19: 34 and 1 John 5: 6. According to the Geneva gloss, water and blood "declare that we have our sinnes washed by him, and he hathe made ful satisfaction for the same".' Fidelia's cup thus also prefigures the Well of Life and the balm from the Tree of Life.[42] The two opposed cups, therefore, replicate in miniature the opposition between the true and the corrupted fountain that underlies the structure of Book 1, as Redcrosse journeys from Errour to the Well of Life. There is perhaps a third element

Full of abhominacions is the drinke of ye execrable faith of that Romishe religion receiued of other, and full of fylthinesse also,' sig. R3ᵛ.

[39] As does Schroeder, 'Spenser's Erotic Drama', 140–59.

[40] Edmund Spenser, *A View of the Present State of Ireland*, ed. Rudolph Gottfried, in Edwin Greenlaw et al., *A Variorum Edition of the Works of Edmund Spenser* (Baltimore: Johns Hopkins University Press, 1932–49), x. 137–8. I am grateful to Andrew Zurcher for locating this reference.

[41] Graham Hough, *The First Commentary on The Faerie Queene* (privately published, 1964), 6.

[42] See below. The Serpent in the cup alludes to the traditional iconography of St John the Evangelist, further evidence of the importance of the Gospel of John—and here, it would seem, the Epistles of John—as well as Revelation for an understanding of Book 1. There is a version of the story of John's resistance to poison in *The Golden Legend*. If the wine and the water in the cup are interpreted also as referring specifically to the Eucharistic chalice, then there is a further anticipation of the operation of 'Balme' as an antidote to poison.

to this pattern of cups, the water jug dropped by Abessa in 1.3. Kathryn Walls has shown that the medieval figure of Synagoga, on whom Spenser draws, is sometimes shown with a broken or upturned chalice.[43] In this case, the pattern of cups or drinking vessels in Book 1 encompasses the old law of the Synagogue (Abessa's jug), the poisoned, corrupting cup of Duessa and the Catholic Church, and the new wine of Fidelia, the Protestant Ecclesia in the House of Holinesse.

When Redcrosse finally learns to read properly, at the House of Holinesse, after his disastrous career as a romance hero and his near destruction by the verbal wiles of Despayre,[44] it is from 'a booke, that was both signd and seald with blood, | Wherein darke things were writt, hard to be vnderstood' (1.10.13). As has been seen, in the exegetical tradition which may have influenced Spenser, as well as in the Bible itself, the Word of God is frequently depicted as a fountain. Here, that Word is implicitly written in the blood of Christ's sacrifice, and so an essentially Protestant connection is made between the Word and the Sacrament, a connection that anticipates the inseparable nature of the Well and the Tree, the water and the balm, baptism and the Eucharist and the Word of God in canto 11.[45] That the context here is explicitly educational encourages the recollection, once again, of *Veritas Temporis Filia* and the gift of the English Bible to Elizabeth, via Spenser's own teacher Richard Mulcaster. A parody of Mulcaster's pageant, in the figure of Errour, has undone Redcrosse, and a positive recapitulation of its ideology and symbolism begins his rehabilitation.

As, during his education in the House of Holinesse, Redcrosse becomes all too aware of his fallen nature, he is himself compared to a blocked and poisoned vessel; in a similar fashion to the way in which the Book's landscape enacts a transition from Catholic miracle-working holy well to providential, sacramental English Protestant healing bath, his own body thus enacts the analogous fountain metaphor of his spiritual transformation:

> But yet the cause and root of all his ill,
> Inward corruption, and infected sin,

---

[43] Walls, 'Abessa and the Lion', 11. This episode is discussed in more detail in Chapter 6.

[44] See the discussion of Despayre by Ann E. Imbrie, ' "Playing Legerdemaine with the Scripture": Parodic Sermons in *The Faerie Queene*', *English Literary Renaissance*, 17 (1987), *passim*.

[45] As John N. King points out, 'Fidelia's carrying of a Bible or New Testament is closely tied to queenly iconography. Although symbolic books also appear in medieval and Renaissance images of saints and other pious women, they were closely linked to Elizabeth as a Protestant queen.' *Spenser's Poetry and the Reformation Tradition*, 131. King also notes (pp. 143–5) the recollection here of Elizabeth's response to the gift of the English Bible in *Veritas Temporis Filia*, as well as the depiction of Faith on the title page of the 1568 Bishop's Bible carrying an open book; Elizabeth herself was also shown.

> Not purg'd nor heald, behind remained still,
> And festring sore did rankle yett within,
> Close creeping twixt the marow and the skin. (1.10.25)

This is finally remedied by his penitence:

> And bitter *Penaunce* with an yron whip,
> Was wont him once to disple euery day:
> And sharpe *Remorse* his hart did prick and nip,
> That drops of bloud thence like a well did play;
> And sad *Repentance* vsed to embay,
> His blamefull body in salt water sore,
> The filthy blottes of sin to wash away.
> So in short space they did to health restore
> The man that would not liue, but erst lay at deathes dore. (1.10.27)

Fittingly, Redcrosse's penitence is partly expressed in terms of the restoration of flow, and of cleansing, reinforced here by the enjambement of the last two lines of stanza 27.[46] Blood is drawn from his own heart—'And sharpe *Remorse* his hart did pricke and nip, | That drops of bloud thence like a well did play'—and he is washed in his own tears: 'And sad *Repentance* vsed to embay, | His bodie in salt water smarting sore, | The filthy blots of sinne to wash away.' Spenser perhaps recalls or even borrows directly here from *Everyman*, in which the protagonist greets the figure of Confession at the House of Salvation as 'O gloryous fountayne y^t all vnclennes doth clarify | Washe from me the spottes of vyces vnclene | That on me no synne may be sene'.[47] There is a further suggestive parallel with the portrayal of Penitence in Cesare Ripa's *Iconologia* (1603, and later editions), and its elaboration by Henry Peacham in *Minerva Britanna* (1612): Ripa's Repentance (Penitentia/Penitenza) is depicted as holding a fish and a scourge (fasting and self-mortification), but the accompanying text (which Peacham illustrates more fully) makes clear that she can be further shown in a soiled dress (baptismal innocence, contaminated by guilt), seated on a rock (Christ), and contemplating a fountain, which is at once the means by which she may literally reflect upon her guilt, and Christ's healing grace.[48] The 1588 inventory of the Earl of Leicester's pictures at Kenilworth includes

---

[46] There is also, perhaps, a recollection of the passage from *Phaedrus* 251 discussed in relation to the *Hypnerotomachia* in Chapter 3, albeit in Christian rather than erotic terms.

[47] *Here begynneth a treatyse how the hye fader of heuen sendeth dethe to somon euery creature to come and gyue a counte of theyr lyues in this worlde and is in maner of a morall playe* (London, 1535) [*Everyman*], sig. B4^v.

[48] See Clifford Davidson, 'Repentance and the Fountain: The Transformation of Symbols in English Emblem Books', in Michael Bath, John Manning, and Alan R. Young (eds.), *The Art of the Emblem: Essays in Honor of Karl Josef Höltgen* (New York: AMS Press, 1993), *passim*. There is no analogue in the emblem books of either Andrea Alciati or Geoffrey Whitney, which clearly influenced Spenser. Davidson notes the fountain image in *Everyman*, but does not link

'the picture of Occasion and Repentance';[49] that Spenser might have known some pictorial version of the figure is far from impossible. In *The Faerie Queene*, Repentance and Remorse turn Redcrosse himself into a fountain, as his sins are expiated by his own blood and tears.

Redcrosse is taught to read, cleansed within and without, properly initiated into the responsibilities of Christian community,[50] and, finally, allowed the sight of the New Jerusalem from the Mount of Contemplation (1.10.53 f.). The connection that Redcrosse makes between the New Jerusalem and Cleopolis and London, as well as the implicit relationship between his tears and blood, the redemptive Water and Blood of Christ's sacrifice, and the Well and the Tree and their effects, suggests the maxim that the kingdom of God is within you: it is the knowledge of self that leads to the transformation of the world at large. It is therefore significant that Redcrosse is named at this point, and brought, through the 'georgos' etymology,[51] and the revelation that he has been brought up by a ploughman (which in turn links him with the proto-Protestant tradition of Langland and pseudo-Chaucer),[52] into a close and symbiotic relationship with his physical environment. His body *is* England, its soil blessed anew by God, and watered with the living waters of the Word; he can experience the blessings and benefits of the Well of Life—as England can enjoy its new-found healing waters—because he has kept the faith.

Much of the critical attention given to the Well of Life has focused on its sacramental implications and therefore its evidence of Spenser's own religious beliefs. Most critics interpret the Well as baptism and the Tree of Life (and the 'trickling streame of Balme' which flows from it 'as from a well') as the Eucharist.[53] While the latter is not as obvious an analogy as the straightforward

it explicitly with the House of Holinesse; he does, however, point out the description of the Eucharist as 'fontem misericordiae'(fountain of mercy) in one of the prayers before communion included in the Sarum Missal, 11.

[49] William J. Thoms, 'Pictures of the Great Earl of Leicester', *Notes and Queries*, 3rd ser. 2, (6 Sept. 1862), 201.

[50] Compare the industry and care for humanity in general at the House of Holinesse and the 'holy Hospitall' (1.10.36) with Archimago's hermitage in 1.1.34, which is 'Far from resort of people, that did pas | In traueill to and froe'.

[51] On the importance of georgic and georgic metaphors to Renaissance educational practices and treatises, see Andrew Wallace, ' "Noursled Up in Life and Manners Wilde": Spenser's Georgic Education', *Spenser Studies*, 19 (2004), 65–92, and Mary Thomas Crane, *Framing Authority: Sayings, Self, and Society in Sixteenth-Century England* (Princeton: Princeton University Press, 1993).

[52] See Norbrook, *Poetry and Politics*, 121, and the essays on *The Plowman's Tale* and Langland in Hamilton (ed.), *Spenser Encyclopedia*.

[53] Harold Weatherby reads the Well of Life as the water of baptism and the balm as the chrism oil used for anointing in baptism, drawing on sources in the Greek liturgy. Although he argues his position forcefully, and makes some interesting use of the St George legends, it remains unconvincing, largely because of the obscurity of the texts upon which his argument

water–baptism equation of the Well of Life, the reasons for drawing it are compelling, and once drawn, it reveals the Tree—in relation to the Well, and to the Book as a whole—as being far richer and more complex than might at first be supposed. For in Spenser's scheme baptism and the Well cannot be separated from the Tree, the balm, and the Eucharist. Both Well and Tree are, in turn, inseparable from a Protestant understanding of the Word of God, and together affirm the importance of understanding and engaging with the Scriptures in the Christian life and mission.

Little interpretative ingenuity is needed to link the Well with baptism. It is associated with rebirth: 'It could recure, and aged long decay | Renew, as one were borne that very day' (1.11.30); 'So new this new-borne knight to battell new did rise' (1.11.34);[54] most explicitly, 'his baptized hands now greater grew' (1.11.36). Hamilton and others note the symbolism of the eagle ('he vpstarted braue | Out of the well, wherein he drenched lay; | As Eagle fresh out of the ocean waue', 1.11.34) in terms of Isaiah 40: 31 and Psalm 103: 4–5, in both of which (as in natural history lore) the eagle is a figure of renewal. In the context of Book 1, however, the eagle also invokes the association with the Gospel of John, being the symbol of the Evangelist as the bird that can fly highest and see furthest. This fits well with the Book's concern with Redcrosse's abilities as a reader, as well as with the importance of this particular Gospel for the Book as a whole. Redcrosse's fall into the Well of Life re-enacts his baptism, and does so implicitly in terms of the profoundly textual nature of the Protestant understanding of baptism.[55] As Thomas M. Dughi puts it,

Book 1's narrative shape and method are rooted in basic Protestant insights into *how* God's Word works its transforming magic. And canto 11's refreshing falls represent

depends. See Harold L. Weatherby, *Mirrors of Celestial Grace: Patristic Theology in Spenser's Allegory* (Toronto: University of Toronto Press, 1994) and 'The True Saint George', *English Literary Renaissance*, 17 (1987). In addition, it is difficult to see why Spenser, whether Puritan or Anglican (but almost certainly not Catholic in his affiliation or sympathies), would represent anything other than the two sacraments retained by the Church of England, baptism and the Eucharist. They were interpreted as such by Ben Jonson in a note in the margin of his copy of *The Faerie Queene*, and there is no reason, despite his own changing religious affiliations, to assume that his interpretation might have been atypical. See James Riddell and Stanley Stewart, *Jonson's Spenser: Evidence and Historical Criticism* (Pittsburgh: Duquesne University Press, 1995), 167. My own discussion of the Well and the Tree has been informed by Gless, *Interpretation and Theology in Spenser*, although I differ from him on some points.

[54] As I was reminded by an anonymous reader, this is imitated by Shakespeare in the description of Prince Hal before the battle of Shrewsbury: 'All furnished, all in arms, | All plumed like ostriches, that with the wind | Bated like eagles having lately bathed', *King Henry IV Part I*, ed. David Scott Kastan, The Arden Shakespeare: Third Series (London: Thomson Learning, 2002), 4.1.96–8.

[55] See the discussion in Chapter 6. The best resolution of any remaining tension between the interpretation of the Well of Life as the sacrament of baptism and as the Word of God can be found, once again, in Erasmus' *Enchiridion*, in the passages discussed in the previous chapter.

the end result of this process: when Redcrosse knight falls, *he falls almost literally into God's Word*; what the reader sees are scenes that figure the working of the Word as it generates—and regenerates—faith within the soul of the righteous man.[56]

His fall into the Well reaffirms Redcrosse's commitment to Christian knighthood. Some critics (notably Rosamund Tuve) have objected that in order to wear the armour of the Christian knight in the first place Redcrosse must have already been baptized and, since it is not possible to be baptized twice, the fall into the Well must represent something else. But this is surely to overemphasize verisimilitude in the interpretation of the allegory. Redcrosse may be an Everyman figure, but he is not an Elizabethan parishioner, and the overt baptismal language and symbolism can simply be seen as demonstrating the knight's renewed commitment to (and, perhaps even more importantly, his increased understanding of) his Christian mission.[57] As Erasmus' once again usefully observes, in his *Paraphrase on Mark*, 'Earth does not suddenly become air; water forms the intermediate stage—it is gradually thinned out into the lighter element'.[58] The earthy, earthly Redcrosse, George, must pass through water before he too can soar like the Johannine eagle, the waters of baptism that are also the waters of Christ's death and Resurrection.

For the Well of Life and the Tree of Life, the water and the balm, cannot be separated because they invoke, as types of baptism and the Eucharist, the water and the blood which flowed from Christ's side at the Crucifixion:[59] 'But one of the souldiers with a speare pearced his side, and foorthwith came there out blood and water' (John 19: 34). With admirable understatement, James Nohrnberg suggests that '[a] certain density seems to have been sought in these symbols: the tree itself is compared to a well, and the waters of the well are said to have become mingled with blood. In either case we are reminded of

---

[56] My emphasis. Thomas A. Dughi, 'Redcrosse's "Springing Well" of Scriptural Faith', *Studies in English Literature*, 37 (1997), 22–3. Dughi also refers to some of the texts (the *Homilies*, for example) which use well or fountain imagery to describe the Scriptures.

[57] 'For a Christian of Spenser's time the word baptism was available and its use prudent. In the 1590s the language stemming from Catholic mysticism carried apparent political dangers: it seemed safer to signify the mystical import of tacit awareness by metaphorizing on scriptural precedent one of the two sacraments still observed by both old and new forms of the Christian religion . . . William Perkins, a Calvinistic English Protestant, could use it in Spenser's day to convey the sense of a radical change of consciousness, spiritually repeatable even if the ritual baptism by water must be enjoyed once only in the life of the individual.' Elizabeth Bieman, *Plato Baptized: Towards the Interpretation of Spenser's Mimetic Fictions* (Toronto: University of Toronto Press, 1988), 144–5.

[58] Desiderius Erasmus', *Paraphrase on Mark*, trans. Erika Rummel (Toronto: University of Toronto Press, 1988), Mark 1.21, p. 21. As Rummel points out, this is clearly influenced by the *Timaeus*, 49.

[59] This interpretation is one of the reasons why I see the Gospel of John, with its particularly pervasive water imagery, as being especially important to the structure and imagery of Book 1. The incident does not appear in the synoptic Gospels.

the sacramental flow from Christ's side'.[60] Spenser's description of the Tree's balm as 'ouerflow[ing] all the fertill plaine, | As it had deawed bene with timely raine' clearly recalls the manna which sustained the Israelites in Exodus 16, another type of the Eucharist:

Then sayd the Lord vnto Moses, Behold, I wil cause bread to rayne from heauen to you, & the people shal goe out, and gather that that is sufficient for euery day, that I may proue them, whether they wil walke in my Law or no.

And so at euen the quailes came and couered the campe: and in the morning the dewe lay round about the hoste. And when the dewe that was fallen was ascended, beholde, a small round thing was vpon the face of the wildernes, small as the hoare frost on the earth. And when the children of Israel sawe it, they sayde one to another, It is MAN, for they wist not what it was. And Moses sayd vnto them, This is the breade which the Lorde has giuen you to eate. (16: 4, 13–15)

As baptism is prefigured by Moses striking the water from the rock of Horeb, so Christ's stricken Body becomes the Rock of 1 Corinthians 10: 3–4,[61] and his healing blood fulfils the promise of the manna.

Spenser's depiction of the Tree of Life and its balm in specifically Eucharistic and Johannine terms additionally invokes the tradition that the Cross stood in the same place as the Edenic Tree of Life.[62] There is a detailed and suggestive version of the tradition in 'The lyfe of Adam' in *The Golden Legend*:

And in the ende of his lyfe when he sholde deye (it is sayde) but of none auctoryte *that* he sende Seth his sone into Paradyse for to fetche the oyle of mercy/where he receyued certayne granes of the fruyte of ye tree of mercy by an angell. And whan he came agayne/he founde his fader Adam yet alyue/& tolde hym what he had done. And than Adam laughed fyrst and than dyed. And than he layde ye graynes or kernelles vnder his faders tongue and buryed hym in the vale of Ebron and oute of his mouthe grewe thre trees of the thre graynes/of whiche the Crosse that our lorde suffered his passyon on was made.[63]

Like the Well of Life and the fountain at Archimago's hermitage (as well as the other parodic or debased fountains of the Book), and indeed the newly discovered or reinvented healing waters of Protestant England in relation to

[60] James Nohrnberg, *The Analogy of The Faerie Queene* (Princeton: Princeton University Press, 1976), 170.

[61] 'And did all eat the same spiritual meat, And did all drinke the same spirituall drinke (for they dranke of the spiritual Rocke that folowed them: and the Rocke was Christ).'

[62] This tradition is discussed in passing by Åke Bergvall, 'Between Eusebius and Augustine: Una and the Cult of Elizabeth', *English Literary Renaissance*, 27 (1997); it is seen, for example, in John Donne's 'Hymne to God my God, in my sicknesse': 'We think that Paradise and Calvary, | Christ's Cross, and Adam's tree, stood in one place; | Look Lord, and find both Adams met in me', lines 21–3, John Donne, *The Major Works*, ed. John Carey (Oxford: Oxford University Press, 1990), 332.

[63] Sig. A4ᵛ.

Figure 1. Amant at the
Fountain of Narcissus, from a
1531 Paris edition of the
Roman de la Rose in the
Cambridge University
Library.

Figure 2. The Fountain of
the Sleeping Nymph: 'The
Mother of All'.
Hypnerotomachia Poliphili
(Venice, 1499), e1. *Photo:
Cambridge University Library.*

ΠΑΝΤΩΝ ΤΟΚΑΔΙ

Per laquale cosa io non saperei definire, sila diuturna & tanta acre se-
te pridiana tolerata ad bere trahendo me prouocasse, ouero il bellissimo
suscitabulo dello instruméto. La frigiditate dil quale, inditio mi dede che
la petra mentiua. Circuncirca dunque di questo placido loco, & per gli
loquaci riuuli fioriuano il Vaticinio, Lilii conuallii, & la floréte Lysima
chia, & il odoroso Calamo, & la Cedouaria, Apio, & hydrolapato, & di
assai altre appretiate herbe aquicole & nobili fiori, Et il canaliculo poscia
e

ΓΕΛΟΙΑΣΤΟΣ

cogitato, Che ponēdo fopra el grado imo iftabile, pondo alcuno, in giu
el femoueua, & in fu traheua lo iftrumēto puerile. Onde cū fubtile exami
ne inueftigato la machina & curiofo artificio, mi fue molto gratiffimo
Et pero nel Zophorulo era infcripto elegante di Atthice formule quefto
titulo. ΓΕΛΟΙΑΣΤΟΣ.

Doppo molto iocofo rifo balneati, & lauatone tutti, cū mille & dolce
amorofe & piaceuole parolette, & uirginali fcherci & blādimēti. Fora del
le thermate aq̄ ufciffimo, faliēdo fopra li affueti gradi cū grāde tripudio &
fefta oue feunxéo cū gli fragrāti odorāti diafpafmatici, & cū myriftico
liquore oblite, ad me ācora offeriteno una buffula & unxime. Diche affai

Figure 3. The 'Trickster' fountain, which drenches Poliphilus as he bathes with the
nymphs of the five senses. *Hypnerotomachia Poliphili* (Venice, 1499), e7. *Photo: Cambridge
University Library.*

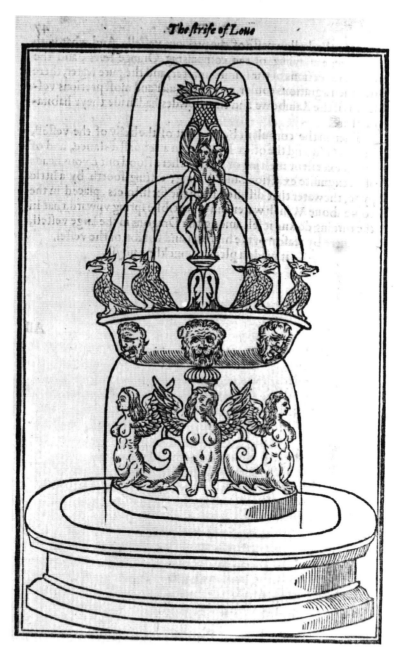

Figure 4. The fountain in the first court of the place of Queen Eleuterylida. Robert Dallington, *Hypnerotomachia: The Strife of Love in a Dreame* (London, 1592), N3ᵛ. *Photo: British Library Reproductions.*

Ilquale ſtylo fermamente infixo uno conſpicuo uaſo di Topacio ſu-
ſteniua, di antiquaria forma, la corpulentia ima del quale era lata, cum tu-
midule ſcindule cincto nell'apertura mirificamente di una coronicetta,
ſotto laquale era una faſciola iclauſtrata d'un'altra ſubiecta. Nellaq̃le liga-
tura, in quatro æquale diuiſione, appacti erano q̃tro alati capituli di pue
rulo cũ q̃tro ſtilláti ſipunculi negli labri. Da poſcia il reſiduo ſi acumina
ua dua táto, q̃to la ima corpulétia, in una obturatióe ſopra l'orificio di una

Figure 5. The fountain on wheels which is brought in at the end of the banquet at
the palace of Queen Eleuterylida, which sprinkles perfume. *Hypnerotomachia Poliphili*
(Venice, 1499), g6. *Photo: Cambridge University Library.*

Figure 6. Poliphilus extinguishes Polia's torch in the sacred well in the Temple of Venus. The priestess wears a mitre and veil; Polia is to her left. *Hypnerotomachia Poliphili* (Venice, 1499), o1. *Photo: Cambridge University Library.*

Figure 7. The Fountain of Adonis and its garden setting. *Hypnerotomachia Poliphili* (Venice, 1499), z7. *Photo: Cambridge University Library.*

Figure 8. The Fountain of Adonis: Polia prepares to tell her story to Poliphilus and the nymphs, at the end of Book 1. *Hypnerotomachia Poliphili* (Venice, 1499), z9ᵛ. *Photo: Cambridge University Library.*

Figure 9. The Fountain of Adonis: Venus and Cupid, and the death of Adonis. *Hypneroto-machia Poliphili* (Venice, 1499), z8. *Photo: Cambridge University Library.*

Figure 10. A Canterbury *ampulla*. *Photo: Anna Cook.*

Figure 11. A Tudor hat badge from a London workshop, *c.*1520–40. *Photo: British Museum.*

The Foūtaynē

oꝛ well of lyfe / out of whiche doth
ſpꝛinge moſt ſwete cōſolatiōs / right
neceſſary foꝛ troubled cōſciences / to then
tent ý they ſhall nat deſpeyꝛe in aduerſite
and trouble. Tranſlated out of latyn
in to Englyſſhe.

Figure 12. The Fountayne or Well of Lyfe (1532). Photo: Cambridge University Library.

Figure 13. Portrait medal of Elizabeth I by Stephen van Herwijk (1565): 'The Divine Fountain of the Realm', *Photo: National Portrait Gallery*, London.

Figure 14. Portrait of a man of the Delves family (Sir George Delves) (1577). *Photo: Walker Art Gallery, National Museums Liverpool.*

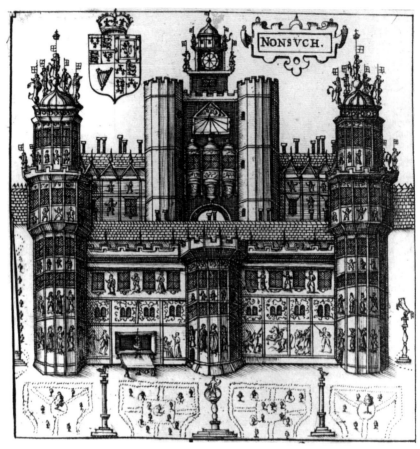

Figure 15. Nonsuch Palace: a view of the Privy Garden. The first Diana fountain (Fig. 16) is in the centre of the foreground; it is flanked by the two 'Falcon Perches', pillars surmounted by Lumley's device of the popinjay or parrot. Another pillar bearing the White Horse badge of Arundel can be seen to the right of the palace, and another fountain, the 'Pelican Bowl' (Fig. 18), is at the front of the building on the left. From John Speed's map of Surrey, in the *Theatre of the Empire of Great Britain* (1611–12). *Photo: Cambridge University Library.*

Figure 16. The Diana Fountain at Nonsuch, from the Lumley Inventory, showing both the crescent moon in the figure's hair and the Lumley crest, with its three 'popinjays', on the basin. See also Fig. 15. *Photo: National Portrait Gallery*, London.

Figure 17. The Imperial Diana Fountain, from the Lumley Inventory, clearly showing the crescent moon on the top of the imperial crown. The precise location of this fountain is uncertain. *Photo: National Portrait Gallery*, London.

Figure 18. The Pelican Bowl at Nonsuch, from the Lumley Inventory; it is shown here with a marble table, on which it may have stood. See Fig. 15. *Photo: National Portrait Gallery*, London.

Figure 19. Design for the Fountain of Imperial Justice at Hampton Court, *c.*1590, by Cornelius Cure. *Photo: Hatfield House.*

the old holy wells, the Tree of Life therefore 'corrects' the trees that have gone before it: the trees, actual and literary, where Redcrosse and Una lost their way, and the two groves, of Fradubio and Fraelissa and of the fountain in canto 7, where Redcrosse made bad interpretative and moral choices. In keeping with this corrective pattern, the 'trickling streame of Balme' which runs from the Tree of Life in canto 11 similarly replaces the 'sweet slombring deaw' of sleep which earlier assailed Redcrosse and Una in Archimago's hermitage and the 'trickling stream from high rocke tumbling downe' that lulls Morpheus. The balm that rejuvenates Redcrosse is elided with his healing sleep, as he lies 'as in a dreame of deepe delight, | Besmeard with pretious Balme' (1.11.50). As healing ointment, the balm from the Tree redresses the damage done to Fradubio by Duessa when she, 'drownd in sleepie night, | With wicked herbes and oyntments did besmeare | My body all' (1.2.42). Fradubio is the old Adam imprisoned by his own carnal nature, and hence a type of Redcrosse, and his Adamite nature is emphasized when Redcrosse attempts to heal his wound by closing it 'with fresh clay' (1.2.44). Christ is the second Adam, whose sacrifice redeems the old, and 'Balme' connotes the healing and restorative powers of the Eucharist. If Spenser is indeed referring to *The Golden Legend* here, the point made is that Christ's sacrifice (and specifically his healing blood) replaces or at least fulfils the notional oil of mercy from the Tree of Life. This is entirely in keeping with Spenser's teleological scheme for the end of the Book: as well as liberating Eden and Una's parents (Adam and Eve), Redcrosse also overcomes the 'old Adam' of his carnal nature. For Barnabe Barnes, writing in 1595, Christ's wounds were specifically Eucharistic—'O blessed sweete wounds fountaines of electre, | My wounded soules balme, and saluations nectre'—but they were also an 'Antidote' to the sins of 'our old wretched father Adam',[64] recalling both the service of public baptism in the Elizabethan Prayer Book—'O mercifull God, grant that the old Adam in these children may be so buried, that the new man may be raised up in them'[65]—and Erasmus' emphasis on the invocation of both the Eucharist and baptism in his paraphrase on John 19: 34. As the Tree and the Well, the water and the balm, are interlinked in their narrative and symbolic functions, so baptism and the Eucharist are presented, in Spenser's Johannine, Erasmian, and Calvinist schema, as inseparable.

---

[64] Barnes (c.1571–1609) is best known for his sonnet sequence *Parthenophil to Parthenope* (1593); he employs similar imagery at several other points in his *Centurie of Divine Sonnets*, from which this is taken.

[65] Hamilton usefully glosses stanza 34 ('So new this new-borne knight to battell new did rise') with reference to the private baptism service in the first Edwardine Prayer Book (1542): 'Graunte that the olde Adam, in them that shalbe baptized in this fountayne, maye so be buried, that the newe man may be raised up agayne.'

The two sacraments (baptism and the Eucharist) identified with the blood and water which flowed from Christ's pierced side, which Spenser expressed in the Well and the Tree of Life, are additionally inseparable from each other because they are both inextricable from the Word of God. In Erasmus' *Paraphrase*, the flow from Christ's side is described as 'making plain in a great mystery that his death would wash us from sin and that it also would bestow on us eternal life'; this makes explicit the connection with the Living Water of John 4, and indeed the Word of John 1. Pre-Reformation English Catholics had been encouraged to meditate on Christ's wounds as wells of comfort, mercy, and grace,[66] but some Protestant devotional practices reconfigured the wounds as specifically baptismal, Eucharistic—and textual. *The Fountayne or Well of Lyfe* (1532) has on its cover a depiction of Christ in a font or fountain that clearly draws on the *imago pietatis* tradition (Fig. 12), yet it is not an affective aid to meditation, but rather a collection of biblical extracts, in English, perhaps intended as a spiritual preparation for the taking of communion.[67] At the very beginning of the *Institutes*, Calvin similarly uses the image of the fountain to describe the goodness of God: 'those blessings which unceasingly distil to us from heaven, are like streams conducting us to the fountain' (1.1.1). For Calvin, as for Spenser, the fountain stands for the ultimate and transcendent source of goodness and truth, and it is a central image in his Eucharistic theology in particular.[68] In Calvin's *Commentary on John*, the image of God as a fountain is further utilized to describe the relationship between Father and Son and the operation of the Son, as the Word, in the world:

[66] See Eamon Duffy's discussion of the cult of the wounds, 'one of the most important and far-reaching in late medieval England, [which] found expression not only in the *Horae* [Books of Hours] but in countless vernacular sermons, prayers, and verses', in *The Stripping of the Altars: Traditional Religion in England c.1400—c.1580* (New Haven: Yale University Press, 1992), 245 and *passim*. Duffy particularly notes the mid-fifteenth-century 'Coventry Ring', which depicts the instruments of the Passion and five mandorla-shaped wounds, labelled as 'the well of comfort', 'the well of grace', 'the well of merci', 'the well of pitty', and (the side-wound) 'the well of everlasting lyffe'; the ring is inscribed with the motto 'vulnera quinque dei sunt medicina mei' (the five wounds of God are my medicine). The Coventry Ring could be usefully seen as a point of transition from the medieval *ampullae* to the Johannine Tudor hat badges which I discussed at the beginning of this chapter. It is also discussed by Gabriele Finaldi in *The Image of Christ* (London: National Gallery Company Limited, 2000), 162–3.

[67] *The Fountayne of Lyfe* is discussed by Davidson, 'Repentance and the Fountain', 13. The *imago pietatis* depicts Christ standing upright in his tomb, which is represented as a square or rectangular Roman sarcophagus and therefore strongly resembles the basin of a fountain (see the discussion of this fountain type in relation to the *Hypnerotomachia*'s Fountain of Adonis in Chapters 3 and 4, above); he is often surrounded by the instruments of the Passion, or is otherwise drawing attention to his wounds.

[68] See B. A. Gerrish, *Grace and Gratitude: The Eucharistic Theology of John Calvin* (Edinburgh: T. & T. Clark, 1993).

It should be noted that three stages of life (*vitae gradus*) are counted here. The living Father occupies the first place: he is the wellspring (*scaturigo*), but distant and concealed. The Son is next: in him we have, as it were, a fountain that is open to us (*fontem nobis expositum*), and through which life is poured to us. Third is the life we draw from him . . . For as the eternal Word of God is the fountain of life (*fons vitae*), so his flesh, like a channel, pours out to us the life that resides intrinsically (as they say) in his deity.[69]

This example of Calvin's Eucharistic theology is a useful and suggestive parallel to the relationship that Spenser constructs between the Word and the sacraments in the figures of the Tree, the balm, and the Well of Life. The water of baptism in the Well of Life renews Redcrosse's Christian commitment and identity, and the Eucharistic balm of the Tree of Life heals and sustains him: both water and balm are additionally the Word of God, the fountain which Redcrosse has finally learnt how to read.

This interconnectedness gives final illumination to the pattern of fountain and well imagery traced throughout Book 1 in this chapter and the two which precede it. The Well and the Tree are the ultimate corrective to Errour,[70] as Christ is the fulfilment (here particularly revealed through the matrix of John and Revelation) of springs and manna in the wilderness, as the Water and Bread of Life. Redcrosse's final, successful encounters with the Well and the balm, and hence with the dragon, at once demonstrate and affirm his assumption (or resumption) of his true baptismal identity as reader and knight and the end of his quest through a landscape in which fountains have been complex and vital, if sometimes ambivalent and unstable, signifiers. In some respects, Well and Tree would not be out of place in the numinous, providentialist, Reformed landscape of late Elizabethan England. They are signs of God's grace and favour to Redcrosse as an Englishman as much as an Everyman; he has approached them in the right spirit of prayerful humility, and they have healed him in body, mind, and spirit. His misguided romance aspirations in the Book's beginning summoned Errour, but the Well and the Tree appear because he has truly believed. As scriptural *teloi* the Well and the balm remake in final, perfected, Christological terms the typological history of humanity; as sacraments they are visible signs of a verbal reality that make and reinforce personal, community, and even national identity. Redcrosse, St George, *georgos* represents in his body the very earth of England. His saturation in the true Word of God evokes Walter Baley's employment of a familiar biblical text in his account of the baths at Newnham Regis:

---

[69] *Commentary on John*, 6: 51, 57, ibid. 132.

[70] The cannibal behaviour of Errour's children can be seen as a parody of the pelican in her piety: this, too, is corrected in the Eucharistic imagery of canto 11. The pelican reference is noted by Donald Cheney, *Spenser's Image of Nature*, 27 and by Pugh, *Spenser and Ovid*, 132.

for most men yet liuing can witnes of many rare and strange cures done by sundrie wels heeretofore vnknowen: which may make manifest to the world that God is well pleased, and in that respect hath blessed this our countrie far more than other nations: and are as it were plaine arguments, to bring other princes to imbrace the Gospell, to roote out all superstition and idolatrie, to plant in their countries true religion out of Gods booke, and aboue all things, to seeke Gods glorie and his kingdome. And it is not altogither a vaine coniecture, to thinke that God in these daies miraculously reuealed wels and springs of medicinall waters neuer knowen before, to worke effects strange and maruellous in our sights, thereby to induce all men to forsake such puddle pits which mans deuise hath digged, and drinke onely of the cleere fountaines of his word, thence onely to fetch remedy for our diseased soules.[71]

The waters of England are a sign of God's revealed truth in Scripture, and a means whereby people may be persuaded of the superior claims of the practices and principles of the new religion, and the image chosen by Baley to express this truth is the same one, from Jeremiah 2: 13, used by Erasmus', Bale, and Jewel, and by Spenser, to endorse and promote new translations of the Scriptures and the Reformed faith.[72] The healing waters of England are also God's reward for the faithful promulgation of the Reformed faith and the English Bible at the same time as they stand for that faith and its Scriptures. The Well of Life is a holy well and a healing spring, Living Water and the Word of God; it is text and sacrament and a real English bath, blessing Redcrosse as an individual and the English nation as a whole. Redcrosse is healed and strengthened by Well and Tree because they are true sacraments, signs of grace, and not because they are miracle-working substances of themselves. In the Well and the balm, baptism and the Eucharist, and in the Word, all things are made new.

[71] Sig. A2^v–A3.   [72] See Chapter 5.

8

Fountains Seen and Unseen

In about May 1575, the diplomat Henry Killigrew wrote to Robert Dudley, Earl of Leicester, to commend to him (and, naturally, to ask for the money to put into execution) a proposal for an elaborate fireworks display, to form part of the entertainments for Queen Elizabeth on her progress to Kenilworth that summer. In the event, the fireworks display seems not to have come off, at least in the exact form proposed here; perhaps it did, in the end, prove too difficult to produce 'Serpents of fire . . . Birds to fly about in the air scattering fire. Two dogs and cats which will fight in the fireworks . . . a fountain throwing wine, water and fire . . . three wheels of wonderful scented fire . . . ', and finally 'A dragon as big as an ox, which will fly twice as high as the tower of St Paul's'.[1] Perhaps the Earl baulked at the quote, which was for £50. In writing to Leicester, however, Killigrew also mentioned that he had already paid some £7 to the unnamed, presumably Italian, craftsman, as he was 'imployd abowt a fountayne which he mindeth to present vnto the quynes majeste. a singuler peace of worke (as I am Informed) wherof the lyk was neuer seane in these partis'. This is a tantalizing piece of information, for it was at Kenilworth, and in time for the Queen's visit in July 1575, that one of the most elaborate (and fully described) fountains in early modern England was erected.[2]

The main source of information about Kenilworth, its gardens, and the entertainments that took place there is the letter of Robert Langham,[3] written

---

[1] 'certi serpenti di fuoco . . . de le aui uiui uolare atorno nel'aria le quali getterano fuoco da per tutto . . . due carni & due gatti uiui li quali artificiosamente combattrano . . . un fonte dal quale scorrera uino acqua & fuoco . . . tre ruote di fuoco mirabili & odorifere . . . un dragone grande come un buc, quale volera due o tre uolte più alto che la torre de san Paolo.' Pepys MS II.607 (the letter), 609 (the enclosed paper). The translation is from Historic Manuscripts Commission, *Report of the Pepys Manuscripts* (London, 1911), 178–9.

[2] 'In a valuation of the Castle of Kenilworth (Cotton MS Tiberius E viii.) without date, but temp. James I and somewhat injured by the fire [1723], is the following item: A fountaine of white marble, engraven round about with storie woork, with the Queenes seat of freestone, both being in the garden—valued at £50.' John Nichols, *The Progresses, Processions, and Magnificent Festivities, of King James the First* (London, 1828), i. 475.

[3] His name was probably 'Langham', although 'Laneham' is the long-established convention. New evidence in support of Langham's authorship has recently been discovered by Elizabeth

semi-publicly to his friend and fellow Mercer Humphrey Martin soon after the events it describes, and published in the same year. Langham records only the one fountain at Kenilworth, but he gives it a prominent position as the last element of note in his lengthy account of the garden. It is spectacular:

In the center (az it wear) of this goodly Gardein, was theer placed, a very fayr Foountain, cast intoo an eight square, reared a four foot hy: from the midst whearof a Colum up set in shape of too *Athlants* joyned togeather a backhallf, the toon looking East, toother west: with theyr hands, uphollding a fayr foormed boll of a three foot over: from wheans sundry fine pipez, did lively distill continuall streamz intoo the receyt of the Foountayn: maynteyned styll too foot deep by the same fresh falling water: whearin pleazantly playing too and from and roound aboout: Carp, Tench, Bream, and for varietee, Pearch and Eel, fysh fayrlyking all and large. In the top, the ragged Staff, which, with the boll, the piller, and eight sydez beneath, wear all heawen oout of rich and hard white Marbl. A one syde, *Neptune* with hiz *Tridental Fuskin* triumphing in hiz Throne, trayled intoo the deep by hiz marine horsez. On an oother, *Thetis* in her chariot drawn by her dollphins. Then *Triton* by hiz fyshez. Heer *Protheus* hearding his sea bulz. Thear *Doris* and her dooughterz solacyng a sea and sandz. The wavez soourging with froth and fome, entmengld in place, with whalez, whirlpoolz, Sturgeonz, Tunneyz, Conchs and Wealks: all engraven by exquisit devize and skyll, so az I may think this not mooch inferioour untoo *Phoebus* gatez, which (*Ovid* sayz) and peradventur a pattern to thiz, that *Vulcan* himself dyd cut: whearof such waz the excellency of art, that the woork in valu surmoounted the stuff, and yet wear the gatez all of clean massy sylver.[4]

This specific detail of the work being more beautiful than the material, together with the imagery decorating the basin, is indeed drawn from the description of the gates made by Vulcan for the Palace of the Sun at the beginning of the second book of the *Metamorphoses* (3–13). This connection, felicitously made in material terms in the Kenilworth fountain, between fountains and gates, water, boundaries, surfaces, and transitions, is one that I am particularly going to explore in this chapter.

I am not going to attempt to give a detailed or systematic account of the fountains in the second and third books of *The Faerie Queene*, as I have with the fountains of Book 1 in the previous three chapters. Neither am I going to revisit, other than in passing, the debates over art and nature, nature and

Goldring: ' "A mercer ye wot az we be": The Authorship of the Kenilworth *Letter* Reconsidered', *English Literary Renaissance* (forthcoming).

[4] *A LETTER: Whearin, part of the entertainment vntoo the Queenz Maiesty, at Killing woorth Castl, in warwik Sheer, in this soomerz Progress. 1575. iz signified* (London, 1575), sig. I4ᵛ-K1. The unconventional orthography used to be thought to represent some regional accent, but it has recently been suggested that it is an attempt at simplified spelling along phonetic lines. I have retained 'Laneham' in the Bibliography for ease of reference, as it remains the name given in most of the older editions of the text, and in the Early English Books Online database.

grace, or indeed the role of Spenser's Italian sources, that have been such a feature of the criticism of Book 2 at least since C. S. Lewis published *The Allegory of Love* in 1936. Perhaps more than any other episode in *The Faerie Queene*, the Bowre of Bliss has something approaching a canon of criticism, from Lewis to Greenblatt and beyond, which adds to, and indeed almost parallels, the 'thick' texture of the passage, the way in which it is overburdened with material description, amplification, and intertextuality. Here, following my practice in discussing Book 1, my focus will be on the reader, on the interactions and interpenetrations of the textual, the visual, the material, and the experiential, and above all on the fountains, seen in Book 2 and unseen in Book 3; in addition, I will consider what it might mean to read these fountains both in terms of a real Renaissance fountain—that at Kenilworth—and the fact that that fountain no longer exists. Michael Leslie has commented on the reluctance of literary critics to look for visual, descriptive, rather than intertextual, literary sources when writing about literary gardens.[5] Building on Leslie's 'gardenist point',[6] the material and experiential dimensions of early modern gardens must also be considered—and fountains exist as a special category with regard to such dimensions.

In its first book, *The Faerie Queene* presents in Redcrosse a hero who goes from fountain to fountain. Fountains punctuate and provide an underlying structure to his physical and spiritual journey, occasioning challenge, reversal, revelation, and transformation. As Alastair Fowler long ago pointed out, the same is true of the fountains in Book 2: 'Guyon's mission is to go from one [fountain] to the other—to form, as it were, a human conduit';[7] more literally than she might have meant, too, Isabel MacCaffrey observed that 'Spenser's allegory continually returns *ad fontes*'.[8] But the initial association of fountains with deception in Book 1, in the figures of Errour, Duessa, and Archimago, is more keenly focused in Book 2 as a concern with the morality of art. Having established the importance and the capacity for symbolic, narrative, and ethical density of the fountain figure in his first book, Spenser progressively destabilizes it in the two that follow. In discussing not only the morality of art, but the morality of looking also, I look back to my discussion of the *Hypnerotomachia*'s Fountain of Venus, and forward to my account of David and Bathsheba, and especially Diana and Actaeon, in relation to Ben

---

[5] Leslie, 'Spenser, Sidney and the Renaissance Garden', 4–6.   [6] Ibid. 5.

[7] Alastair Fowler, *Spenser and the Numbers of Time* (London: Routledge and Kegan Paul, 1964), 94. Fowler also suggested that Book 2 as a whole is, as it were, governed by Aquarius, whose iconography is very similar to that of Temperance, and that the prominent fountains are part of this zodiacal allegorical schema.

[8] Isabel G. MacCaffrey, *Spenser's Allegory: The Anatomy of Imagination* (Princeton: Princeton University Press, 1976), 188.

Jonson's *The Fountaine of Selfe-Love*. By the end of Book 2 of *The Faerie Queene*, fountains have been exposed as decidedly ambivalent, and in Book 3, they have disappeared almost completely, yet retain an unseen presence. As sites loaded with intertextual associations and interpretative imperatives, they at once shape the journeys of the protagonists, structure the reading of them, and themselves demand to be read.

Leslie has noted how early modern gardens were structured around 'certain liminal points . . . thresholds where [visitors] must learn, decide, take stock', and that Guyon (and the reader) have a similar experience in the Bowre of Bliss.[9] This is perhaps even more true of the experience of Britomart and the reader in Book 3. Because of their materialization, dramatization even, of the intersection of art and nature, nature and culture, and the attention that they draw to the nature of surfaces, fountains are very often crucial limens. The fountains of Book 1 certainly function this way, as do those of the *Hypnerotomachia Poliphili* and Sidney's revised *Arcadia*, as previous chapters have shown. Langham's description of the Kenilworth fountain notes that there are fish both inside and outside the fountain, with 'whalez . . . Sturgeonz, Tunneyz, Conchs and Wealks' and other fish included among the decoration of the basin and—rather implausibly—'Carp, Tench, Bream, and for varietee, Pearch and Eel' swimming happily together in the water it encloses. The fountain has become a kind of mirror zone, like the surface of the pool in the Garden of Kalander a limen between image and reality; it is a site where art imitates nature and nature art. That its imagery recalls the gates of Phoebus reinforces this liminal quality, and indeed that invocation of gates has a further analogue in the ivory gates of Spenser's Bowre of Bliss. Like Book 1, Book 2 is framed by fountains, that of the chaste nymph, scene of Mordant's death and Amavia's suicide (2.1), and the fountain at the centre of the Bowre of Bliss (2.12). Perhaps appropriately, it can be easy to skip over the earlier episode of the Fountain of the Chaste Nymph when considering the fountains in Book 2, to arrive all the more quickly at the attractions, both aesthetic and critical, of the Bowre of Bliss and its central fountain. Yet Amavia's fountain is itself a crucial limen in the unfolding narrative of *The Faerie Queene* as a whole. As much as Guyon's mistaken combat with Redcrosse (2.1.1–31), it marks an ethical and aesthetic transition from Book 1 to Book 2.

Guyon and his companion, the Palmer, find a woman bleeding to death beside a fountain in the forest:

> In whose white alabaster brest did stick
> A cruell knife, that made a griesly wownd,
> From which forth gusht a stream of goreblood thick,

---

[9] Leslie, 'Spenser, Sidney and the Renaissance Garden', 16.

That all her goodly garments staind arownd,
And into a deepe sanguine dide the grassy grownd.

Pittifull spectacle of deadly smart,
Beside a bubling fountaine low she lay,
Which shee increased with her bleeding hart,
And the cleane waues with purple gore did ray;
Als in her lap a louely babe did play
His cruell sport, in stead of sorrow dew;
For in her streaming blood he did embay
His litle hands, and tender ioints embrew;
Pitifull spectacle, as euer eie did vew. (2.1.39–40)

Crucial to this episode is the word 'spectacle', which itself frames stanza 40, and the issue of the spectacular and the specular is central to the fountains of Books 2 and 3. Redcrosse has learned how to read and has been born again in the waters of the Well of Life, but in Books 2 and 3, Guyon and Britomart are confronted with the question of how to look. Accordingly, both they and the reader are presented with a series of spectacles. What Guyon and, through him, the reader are invited to look at is concrete, visual, yet tangible; what Britomart must address is far more interior, shifting, and uncertain, questioning the very nature of perception.

Confronted with this bloody and compelling spectacle of a dying woman and her child beside a fountain, Guyon manages temporarily to revive the woman, Amavia. She tells them that when she was pregnant, her lover Mortdant—whose body also lies beside the fountain—had gone adventuring and been bewitched by the evil witch Acrasia, and taken by her to the sensual paradise called the Bowre of Bliss. Although Amavia had managed to rescue Mortdant, Acrasia's final vindictive action had been to give him a drink of poisoned wine, cursed in such a way that he will die as soon as he takes a drink of water:

> With cup thus charmd, him parting she deceiued;
> *Sad verse, giue death to him that death does giue,*
> *And losse of loue, to her that loues to liue,*
> *So soone as Bacchus with the Nymphe does lincke.* (2.1.55)

And this is what has happened at the fountain where Guyon and the Palmer have come across Amavia, her baby, and the body of Mortdant. Her tale told, Amavia dies, and Guyon buries her with Mortdant. He takes the baby, but when he tries to wash the infant's hands, which are covered in his mother's blood, he cannot. The Palmer tells him that the fountain itself had once been one of Diana's nymphs, who had sought to escape the pursuit of the amorous Faunus:

> At last when fayling breath began to faint,
> And saw no meanes to scape, of shame affrayd,

> She set her downe to weepe for sore constraint,
> And to *Diana* calling lowd for ayde,
> Her deare besought, to let her die a mayd.
> The goddesse heard, and suddeine where she sate,
> Welling out streames of teares, and quite dismayd
> With stony feare of that rude rustick mate,
> Transformd her to a stone from stedfast virgins state.
>
> Lo now she is that stone, from whose two heads,
> As from two weeping eyes, fresh streames do flow,
> Yet colde through feare, and old conceiued dreads;
> And yet the stone her semblance seemes to show,
> Shapt like a maide, that such ye may her know;
> And yet her vertues in her water byde:
> For it is chaste and pure, as purest snow,
> Ne lets her waues with any filth be dyde,
> But euer like her selfe vnstayned hath beene tryde. (2.2.8–9)

The descriptions of the tragic Amavia and the Fountain of the Chaste Nymph which is the scene of her death anticipates the importance of the materiality and the sculptural content of the fountain in the Bowre of Bliss. The fountain itself retains a physical form reminiscent of the chaste nymph, but the body of Amavia herself is also described in sculptural terms, with her 'white alabaster brest . . . From which forth gusht a stream of goreblood thick'; there is almost a ghastly parody here of the fountains in which water streamed from the breasts of nymphs and goddesses, familiar from the *Hypnerotomachia* and, indeed, several Elizabethan gardens, as well as an anticipation of another spectacle, that of Amoret in the House of Busirane in 3.12.31. In Spenser's 'pittifull spectacle', the real fountain looks like a woman's body, and the real woman's body looks like a fountain. The attention of both protagonist and reader is being drawn from the watery aspects of the fountain figure, emphasized in Book 1, to its sculptural qualities.

There is a strong recollection in the Palmer's story of the chaste nymph of the pseudo-Ovidian metamorphosis of another of Diana's maidens, into the enervating fountain which is the scene of Redcrosse's disastrous encounter with Duessa in 1.7.[10] Yet the fountain 'in the midst' of Book 1, and the fateful encounter for which it is the setting, are associated with moral failure, both the nymph's, in her laziness, and Redcrosse's. On a first reading the Fountain of the Chaste Nymph would seem to be quite the opposite, representing purity and moral fortitude, but, as Linda Gregerson puts it, 'the poem has taught

---

[10] As Hamilton points out, this metamorphosis draws in particular on those of Daphne in *Metamorphoses*, 1.548–52 and Arethusa, 5.621–3. See also the discussion of the episode by Pugh, *Spenser and Ovid*, 83–9.

us to think more sceptically about such purity'.[11] That little Ruddymane's hands must remain bloodstained, and he is named accordingly, as a sign of his mother's innocent suffering, seems cruel and excessive, out of keeping with the generous, cleansing, baptismal associations for the fountain established at the end of the previous book. The failure of the fountain's waters to cleanse his hands may well be about original sin—but it does not have to be exclusively so; as Colin Burrow points out, when the Palmer explains that the child's hands 'may not be cleansed with water of this well' '[t]he emphasis falls on "*this* well"': others without this extraordinary history of abstinence might work rather better'.[12] Burrow further notes that although the fountain's aetiology recalls the stories of Daphne and Arethusa, the Ovidian protagonist of whom the fountain is most reminiscent is Anaxarete, 'whose stony chastity is expressed in her eventual form . . . by no means a pleasant creature'.[13] Anaxarete, we might recall, is the nymph invoked by Polia in the *Hypnerotomachia*, when she reproaches herself for her heartlessness and cruelty towards the besotted Poliphilus. At this moment of origin for Guyon's quest as the Knight of Temperance, the story of Acrasia and Mortdant, Amavia, Ruddymane, and the Fountain of the Chaste Nymph establishes some problematic and uncomfortable precedents for the rest of the book and Guyon's conduct within it.

The means of the unfortunate Mortdant's death, whereby a curse is activated when he drinks water after drinking wine, evokes common medieval and early modern emblematic representations of temperance as a woman mixing water with wine. Yet the tempering of Acrasia's wine with the fountain's water is not beneficial, but deadly. The fountain's extreme purity[14]—and, accordingly, its ambivalent representation of the virtue of temperance—anticipates Guyon's paradoxically extreme temperance, and his destruction of the Bowre of Bliss in particular. Amavia and Mortdant bring together love, life, and death at the fountain, which should itself give life but instead brings death to both knight and lady. The conduct of both lovers has been intemperate, as the fountain is intemperate in its purity and its inability to fulfil its emblematic functions of both washing and tempering wine. Guyon's ultimately qualified achievement of his quest as the knight of temperance is thus neatly foreshadowed by the very device that initiates that quest, the fountain.

---

[11] Gregerson, *The Reformation of the Subject*, 27 ff.

[12] Colin Burrow, 'Original Fictions: Metamorphoses in *The Faerie Queene*', in Charles Martindale (ed.), *Ovid Renewed: Ovidian Influences on Literature and Art from the Middle Ages to the Twentieth Century* (Cambridge: Cambridge University Press, 1988), 105.

[13] Ibid. 105. This is also noted by Pugh, *Spenser and Ovid*, 85.

[14] See the discussion by Lewis H. Miller, 'A Secular Reading of *The Faerie Queene* Book II', *English Literary History*, 33 (1966), 158 and *passim*.

The two fountain episodes which frame Book 2 are additionally linked by a series of cups, just as the opposition between the true and false fountains of Book 1 is echoed by that between the cups borne by Duessa and Fidelia.[15] Indeed, in the Bowre of Bliss and its analogues, fountains and cups seem interchangeable, as James Nohrnberg has pointed out.[16] The 'cup thus charmd', the fatal parting pledge between Acrasia and Mortdant, is anticipated by Amavia's description of the way in which her rival 'makes her louers dronken mad' (2.1.52.2); there is an elision in the book between the visual and the oral, most famously in the description of Acrasia herself in the Bowre with Verdant, 'With her false eyes fast fixed in his sight . . . And through his humid eyes did sucke his spright' (2.12.73.2, 9). The cups of Book 2 differ from those in Book 1, however, because they are presented in the context of social ritual. The decadent porter who nominally keeps the gate of the Bowre has at his side 'a mighty Mazer bowl of wine', while his female counterpart, Excesse, who keeps the second gate, presents visitors with 'a Cup of gold'. To offer wine to guests is hospitable, yet these cups, and those who proffer them, are decadent, and display and excess have corrupted social rituals and relationships, just as Acrasia herself abused the ritual of the parting or stirrup cup in her delayed-action murder of Mortdant.[17] The 'mazer' gains an additional ironic significance in the derivation of its name from the wood traditionally used to make it, maple, described by Spenser as 'seeldom inward sound' (1.1.9.9). The cup that all these cups stand for is Circe's cup, unsurprising given Acrasia's debt to Homer's enchantress. Karen Britland has explored the role of the Circe myth in early modern drama, and she notes that Circe's power is 'connected to a notion of hospitality . . . Her island could be a comedic, pastoral space of retreat and recuperation. Instead, it offers a threat: the threat of luxury and idleness, enervation and effeminisation . . . Circe's hospitality to the Greeks is shown to be excessive'.[18] Acrasia's blowsy porters may be unappealing, even repellent in their decadence, but they too, like Acrasia and like Circe,

---

[15] John N. King additionally points out that '[t]he iconoclastic action of Book 2 repeats the shattering of cups and destruction of idols [in Book 1]'. *Spenser's Poetry and the Reformation Tradition*, 100. I am indebted, in my discussion of cups, to many conversations with Lucy Razzall.

[16] 'The earthly paradise in Trissino's epic [*Italia liberata*]—presided over by the sorceress Acratia—is specifically approached through an ivory gate. The other two ingresses to Acratia's realm are by way of fountains where the traveler is offered unmanning drinks. The various cups associated with Spenser's Acrasia and Trissino's Acratia have their original in the cup of Ariosto's Alcina.' Nohrnberg, *The Analogy of The Faerie Queene*, 440.

[17] It is interesting to note that poisoning traditionally attracts greater opprobrium as a means of killing both because it must perforce be premeditated, and because it so often violates the bond of hospitality.

[18] 'Circe's Cup: Wine and Women in Early Modern Drama', in Adam Smyth (ed.), *A Pleasing Sinne: Drink and Conviviality in Seventeenth-Century England*, Studies in Renaissance Literature (Woodbridge: D. S. Brewer, 2004), 114, 115.

are offering hospitality. When Guyon overthrows the mazer 'disdainfully' and 'the cup to ground . . . violently cast[s], | That all in peeces it was broken fond' (2.12.49, 57), he is simply being rude. Here in the cups, and in the Bowre itself, is the counterpart to the excessive chastity of the stony nymph: excessive hospitality, met with an excessive rebuff. What Guyon is called upon to demonstrate and embody in his temperance is not righteous indignation and the violent destruction of excess in all its guises, but rather discernment and discrimination. Whereas Redcrosse has to slay the dragon, it is imperative that Guyon let Acrasia live, albeit exposed and restrained.[19] As generations of critics have shown, it remains unclear whether we should approve his destruction of Acrasia's Bowre.

The Bowre of Bliss's gorgeous fountain is surely one of the most analysed passages in the whole of *The Faerie Queene*, and critics from C. S. Lewis onwards have discussed it as epitomizing the conflict between art and nature that the Bowre depicts. Emphasizing its underlying connection with the enervating fountain in the glade which is in the middle of Book 1, associated with the nymph who sat down to rest 'in middest of the race' (1.7.5.4), the fountain is at the centre of the bower:

> And in the midst of all, a fountaine stood,
> Of richest substance, that on earth might bee,
> So pure and shiny, that the siluer flood
> Through euery channell running one might see;
> Most goodly it with curious ymageree
> Was ouerwrought, and shapes of naked boyes,
> Of which some seemd with liuely iollitee,
> To fly about, playing their wanton toyes,
> Whylest others did them selues embay in liquid ioyes,
>
> And ouer all, of purest gold was spred,
> A trayle of yuie in his natiue hew:
> For the rich metall was so coloured,
> That wight, who did not well auis'd it vew,
> Would surely deeme it to bee yuie trew:
> Low his lasciuious armes adown did creepe,
> That themselues dipping in the siluer dew,
> Their fleecy flowres they fearfully did steepe,
> Which drops of Christall seemd for wantones to weep. (2.12.60–1)

There is no suggestion here that the fountain's decoration has any narrative content or 'storie woork', like that at Kenilworth, but there are other strong

---

[19] This contrast between the 'beacon of moral clarity' that is Redcrosse's mission and the 'moral ambivalence' of Guyon's quest is discussed by Paul Suttie, 'Moral Ambivalence in the Legend of Temperance', *Spenser Studies*, 19 (2004), 126 and *passim*.

parallels; we might recall, too, that the Kenilworth fountain was 'in the center... of this goodly Gardein'. Spenser certainly knew the passage from the *Metamorphoses* upon which Langham drew in his *Letter*, and which (one can only assume) was the decorative source for the Kenilworth fountain itself; it is not impossible, either, that Spenser knew Langham's *Letter* also, or indeed that he had seen the Kenilworth fountain. Spenser's fountain is not made of marble, but of some unnamed substance through which the running water can be seen, probably crystal;[20] like Vulcan's gates, the effect is of silver, and of richness.[21] More crucially, Ovid's gates are not intended to titillate, but in their metamorphosis at Kenilworth, and in Langham's text, they are certainly presented as a source of visual, and erotic, pleasure, as Spenser's fountain is. Langham followed his description of the sculptural content of the fountain with the comment that 'Heer wear things ye see, moought enflame ony mynde too long after looking': this is true of Spenser's fountain even before the naked women who bathe in it are considered, given the accumulation of adjectives in the two stanzas used to describe it.

The golden ivy, coloured 'in his natiue hew', has attracted much critical attention,[22] with Lewis reserving particular opprobrium for it.[23] Two things could be added, however, to this rather over-worn discussion. The first is to note in passing the way in which the detail of the ivy can be used to link the fountain back into the Book's pattern of cups, via a passage in *The Shepheardes Calender* which describes 'A mazer ywrought of the Maple warre ... | Entrailed with a wanton Yuie twine'.[24] Ivy is a traditional remedy for drunkenness, whence its association with Bacchus and its use in early modern London as an inn sign; this would explain its appearance on a mazer or drinking bowl. Second, and more substantially, Spenser's ivy that is not ivy, in its close association with the fountain, recalls a key passage in Erasmus'

---

[20] See the discussion by John B. Bender in *Spenser and Literary Pictorialism* (Princeton: Princeton University Press, 1972), 186.

[21] The ivory gates of the Bowre also recall those of Phoebus' palace in *Metamorphoses* 4, although they depict not sea creatures but the story of Jason and Medea. There is also, intriguingly, an echo of Langham's description of the waves carved on the fountain—'soourging with froth and fome'—in Spenser's description of the voyaging Argo: 'Ye might have seen the frothy billowes fry | Vnder the ship', 2.12.45.1–2; this detail does not appear in Ovid.

[22] In many respects it is simply a romance trope of exoticism and artifice: Stephen Hawes (d. 1523) includes in the palace courtyard in his *Pastyme of Plesure* 'a right crafty vyne' which 'of golde was made... In stede of grapes | the Rubies there did shyne'. *The historie of graunde Amoure and la bell Pucel, called the Pastime of plesure* (1554), sig. B3. This golden vine's proximity to an exotic fountain is suggestive.

[23] 'Whether those who think that Spenser is secretly on Acrasia's side, themselves approve of metal vegetation as a garden ornament, or whether they regard this passage as a proof of Spenser's abominable bad taste, I do not know', *The Allegory of Love: A Study in Medieval Tradition* (Oxford: Oxford University Press, 1936; repr. 1959), 325.

[24] *August*, 26, 30 in *Edmund Spenser: The Shorter Poems*, ed. McCabe, 108.

colloquy *The Godly Feast*. In many of his educational treatises, Erasmus extolled the capacity of wall paintings and inscriptions to instil good morals and even eloquence in the young, and it is known that the gardens and houses of several of his friends and fellow humanists in England—notably John Colet's at the Charterhouse at Sheen—were decorated in this way.[25] In *The Godly Feast*, Erasmus describes such an environment and its garden in particular, which is the setting for the main part of the colloquy's discussion.[26] There is a fountain in the centre of Eusebius' garden, which he explains to his friend Timothy as a spiritual symbol. Its water runs into a channel, of which Timothy asks

Timothy . . . is it made of marble?
Eusebius Don't say that. Where would marble come from? It's imitation marble made of cement. The colour is added later by means of a white coating.
Timothy Where does such a pretty stream finally bury itself?
Eusebius See how crude we are: after it has delighted our eyes here sufficiently, it drains the kitchen and carries that waste along to the sewer.
Timothy That's callous, so help me!
Eusebius Callous, unless the goodness of the eternal Will had made it for this use . . . We do not misuse this water if we employ it for the various purposes for which it was given by him who provides everything abundantly for human needs . . .

Underlying this passage are a number of significant assumptions and prescriptions about what might be termed visual morality.

Intriguing in the context of a discussion of Spenser's fountain and its imitation ivy is Eusebius' admission that the 'channel'—and perhaps the fountain also—is not made of marble, as it appears, but instead of 'imitation marble made of cement [with] [t]he colour . . . added later by means of a white coating'. Fake (golden) ivy and fake (concrete) marble are of different aesthetic—and perhaps moral—orders. But Erasmus' apparent endorsement of artifice in the garden suggests that the overall effect, and, in this case, the way in which that effect is then moralized as an image for both the beauty and the practical utility of Scripture, is more important than the integrity of the means employed in its devising. Eusebius does not aim to deceive—he answers Timothy's question honestly and with evident pride in his ingenuity

---

[25] Colet's *ODNB* biographer notes that 'his will of 1519 requires that all "boardwork" [presumably decorative panels, although not in *OED* in this sense] and "painted images upon the walls" remain there'. He also points out that Colet is thinly disguised as one of the interlocutors in Erasmus' satirical *A Pilgrimage for Religion's Sake*, discussed above. J. B. Trapp, 'Colet, John (1467–1519)', *Oxford Dictionary of National Biography* (www.oxforddnb.com/view/article/5898, accessed 25 Jan. 2006)

[26] Desiderius Erasmus, *Colloquies*, trans. Craig R. Thompson (Toronto: University of Toronto Press, 1997), 178–9.

(and thrift). What is most telling is his final statement on the subject of the fountain, that 'We do not misuse this water if we employ it for the various purposes for which it was given by him who provides everything abundantly for human needs...' By extension, the water, as it reflects the garden, the fountain itself, and the imitation marble channel stand not only for the Word of God but for art and artifice also. In Christ's garden, not only all creation, but all human creative acts, are good.

Elizabethan gardens were full of such devices: the great fountain at Kenilworth may have been made of marble, but other ornaments in the garden were made from wood painted to look like stone (or at least cheap stone painted to look like expensive stone), and one of the garden's most famous features was an elaborate aviary, with ornamental plasterwork gilded and painted to look like precious stones.[27] It is the use to which such things are put, not the things themselves, that is morally inflected; it is also the way in which they are presented and perceived, the way in which they are looked at. Eusebius' imitation marble is presented by him as such, and he is anxious that Timothy should look beyond such incidental details to recognize the moral and spiritual goodness of the fountain, and the garden, as a setting and a sign.[28] The golden ivy which twines lasciviously around Spenser's fountain is more morally ambivalent—it is, perhaps, designed to deceive—but only those who do 'not well auis'd it vew' (2.12.61.4). The shrewd, the well prepared, the well educated, the moral, will not be deceived; they will instead, like Eusebius' friend Timothy, appreciate the artifice and the effect. The message of the ivy is 'caveat spectator', and its presence here shows that Guyon is neither a careful nor a discerning looker. Syrithe Pugh points out that, from the beginning of the Book, Guyon is (like Redcrosse) 'a bad reader, unaware of the true meaning which lies beneath the deceptive surface of the text in which he is embedded';[29] like Redcrosse, too, he is as unaware of the process whereby he might safely access such meanings as he is of the meanings themselves. In Book 1 of *The Faerie Queene*, Redcrosse's downfall has been his unarmed mind, in the terms outlined in Erasmus' *Enchiridion*; in Book 2, the analogous problem is Guyon's unarmed eyes.

---

[27] 'Under the Cornish again, euery part beautified with great Diamonds, Emerauds, Rubyes and Saphyres: poynted, tabld, rok & roound: garnisht with theyr golld, by skyllfull hed & hand, and by toyl & pensyl, so lyuely exprest, az it moought bee great marueyl, and pleazure too consider hoow neer excellensy of art coold approch vntoo perfection of nature,' 'Laneham', *A LETTER*, sig. I3ᵛ.

[28] 'Many early Protestants shared the Erasmian view that images in themselves are spiritually neutral because their value depends upon how they are applied.' King, *Spenser's Poetry and the Reformation Tradition*, 69.

[29] Pugh, *Spenser and Ovid*, 79.

Even more than the golden ivy, the two young women who bathe in the
fountain have, appropriately enough, been a focus of critical attention, as they
are of Guyon's:

> As *Guyon* hapned by the same to wend,
> Two naked Damzelles he therein espyde,
> Which therein bathing, seemed to contend,
> And wrestle wantonly, ne car'd to hyde,
> Their dainty partes from vew of any, which them eyd.
>
> Sometimes the one would lift the other quight
> Aboue the waters, and then downe againe
> Her plong, as ouer maystered by might,
> Where both a while would couered remaine,
> And each the other from to rise restraine;
> The whiles their snowy limbes, as through a vele,
> So through the christall waues appeared plaine:
> Then suddeinly both would themselues vnhele,
> And th'amarous sweet spoiles to greedy eyes reuele. (2.12.63–4)

Spenser borrows the women from Tasso,[30] although in the *Gerusalemme
liberata* they are swimming rather than wrestling, and much has been made of
the (faux) lesbian eroticism of the scene. There is no question that the scene
is meant to titillate both Guyon and the reader, especially when one of the
women, on becoming aware of Guyon's presence, deliberately displays herself
to him:

> The wanton Maidens him espying, stood
> Gazing a while at his vnwonted guise;
> Then th'one her selfe low ducked in the flood,
> Abasht, that her a straunger did auise:
> But thother rather higher did arise,
> And her two lilly paps aloft displayd,
> And all, that might his melting hart entyse
> To her delights, she vnto him bewrayd:
> The rest hidd vnderneath, him more desirous made (2.12.66).

This is all very well—at least one of these two is a Bad Woman, or at least
a Silly Woman (for Lewis, the two seem synonymous)[31]—but it does not

---

[30] *Gerusalemme liberata*, 15.58–66; as Hamilton points out, Fairfax's translation, under
Spenser's influence, has them wrestling also.

[31] His comments that 'their names are obviously Cissie and Flossie' and that they 'are
ducking and giggling in a bathing-pool for the benefit of a passerby: a man does not need to
go to faerie land to meet them' (Lewis, *The Allegory of Love*, 331)—'giggling' is entirely his
addition—are much quoted. Two more nuanced accounts of the women in the fountain are by
Howard Hendrix, ' "Those Wandring Eyes of His": Watching Guyon Watch the Naked Damsels

explain why they should be portrayed as wrestling. As is well known, Guyon is a wrestler, but what has not hitherto been noted is the importance of wrestling to the educational writings of Richard Mulcaster, Spenser's schoolmaster and mentor.[32]

There are considerable echoes of Mulcaster's work *Positions Concerning the Training Up of Children* (1581) in Spenser's 'Letter to Raleigh', and particularly of Mulcaster's discussion of virtue and nobility.[33] Like most writers of educational treatises and conduct books, Mulcaster includes discussion of the importance of physical exercise in the fashioning of a gentleman. His choice of wrestling, however, is unusual,[34] and he devotes considerable space to both explaining and defending it:

For wrestling as it is olde and was accounted cunning sometimes, so now both by Physicians in arte, and by our countreymen in use, it seemeth not to be much set by, being contemned by the most, and cared for but by the meanest. Yet the auncient *Palestra* a terme knowen to the learned, and joined with letters, and Musick, to prove the good bringing up of youth as a most certaine argument of abilitie well qualified, fetcht that name of the Greek παλη, which we in English terme wrastling, and was alwaye of good note, as wrastling it selfe in games gat victories, in warre tried forces, in health helped haviour, in the bodye wrought strength.[35]

Mulcaster does not himself draw out the inference that wrestling can be employed as a metaphor for a wider pedagogical approach, but in the figure of Guyon, and especially, I would argue, in his encounter with the women wrestling in the fountain, Spenser does.

The women in the fountain are specifically wrestling because they, and the fountain, epitomize what Guyon must himself wrestle with, his own propensities to both reactionary censure and concupiscence, in his quest to become truly temperate and, in terms outlined by both Spenser and Mulcaster, a virtuous gentleman. He must learn how to look, and without the Palmer's externalized force of moral intervention, which comes no more naturally to

---

Wrestling', *Assays*, 7 (1992), 71–85 and Arlene M. Okerlund, 'Spenser's Wanton Maidens: Reader Psychology and the Bower of Bliss', *PMLA* 88 (1973), 62–8.

[32] On Mulcaster's influence on Spenser, see Chapter 5.

[33] 'Now then nobilitie emplying the outward note of inward value, and gentilitie signifying the inward value of the outward note, it is verie easie to determine, what it is to be a *nobleman*, in excellencie of vertue shewed, and what it is to be a *gentleman* to have excellent vertue to shew. Whereby it appeareth that vertue is the ground to that whole race, by whether name so ever ye call it, *wisedome* in *policie*, *valiance* in *execution*, *justice* in *deciding*, *modestie* in *demeanour* ...' Mulcaster, *Positions*, 199.

[34] Castiglione had included it as one of the skills in which the courtier should be proficient, but which should be displayed 'Sildome in open syght of the people but privilye with himselfe alone, or emonge hys friendes and familiers'. Castiglione, *The Book of the Courtier*, tr. Thomas Hoby, 369.

[35] Mulcaster, *Positions*, 83.

him than its equivalent in the fountain at Kenilworth. For, having described the Ovidian scenes on the fountain's basin, Langham adds, 'Heer wear things ye see, moought enflame ony mynde too long after looking: but whoo so waz foound so hot in desyre, with the wreast of a Cok waz sure of a coolar: water spurting upward with such vehemency, az they shoold by and by be moystned from top too to'.[36] This device of the 'water joke' was common in Elizabethan gardens, and in their European counterparts. Here it has a particularly moral cast. As Michael Leslie observes, 'the water-jokes catch the unwary, the morally lax', and elsewhere he comments on the automata found in *The Faerie Queene*: 'The statues threateningly move from their proper realm as mute and subject to the eye and assume power over the beholder; they are emancipated from the temporal world of the verbal and dominate the spatial imagination'.[37] Yet this quality of movement in four dimensions is always already present in a fountain. It is the hermeneutic instability, the almost literal fluidity of the Kenilworth fountain—its playing water, its swimming fish, the watery scenes which decorate it—that over-stimulates the onlooker, as much as the erotic content of its decoration. The bathing women in the Bowre's fountain take this instability further: like Venus at the climax of Book 1 of the *Hypnerotomachia*, and as Amavia's 'pittifull spectacle' anticipates, they are the fountain as well as being in it, nymphs who have sprung to life and movement through the metamorphic, transformative element of water. Guyon's crisis is a moral one because it is a crisis of interpretation as well as of improper desire; the beasts in the bower, of which Grille is only the most prominent, have also gazed too long on forbidden sights as much as—or, indeed, at the same time as—they have drunk from Circe's cup.

To wrestle morally with the sight of the wrestling naked women in the cool and alluring waters of the beautiful fountain decorated with 'lasciuious' ivy and naked boys engaged in 'wanton ioyes' is the Book's final test, even more so than the sight of Acrasia herself, and it is a test which Guyon almost fails. He cannot succeed without the Palmer's intervention, and indeed becomes, in his arousal, the 'filthy Priapus' identified by Erasmus' Eusebius as a more common statue in the garden than the figure of Christ which is the guardian of his own.[38] In the Bowre of Bliss, to look is to drink; to do either in the wrong

---

[36] Sig. K1.

[37] Leslie, 'Spenser, Sidney, and the Renaissance Garden', 7, 22. He also notes the equivalence between the apparently moral function of the water joke at Kenilworth and the Palmer's admonishment (18), and revisits the issue of automata in his British Academy lecture, pp. 99–100.

[38] Erasmus' location of such a statue in the setting for his colloquy makes the garden space a sacred and a moral one, but also acts as a reminder that all of creation is God's, and that it is

way, without being 'well auis'd', is to be morally compromised: in Simon Shepherd's succinct formulation, 'the scene is not simply about dangerous female beauty, but about how the male gaze is trapped'.[39] Assessments such as Judith Dundas's, when she suggests that 'in Spenser's descriptions of evil art, he emphasizes above all the manipulation of the spectator',[40] in some respects miss the point: in the case of the fountain in the Bowre of Bliss at least, it is not evil art that is the problem, but an unwary and undiscerning spectator who is ready and willing to be manipulated. It is Guyon's 'wandring eyes' that the Palmer rebukes (2.12.69.2), and the reader, too, must be implicated in this.[41]

Book 2, and especially the account of the Bowre of Bliss and its destruction, can be read as part of a wider pattern operating in *The Faerie Queene* as a whole.[42] Yet the critical focus on the nature and extent of Spenser's iconoclasm in Book 2 has perhaps obscured the simultaneous emphasis in the book on the construction of a morally informed, discerning, and discriminating reader. There is little point in eradicating the false and constructing the true if neither Guyon nor the reader can tell which is which: to borrow Raphael Lyne's formulation, the Bowre of Bliss 'confronts the reader with the problem of unscrambling mixed messages'.[43] More subtly, Spenser suggests that the impulse to destroy that which is false, immoral, and corrupting must itself be tempered by the moral fortification of the reader. The debate is over censorship as much as iconoclasm: better to equip the reader to confront immoral art than to rely on the externalized censure of the Palmer or the cold shower. Art with the potential to corrupt can be destroyed, as Guyon does with the Bowre. Access to art of whatever kind, or to sensory experiences in

inherently good. Statues of Christ in the garden, and presumably dressed as a gardener (as in John 20: 15), were rare but not unheard of: William Cecil, Lord Burghley, apparently had such a statue in his garden at Theobalds. It is mentioned, however, in only one contemporary source (the account of Waldstein in 1600), and Paula Henderson has suggested that he may in fact have been influenced in this by Erasmus' well-known colloquy. See *The Tudor House and Garden*, 203.

[39] Simon Shepherd, *Spenser*, Harvester New Readings (New York: Harvester Wheatsheaf, 1989), 85. See also the discussion of related ideas in Book 3 by Richard J. DuRocher, 'Guiding the Glance: Spenser, Milton, and "Venus looking glas" ', *Journal of English and Germanic Philology*, 92 (1993), 325–41.

[40] Judith Dundas, *The Spider and the Bee: The Artistry of Spenser's* Faerie Queene (Urbana: University of Illinois Press, 1985), 54.

[41] 'This episode [the Bowre of Bliss] is another example of the need for both readers of the poem and the heroes of the poem to *read carefully*,' John S. Pendergast, 'Christian Allegory and Spenser's "General Intention" ', *Studies in Philology*, 93 (1996), 283.

[42] 'Although *The Faerie Queene* incorporates an iconoclastic attack against the abuse or misapplication of art, Spenser never equates art with idolatry. Instead, he juxtaposes the eradication of "false" products of the imagination with the reciprocal construction of "true" literature and art', King, *Spenser's Poetry and the Reformation Tradition*, 109.

[43] Raphael Lyne, 'Grille's Moral Dialogue: Spenser and Plutarch', *Spenser Studies*, 19 (2004), 160.

general, can be controlled. We are familiar with the conventions of privacy and secrecy surrounding the display of portrait miniatures,[44] and analogous conventions sometimes governed the display of larger portraits also.[45] In Langham's description of the fountain at Kenilworth and the privy garden in which it stood, he makes much of having gained access to it semi-illicitly, while the Queen, Leicester, and their attendants were out hunting.[46] Most crucially, however, ideal readers (and viewers) can be educated and trained so that they can look on that which 'moought enflame ony mynde too long after looking' without being moved either to immorality themselves or to destruction.

The Proem to Book 3 of *The Faerie Queene* is perhaps best known for its invitation to Elizabeth to see herself 'in mirrors more than one'. While the ideas of reflection and plurality that this suggests are incidental to this discussion, the second stanza introduces a different focus when it considers 'the pourtraict of her hart':

> But liuing art may not least part expresse,
> Nor life-resembling pencill it can paynt,
> All were it *Zeuxis* or *Praxiteles*:
> His dædale hand would faile, and greatly faynt,
> And her perfections with his error taynt. (3 Proem 2.1–5)

This topos of inexpressibility is well worn, but two aspects of Spenser's use of it have attracted less critical attention than his advertising of Elizabeth's plural nature. The first is the invocation of forms of artistic expression other than literature: painting, sculpture, and, in the phrase 'dædale hand', perhaps other, more ambiguous forms of artistic cunning, of the sort concerned with automata and *trompe l'œil*; even, perhaps, the creation of water jokes, crystal fountains, and golden ivy. The quest to portray Elizabeth cuts across the boundaries of genre and media; it is concertedly interdisciplinary. Second, Spenser explicitly presents his project as hard and even dangerous work. In Book 3 he draws attention to his own labour by making the reading hard work too, but he makes this difficult reading a labour with its own particular rewards. In Linda Gregerson's formulation, *The Faerie Queene* 'flatters and empowers its readers much as it flattered and empowered a Renaissance queen—by giving us copious work to do'.[47] Spenser solicits a particular kind

---

[44] Fumerton, *Cultural Aesthetics*, chapter 3 *passim*.

[45] Of the pictures listed as being at Kenilworth in the 1588 probate inventory of Leicester's goods, the vast majority were furnished with curtains. This was partly for their protection, but it also meant that access to them could be controlled and directed. Thoms, 'Pictures of the Great Earl of Leicester', 201–2.

[46] 'Laneham', *A LETTER*, sig. I4.

[47] Gregerson, *The Reformation of the Subject*, 20.

of reading, one that is itself pluralistic and interdisciplinary, feeling its way by grasping at every possible clue. If Book 1 has been about learning to read the Bible, and Book 2 has concerned itself with learning how (or how not) to read images, then Book 3 builds on both of these, even as it calls into question the nature of reading, the nature of looking, and the nature of love.

In Book 3 the only real fountain encountered by Britomart is the one where she meets the hapless Scudamour in 3.11.7. There are, however, other kinds of fountains in Book 3, which shape both Britomart's journey and the reader's experience. That experience is qualitatively different from that of reading Books 1 and 2, although it builds upon it: in particular, it is harder. Britomart's meeting with Scudamour is a discreet nod back at the preceding two books and the wider romance tradition, in which the forest fountain is the *locus classicus* for such encounters. But the appearance of the motif here in fact reveals how unlike the other two books Britomart's has been in its structure and ethos, and how much it has apparently violated the expectations that they have established. Although Book 3 is titled 'The legende of Britomartis', she is far less present in her own legend than are Redcrosse and Guyon in theirs, being active in only seven cantos. Where Books 1 and 2 are essentially linear, Book 3 makes more extensive use of interlace. The ambiguity given to the book by the cancellation of its original ending in the 1596 edition emphasizes its plurality and lack of closure. Especially in comparison with Books 1 and 2, Book 3 is hard to read. Spenser makes Britomart a reader figure of a kind that goes beyond the usual reader-surrogate, drawing attention to the processes and pitfalls of the act of reading. He solicits a particular kind of reading, asking both Britomart and the reader to read dangerously. The reading solicited by Spenser in Book 3 is active, moral, didactic, and dialogic, and Book 3's apparently invisible fountains play an important part in this.

Like Book 1, Book 3 has a 'fountain' at its centre, a version of the Diana–Actaeon encounter that appears in all three books of the 1590 *Faerie Queene*.[48] That it is significantly reinvented is a sign that a new, more active form of reading is being asked for. The encounter with Diana occurs in the context of the relation of the miraculous conception and birth of Amoret and Belphoebe. It tells how Venus, having lost her son Cupid, seeks him in the forest, Diana's territory. She encounters her sister-goddess as she bathes in a forest spring with her nymphs after the hunt; Diana is displeased to be interrupted, and the meeting between the two sister-goddesses does not begin well. Diana dismisses Venus as trivial and immoral, and threatens to clip

---

[48] Fradubio in Book 1 (1.2.40), Guyon in Book 2; the motif is significantly reworked again in the *Mutabilitie Cantos*. These multiple rewritings are considered by Brown, 'Arachne's Web', 123–7.

Cupid's wings if she finds him in her woods—so Venus quite literally 'turns on the charm':

> so [Diana] she soone appeasd,
> With sugred words and gentle blandishment,
> From which a fountaine from her sweete lips went,
> And welled goodly forth, that in short space
> She was well pleasd, and forth her damzels sent
> Through all the woods, to search from place to place,
> If any tract of him or tydings they mote trace. (3.6.25)

The Diana–Actaeon story is here rewritten in a number of ways. Most obviously, it is not Actaeon, whether gloating voyeur or hapless hunter, who invades Diana's private space with his presence and his gaze, but another goddess. As Theresa M. Krier describes it,

[t]his bathing of the goddess is beautifully and surprisingly non-narcissistic for Diana, and non-voyeuristic for the reader . . . What Spenser represents is not naked women as the object of a male gaze, or even of their own regard, but the purified voluptuousness of those bodily sensations after strenuous and disciplined exertion, of inhabiting one's body fully.[49]

The situation is no longer one of transgression and drastic punishment, as in the case of Fradubio in Book 1, or lingering voyeurism followed by the violent destruction of all possible forms of temptation, as in Guyon's eventual response to the Bowre of Bliss. Compromise is reached and the outcome is a happy one, for the nymphs find, not Cupid, but the newborn Amoret and Belphoebe. A topos of transgressive looking, or misreading, which is punished by a loss of identity and further misreadings (Actaeon's hounds cannot recognize their master and erase even his new identity as they dismember him) is transformed into something positive and hopeful. Venus' initial transgression becomes the catalyst for the eventual revelation of a new vision of love, one that emphasizes balance and mutuality. The voyeurism and cruelty implicit in the Actaeon motif and expressed in graphic detail in the House of Busirane are shown not to be inevitable. Both Diana and Venus–Actaeon are hunters, and Britomart is too, but (in Lauren Silberman's pithy phrase) 'although the motif of the chase underlies much of Book 3, the book—and the entire poem—in 1590 closes with a clinch rather than a kill'.[50] The meeting of Venus and Diana, at the heart of Book 3, therefore enacts and even ensures the possibility of new

---

[49] Krier, *Gazing on Secret Sights*, 120. See also her discussion of the Fradubio episode, p. 133. Krier's reading is developed by Jason Gleckman, 'Providential Love and Suffering in *The Faerie Queene*, Book III', *Spenser Studies*, 19 (2004), 209–35.

[50] Lauren Silberman, *Transforming Desire: Erotic Knowledge in Books III and IV of* The Faerie Queene (Berkeley and Los Angeles: University of California Press, 1995), 49.

ways of looking and being looked at, and of alternative ways of both reading and acting upon what is seen.

This principle of reinvention underlies the whole Book. In 3.2, the origin of Britomart's quest is retrospectively revealed. She has looked into her father's magic mirror and seen the face of a knight, Artegall, with whom she has instantly fallen in love. She pines away and eventually reveals her plight to her faithful nurse: 'I fonder, then *Cephisus* foolish child, | Who hauing vewed in a fountaine shere | His face, was with the loue thereof beguild; | I fonder loue a shade, the bodie farre exild' (3.2.44). In the first of the Book's fountain images, Britomart thus compares herself with Narcissus, as she regards Artegall as even more ridiculously unattainable than her own reflection. The surface of the mirror/fountain becomes an impermeable meniscus, and its status as an instrument of revelation and self-knowledge is undermined. Yet before seeing the vision of Artegall, Britomart has for a time gazed, in a state of equal perturbation, on her own reflection in the glass. Her quest will be as much for her own identity as for the unknown Artegall. In Helen Cooper's formulation, '[t]he "looking glass" is at once an allegorization of loving at first sight, since a mirror offers nothing except sight; and of the growth into self-awareness consequent on falling in love . . . It is Britomart herself who names [Artegall], as if he were a part of her own subjectivity rather than an independent character'.[51] Yet what the invocation of Narcissus also reminds us, beyond the conventional association with self-love and self-delusion, is that reflection is never exact: as Linda Gregerson notes, '[a] mirror's truth . . . may lie precisely in its refusal to give back a straight rendition of the image before it . . . A history of Ovidian metamorphosis may considerably broaden a pool's reflective capacity, or a poet's ability to manipulate reflection, until plain visual experience is at once deeply mined and seriously compromised'.[52] The surface of water is a shifting and imperfect glass, and the Renaissance mirror was not the shiny precision instrument familiar to modern readers but similarly prone to softenings, shadowings, and distortions.[53]

Even before the recounting of why exactly it is that Britomart is travelling incognito as a knight errant, her concealed or disguised identity is the catalyst for the introduction of the motif of misreading which recurs throughout the Book. Most notorious is Malacasta's attempted seduction of Britomart in 3.1, but throughout the other plots of the Book, unrelated to Britomart, the motif of wrong reading recurs. There is to some extent a continuation here of the motif of the duplicity and deceit personified in the earlier books by

[51] Cooper, *The English Romance in Time*, 254, 255.

[52] Gregerson, *The Reformation of the Subject*, 34.

[53] See the discussion by Michael O'Connell, *Mirror and Veil: The Historical Dimension of Spenser's* Faerie Queene (Chapel Hill: University of North Carolina Press, 1977), 19.

Duessa: but these misinterpretations of Book 3 are less the result of malice, and more understandable, as instances of wrong reading in a difficult text. As the plot weaves in and out, without the linearity, emblematic characterization, and certain closure of the quest-structured earlier books, the characters' misapprehensions mirror the difficult experience of the reader. In his useful essay on 'the narrator' in *The Spenser Encyclopedia*, Jerome S. Dees notes that 'forms of the verb *to read* with at least 15 denotations appear over 130 times in the poem'. More than a quarter of these are in Book 3. Dees also comments that 'the narrator capitalizes on the full range of the verb with its emphasis on judgement, discernment, interpretation and counsel. To be fashioned is to fashion, no innocent act, but always one of interpreting, of seeing aright when one might as easily see wrong'.[54] This is precisely the kind of reading that the reader has been implicitly prepared for by the end of Book 2, and that is essential in Book 3, which demonstrates that one can only become a better lover by reading avidly, actively, and receptively; by becoming a better reader. For all her misreadings and lack of self-awareness, Britomart sees herself as a reader. As Syrithe Pugh puts it, she 'mediates her very self-reflection through her reading of Ovid',[55] melodramatically comparing herself to Ovidian heroines, as well as to Narcissus, and later proves a ready audience for Paridell's tale of his Trojan descent and the founding of Albion. That Britomart and Glauce seek help from Merlin, who responds with chronicle history in the guise of prophecy, shows the trust that she is prepared to place in record. She is by nature intertextual and allusive in her reading—but she must broaden her referential base by reading texts that are not necessarily written, and be more sceptical of those that are.

For, as Britomart's story progresses, Spenser questions the privileged status of the written word, and of sensory, particularly visual, evidence by demonstrating instances of its instability or abuse, most notably in the Castle Joyous and the Masque of Cupid. Book 3 is work in progress, a permeable, unstable, open text. Its outcome, the union of Britomart and Artegall, is apparently providentially assured, but Britomart must nevertheless work hard at it; she must actively read, and so write, her own destiny. The ambivalence and danger of reading and writing is seen most explicitly in the Book's climax at the House of Busirane, where Britomart encounters mysterious inscriptions, a masque of emblematic characters each displaying his or her name, and, finally, the grisly sight of the enchanter himself, torturing Amoret:

> And her before the vile Enchaunter sate,
> Figuring straunge characters of his art,
> With liuing blood he those characters wrate,

[54] Hamilton (ed.), *Spenser Encyclopedia* 499.   [55] Pugh, *Spenser and Ovid*, 119.

> Dreadfully dropping from her dying hart,
> Seeming transfixed with a cruell dart,
> And all perforce to make her him to loue. (3.12. 321)

This scene has been interpreted as a parody of the mechanics of the Petrarchan poetic. But Amoret's bleeding body is also a macabre version of a fountain, the fountain of the Muses, or the life-giving fountain of Christ crucified. The anxieties about writing poetry explored in Book 1 in the figure of Errour are here revisited in a more refined and shocking form.

This 'pittifull spectacle' is subsequently corrected by the second fountain image that frames Book 3, the vision of the Hermaphrodite that was excised and replaced in the 1596 text but has never been forgotten, not least by critics. Britomart has reunited Amoret and Scudamour:

> Lightly he clipt her twixt his armes twaine,
> And streightly did embrace her body bright,
> Her body, late the prison of sad paine,
> Now the sweet lodge of loue and deare delight:
> But she faire Lady ouercommen quight
> Of huge affection, did in pleasure melt,
> And in sweete rauishment pourd out her spright:
> No word they spake, nor earthly thing they felt,
> But like two senceles stocks in long embracement dwelt.

> Had ye them seene, ye would haue surely thought,
> That they had beene that faire *Hermaphrodite*,
> Which that rich *Romane* of white marble wrought,
> And in his costly Bath causd to bee site:
> So seemd those two, as growne together quite. (3.12.45a–46a)

This is an obvious correlative to the Narcissus reference in 3.2, providing the Book with an ending that is both logical and suggestive.[56] The two images are fundamentally connected by their basic point of reference for, although it has many more associations, the Hermaphrodite is also another example of Ovidian metamorphosis associated with a fountain. In a final twist, Spenser emphasizes this watery context by comparing the lovers' embrace to a statue set in a pool:

The complex reference to the Hermaphrodite alludes to Ovid's text at the same time that it subtly calls attention to an absence. The image is not a direct reference to a Hermaphrodite, nor to a statue of the Hermaphrodite, nor is it even a simple metaphor

---

[56] The description of Amoret in particular recalls the same passage from the *Phaedrus* which underlies the description of the ecstasy of union at the Fountain of Venus in the *Hypnerotomachia*. See Chapter 3, and also Krier's discussion of the passage in *Gazing on Secret Sights*, 85–7. Spenser also clearly draws on the account of the origins of love in the *Symposium*, 189–93.

likening the embracing Amoret and Scudamour to a Hermaphrodite. Spenser refers
to a specific statue that is not present in the scene he is describing.[57]

That this statue that does not exist is set in a pool adds the further dimension
of reflection: the image of the Hermaphrodite is one of both fusion and
doubleness, like the names of the lovers themselves, which can be mapped
on to each other yet retain their own discrete identities: 'the picture of chaste
love presented for our edification does not evoke the traditional notion of
two becoming one. Rather, the two lovers become a new entity: a couple'.[58]
Britomart's vision of the Hermaphrodite is a true reflection of something
that is not there, but that could be. Furthermore, Scudamour's greeting of
Amoret 'Like as a Deare, that greedily embayes | In the coole soile, after long
thirstinesse' makes explicit another fountain topos, the *sicut cervus* image of
Psalm 42.[59] The motif of chase, introduced at the very beginning of the Book
by the fleeing Florimell, itself achieves closure in this preliminary image of
refreshment and rest. But the 'bookending' of Britomart's quest with these
two fountain images is more than a neat Ovidian framing device, for the
pairing of Narcissus and Hermaphroditus was not unknown in Renaissance
art. Edgar Wind noted that the Fountain Room at the Château d'Anet
was decorated with pairs of fountains or rivers, including Narcissus and
Hermaphroditus, following Pontus de Tyard's *Douze fables des fleuves ou
fontaines* (1585).[60] Tyard's work is, like Spenser's Hermaphrodite, ekphrastic:
each river or fountain first has its mythical origin related, followed by '*The
description for the painter*'[61] and an epigram, and the dedicatory epistle notes
the architectural context, 'this superb castle of Anet, which has gained its
greatest lustre from your beautiful devices'.[62] In Tyard's sequence, quite
possibly known to Spenser, the pairing occupies a slightly anomalous position,
for—although they are obviously meant to be read as a pair—they are not
adjacent in the sequence:

[57] Lauren Silberman, 'The Hermaphrodite and the Metamorphosis of Spenserian Allegory',
in Mihoko Suzuki (ed.), *Critical Essays on Edmund Spenser* (New York: G. K. Hall and Co., 1996),
163. Despite the specificity of the reference, no description of such a real statue has ever been
traced, and representations of hermaphrodites in sculpture tend to be of beautiful androgynes,
rather than displaying the doubleness implied by Spenser's description.

[58] Silberman, *Transforming Desire*, 69.

[59] See the discussion of Psalm 42 in relation to the *Hypnerotomachia* in Chapters 2 and 3.

[60] See Wind, *Pagan Mysteries*, 77 n. 84, and Frances Yates, *Astraea: The Imperial Theme in
the Sixteenth Century* (London: Routledge and Kegan Paul, 1975), 135. The connection between
Narcissus and Hermaphroditus in the context of Book 3 is also discussed by Nohrnberg, *The
Analogy of The Faerie Queene*, 474.

[61] '*la description pour la Peintre*'; this appears on the title page. The two fables are found in
sig. B3ᵛ–B6ᵛ.

[62] 'cette superbe maison d'Anet, qui a pris son plus grand lustre de vos belles inuentions', sig.
A2ᵛ.

Tyard . . . gave his sequence a clearly binary structure . . . At a given moment, however, this symmetry is ruptured, and replaced by a chiasmus. Two wrongdoers [Inde and Chrysoroas] who, in fleeing from their persecutors, throw themselves into the water, are juxtaposed in poems 7 and 10. This diagonal axis intersects with the axis joining poems 8 and 9, those of Narcissus and Salmacis.[63]

This mysterious chiasmus in Tyard's otherwise strictly ordered sequence parallels the productive instability of the fountain figure in Book 3, as it formally represents a boundary and a surface that can simultaneously reflect and be permeated. Britomart's identification with Narcissus has led her to regard the surface of the mirror-fountain as an impenetrable, impassable barrier and her sudden love for the unknown Artegall as therefore doomed. Since many of the other actions of Book 3 highlight the deceptive nature of sight and the danger of misreading, by its end the reader is as confused about character, plot, ethics, aesthetics, and even genre as is Britomart. But the Hermaphroditic vision suggests that the closure of union is possible; that the mirror-surface of the meniscus is a boundary that can be illusory. In the story of Hermaphroditus, 'Ovid conceives of a selfhood defined by boundaries and surfaces, which are unpredictably fluid or penetrable'.[64] The surface of water, as Leonard Barkan has pointed out, can stand for the possibility of change, growth and transformation, a creative and erotic entering-in;[65] like the *Hypnerotomachia*'s Polia at the Fountain of Venus, Spenser's lovers' bodies are identified with the penetrable surface of the water. The fountains in the Bowre of Bliss and at Kenilworth were morally problematic in their fluidity, their elision of the categories of stone and water, sculpture, fish, bathers, and observers. Here that fluidity, that hermeneutic instability, is welcomed and cherished.

In Books 1 and 2 of *The Faerie Queene*, the linear process of reading, of simply turning pages, mirrors the relatively straightforward quests of Redcrosse and Guyon. While the fountains that they encounter often encode many layers of symbolism, and increasingly raise aesthetic and moral questions, they also have a purely structural function, remaining real and locatable landmarks in the quest landscape. The three fountains of Book 3, however (those of

---

[63] 'Tyard . . . a donné à son cycle une structure nettement binaire . . . À un moment donné, pourtant, cette symmetrie est brisée et remplacée par un chiasme. Deux malfaiteurs qui, en fuyant devant leurs persécuteurs, se jettent dans l'eau, se trouvent juxtaposés dans les poèmes no 7 et 10. Cet axe diagonal se croise avec l'axe des poèmes no 8 et 9, ceux de Narcisse et Salmacis.' Heidi Marek, 'Narcisse et Salmacis: le thème de l'unité et de la diversité dans *Les Douze fables de fleuves ou fontaines* de Pontus de Tyard', in *Sources et fontaines du Moyen Âge à l'Âge Baroque*, 289–90.

[64] Krier, *Gazing on Secret Sights*, 50.

[65] See the discussion of this in relation to Narcissus and the *Hypnerotomachia*'s Fountain of Venus in Chapter 3.

Narcissus, Diana, and the Hermaphrodite) are, as more intertextual, allusive sites, far more subjective, and they foreground and question the nature and process of perception itself. While Redcrosse has Una, Coelia, and the hermit and Guyon the Palmer, Britomart has no guide: Glauce, although implicitly present, is an inconsequential character for much of the action. In Book 3, there are no great scenes of teaching or telling (compare the House of Holinesse and the House of Alma): there is only the prophecy of Merlin and a seemingly unattainable vision in a mirror. Britomart is shown, not told, and in an environment where the evidence of the eyes can be untrustworthy or ambiguous. The comparison with Book 1 is striking, yet Book 3 would be impossible without its hermeneutic precedent; it 'reasserts the role of the reader in making meaning... Instead of training the reader to discover predetermined truth, Spenser emphasizes how precariously meaning is created out of uncertainty and ignorance in the fallen world'.[66] In the Book most concerned with the very nature of reading, Britomart reads alone. The reader shares her disorientation, with the burden of constant (re)interpretation and appraisal being encoded into the reading experience itself. Both protagonist and reader are impelled to become less passive, more unconventional in their strategies of interpretation and consequent action.[67]

Britomart takes her first step towards becoming a more writerly reader[68] when she arms herself (3.3.60). Her lance is a phallic signifier of her newly assumed masculine identity, but it is also an authorial pen, the means by which she will inscribe her own deeds and destiny into the annals of British history. It signifies active, writerly readership. Only Britomart and the reader can free Amoret from where, punningly, she is 'cruelly pend', by seizing the writerly initiative, arriving at a new vision of love, where words are no longer necessary: 'No word they spake, nor earthly thing they felt.' This is not an

---

[66] Silberman, 'The Hermaphrodite', 154.

[67] 'As both Linda Gregerson and Suzanne Wofford have argued, *The Faerie Queene* constructs two alternative models of reading, one which Gregerson terms "idolatrous" and Wofford "allegoric", and which functions by attempting to firmly solidify meaning and control interpretation. The other, called "interpretive" by Gregerson and "errantry" by Wofford, is represented primarily by Britomart, and is a mode of reading that generates indeterminacy or narrative.' Gleckman, 'Providential Love', 229.

[68] One might say that both Britomart and the reader are experienced in the ways of what Barthes termed the readerly text, the *lisible*, further defined by Ann Jefferson as 'what we recognise and already know... that as readers we passively consume' ('Structuralism and Post-Structuralism', in Ann Jefferson and David Robey (eds.), *Modern Literary Theory: A Comparative Introduction* (London: B. T. Batsford, 1986), 108). In Book 3, however, both Britomart and the reader are called upon to engage with the writerly text, the *scriptible*, which '[makes] the reader no longer a consumer, but a producer of the text' (ibid.). Barthes speaks of the reader 'gaining access to the magic of the signifier, to the pleasure of writing' (Roland Barthes, *S/Z*, trans. Richard Miller (London: Jonathan Cape, 1975), 4).

easy process, but it is a compelling one. Throughout Britomart's story reading is seen as work, as a labour of interpretation, involving total commitment and openness to possible clues, to intertextual assistance of all kinds, and to risk-taking. Lauren Silberman suggests that 'Britomart's quest for Artegall involves braving the hermeneutic gap between self and other; Book 3 defines reading as an act of courage, with both moral and sexual connotations of the word "courage" relevant to the hermeneutic enterprise'.[69] Where Books 1 and 2 have illustrated the perils of the unarmed mind and the unarmed eyes, Book 3 explores the perilous necessity—and the potential rewards—of the unarmed heart. As Merlin tells Britomart, 'let no whit dismay | The hard begin, that meets thee in the door'.

The final stanza of Book 3, like its Proem, explicitly addresses this idea of writing and reading as work: 'But now my teme begins to faint and fayle, | All woxen weary of their iournall toyle: | Therefore I will their sweatie yokes assoyle | At this same furrowes end, till a new day' (3.12.47a). The writer, like the oxen, deserves a break. From the work of reading, writing, and imagination to that of real excavation: the Kenilworth fountain—so vividly described by Robert Langham—was rediscovered in the summer of 2005, although a nondescript octagonal base of rubble and cement, together with three small flakes of white marble, are all that survive. It had been missed in a number of previous archaeological investigations of the privy garden site because the site had been looked at and interpreted in the wrong way, based on mistaken assumptions as to the dimensions and axes of the garden. This is not a metaphor that can be taken much further, but it is a suggestive one with which to conclude this discussion of the fountains of *The Faerie Queene*: to look for and at things in new ways can be revelatory. And the poem goes on to conclude 'And ye faire Swayns, after your long turmoyle, | Now cease your worke, and at your pleasure play; | Now cease your worke; tomorrow is an holy day' (3.12.47a). The 'swayns' are Scudamour and Amoret, but the readers of the poem are also being addressed. While 'Tomorrow is a holiday' it is also a 'holy day', and Psalm 42 ('As the hart panteth after the water brooks') is proper to Easter Saturday.[70] Book 3 has nothing like the eschatological framework of Book 1, or even of Book 2, but it too concludes with a revelatory, transformative vision of a fountain, after a legend in which fountains have themselves been a significant aid to seeing, and reading, and loving, in a new way.

[69] Silberman, 'The Hermaphrodite', 158.

[70] See Anne Lake Prescott, 'The Thirsty Deer and the Lord of Life: Some Contexts for *Amoretti* 67–70', *Spenser Studies*, 6 (1985).

Part III

Poisoned Springs:
Jonson's *The Fountaine of Selfe-Love* (1600)

9

The Public Fountain: Elizabethan Politics and the Humanist Tradition

Sometimes displayed among the Elizabethan and Jacobean miniatures in the National Portrait Gallery in London, but all too easily overlooked amidst the jewel-like Hilliards and Olivers, is a small, worn portrait medal in lead, less than two inches in diameter (Fig. 13).[1] Not surprisingly, its obverse portrays Elizabeth in traditional profile, surrounded by a conventional inscription: ELIZABETH. D.G. AN[GLI]AE. ET HIBE[RNIAE. R]EGINA.[2] The reverse, however, depicts a rarer subject, difficult to make out because of both its unfamiliarity and the medal's worn state. A woman, clasping a cross to her breast, sits beside a fountain, the waters of which stream out and down from its top, and a Greek motto states that this is ZAΘEH.BA[Σ]IΛIHΣ.AIBAΣ, 'the Divine Fountain of the Realm'. The woman is Fides, and the motto is an anagram of EΛIZABHΘ H BAΣIΛIΣΣA, 'Elizabeth the Queen'. Although this significance is obviously only available, at least initially, to those with a facility in Greek anagrams, the implication once the anagram is decoded is clear: 'Elizabeth the Queen' *is* 'the Divine Fountain of the Realm'. The medal was the project of Stephen van Herwijk, a Flemish metalworker living in England in the mid-1560s, and Charles Utenhove, a Flemish Protestant poet, who designed its programme. Utenhove's correspondence with William Cecil, seeking approval for the medal and its anagrammatical symbolism, survives; it includes a French poem describing Elizabeth as 'la Divine fontaine | En vertu, en savoir, en beauté souveraine' (the Divine fountain, sovereign in virtue, wisdom, and beauty).

There is an obvious continuity here with the material discussed in previous chapters, and above all with Elizabeth's 1559 coronation entry: the Queen is

---

[1] NPG 4294. The medal is succinctly discussed by Roy Strong in *Gloriana*, 62–3, and in more detail by Jan Van Dorsten, 'Steven Van Herwijk's Elizabeth (1565): A Franco-Flemish Political Medal', *Burlington Magazine*, 111 (1969) and *The Radical Arts: First Decade of an Elizabethan Renaissance* (Leiden: Leiden University Press, 1970). It is also noted by John N. King, *Tudor Royal Iconography: Literature and Art in an Age of Religious Crisis* (Princeton: Princeton University Press, 1989), 107.

[2] The medal has some damage around the edges, but the inscription is easily reconstructed.

associated with the unsullied springs of pure Scripture and doctrine and as she is refreshed at faith's fountain, so she in turn conveys that same spiritual refreshment to her people. Yet the medal, its emblem, and motto also draw upon and affirm the broader political symbolism of the fountain figure. This is perhaps unsurprising, for both van Herwijk and Utenhove were known for their Protestant internationalist sympathies, and the medal commemorated the 1565 Treaty of Troyes. The fountain is an ancient and complex political symbol which, as will be seen here, was specifically associated with Elizabeth I in subtle, yet increasingly complicated and ambivalent ways. This chapter first establishes a nexus of classical and humanist texts concerned with princely power and authority, and then examines some of the ways in which the Queen's image was reflected and refracted in terms of the fountain in art and literature, thus establishing a literary and cultural frame both for Elizabethan gardens and for a play by Ben Jonson.

Near the end of Elizabeth's reign and in the context of its last great crisis, the fall of the Earl of Essex (as Chapter 12 in particular explores), Ben Jonson wrote *The Fountaine of Selfe-Love. Or Cynthias Revels*, which appeared in print in 1601, soon after its first performances. It has attracted relatively little critical attention, and has often been judged harshly by the little attention it has drawn, as embarrassingly conventional praise of the ageing Queen Elizabeth, the 'Cynthia' of its title, tempered with under-developed court satire. Perhaps because, following the reversal of its title in the 1616 Folio,[3] the play is generally known simply as *Cynthia's Revels*, the centrality of the titular fountain to the play has been lost. Taking the fountain as a point of interpretative departure, however, recovers the play's underlying unity and cohesion, in its thematic concerns and in the imagery through which they are presented. Refocusing on this device recovers the play's theatrical innovation, polemical daring, and its acute specificity to its historical moment. Its lack of plot, static, wordy action, and flat, unsympathetic characters have been allowed to obscure some of its more radical features, such as its pervasive metatheatricality and its complex and not unambivalent vision of the Queen. In its fountain, *The Fountaine of Selfe-Love* makes notable use of a visual symbol as a syncretic device that keeps the play's concerns before the audience

---

[3] In the quarto the title page names the play as *The Fovntaine of Selfe-Love. Or Cynthias Revels*. In the 1616 Folio the play appears as *Cynthias Revels, or The Fountayne of selfe-Loue. A Comicall Satyre*, and it has been known as *Cynthia's Revels* ever since. Janet Clare discusses some of the other differences between the two versions, and the various ways in which they can be interpreted in *Art Made Tongue-Tied by Authority: Elizabethan and Jacobean Dramatic Censorship* (Manchester: Manchester University Press, 1999), 104–6. Criticism of the play has perhaps also been hampered by the fact that Herford and Simpson printed only the Folio version in their edition, which is a much enlarged text.

even when they are long absent from its action. Jonson used the fountain to expose and interrogate the nature and function of the court and of the poet, and in so doing he employed a figure that already inhered with a rich variety of associations and meanings. He therefore did not need continually either to explicate them or even to draw more than token attention to the device itself, which retains an eloquent and significant presence for most, if not all, of the play. To approach *Cynthia's Revels* once again as *The Fountaine of Selfe-Love* does not make it a great play, but it helps to make better sense of both the play itself and its cultural and historical context, and the intertextual strategies of interpretation, in the broadest possible sense, that it solicits.

When Jonson substantially rewrote *The Fountaine of Selfe-Love* for its inclusion in the 1616 Folio of his works, he introduced it with a dedication 'To the Speciall Fovntaine of Manners: The Court':

Thou art a bountifull, and braue spring: and waterest all the noble plants of this Iland. *In thee, the whole Kingdome dresseth it selfe, and is ambitious to vse thee as her glasse. Beware, then, thou render mens figures truly, and teach them no lesse to hate their deformities, then to loue their formes: For, to grace, there should come reuerence; and no man can call that louely, which is not also venerable. It is not pould'ring, perfuming, and euery day smelling of the taylor, that conuerteth to a beautiful obiect: but a mind, shining through any sute, which needes no false light either of riches, or honors to helpe it. Such shalt thou find some here, euen in the raigne of* CYNTHIA *(a* CRITES, *and an* ARETE.*) Now, vnder thy* PHŒBVS, *it will be thy prouince to make more: Except thou desirest to haue thy source mixe with the* Spring *of* selfe-Loue, *and so wilt draw vpon thee as welcome a discouery of thy dayes, as was then made of her nights.* Thy seruant, but not slaue, BEN. IONSON.[4]

The image of the fountain as applied to the relationship between prince and state is an old one, with many variations, but it seems to have been particularly current in the late sixteenth century. It is surprising, therefore, that no sustained attempt seems to have been made to read *The Fountaine of Selfe-Love* in the light of this popular motif, nor yet to use the play as a lens through which to re-examine the many other appearances of the fountain figure, albeit generally less extended ones, in court and political contexts in the late sixteenth century. In Jonson's play in particular, the political fountain is entwined with other strong associations of the fountain figure, with poetry and language, for example, as well as the obvious Narcissus connection. Although Leonard Barkan has observed in passing that '[t]he image of the fountain as source from which the purity or impurity of the monarch flows through the commonwealth is quite common in English Renaissance

---

[4] Ben Jonson, *The Workes of Beniamin Ionson* (London, 1616), sig. P6ᵛ.

literature, turning up in such disparate texts as the *Faerie Queene* and *The Duchess of Malfi*. Jonson cleverly unites this tradition with mythological sources of water, especially Narcissus' pool',[5] there is a great deal more to be said, especially as Barkan makes the assumption that *The Fountaine of Selfe-Love* celebrates the Queen as Cynthia/Diana without ambiguity. As Jonson's dedication makes clear, his play tropes on two by now familiar and paradoxically interrelated qualities of the fountain figure: its capacity to reflect, and its ability to transmit, the way in which it is both 'glasse' and 'spring'. Elizabeth's accustomed persona of the goddess Diana (represented as 'Cynthia' by Jonson) was 'among the Poets . . . called the goddesse of hunting, and imperiall gouernesse of pleasant groues, shrub-bearing hils, and christal-faced fountaines'.[6] Sir John Davies could therefore describe his queen, in the space of a stanza, as

> The Christall glasse that will no venome hold,
> The mirror wherein Angels loue to looke:
> DIANAES bathing fountaine, cleare and cold,
> Beauties fresh Rose, and vertues liuing booke.[7]

The fountain's reflecting surface can stand for exemplarity, while its flowing waters are the means by which that exemplarity is to be transmitted. Yet in both these capacities, as Jonson's dedication and his play reveal, the fountain of the prince or of the court is vulnerable to distortion and corruption. One is reminded here of Horace's Ode to the Fons Bandusiae, the purity of which is praised in part so that its subsequent pollution may be the more strikingly described.[8]

This vulnerability is implicit in the many appearances of the figure in the humanist political texts upon which Jonson apparently draws, and which would have been very familiar to his audience.[9] An extended contemporary example of the fountain being used to describe the relationship between the prince and the state can be found, for example, in Sir Thomas Elyot's *The Image of Gouernaunce* (1556).[10] At the beginning of his reign, the young emperor Alexander Severus is urged by his mother Mammea to reform his court for the good of the nation: 'the princes palaice is like a common fountayne or springe

[5] Leonard Barkan, 'Diana and Actaeon: The Myth as Synthesis', *English Literary Renaissance*, 10 (1980), 333 n. 33. See also Brown, 'Arachne's Web', 128.

[6] Richard Lynche, *The Fountaine of Ancient Fiction* (London, 1599), sig. H1ᵛ.

[7] Sir John Davies, 'A Contention betwixt a Wife, a Widdow, and a Maide', in Francis Davison, *A poetical rapsodie* (London, 1611), sig. B7ᵛ.

[8] Discussed in Chapter 6.

[9] See the useful related discussion of the 'troubled fountain' figure by Rolf Soellner, 'The Troubled Fountain: Erasmus Formulates a Shakespearian Simile', *Journal of English and Germanic Philology*, 55 (1956), 70–4.

[10] This is the latest edition, and the one from which I quote. The first appeared in 1541.

to his citee or countrey, wherby the people by the cleanesse therof be long preserued in honestiee, or by the impurenesse therof, are with sundry vices corrupted. And vntyll the fountaine be purged, there can neuer be any sure hope of remedie.' Alexander himself then employs the same image when outlining his planned reforms to the Senate:

we desyre none other prerogatiue, but that it maye take his fyrst begynnynge at our propre palayce and householde, and in our owne persone to be fyrste executed, to the intente that the principall fountayne, beyng founde cleane, the remnant of our subiectes, whose order of lyuing procedeth of our exaumple, as riuers and sundry lakes from a heade sprynge, whiche is sette on a mountayne, may with lyttle dyfficultee be more easely pourged.[11]

In the Cambridge University Library copy, this passage has been annotated in a contemporary hand, most heavily in this portion of the text, which is by no means annotated throughout.[12] The two notes on F1ᵛ read 'Alexander wold haue reformation to begyn at his owne palace & in his own person' and 'subiectes resemble their princes liuing as the rivers doe *the* springes'. Both the principle and the metaphor seem therefore to have had particular appeal to at least one reader in the second half of the sixteenth century.

In *The Education of a Christian Prince* Erasmus (once again), using a related image, had made much the same point:

The common people imitate nothing with more pleasure than what they see their prince do. Under a gambler, gambling is rife; under a fighter, everyone gets into fights; under a gourmandizer, they wallow in extravagance; under a voluptuary, they become promiscuous; under a cruel man, they bring charges and false accusations against each other. Turn the pages of history and you will always find the morality of an age reflecting the life of its prince . . . He is supreme in goodness, and his goodness flows from him to other men as from a spring.[13]

In the last decade of Elizabeth's reign, Anthony Fletcher expressed the principle more aphoristically: 'Euen as a brooke doth follow the nature of the fountaine, from whence it commeth: So people do follow the disposition of their prince: the fountaine being troubled, the brooke is troubled also, and the prince disquieted, the people finde no peace'.[14] As one would expect, in *The*

[11] Sir Thomas Elyot, *The Image of Governaunce* (London, 1556), sig. E5ᵛ, F1ᵛ.
[12] The copy (Pet.F.4.30), originally from the library of Peterborough Cathedral, is in good condition and appears still to be in its original vellum binding, as none of the marginal annotations have been cropped by rebinding.
[13] Desiderius Erasmus, *The Education of a Christian Prince*, trans. Neil M. Cheshire and Michael J. Heath (Toronto: Toronto University Press, 1986), 219–20.
[14] Anthony Fletcher, *Certaine Very Proper, and Most Profitable Similies* (London, 1595), sig. B3.

Education of a Christian Prince Erasmus was particularly concerned with the advice that is given to a monarch, and he once again used the fountain image to express this:

no man does the state a greater service than he who equips a prince's mind, which must consider all men's interests, with the highest principles, worthy of a prince; and that no one, on the other hand, brings such appalling disaster upon the affairs of mortal men as he who corrupts the prince's heart with wrongful opinions or desires, just as a man might put deadly poison in the public spring . . . Just as someone who poisons the public fountain from which everybody drinks deserves the severest of punishments, so someone who implants in a prince's mind perverted ideas, which will eventually be the ruin of a great many people, is the most vicious of men. Given that anyone who debases the prince's coinage is punished with death, how much more deserving of that punishment is someone who corrupts his mind?[15]

As Erasmus himself indicates, his ultimate source was Plutarch's *Moralia*: 'the slanderers, backbiters, and flatterers who constantly corrupt rulers or kings or tyrants, are driven away and punished by everyone, as if they were putting deadly poison, not into a single cup, but into the public fountain which, as they see, everyone uses'.[16] Both Erasmus and Plutarch emphasize the autonomous power of the prince, but also that it is an autonomy the moral character of which is largely determined by environment.

John Webster gave the idea probably its most explicit and striking expression in the first years of the reign of James I, in the opening scene of *The Duchess of Malfi*:

> a Princes Court
> Is like a common Fountaine, whence should flow
> Pure silver-droppes in generall: But if't chance
> Some curs'd example poyson't neere the head,
> Death, and diseases through the whole land spread.[17]

Webster's words are in fact strongly reminiscent of the concluding lines of *The Fountaine of Selfe-Love*:

> Princes that would their People should do well
> Must at themselues begin, as at the heads;
> For men by their example patterne out
> Their Imitations, and reguard of Lawes:
> A vertuous Court, a world to vertue drawes.
>
> (5.5, M1ᵛ)

[15] Erasmus, *The Education of a Christian Prince*, 203, 211.
[16] Plutarch, *Moralia*, 778 D.
[17] *The Works of John Webster*, 1: *The White Devil, The Duchess of Malfi*, ed. David Gunby, David Carnegie, and Antony Hammond (Cambridge: Cambridge University Press, 1995), 1.1.11–5.

This is unsurprising given their shared humanist sources. But Jonson gives his version of these sentiments to his character of Cynthia, his Elizabeth figure, rather than to a courtier as Webster does, and at the end of his play rather than in its opening scene. Webster's play in fact uses the figure of the fountain to explore particular issues surrounding female rule: it is not simply a court vulnerable to corruption, but the Duchess's unchaste female body that becomes the common fountain. For both Webster and Jonson, and their classical and humanist antecedents, the prince is vulnerable to the influence of courtiers and advisers, who must therefore be carefully chosen and monitored, for they influence not only the ruler as an individual, but the realm. That Webster could begin his Jacobean play with such an image, in a way that Jonson could surely not, save implicitly, suggests the particular potential for tension between the conventional nature of the fountain image, applied to the operation of monarchical government at least since Plutarch and especially by Renaissance humanists, and its simultaneous specificity to Elizabeth, Mulcaster's Protestant Veritas, van Herwijk's 'Divine Fountain of the Realm', and Cynthia, Diana, 'goddesse . . . of christal-faced fountaines'.

Many occurrences of fountain imagery associated with Elizabeth were straightforward, merely troping on the conventions of royal favour and bounty. The oration by the Norwich schoolmaster Stephan Limbert on the occasion of Elizabeth's visit to the city in August 1578 is typical:

It is reported (moste gracious Queene) that Ægypte is watered with the yerely overflowing of the Nilus, and Lydia with the golden streame of Pactolus, whyche thing is though to be the cause of the greate fertilitye of these countries: but uppon us, and farther, over all Englande, even into the uttermoste borders, many and maine rivers of godlynesse, justice, humilitie, and other innumerable good things, in comparison of the whyche golde is vile and noughte worth, do most plentifully gushe out, and those not from Tmolus or other hilles I knowe not whiche, but from that continuall and most aboundant welspring of your goodnesse . . . [18]

In a similar vein, a visitor to Whitehall, Thomas Platter, saw a motto forming part of a mural in one of her chambers:

Again I noticed a hand stretching a fore finger out of the clouds, accompanied by this verse:

> Tu lux unde suam deducunt cetera lucem
> Tu fons unde suos depromunt singula succos
> Tu medicina alijs quae fers (Regina) salutem
> Tu mihi lux, mihi fons, tu medicina mihi,

[18] Nichols, *The Progresses and Public Processions of Queen Elizabeth*, ii. 157.

being in English

> Thou art the light from whom others take their brilliance
> Thou art the fount of others' springs
> Thou art an elixir, thou Queen, bringest health
> Thou art my light, my fount, my elixir,[19]

and Baron Waldstein had noted a similar motto—'Vivat regina Elisabetha, in qua fons omnis prudentiae' ('Long live Queen Elizabeth, in whom is the source of all wise dealing')—inscribed into a mantelpiece at Hampton Court.[20] In a straightforwardly Ovidian vein the Queen's bathroom at Whitehall was a grotto-like affair, surely meant to recreate the bath of Diana, in which 'the water pour[ed] from oyster shells and different kinds of rock'.[21]

'Real' fountains (as opposed to their simple evocation) also appeared as embroidered motifs on Elizabeth's clothes, and among her jewellery, although they were far from being a common motif. As well as the flowers and foliage which might seem conventional to modern sensibilities, Elizabeth possessed garments embroidered with flies, worms, and snails, shrimps, flames, and stars, the signs of the zodiac, rocks, ships, and fishes and (in a particularly unlikely combination) scallop shells and bagpipes.[22] The Nine Muses made appearances on two garments, a petticoat with a border of 'pomegranetts pyne aple trees frutidge and the nyne Muses' and another, of white satin, 'embroidered allover with peramydes pillers and Muses in cloudes with

---

[19] Clare Williams, *Thomas Platter's Travels in England, 1599* (London: Jonathan Cape, 1937), 164–5.

[20] G. W. Groos, *The Diary of Baron Waldstein: A Traveller in Elizabethan England* (London: Thames and Hudson, 1981), 147.

[21] Ibid. 51. Waldstein was in England in 1600. Unfortunately Philip Julius, Duke of Stettin-Pomerania, travelling through England two years later only noted that at Whitehall the Queen had 'a nice bathroom' ('eine feine Badestube'), 'Diary of the Journey of Philip Julius, Duke of Stettin-Pomerania, through England in the year 1602', ed. Gottfried von Bülow, *Transactions of the Royal Historical Society*, 6 (ns) (1892), 24–5.

[22] References to these, and many others, can be found in Janet Arnold, *Queen Elizabeth's Wardrobe Unlock'd: The Inventories of the Wardrobe of Robes Prepared in July 1600 Edited from Stowe MS 557 in the British Library, MS LR 2/121 in the Public Record Office, London, and MS V.b.72 in the Folger Shakespeare Library, Washington DC* (London: Maney, 1988); these examples are found on pp. 284, 291, 292, 341. There is perhaps a rare pictorial record of one of these garments in the portrait of a woman thought to be of Mary Edmondes, née Clerke, the wife of Sir Clement Edmondes, who had been a waiting gentlewoman to Lady Stafford, herself one of Queen Elizabeth's women for forty years. This relationship would certainly fit the patterns of distribution known for Elizabeth's cast-off clothes. Clearly visible under her elaborate black and white costume is a brightly embroidered petticoat, upon which a castle, sun, rain, and a sea filled with fish and sea monsters can be seen. See the catalogue entry in Karen Hearn (ed.), *Dynasties: Painting in Tudor and Jacobean England 1530–1630* (London: Tate Gallery, 1995), 197–8.

a faire broade border embrodered like clouds and pavilions of venice golde silver and silke of sondrie colours'.[23] Even given the already crowded nature of this last garment, one wonders if there might yet have been some room for Helicon and its spring. Surviving garments and fragments in the Victoria and Albert Museum and elsewhere attest to the density and liveliness of the embroidered decoration on the clothing of the rich at the end of the sixteenth century. Sometimes such devices on the garments of the Queen were merely decorative; on other occasions (and particularly when the garments had been presented to the Queen as gifts) they may well have been making a political or ideological point on behalf of the giver.

This embroidery was executed by both professionals and talented amateurs, and it is not unlikely that some of the petticoats given to Elizabeth in particular might have been the work of their female givers. The great portrait of Elizabeth at Hardwick Hall probably records one such gift by Bess of Hardwick, Countess of Shrewsbury, to the Queen as modelled by its recipient. The Countess was a notable embroiderer, and much of her work, including that created in collaboration with Mary Stuart, who was in the official custody of the Countess's fourth husband George Talbot, Earl of Shrewsbury, 1568–84, survives. The portrait of the Queen dates from 1599–1601, and Janet Arnold notes a payment of £50 to the Queen's tailor William Jones, in 1601, which could conceivably be for the gown's making up.[24] The gown, covered in flowers, birds, and aquatic animals, is the most elaborate example of embroidery in any of the Queen's portraits. It is probably overly fanciful to relate it too closely to this discussion of fountains, but the way in which the flowers, fish, animals, and birds decorating it are frequently depicted as emerging from their own discrete patches of water makes the gown itself, and even its intended wearer, the Queen herself, a pond or stream.

In the last years of the sixteenth century there seems to have been a particular vogue for garments with 'piramides' or obelisks: five petticoats embellished thus were given as New Year's gifts to the Queen in 1598–1600 alone.[25] Fountains were perhaps in some respects a sub-category of this particular architectural device, like the pillars and spires also encountered embellishing the Queen's clothes at about this time. In Whitney's *Choice of Emblemes* (1586), the 'pyramid' (like the device of the pillar, notably in the 'Sieve'

---

[23] Arnold, *Queen Elizabeth's Wardrobe Unlock'd*, 300, 302.

[24] Ibid. 76–80. For a surviving example of the Countess' embroidery, see cover illustration.

[25] The 1600 inventories list five gowns (both 'round' and 'loose'), seven kirtles (an undergown, of which only the front was usually seen), a forepart (the apron-like detachable front of a skirt), a cloak, a 'juppe and safeguard' (a long protective coat and matching skirt, worn for riding), a doublet, and no fewer than nine petticoats. Ibid. 272, 274 (3), 277, 283, 284 (2), 285 (4), 294, 315.

portrait) stood for the constancy and steadfastness of the Prince, while the ivy or vine it sometimes supported was the Church;[26] the accompanying motto reads 'Te stante, virebo' ('While you endure, I will flourish').[27] The fountain had a similarly political significance, and it may have appeared as a specifically political or ideological device on Elizabeth's clothes at much the same time. As Janet Arnold observed, '[t]he often complex symbolism expressed in the rich embroideries was in many cases carefully chosen by close friends and loyal subjects as well as those trying to climb the ladder of preferment'.[28] That the gifts of jewellery given to Elizabeth often had (barely) hidden meanings is well known, Philip Sidney's gift of a whip of gold and diamonds with cords of seed pearls in 1580–1 being but the most often-cited example. While in 1575 the gift of a gold pendant in the shape of 'a very smale fountayne' seems to have been purely ornamental, in the late 1570s and early 1580s the emblematic nature of the jewels and other items presented to the Queen appears to have become more prominent, with some of the gifts apparently referred to the vexed question of her proposed marriage with Anjou. In 1578–9 the anti-marriage Sir Henry Sidney gave 'a feyer juell of golde, with a Dyana', while two years later the pro-marriage Earl of Arundel presented 'a bodkin of goulde, with a pendante, being a cradell garnished with small dyamondes'.[29]

In 1577–8, however, the Queen was presented with a less ostentatious gift, 'A feyer cushyn of purple vellat, very feyerly embrawdred with the story of Truth set with garnetts and sede perle, the backsyde purple satten frynged, and tassells of Venice golde and sylke'.[30] It was presented (and, one assumes, commissioned, perhaps even executed) by the Duchess of Suffolk, and its 'story of Truth' was presumably some representation of *Veritas Temporis Filia*, the central pageant of Elizabeth's coronation entry in 1559. Katherine Bertie, Duchess of Suffolk (1519–80), was one of the last, and most formidable, survivors of the circle of Katherine Parr. Born Katherine Willoughby, daughter of William Willoughby, eleventh Baron Willoughby de Eresby, and Maria de Salinas, maid of honour to Katherine of Aragon, in 1533 she had become at 14 the fourth and last wife of Charles Brandon, Duke of Suffolk, and she remained prominent in court circles after his death in 1545. In the reign of Edward VI, she had been one of the greatest patrons of the reformers, the dedicatee of Erasmus' *Paraphrases* and the especial champion of Hugh Latimer; she and her second husband Richard Bertie (m. 1552?) had been celebrated Marian exiles, their wanderings (as far as Poland, where their son Peregrine was

---

[26] Geoffrey Whitney, *A Choice of Emblemes* (London, 1586), sig. A1.
[27] Arnold, *Queen Elizabeth's Wardrobe Unlock'd*, 87.   [28] Ibid. 2.
[29] Nichols, *The Progresses and Public Processions of Queen Elizabeth*, i. 413, ii. 257, 301.
[30] Ibid., ii. 67.

born) being recorded by Foxe and also the subject of a ballad and a play.[31] Katherine Bertie's royal connections ensured her a place in court circles, but her Protestant convictions and activities meant that her relationship with Elizabeth was increasingly strained. The year of her gift, 1577–8, marked the end of the first phase of Anjou's (formerly Alençon's) courtship of the Queen, brought to an end (among other factors) by Elizabeth's reluctance to intervene in the Low Countries. As in the case of the original tableau, the materiality and ritual context of the Duchess' gift seems to have made it oblique—the 'story of Truth' was a cushion, just as in 1559 the fountain of spiritual truth was a conduit and the Word of Truth was a book (and a gift)—its slightly coded nature perhaps taking the edge off its reproach in a way that would not be possible in the case of a textual or even a more purely visual device. But in the context of the moment, the Duchess' choice of subject for her gift, if it was indeed an allusion to the coronation pageant of *Veritas Temporis Filia*, was a pointed reminder to Elizabeth of her obligations and identity as a Protestant Queen.

Even the gifts of clothing to the Queen at New Year on occasion contrived to instruct as well as to delight and flatter her, although perhaps none was quite so overt as the Duchess of Suffolk's cushion. In 1599 Sir Thomas Jarratt presented as a New Year's gift to the Queen 'the Nether skirtes of a pettycote of white satten embrothered all over like fountaynes and flowers with a broade border likewise embrothered', and a second petticoat, also of white satin, but 'embroidered allover with blacke flies with a border of fountaines and Trees embroidered rounde aboute it and waves of the Sea',[32] was also in the Wardrobe in 1600. Particularly interesting, and more concrete, in the context of the political symbolism of fountains is another garment given to the Queen as a New Year's gift, although at an earlier date. In 1585 Fulke Greville had presented the Queen with 'A Covering for a French gowne of Lawne Imbraudered with Fountaynnes snakes and swordes all over', which was evidently still in the Wardrobe in 1600.[33] It is surely not far-fetched, given Greville's commitment to what his most recent biographer terms 'the

---

[31] John Foxe, *Actes and Monuments* (1583), 2078–81 (Yyyyy3–Yyyyy4ᵛ). The ballad by Thomas Deloney, 'The most rare and excellent History Of the Dutchesse of Suffolkes calamity', was reprinted at least seven times in the seventeenth century, and had originally appeared in Deloney's *Strange Histories* (1602). Thomas Drue's play *The life of the dutches of Suffolke*, which does not go much beyond the events described in the ballad, was published in 1631.

[32] Arnold, *Queen Elizabeth's Wardrobe Unlock'd*, 299, 301.

[33] Ibid. 270. There is some confusion because the 1600 inventory lists what is clearly the same garment as being 'embrodered allover with Fountaines, Snailes, swordes and other devices', and Arnold suggests that this is either scribal error or else both snakes and snails appeared; they were both common decorative motifs. A covering was an over-garment of semi-transparent fabric; there is a good example in the 'Pelican' portrait.

humanist notion of service to one's prince',[34] to speculate that this decoration referred to government, prudence, and justice. At about the same time, the currency and centrality of the image of the fountain of royal patronage and favour allowed Philip Sidney, less than a decade after the loyal Norwich schoolmaster, to declare that Elizabeth might not be the only such fountain. He wrote in a letter to Walsingham, '[i]f her majesty were the fountain I would fear considering what I daily find that we should wax dry, but she is but a means whom God useth and I know not whether I am deceived but I am faithfully persuaded that if she should withdraw herself other springs would rise to help this action'.[35] Like Katherine Bertie, Duchess of Suffolk, a few years earlier, Sidney was concerned with the plight of Protestants in the Netherlands, the English intervention, led by Leicester, and Elizabeth's wavering patronage of the campaign. He suggested in his choice of image that Elizabeth was no longer necessarily unique or irreplaceable as 'the fount of others' springs',[36] and he perhaps also glanced at the specifically Protestant associations of the identification of Elizabeth with the fountain. A few years later, these associations were once more revisited in George Peele's mayoral pageant *Descensus Astraeae*.[37]

A tapestry now in the Victoria and Albert Museum is perhaps more ambiguous—if less obviously pointed—than these glimpses into Elizabeth's wardrobe and gift inventories, although it is suggestively similar to Greville's 'covering' in date. It was woven for the Earl of Leicester in about 1585, probably for his London residence, Leicester House.[38] The massive panel depicts in its centre Leicester's arms and motto, flanked on either side by an elaborate fountain. The two fountains are very similar, but not identical, and the one on the left, in particular, has several features in common with the great fountain at Kenilworth,[39] both being topped with Leicester's bear and ragged staff. Anthony Wells-Cole has shown, however, that the fountain designs are in fact copied from designs by Vredeman de Vries, published by Gerard de Iode in his *Artis Perspectivae* (Antwerp, 1568). He suggests further that the tapestries may have been woven by workers closely connected with the Sheldon works, but working in a workshop attached to the Great Wardrobe in London, noting payments at that time to Richard Hickes, who was the

---

[34] John Gouws, 'Greville, Fulke, First Baron Brooke of Beauchamps Court (1554–1628)', *Oxford Dictionary of National Biography* (www.oxforddnb.com/view/article/11516, accessed 16 Mar. 2006).

[35] Quoted by Worden, *The Sound of Virtue*, 46; see also *The Major Works*, 295.

[36] As she had been described in one of the painted mottoes at Whitehall; see above.

[37] This is noted in Chapter 5, and discussed in Chapter 10.

[38] Two associated side panels are now in the Burrell Collection in Glasgow; a second horizontal panel known to have been in Drayton House in the 1920s is now lost.

[39] Discussed in Chapter 8.

head of one of the Sheldon workshops but who also worked in London.[40] The records suggest that the tapestries were destined for a banqueting house, a location certainly in keeping with their opulence and exotic decoration; one might also observe that banqueting houses, like fountains, often related as much to the garden as to the house, and were similarly situated in a position that was liminal to both the natural and the built environment of an estate. The Sheldon factories were at Barcheston (or Barston) in Warwickshire and Bordesley in Worcestershire, both close to Kenilworth, and it has been observed of the large-scale tapestry county maps for which the Sheldon works were best known that they 'suggest a personal knowledge of the country by the designer of each map, for usually the churches are correctly represented, with or without a spire'.[41] It is surely not unlikely that Leicester would commission as decoration for his London home a tapestry representing or at least recalling one of the most celebrated features of his greatest house, and that the tapestry's designers and weavers might also have used their own knowledge of Kenilworth in its execution, adapting their known visual source in the process.

A fountain, whether 'real' or imaginary, such as might be represented in a grand tapestry, is on one level simply a familiar trope of elaborate and luxurious display; that the Leicester tapestry draws on a Dutch engraving of an imaginary scene affirms that. But here the possibility of reading the fountains as images of monarchy and government, and their juxtaposition with Leicester's personal motto, 'Droict et Loyal' (just and loyal), the fountains being surmounted with his badge, hints at the contingent nature of such government. Leicester perhaps marked the importance of his many years of loyal and devoted service to the Queen by crowning an image of her rule with his own personal device. He had been just and loyal in his service to the Queen, and her successful rule had in some senses depended upon that continued loyalty. As Plutarch and Erasmus had taught, the public fountain's influence and the prince's power were inseparable from their vulnerability and, as Jonson himself explores in *The Fountaine of Selfe-Love*, language itself could be described in much the same terms, being intimately connected to princely power and moral and cultural order, and similarly vulnerable to corruption.[42]

This vulnerability is given perhaps its most graphic expression in the period in one of the most shocking moments in early modern drama, the speech

[40] Wells-Cole, *Art and Decoration in Elizabethan and Jacobean England*, 79, 222–3.

[41] John Humphreys, *Elizabethan Sheldon Tapestries* (London: Oxford University Press, 1929), 16. Humphreys suggests that the tapestry depicts the Kenilworth fountain and that it was woven to decorate Elizabeth's bedchamber at Kenilworth in 1575. This is extremely unlikely.

[42] The corruption of language is discussed in Chapter 11.

of Marcus on the appearance of his niece Lavinia, her hands cut off and her tongue cut out, following her rape, in Shakespeare's *Titus Andronicus* (1594):

> Alas, a crimson river of warm blood,
> Like to a bubbling fountain stirred with wind,
> Doth rise and fall between thy rosed lips,
> Coming and going with thy honey breath . . .
> Ah, now thou turn'st away thy face for shame,
> And notwithstanding all this loss of blood,
> As from a conduit with three issuing spouts,
> Yet do thy cheeks look red as Titan's face,
> Blushing to be encountered with a cloud.[43]

Titus Andronicus was one of the most popular plays of the 1590s, and Jonson may have known it better than many: it had been the property of the Admiral's Men, before passing to the Chamberlain's Men in the late 1590s, a second quarto was printed in 1600, and Jonson himself referred to it dismissively in his Induction to *Bartholomew Fair* (1614). More than Marcus' vivid image of a fountain of blood makes it relevant to a discussion of Jonson's *The Fountaine of Selfe-Love*, however, for as Jonathan Bate has persuasively argued, in *Titus Andronicus* 'Shakespeare is interrogating Rome, asking what kind of example it provides for Elizabethan England'; even more, the play is 'both a revisionary reading of the Ovidian text and an examination of the efficacy of humanist education'.[44] Like Jonson, Shakespeare uses the fountain not simply as a humanist image, but as an image for humanism itself. His play's Ovidianism has been brilliantly elucidated by Bate and others, as has the way in which it is Lavinia in particular who is portrayed as a repository of classical texts and values, in her Virgilian name and her recollection of the iconic figures of Lucretia and Virginia, as well as her strong association with Ovid: it is Lavinia who has begun young Lucius' Roman education by reading to him 'Sweet poetry, and Tully's *Orator*', and who finally reveals the nature of the crimes against her through a material intertext, a copy of the *Metamorphoses*.[45] Yet

---

[43] 2.3.22–5, 28–32. Quotations from *Titus Andronicus* are taken from *Titus Andronicus*, ed. Jonathan Bate, The Arden Shakespeare: Third Series (London: Routledge, 1995). There is a related image in Julius Caesar, when Caesar relates to Decius that his wife Calphurnia 'dreamt tonight she saw my statue, | Which, like a fountain with an hundred spouts, | Did run pure blood; and many lusty Romans | Came smiling and did bathe their hands in it', ed. David Daniell, *Julius Caesar*, The Arden Shakespeare: Third Series (London: Thomas Nelson and Sons, 1998), 2.2.76–9. As Daniell points out, 'Plutarch gives the dream, but of a fallen pinnacle . . . The statue running blood, and anticipation of the conspirators bathing their hands in his blood (below, 3.1.105–10), are Shakespeare's.'

[44] Jonathan Bate, 'Introduction', in *Titus Andronicus*, 17, and *Shakespeare and Ovid* (Oxford: Clarendon Press, 1993; repr. 2001), 104.

[45] 4.1.14, 42.

it is the lesson of the *Metamorphoses* that has led Chiron and Demetrius to cut off Lavinia's hands, lest she be able to write (or weave) her attackers' names like Philomel:[46] Rome has become a 'wilderness of tigers',[47] and its most fetishized texts have been exposed as sites of violence and violation. The *fontes* run with blood.

Titus himself repeats the image of the polluted fountain when he in turn sees his wounded daughter:

> Shall thy good uncle and thy brother Lucius
> And thou and I sit round about some fountain,
> Looking all downwards to behold our cheeks,
> How they are stained like meadows yet not dry,
> With miry slime left on them by a flood?
> And in the fountain shall we gaze so long
> Till the fresh taste be taken from that clearness
> And made a brine pit with our bitter tears?[48]

To sit around a fountain should be to prepare to tell and listen to courtly stories of love;[49] to look into its waters should be to seek self-knowledge and revelation. But the surface of the fountain that Titus imagines will show only faces 'stained . . . with miry slime left on them by a flood', recalling his invocation of 'Nilus [which] disdaineth bounds' some sixty lines earlier and so the chaotic, threatening fecundity of the Nile which spontaneously generates life;[50] its pure waters will be made bitter with weeping. The world of *Titus Andronicus* is one where '*Terras Astraea reliquit*'; it 'imagines a time when justice has left the earth':[51] Jonson's play, in its own way, has a similar concern with the absence of justice.[52] When he is finally about to revenge himself on Chiron and Demetrius, Titus describes his daughter to them as 'the spring whom you have stained with mud', and, in a final grisly, visual recurrence of the image of the polluted fountain, it is Lavinia who ''tween her stumps doth hold | The basin that receives your guilty blood'.[53] Like *Titus Andronicus*, and

---

[46] This is discussed by Bate, *Shakespeare and Ovid*, 107–8: 'What is the point of a humanist education if, instead of instilling in you *integer vitae*, it makes you into a craftier Tereus?' See also the rich discussion of the episode and its wider context in chapter 2 of Sean Keilen's *Vulgar Eloquence: On the Renaissance Invention of English Literature* (New Haven: Yale University Press, 2006).

[47] 3.1.54.   [48] 3.1.123–30.

[49] See the discussion of the *Hypnerotomachia*'s Fountain of Adonis in Chapter 3.

[50] Ovid, *Metamorphoses*, 1.416–37; this passage is discussed in relation to Spenser's Errour in Chapter 6. There are also, perhaps, in Titus' speeches in this scene, recollections of Psalm 69, which begins 'Save me, O God; for the waters are come in unto my soul. I sink in deep mire, where there is no standing: I am come into deep waters, where the floods overflow me.'

[51] 4.3.4; Bate, 'Introduction', in *Titus Andronicus*, 28.   [52] See Chapter 12.

[53] 5.2.170, 182–3.

perhaps following its specific example, *The Fountaine of Selfe-Love* is 'a play replete with literalized metaphors' or rather with one, that of the fountain. It is a play that similarly depends on the tropes and traditions of Ovid as much as those of humanist political discourse and, like *Titus Andronicus*, it forces the re-evaluation of such figures and inheritances in both moral and aesthetic terms.

As with *Titus Andronicus'* debt to the story of Philomel, and specifically like Book 3 of Spenser's *The Faerie Queene*, discussed in the previous chapter, *The Fountaine of Selfe-Love* is underpinned by invocations of Ovidian stories, those of Narcissus, Hermaphroditus,[54] and Diana and Actaeon. The third of these is the most important and also the most subject to re-evaluation, and one of the ways in which this happens is by subtle recollections of what might be termed the biblical analogue of Diana and Actaeon, the account of the adultery of David and Bathsheba in 2 Samuel 11: 2–5.[55] As the next chapter shows, the staging of *The Fountaine of Selfe-Love* particularly recalls a contemporary play on that theme. The biblical account is brief:

And it came to pass in an evening-tide, that David arose from off his bed, and walked upon the roof of the king's house: and from the roof he saw a woman washing herself; and the woman was very beautiful to look upon. And David sent and enquired after the woman. And one said, Is not this Bath-sheba, the daughter of Eliam, the wife of Uriah the Hittite? And David sent messengers, and took her; and she came in unto him, and he lay with her; for she was purified from her uncleanness: and she returned unto her house. And the woman conceived, and sent and told David, and said, I am with child.

By the early sixteenth century, David's adultery with Bathsheba, even more than his subsequent murder of her husband Uriah, was interpreted as occasioning his composition of the seven penitential psalms, and above all Psalm 51, the *Miserere*.[56] In medieval and early modern art and literature, David is as

---

[54] *The Fountaine of Selfe-Love*'s debt to the Ovidian Fountain of Salmacis is discussed in Chapter 11.

[55] The strong connection between the two stories, and in particular the ways in which George Peele's dramatic version of the David and Bathsheba story (which is considered at some length in Chapter 10) draws on the conventions of Elizabethan Ovidianism and the epyllia, is discussed in a useful note by Inge-Stina Ekeblad, '*The Love of King David and Fair Bethsabe*: A Note on George Peele's Biblical Drama', *English Studies*, 39 (1958), 57–62.

[56] A headnote in the 1568 Bishops' Bible introduces Psalm 51 as 'Dauid acknowledgyng his great offence in committyng adulterie, besecheth most humbly God of his great mercie to pardon his sinnes', and in the 1587 Geneva Bible it is subtitled 'A Psalme of Dauid, when the Prophet Nathan came vnto him, after he had gone in to Bath-sheba'; this is repeated in the 1611 Authorized Version. An image of Bathsheba bathing in her fountain frequently introduced the Psalter in Bibles and Books of Hours, including the Great Bible. See Clare L. Costley, 'David, Bathsheba, and the Penitential Psalms', *Renaissance Quarterly*, 57 (2004), 1235–77. On the tradition of its illustration, see Max Engammare, 'La Morale ou la beauté? Illustrations des

much a model of repentance as of kingship or heroism,[57] and his repentance is occasioned above all by his sexual sin, his adultery with Bathsheba, represented both pictorially and poetically by the scene of his observing her naked in the fountain.

Like the story of Diana and Actaeon, that of David and Bathsheba is one of transgressive looking; even more, it shares with the Ovidian story a concern with both guilt and power. Given these associations, it is surprising that Sir John Harington addressed his epigram 'Of King Dauid' specifically to the Queen herself:

> Thou Princes Prophet, and of Prophets King,
> Growne from poore Pastoralls, and Shepheards fold,
> To change the sheephooke to a Mace of gold,
> Subduing sword and speare, with staffe and sling:
> Thou that didst quell the Beare and dreadful Lyon,
> With courage vnappald, and actiue lymmes;
> Thou that didst praise in it, induring Himms
> With Poetry diuine the God of Syon;
> Thou sonne in Law to King & Prince appointed:
> Yet, when that king by wrong did seek thy harme,
> Didst helpe him with thy Harp, and sacred charme:
> And taught, no not to touch the Lords Anointed.
> Thou, thou great Prince, with so rare gifts replenished
> Could'st not eschew blind Buzzard Cupids hookes,
> Lapt in the bayt of Bersabees sweet lookes:
> With which one fault, thy faultles life was blemished.
> Yet hence we learne a document most ample,
> That faln by fraylty we may rise by faith,[58]
> And that the sinne forgiuen, the penance staieth;
> Of Grace and Iustice both a sweet example.
> Let no man then himselfe in sinne imbolden
> By thee, but thy sharpe penance, bitter teares,
> May strike into our harts such godly feares,

amours de David et Bethsabée (II Samuel 11–12) dans les bibles des xve–xviie siècles', in Bertram Schwarzbach (ed.), *La Bible imprimée dans l'Europe moderne* (Paris: Bibliothèque Nationale de France, 1999), 447–76, and 'David côté jardin: Bethsabée, modèle et anti-modèle littéraire à la Renaissance', in *Cité des hommes, cité de Dieu: travaux sur la littéraire de la Renaissance en l'honneur de Daniel Ménager* (Geneva: Droz, 2003), 533–42.

[57] See Charles A. Huttar, 'Frail Grass and Firm Tree: David as a Model of Repentance in the Middle Ages and Early Renaissance', in Raymond-Jean Frontain and Jan Wojcik, (ed.), *The David Myth in Western Literature* (West Lafayette, Ind.: Purdue University Press, 1980), 38–54.

[58] In the 1618 edition of the epigrams, this line appeared as 'Our flesh then strongest is, when weak'st our faith'. The text here is given from the 1600 manuscript, and quoted from *The Epigrams of Sir John Harington*, ed. N. E. McClure (Philadelphia: University of Pennsylvania Press, 1926).

As we may be thereby from sin with-holden.
Sith we, for ours, no iust excuse can bring,
Thou hadst one great excuse, thou wert a King.

Harington (1560–1612) was probably composing his epigrams throughout the 1590s, and he assembled them into two manuscript collections for his mother-in-law Jane Rogers and Lucy, Countess of Bedford, in December 1600.[59] His addressing of this particular epigram to the Queen is intriguing, as a comparison between Elizabeth and King David—or, indeed, Bathsheba herself—in these terms is hardly flattering.[60] Harington's point appears to be that Elizabeth has escaped censure for some fault—implicitly sexual—because of her rank, and it is perhaps telling that here it is Bathsheba who is the active party, her 'sweete lookes' described as 'bayt'. Although more precise dates of composition are impossible to know, it is not impossible that in his epigram 'Of King David' Harington is glancing both at the Queen's supposed erotic intrigues[61] and her apparent double standard with respect to the transgressions of others. For Harington, Bathsheba is at least partly to blame.

This is a conclusion implicitly shared by Jonson in his depiction of Diana/Cynthia in *The Fountaine of Selfe-Love*, one that he points at both

---

[59] See the discussion by Jason Scott-Warren in *Sir John Harington and the Book as Gift* (Oxford: Oxford University Press, 2001), 136–41.

[60] Given the contemporary preoccupation with David's sexual sin, and Harington's direct allusion to it here, it is unsurprising that Patrick Collinson cites this epigram in his *Oxford Dictionary of National Biography* article on the Queen, observing that it 'is not evidence that Elizabeth was a nymphomaniac but an indication of what some people were prepared to believe', Patrick Collinson, 'Elizabeth I (1533–1603)', *Oxford Dictionary of National Biography* (www.oxforddnb.com/view/article/8636, accessed 20 Mar. 2006).

[61] Presumably with Leicester: the 'Beare' of line 5 does appear in 1 Samuel 17: 34–7, but could equally allude to the Earl, as it apparently does in Harington's slighting reference elsewhere to Leicester as 'the greate Beare that caried eight dogges on him when Monsieur was here', *The Metamorphosis of Ajax*, ed. Elizabeth Story Donno (London: Routledge and Kegan Paul, 1962), 171. Donno links this to a feat by a real bear at the time; Jason Scott-Warren, however, interprets it as meaning Leicester, and suggests that it caused Harington to '[languish] . . . some time in royal disfavour', Jason Scott-Warren, 'Harington, Sir John (bap. 1560, d. 1612)', *Oxford Dictionary of National Biography* (www.oxforddnb.com/view/article/12326, accessed 16 Mar. 2006). Leicester was himself identified with David, committing adultery with, and subsequently marrying, another man's wife, in the libellous tract circulated in manuscript in 1584, shortly after the publication of the similarly libellous *Leicester's Commonwealth*. The so-called 'Letter of Estate' accused both Leicester and Lettice Knollys of the murders of their previous spouses, and drew an implicit parallel between David's sending of Uriah into the vanguard of the battle and Walter Devereux's doomed mission in Ireland. This makes the gift, in 1579, of a small, opulent metal box to Leicester, depicting David and Bathsheba on the lid and the bear and ragged staff on the inside, particularly intriguing: its background decorative scheme, full of symbols of fertility and marriage, suggests a connection to Leicester's marriage to Lettice. It is now in the Victoria and Albert Museum (Museum number M.665–1910).

through his use of the Actaeon myth and also, possibly (as the following chapter shows), through a strong dramaturgical recollection of a contemporary play on the theme of David and Bathsheba. In visual art in particular, the stories of both Diana and Actaeon and David and Bathsheba call into question the morality of looking and the propriety of art itself. In a persuasive discussion of seventeenth-century Dutch art, Eric Jan Sluijter notes that

as soon as depictions of nude women were depicted with some frequency in Holland several of the themes that became most popular were about men being excited by gazing at beautiful women. These include not only the subject of Rembrandt's painting, the bathing Bathsheba seen by David, but also the bathing Susanna spied upon by the Elders (the two most popular subjects from the Old Testament in the northern Netherlands) and the bathing Diana and her nymphs seen by Actaeon (the most popular mythological subject in Holland). Seventeenth-century treatments of all three subjects locate the viewer in the same position and watching the same enticing beauty as the men in the stories depicted—men who were aroused by looking and were afterward severely punished.[62]

Such paintings were obviously a respectable (or semi-respectable) means of portraying the nude female body, but they also 'functioned as one of the most obvious moralizing examples about the dangers of sight'.[63] They can be found in sixteenth-century English collections: at the time of his death Leicester had at Leicester House a number of naked pictures, including 'One of Susanna and the Judges', 'Diana bathyng hirselfe with her Nimphes', 'A Picture of a naked Lady [Venus?] sleeping and Cupid menaicing hir with his darte', and 'A Picture of Diana and Acteon', and there was a second 'Picture of Susanna' at Wanstead.[64] It is perhaps significant, however, that at least two of these were not on public display 'in the greate Gallerye' but 'in Mr. Garnettes Chamber' ('a picture of Venus and Cupid manecing her with his darte', valued at 3*s.* 4*d.*) and in a 'Withdrawing Chamber' ('a picture of Diana', valued at 5*s.*).[65] Moreover, the story of Diana and Actaeon is a topos of transgressive looking not only in visual art, but also in literary ekphrasis; the mind's eyes can also

[62] Eric Jan Sluijter, 'Rembrandt's Bathsheba and the Conventions of a Seductive Theme', in Ann Jensen Adams (ed.), *Rembrandt's Bathsheba Reading King David's Letter* (Cambridge: Cambridge University Press, 1998), 76. Rembrandt's painting dates from 1654. Hélène Casanova-Robin makes much the same point with reference to Diana and Actaeon: 'L'œil d'Actéon, contemplant une scène de bain évoque inévitablement l'œil d'un spectateur contemplant un tableau' (Actaeon's eye, looking at a bathing scene, inevitably evokes the eye of a spectator looking at a painting). Her discussion of the Diana and Actaeon story is very useful. Casanova-Robin, *Diane et Actéon*, 200.

[63] Sluijter, 'Rembrandt's Bathsheba', 79.

[64] Thoms, 'Pictures of the Great Earl of Leicester', 224–6.

[65] Charles Lethbridge Kingsford, 'Essex House, Formerly Leicester House and Exeter Inn', *Archaeologia*, 73 (1922–3), 30, 32.

look on that which they should not, and in terms of the identification of Elizabeth with Diana, this is *lèse-majesté*. The *locus classicus* for this is near the beginning of Apuleius' *The Golden Ass*:

In the exact centre of the hall stood a Diana in Parian marble. It was a brilliant *tour de force* of sculpture: as one entered the room the goddess with flowing tunic seemed to be coming straight at one in her swift course, inspiring awe by her powerful godhead. To right and left she was flanked by hounds, also of marble . . . Behind the goddess there arose a rock in the shape of a grotto, with moss and grass and leaves and branches, vines here and shrubs there, a whole plantation in stone . . . From the middle of the foliage there peered out the figure of Actaeon in stone with his prurient gaze fixed on the goddess, the transformation into a stag already begun; one could see both him and his reflection in the spring as he waited for Diana to take her bath.[66]

In the course of *The Golden Ass* the narrator himself is transformed not into a stag but an ass, and this process is set in train shortly after his encounter with this Diana; after a series of adventures, many of them highly erotic, he recovers his human shape only after seeing a vision of Isis/Diana. The motif recurs in Shakespeare's *Cymbeline* (*c*.1606–11), where the villain Iachimo describes to Posthumus, as evidence of his wife Innogen's adultery, the appearance of her naked body, sleeping, and the furnishings of her bedroom, which include 'the chimney-piece, | Chaste Dian, bathing'.[67] Iachimo is here Actaeon, but the audience are placed in a like position, having spied, like him, on the innocent Innogen, and having reimagined both naked princess and naked goddess, whom they have not themselves seen, even as he describes the scene to Posthumus. That the scene is already ekphrastic in its associations makes all the more pointed its recurrence in both visual and literary interrogations of the morality of art and of looking (not least at goddesses), such as are encountered in Elizabethan gardens and in Jonson's *The Fountaine of Selfe-Love*.

It is, above all, his play's titular fountain that allows Jonson to gesture so forcefully at all these concerns—politics and corruption, the nature (and prerogatives) of majesty and how it should be looked at—and more besides. There is perhaps a division apparent here between the shared humanist (and indeed Ovidian) symbolic vocabulary common to most educated people, and the more rarefied, multi-layered, and oblique devices employed by those in court circles, whereby a greater familiarity with the complex symbolic and ideological potential of images and objects gave rise to a denser and more nuanced approach, seen in the New Year's gifts and Harington's epigrams,

[66] Apuleius, *The Golden Ass*, 2.4, pp. 23–4. *The Golden Ass* and the Actaeon myth are discussed by Brown, 'Arachne's Web', 126, and with particular reference to Shakespeare's *A Midsummer Night's Dream* by Leonard Barkan, 'Diana and Actaeon', 352 ff.

[67] *Cymbeline*, ed. J. M. Nosworthy, The Arden Shakespeare: Second Series (London: Methuen, 1955; repr. Routledge, 1994), 2.4.81–2.

for example. In *The Fountaine of Selfe-Love*, as the following chapters show, Jonson draws on such coterie knowledge and, more, such an elite familiarity with the strategies of interpretation that such knowledge and its manifestations required, in much the same way as early modern gardens solicited a variety of responses from those who visited them.[68] In staging the fountain as his play's controlling metaphor, Jonson focuses his audience's attention upon humanist concepts not simply in the abstract, but in visual and material terms, and 'in action'. Like Harington, Greville, and Sidney (and many others who gave gifts to the Queen) he implicitly solicits an analogous consideration of these concepts and principles in the culture of the Elizabethan court.

[68] The Grove of Diana at Nonsuch exemplified this principle; its relationship to Jonson's play is discussed in detail in Chapter 12.

10

A Visual Metaphor: Staging the Fountain

The young Edmund Spenser had been connected with, and perhaps influenced by, the pageants which had greeted Elizabeth Tudor when she made her official 'coronation' entry into London in January 1559, through his teacher and mentor Richard Mulcaster.[1] Some thirty years later, Spenser's own *Faerie Queene* clearly influenced another pageant writer, George Peele (1556–96). In *Descensus Astraeae*, Peele staged the fountain as an emblem of the realm and of the Protestant religion, and he appears in general to have had something of a fascination with fountains as theatrical settings, for three of his seven extant plays and pageants feature the device in some form.[2] It is my contention here that Peele's staged fountains in turn significantly influenced Ben Jonson's *The Fountaine of Selfe-Love*.

Descensus Astraeae was written for the installation of William Webb as Lord Mayor in 1591. Compared with the later publication of the mayoral pageants of Middleton, Munday, and Heywood, Peele's publication is both slender and straightforward: it is, in fact, only the second such pageant for which a printed

---

[1] See Chapter 5.

[2] Peele's surviving plays and pageants, in addition to *Descensus astraeae the device of a l'ageant [sic] borne before M. William Web, lord maior of the citie of London on the day he tooke his oath, beeing the 29. of October. 1591* (1591), are *The araygnement of Paris a pastorall. Presented before the Queenes Maiestie, by the Children of her chappell* (c.1581–4), *The deuice of the pageant borne before the Woolstone Dixi Lord Maior of the citie of London. An. 1585* (1585) (this mayoral pageant is the first such to survive in print), *The battell of Alcazar fought in Barbarie, betweene Sebastian king of Portugall, and Abdelmelec king of Marocco. With the death of Captaine Stukeley* (c.1588–94), *The famous chronicle of king Edward the first, sirnamed Edward Longshankes with his returne from the holy land. Also the life of Lleuellen rebell in Wales. Lastly, the sinking of Queene Elinor, who sunck at Charingcrosse, and rose againe at Pottershith, now named Queenehith* (c.1593), *The old wiues tale A pleasant conceited comedie* (c.1595), and *The loue of King Dauid and fair Bethsabe With the tragedie of Absalon* (c.1591–4). Peele also wrote many poems, several for court occasions, and other dramatic fragments survive; it has frequently been suggested that he collaborated with Shakespeare on *Titus Andronicus*. See the discussion by Brian Vickers in *Shakespeare, Co-Author* (Oxford: Oxford University Press, 2002), chapter 3 *passim*. Jonathan Bate has suggested that Shakespeare revised Peele (personal communication); the identification of the fountain image as one of Peele's authorial 'fingerprints' would tend to support this, although as Vickers notes (160), *Titus* shares two of its notable fountain images (and much more besides) with *The Rape of Lucrece*. See the discussion in the previous chapter.

record survives. The pageant, too, was simple, comprising only one 'device', in contrast to the elaborate floats or carts, on both land and water, which were to become the norm in the seventeenth century. The device presented '*Astraea*', the imperial virgin of justice and a familiar persona of Elizabeth (she is later referred to as 'Our faire *Astraea*, our *Pandora* faire, | Our faire *Eliza*, or *Zabeta* faire'),[3] dressed as a shepherdess. Peele's Astraea, however, did not defend her flock, except by implication: rather, her task was to protect a fountain. The fountain itself is not described, but it was clearly substantial, for it was large enough for two men to be seated beside it, representing Superstition and Ignorance, a Friar and a Priest respectively, together with the Three Graces and the Three Virtues, Honor, Maiestie, Stedfastnesse, Mercy, a Champion, and two Malcontents. Not all of these were speaking parts.

The pageant has little plot or action. The Presenter introduces and eulogizes Astraea as a 'Celestiall sacred Nymph, that tendes her flocke | With watchfull eyes, and keep this fount in peace: | Garded with Graces, and with gratious traines, | Vertues diuine, and giftes incomparable'.[4] The fountain clearly represents the realm, and in its pastoral aspect recalls the 'flourishing commonwealth' of the 1559 tableau. Most pressingly, Astraea is exhorted not to let 'blind superstitious ignorance, | Corrupt so pure a spring'.[5] After fulsome praise of the Queen's virtue and government, the presenter concludes his panegyric in lines that implicitly elide Astraea/Elizabeth with her realm in the image of the fountain:

> Goddesse liue long, whose honors we aduance,
> St[r]engthen thy neighbours, propagate thine owne:
> Guide well thy helme, lay thine annointed hand
> To build the temple of triumphant Trueth,
> That while thy subiects draw their peace from thee,
> Thy friends with ayd of armes may succor'd be.[6]

The pageant thus has an obvious Protestant internationalist agenda, in its reference to 'thy friends', presumably the Dutch. In her only, short, speech, Astraea herself describes her realm as blessed by God. Superstition, the Friar, instructs his priest companion 'Stirre Priest, and with thy beades poyson this spring, | I tell thee all is banefull that I bring'; the Priest, however, demurs: 'It is in vaine hir eye keepes me in awe, | Whose heart is purely fixed on the law: | The holy law, and bootlesse we contend, | While this chast nimph, this fountain doth defend'.[7] Peele's two-dimensional characters recall not only Spenser's Archimago and Ignaro, but also those who appeared in one of the other pageants of the 1559 entry, where they were trodden down by 'Pure

---

[3] *Descensus Astraeae*, sig. A2[v].   [4] Ibid., sig. A2.   [5] Ibid., sig. A2.
[6] Ibid., sig. A2[v].   [7] Ibid., sig. A3.

Religion' in the pageant in Cornhill. Peele's Astraea herself can be related to the figure of Truth, given that the appearance of both is associated with the momentous passage of time. Eventually, the 'Malecontents' are forced to admit that they cannot harm her:

—What meaneth this, I striue and cannot strike,
She is preserued by myracle belike:
If so then, wherefore threaten we in vaine,
That Queene, whose cause the gracious heauens maintain.
—No maruell then although we faint and quaile,
For mightie is the truth and will preuaile.[8]

The fountain therefore not only stands metonymically for the idealized pastoral realm of the flourishing commonwealth, but for Protestantism also, and perhaps specifically for that Protestant totem, the English Bible. In the 1559 tableau the silent presence of the Little Conduit had brought these two strands of imagery together: Peele, perhaps drawing on that famous pageant, does the same. *Descensus Astraeae* can be seen, therefore, as a Spenserian reworking of some of the most salient themes of Elizabeth's coronation entry in 1559, and *Veritas Temporis Filia*, complete with its fountain location, in particular.

It is not impossible that Ben Jonson might have seen *Descensus Astraeae* in print, although he was probably fighting in the Low Countries at the time of its performance in the autumn of 1591. It seems more than likely, however, that in writing *The Fountaine of Selfe-Love* he was influenced by the practicalities and, even more, the conceptual possibilities suggested by Peele's not dissimilar staging of the fountain in *The Love of King David and Fair Bethsabe*. Peele's play was published posthumously in 1599, although it had been entered in the Stationers' Register on 14 May 1594. His editors date it to the period 1591–4; it is thus close in date to *Descensus Astraeae*. The surviving text is corrupt, including the notorious instance of a character dying in one scene and subsequently reappearing unharmed, and its place and date of first performance, and the company for which it was written, are unknown. At least one of Peele's plays, *The Arraignment of Paris*, however, was written for the Chapel Children, and performed at the first Blackfriars theatre, and it is not unlikely that *David and Bethsabe* was also performed there; it has very similar staging requirements to other plays known to have been played at both the first and second Blackfriars theatres.

After the play's conventional Prologue, a stage direction instructs its speaker to draw 'a curtaine, and discover . . . Bethsabe with her maid bathing over a

---

[8] *Descensus Astraeae*, sig. A4.

spring: she sings, and David sits above vewing her'.[9] The situation is exactly that familiar from illustrations of the scene in psalters, prayer books, and other sources. As in similar instances—Colonna's Fountain of the Sleeping Nymph in the *Hypnerotomachia*, or Guyon's encounter with the bathing damsels in the Bowre of Bliss,[10] for example, or in the seventeenth-century Dutch paintings discussed in Chapter 9—the audience's identification with the spectator's gaze, here David's, is assumed and encouraged. The tableau is initially static as Bathsheba sings and, although her song is ostensibly addressed to Zephyr, the gentle spring or summer breeze, it is as if she is at once describing her own body, and encouraging its identification with the fountain in which she sits: 'Thy body smoother then this wavelesse spring. | And purer than the substance of the same'.[11] This elision of the fountain and Bathsheba's body is taken over and elaborated by David, for he responds thus to the sight of Bathsheba in her bath:

> May . . .
> That precious fount, beare sand of purest gold,
> And for the Peble, let the silver streames
> That pierce earths bowels to mainteine the source,
> Play upon Rubies, Saphires, Chrisolites . . . [12]

David promises to ornament the fountain, but he is also implicitly outlining his plans similarly to deck with jewels the chaste body of Bathsheba. He summons her, in order that she may 'wash in Davids bower, | In water mix'd with purest Almond Flower, | And bath her beautie in the milke of kids'.[13] Bathsheba is inseparable from her fountain; thus elided, the two become trophy, art object, and erotic icon, which Peele's dramaturgy and *mise-en-scène* explicitly frame as such within the confines of the discovery space as deftly as any artist in ink, paint, or stone.

As the play unfolds, however, the image of the fountain, established in such strongly visual and material terms in its opening scene, recurs in other, equally charged ways. Bathsheba's husband Uriah is laying siege to the city of Rabbah, sent by the King to his certain death in 'the forefront of the hottest battle'.[14] Outside the city walls, he tells his companion Joab, 'Let us assault and scale this kingly Tower, | Where all their conduits and their fountaines are, | Then we may easily take the citie too.' When the battle is over and being reported, the same detail is repeated:

> And tell my lord the King that I have fought
> Against the citie Rabath with successe,
> And skaled where the royal pallace is,

---

[9] *The Love of King David and Fair Bethsabe* (London, 1599), sig. B1–B1ᵛ.
[10] *The Faerie Queene*, 2.11.   [11] *The Love of King David and Fair Bethsabe*, sig. B1ᵛ.
[12] Ibid., sig. B2.   [13] Ibid., sig. B2.   [14] 2 Samuel 11: 15.

The conduit heads and all their sweetest springs . . .
Thy servant Joab . . .
Hath by the finger of our sovereines God,
Besieg'd the citie Rabath, and atchieved
The court of waters, where the conduits run,
And all the Ammonites delightsome springs . . . [15]

Peele here enlarges upon a small detail of the biblical text: 'And Joab sent messengers to David, and said, I have fought against Rabbah, and have taken the city of waters'.[16] As has been seen already in Chapter 5 and those following, the struggle to control water sources is an unsurprising feature of many Old Testament narratives, and indeed of siege warfare in all periods of history.[17] His amplification of this detail in the context of the play as a whole is surely deliberate and calculating: Uriah lays siege to the fountains of Rabbah just as David importunes Bathsheba, in the process identifying her with, and fetishizing her as, the fountain in which he has first seen her bathing. In Peele's juxtaposition or paralleling of these two strands of his play, their shared metaphor in turn allows their elision, for David's sexual intrigue has lasting political, as well as personal and spiritual, repercussions. In *The Fountaine of Selfe-Love*, written soon after the publication of Peele's play, Jonson used the staged device of the fountain in a dramaturgically analogous way.

In order to piece together an idea of how the fountain in *The Fountaine of Selfe-Love* might have been staged, and to establish additional possible precedents for its physical presence in the theatre, it is necessary to set the play in its proper theatrical and historical context, in the repertoire of the Children of the Chapel at the second Blackfriars theatre. If not their very first play performed at that venue, *The Fountaine of Selfe-Love* was certainly one of the first. It was published 'As it hath beene sundry times *priuately acted in the* Blackfriers *by the* Children *of her* Maiesties *Chappell*' in 1601, having been entered in the Stationers' Register on 23 May. Harbage gives the date of its first performance only as 1600–1, but Kawachi, following Chambers and others, assumes that it was the 'Show like a Mask' performed at court (presumably at Whitehall, where Elizabeth usually spent the Christmas season) on 6 January 1601, and accordingly lists its first Blackfriars performance as

---

[15] *The Love of King David and Fair Bathsabe*, sig. B3^v, B4^v, C3^v.   [16] 2 Samuel 12: 27.

[17] In Judith, for example, the army of Holofernes takes control of Bethulia's water supply: 'For all the inhabitants of Bethulia have their water thence; so shall thirst kill them, and they shall give up their city' (7: 13). A similar motif recurs in Tasso's *Gerusalemme liberata*, where the city is referred to on many occasions as well watered, and the control of its supply presented as crucial in both literal and symbolic terms. See *Jerusalem Delivered: An English Prose Version*, trans. and ed. Ralph Nash (Detroit, Mich.: Wayne State University Press, 1987), 1.89, 3.56, 13.14, 13.67, 71, 76–9, 19.121.

1600.[18] Chambers suggested that '[t]he original production will have been in the winter of 1600'.[19] The title page of the 1616 Folio states that the play was 'Acted, in the yeere 1600. By the then Children of Queene ELIZABETHS *Chappell*', and, discussing Jonson's previous play, *Every Man out of his Humor*, Herford and Simpson noted that 'Jonson at this stage [1599] adopted the Calendar date which began the year on 1 January',[20] thereby implying that *The Fountaine of Selfe-Love* was first performed some time before the end of the calendar year. In any case, *The Fountaine of Selfe-Love* cannot have been performed at the Blackfriars any earlier than October 1600, as Burbage's lease of that theatre (for £40 p.a.) to Henry Evans, the manager of the Chapel Children, was signed on 2 September, coming into effect that Michaelmas (29 September).

One play that does seem likely to have been performed by the Chapel Children at the Blackfriars before *The Fountaine of Selfe-Love* is John Lyly's *Loues Metamorphosis*. Like George Peele, Lyly had worked with Henry Evans and the first Blackfriars company in the 1580s. *Loues Metamorphosis* was entered in the Stationers' Register on 25 November 1600, and when it was published the following year its title page stated that it was 'First playd by the Children of Paules, and now by the Children of the Chappell'. Lyly's play, therefore, could well fit the reference made by the third boy in the Induction to *The Fountaine of Selfe-Love*: 'the Vmbrae, *or Ghosts of some three or foure* Playes, *departed a dozen yeares since, haue been seene walking on your Stage here*' (A4ᵛ). As Chapter 12 will suggest, there are also historical reasons for inferring that *The Fountaine of Selfe-Love* may have had its first public performances at the Blackfriars in late October or early November 1600, relating to the fortunes of the Earl of Essex.

Like the fountain in *David and Bethsabe*, the eponymous fountain of Jonson's play was surely a reasonably elaborate and possibly quite large piece of three-dimensional scenery. It could have appeared through the trap in the middle of the stage, in which case Echo would have risen (the stage direction is

[18] Alfred Harbage, *Annals of English Drama* (London: Routledge, 1989), 80; Yoshiko Kawachi, *Calendar of English Drama 1558–1642* (New York: Garland, 1986), 117. James Bednarz doubts that *The Fountaine of Selfe-Love* was performed at court in the Christmas season of 1600–1, suggesting that if it were ever performed at court (which, given the lack of an explicit statement to that effect on the title page of either quarto or folio, he doubts) it was at Candlemas, 22 February. See *Shakespeare and the Poets' War* (New York: Columbia University Press, 2001), 269. Given that this was after the Essex rebellion (and less than a week before Essex's execution), this seems to me unlikely, given the more sympathetic attitude towards Essex that I see the play as taking. This is discussed in Chapter 12.

[19] E. K. Chambers, *The Elizabethan Stage* (Oxford: Clarendon Press, 1923), iii. 364.

[20] *Ben Jonson, ix: An Historical Survey of the Text, The Stage History of the Plays, Commentary on the Plays*, ed. C. H. Herford and Evelyn and Percy Simpson (Oxford: Clarendon Press, 1950), 186.

'Ascendit', B3) either from behind it or, indeed, from within it. Or else, again like Bethsabe's fountain, it could have been revealed in the inner stage/rear stage/discovery space, perhaps by the drawing aside of the '*silke* Curtine' alluded to by the third boy in the Induction (A4) and then pushed forward, allowing Echo to appear either from behind it or using the mid-stage trap, and then being returned to the discovery space later. Indeed, it may have been the '*peice of* Prospectiue' to which the boy also refers. If there were, as Andrew Gurr suggests, three entrances at the back of the Blackfriars stage (perhaps double doors or a curtain flanked by two single doors) then the necessary entrances and exits while it was in place could be effected using the side doors alone.[21] A physical structure, perhaps made of canvas and wood like those which appear in the records of the Office of the Revels,[22] with Echo (played, after all, by a child rather than an adult actor) simply concealing himself behind or within it in performance, could easily have been transported to court.

If the fountain in Jonson's play had a similarly central thematic importance to the one in Peele's *David and Bethsabe*, and if it too were visually reinforced by a physical prop fountain for some or all of the play, what evidence is there in surviving theatre records for such a device? Such evidence is disparate and must in the main proceed by analogy, but it is certainly possible to make such a case, by drawing on plays from similar milieux and with apparently similar prop requirements, as well as on the pageant tradition in which *The Fountaine of Selfe-Love* to some extent participates. In addition to *David and Bethsabe*, three plays are particularly relevant, two by John Lyly, *Loues Metamorphosis* and *Endimion*, which probably had its first court performance on 2 February 1588[23] and was published in 1591, and George Peele's *The Old Wiues Tale*, published in 1595.

A comparison between *The Fountaine of Selfe-Love* and *Loues Metamorphosis* is useful not only for what it may imply about their relative positions in the very early repertoire of the Chapel Children, but also for some suggestive similarities in their staging requirements. *Loues Metamorphosis* is very loosely

---

[21] Andrew Gurr, *The Shakespearean Stage* (Cambridge: Cambridge University Press, 1992), 159–60. While the fountain is needed only for the action in the first act, it could (following the conventions of 'simultaneous staging', outlined by Bevington) have remained on stage at least until the end of Act 4, when it is likely that the stage would have been reset to accommodate the 'tableau' of Cynthia and her attendants. It may be, however, that Cynthia appeared in the gallery—although from the way in which Echo's song is introduced, it seems that this was where the musicians were located—in which case the fountain may well have remained on stage throughout.

[22] Discussed below, pp. 228–9.

[23] See John Lyly, *Endymion*, ed. David Bevington (Manchester: Manchester University Press, 1996), 8.

based on the myth of Erisicthon, who in the play is punished by Ceres for felling a sacred tree. In the first scene, three foresters hang imprese on the tree, and in the second the three nymphs garland the tree and sing and dance around it. Their ceremonies are interrupted by Erisicthon, who takes an axe to the tree. Nisa the nymph cries, 'but see, the tree powreth out bloud, and I heare a voice'. Erisicthon retorts, 'What voice? If in the tree there be any bodie, speake quickly, lest the next blow hit the tale out of thy mouth.' This prompts a long dying speech from the nymph of the tree, Fidelia.[24] She is presumably concealed either beneath the stage or within the tree's trunk: as the long speech would have been unduly muffled if delivered entirely from below stage, and as the tree is subsequently hacked to pieces, it seems likely that the actor playing the nymph was able to rise up from under the stage inside the tree, exiting by the same means. There is an obvious parallel here with the appearance of Echo, at a very similar point, in *The Fountaine of Selfe-Love*. Even more obvious from a staging perspective is the Prologue to *Poetaster*, Jonson's next play for the Chapel Children at the Blackfriars (1601). It is delivered by Envie, who '*arises in the midst of the stage*'. This unambiguously suggests the use of a trap, and it is clear from the stage directions for one of the plays performed at the first Blackfriars that such a device was in use then.[25] In Peele's *Arraignment of Paris* (c.1584) there are directions that '*Heereuppon did rise a Tre[e] of gold laden with Diadems & Crownes of golde*', and then that '*The Tree sinketh*'; later '*Pluto ascendeth from below in his chaire*'.[26] It can therefore reasonably be inferred that this trap was used for Fidelia and the tree in *Loues Metamorphosis*, for Envie in *Poetaster*, and for Echo and the fountain in *The Fountaine of Selfe-Love*.

Irwin Smith noted that Echo's first words are heard from under the stage, perhaps assigned to another actor, and that Mercurie's striking the stage with his caduceus (1.2, B3) is 'a sound cue to the trap operators below'.[27] He posited, however, that the second Blackfriars had two traps, one in the middle of the platform and one in the rear stage, or discovery space: 'The rear-stage trap serves throughout the act as the spring called the fountain of self-love . . . In preparation for its role as a spring, the opening in the floor has perhaps been edged with rushes or flowers to disguise the trap itself and the basin of water suspended in it'.[28] Smith's pseudo-naturalistic interpretation of the fountain as a forest pool fringed with aquatic plants is both anachronistic and at odds with Jonson's text. Echo laments of the fountain 'And here, (ay me,

---

[24] Sig. B3; B3–B4.
[25] Irwin Smith, *Shakespeare's Blackfriars Theatre: Its History and Design* (London: Peter Owen, 1966), 141–2.
[26] George Peele, *The araygnement of Paris* (London, 1584), sigs. B4ᵛ, D2ᵛ.
[27] Smith, *Shakespeare's Blackfriars Theatre*, 314.   [28] Ibid. 359.

the place is fatall) see, | The weeping *Niobe*, translated hether | From Phrygian mountaines: and by *Phoebe* reared | As the proude Trophaee of her sharpe reuenge' (1.2, B4). 'Reared' implies both verticality and the erection of a physical structure,[29] and 'Trophaee' a monument. The fate of Niobe in myth was to be transformed into a quasi fountain: 'There, set on a mountain's peak, she weeps; and even to this day tears trickle from the marble'.[30] Emblems and other illustrations frequently show both Narcissus and Actaeon coming to grief not in the naturalistic forest settings implied by Ovid, but beside far more architectural fountains.[31] Finally, to assume that the fountain which so shapes the opening action of the play, and which is a symbol establishing the play's controlling metaphor and so its moral agenda in visual terms, was represented by a hole at the back of the Blackfriars stage leaves unsolved the problem of the staging of the apparent court performance, which (from the surviving records)[32] can have taken place at the most four months after its opening at the Blackfriars, presumably with considerably less notice.

Several critics have noted similarities between *The Fountaine of Selfe-Love* and Lyly's *Endimion* (1588), both plays written for boys' companies and with court performance in mind. Oscar Campbell suggested that 'four of the women in *Endimion* can be regarded as furnishing a model for Jonson's college of etiquette. Tellus, Semele, Scintilla, and Favilla all represent false ideals of courtly conduct, as opposed to those illustrated by the divine Cynthia,' and more recently Anne Barton has noted that 'Like her namesake in Lyly's *Endimion* (1588), Cynthia is an allegorized Elizabeth'.[33] In *Endimion*, Lyly employs the legend of the human youth beloved of the moon goddess in an examination of love and friendship and the nature of the ideal courtier. In the play's third act, the courtly knight Eumenides, who is 'going to Thessalie, to seeke remedie for *Endimion* . . . who hath beene cast into a dead sleepe, almost these twentie yeeres', comes to a fountain, of which it is said that 'who so can cleerely see the bottome of thys Fountaine, shall haue remedie for any thing'.[34] As David Bevington has observed, 'Eumenides is a wandering knight out of medieval romance',[35] and the magic fountain is a stock romance device: only faithful lovers can see its bottom. Eumenides is successful: 'I plainelie see the bottome, and there in white marble engrauen these wordes, *Aske one for*

---

[29] *OED* 1a, 7a.   [30] Ovid, *Metamorphoses*, 6.311–12.

[31] As can also be seen in two of the woodcuts illustrating Spenser's *Shepheardes Calender*, discussed in Chapter 6.

[32] See above, pp. 222–3.

[33] Oscar Campbell, *Comicall Satyre and Shakespeare's Troilus and Cressida* (San Marino, Calif.: Huntington Library, 1938), 99; Anne Barton, *Ben Jonson, Dramatist* (Cambridge: Cambridge University Press, 1984), 79.

[34] John Lyly, *Endimion, the Man in the Moone* (London, 1591), sig. E4.

[35] Lyly, *Endymion*, ed. Bevington, 38.

all, and but one thing at all.' Eumenides asks for Endymion's release, and the magic fountain 'responds' by revealing the words '*When shee whose figure of all is the perfectest, and neuer to bee measured, alwaies one, yet neuer the same: still inconstant, yet neuer wauering, shall come and kisse* Endimion *in his sleepe, hee shall then rise, els neuer*'.[36] 'She' is, of course, Cynthia.

David Bevington has discussed the staging of *Endimion*'s fountain in some detail. Having suggested that Lyly used the device of stage 'mansions' or 'houses', perhaps made of canvas, to represent the various fixed locations of the play, he infers that

> the fountain is to be located near the lunary bank but not precisely on the same spot . . . allow[ing] both to exert their felt presences when they are not actively in use. Both would profit from the use of a curtain, to screen off Endymion during his long sleep and to conceal the fountain (if it was a practical stage structure) when it is no longer needed; alternatively, the fountain could be painted on such a curtain.[37]

Given that the action in 3.4 requires Eumenides to look *into* the fountain, in order to read the words written on its bottom, it is tempting to deduce that a 'practical stage structure' rather than a painted curtain was employed and, if so, that it was perhaps a simple well or basin, as the 'brim', wide enough to have words engraved upon it, is referred to several times. Similarly, Bathsheba's fountain in *David and Bethsabe* must surely have been sufficiently three-dimensional for her to sit beside, if not in it. Such a structure, perhaps made of canvas, could be easily transported for a production outside the playhouse. It is tempting to wonder whether, given the allusion to the 'Vmbrae' of old plays, quoted above, another of the very early plays performed at the second Blackfriars might have been Lyly's *Endimion* or, indeed (given its publication date), Peele's *David and Bethsabe*. Could *The Fountaine of Selfe-Love* in fact have 'recycled' its key piece of scenery from one of these?

George Peele's *The Old Wiues Tale* (*c*.1595), which like *David and Bethsabe* survives only in a confusingly corrupt text, specifically calls for a well, which plays an important part in its action. Lampriscus has been told by the Old Man to send his two daughters 'to the Well for the water of life'. When Zantyppa ('*the curst Daughter*') '*offers to dip her Pitcher in, and a head speakes in the Well*', she, true to her name, '*breakes hir Pitcher vppon his heade*'. In the play's final act Celanta, her 'sweete sister', repeats the action and is duly rewarded for her obedience to the Head's instructions, first with corn and then with gold from the well.[38] It is clear from this action that the well in Peele's play could not have been the painted curtain posited as an alternative by Bevington

---

[36] Lyly, *Endimion*, sig. F1, F2[v]. [37] *Endymion*, ed. Bevington, 50, 53.
[38] George Peele, *The old wiues tale A pleasant conceited comedie* (London, 1595), sig. B4, D4, D4[v], E3[v]–E4.

in his discussion of *Endimion*; it must have been a physical structure into which pitchers could be lowered and from which a 'head', whether belonging to an actor or represented by a mask or mannequin, could rise. The need even for a trap would have been avoided if the well structure itself were large enough to conceal an actor. William Percy's *The Faery Pastorall*, of which no performance is recorded, but which seems to have been written with some knowledge of the staging practices in the private theatres, similarly includes among its extensive requirements 'A Lowe well with Roape and Pullye', large enough for a man to hide in.[39] It survives in a manuscript dated 1603. Of a similar date is an Oxford entertainment entitled *Narcissus*, in which the fountain is ingeniously staged by '*one with a buckett and boughes and grasse*', who is listed in the dramatis personae as 'The Well', like Wall and Moonshine in *A Midsummer Night's Dream*.[40]

Speculating as to whether *The Old Wiues Tale* might have been performed at court, A. R. Braunmuller suggested that

it certainly seems to envisage what is known as 'simultaneous staging', where several different locations (for example, Sacrapant's lair, the well, the cross where Erestus stands) appear on stage at once. This form of staging was much more common at court than on the public stage . . . The large number of props again suggests a well-equipped troupe, or perhaps one which could call on the resources of the Queen's Office of the Revels.[41]

The kind of 'simultaneous staging' envisaged by editors of both *Endimion* and *The Old Wiues Tale*, as well as their employment of a prop fountain and well respectively, suggests both that such a physical structure could have appeared in *The Fountaine of Selfe-Love*, and that it could also have remained on stage throughout much, if not all, of the play's action. A prop described as 'ye wel counterfeit' does indeed appear in the records of the Office of the Revels for February 1576/7. On 18 February 1564 payments were made for 'provicions for A play maid by *Sir* percivale hartts Sones *with* . . . a Rocke, or hill ffor the IX musses to Singe vppone *with* a vayne of Sarsnett Dravven vpp and downe', and in June 1572 the accounts record 'A Chariott of xiiij foote Long & viij foote brode with a Rock vpon it & A fowntayne therin with the furnishing and

---

[39] William Percy, *The Cuck-Queanes and Cuckolds Errants, or the Bearing Down the Inne, a Comedy. The Faery Pastorall, or Forrest of Elues* (London, 1824), 94.

[40] *Narcissus: A Twelfe Night Merriment*, ed. Margaret L. Lee (London: David Nutt, 1893), pp. xxi, 18. The text survives among the Rawlinson MSS. It is not impossible that this Oxford entertainment might be specifically referencing Jonson's play, not only in its subject matter but in its similarly ostentatious 'staging' of the fountain. At the end of the play 'Francis the Porter' appears to reclaim his bucket: 'Are those the ladds that would doe the deede? | They may bee gone, & God bee their speede; | Ile take vpp their buckett, but I swear by the water, | I have seene a farre better play at the theater', 27.

[41] A. R. Braunmuller, *George Peele* (Boston: Twayne Publishers, 1983), 63.

garnishing therof for Apollo and the Nine Muzes'. In 1584 there is an entry for 'An Inuention called ffiue playes in one presented and enacted before her ma*ie*stie . . . by her highnes servaunt*es* wheron was ymployed a greate cloth and a battlement of canvas and canvas for a well and a mounte' (1584).[42] Frustratingly, the detailed Revels accounts peter out long before *The Fountaine of Selfe-Love*, but it is nevertheless encouraging to see a record such as the one quoted which links a professional company with 'canvas for a well'. The device seems to have been a popular one in court pageants, as well as in civic pageantry. Furthermore, while there is no mention of either a fountain or a well in Henslowe's inventory (1598), it does record other, presumably large, prop structures, such as 'i rocke, i cage, i tombe, i Hell mought'.[43]

There are of course several problems in citing these entries from the records of the Office of the Revels in an attempt to argue that *The Fountaine of Selfe-Love* featured some sort of reasonably substantial prop fountain on stage. The first and most indisputable is that of dates: the latest entry cited is 1584, sixteen years before Jonson's play. The second is that Jonson was not writing for a unique court performance but, initially at least, for public performance at the Blackfriars, although probably with a subsequent court performance in mind. Yet in *The Fountaine of Selfe-Love* (in contrast to, for example, *Every Man out of his Humor*) Jonson was writing about and representing a court, with a court masque as his play's climax. It is also known that he at some point owned a copy of Baltasar Beaujoyeulx's *Balet comique de la Royne* (1581). Performed at the celebrations of the marriage of the Duc de Joyeuse and Mademoiselle de Vaudemont at the court of Henri III, it included a chariot made in the shape of a fountain large enough to carry Louise of Lorraine, her ladies, and an ensemble of musicians, which appears among the edition's illustrations.[44] It is not inconceivable that Jonson, in his exposure and interrogation of the court, might have intentionally adapted some of the scenic conventions (and ostentations) of the court's own elaborate pastimes.

Of *Endimion*, Bevington observes that 'Fundamental to Lyly's dramaturgy are simultaneity and juxtaposition. The theatrical signs of Cynthia's court are ever-present, even as we journey to the desert castle or to the lunary bank or to the magic fountain. Conversely, those symbolic locations exert a felt presence even when not actually visible in the theatre'.[45] The same might well

---

[42] Albert Feuillerat, *Documents Relating to the Office of the Revels in the Time of Queen Elizabeth* (Louvain: Bang, 1908), 277, 365, 117, 57.

[43] Gurr, *The Shakespearean Stage*, 187.

[44] John Meagher, *Method and Meaning in Jonson's Masques* (Notre Dame, Ind.: University of Notre Dame Press, 1966), 22. An illustration is reproduced in Roy Strong, *Art and Power: Renaissance Festivals 1450–1650* (Woodbridge: The Boydell Press, 1984), 82.

[45] *Endymion*, ed. Bevington, 56.

be observed of Jonson's dramaturgy, especially in his early plays, and even in some of his great works, such as *Volpone* (Volpone's 'shrine', the city of Venice itself), *The Alchemist* (the alchemist's 'laboratory' and the house in which it is located), and, above all, *Bartholomew Fair*. In 'Tree Properties and Tree Scenes in Elizabethan Theatre', Werner Habicht discusses 'the considerable extent to which meaningful visual and "emblematic" elements must have contributed to dramatic performances on the Elizabethan public stage'. Citing such instances as the garden scenes in *1 Henry VI* (2.4) and *Richard II* (3.4), he observes that the 'Elizabethan tree property . . . far from merely specifying a locality, is a symbolically charged focal point', and concludes that a tree property could have acted as 'a unifying element . . . a permanent visual reminder of a play's central themes'.[46] This is the sense in which the putative prop fountain in *The Fountaine of Selfe-Love* functions, and likewise the fountain in Peele's *David and Bethsabe*. Habicht also notes the 'traditional associations of the garden with the State': the fountain in *The Fountaine of Selfe-Love* evokes the garden of the state in much the same way as had been commonplace for generations, if not centuries, in royal and civic pageants and entries, as, for example, in Elizabeth I's own coronation entry.[47] This is of course closely related to the symbolism of the humanist and classical political texts discussed in Chapter 9, if a more popular expression of their ideas and imagery.

Recalling the multiple occurrences of fountains of Apollo and the Muses in the Revels accounts, it is perhaps not too much to suggest that the fountain in *The Fountaine of Selfe-Love*, at least by a court audience accustomed to both court and civic pageantry, might have been read as referring both to the realm and to the classical Helicon. George Parfitt has suggested that at the beginning of *Volpone*, the way in which Volpone's golden treasure is staged shows the way in which Jonson uses a visual image 'as the key to a play's central meaning'.[48] The opening of *The Fountaine of Selfe-Love*, as of George Peele's *David and Bethsabe*, is surely an even more striking instance of this device. Quickly and economically, Jonson uses a combination of image, text, and unspoken cultural association to frame his play, announcing its concerns and moral purpose, and suggesting the interpretative approach that his audience and, later, readers should take to it. In the 1616 Folio, his elaborate dedication 'To the Court' in fact replicates in printed form a frame for the play which, in the theatre, was established in purely visual and material terms.

[46] Werner Habicht, 'Tree Properties and Tree Scenes in Elizabethan Theatre', *Renaissance Drama*, 4 (1971), 69, 92.

[47] Ibid. 87. See my discussion in 'Location as Metaphor' and in Chapter 5.

[48] George Parfitt, *Ben Jonson: Public Poet and Private Man* (London: J. M. Dent and Sons, 1976), 90.

As in Peele's *David and Bethsabe*, it seems likely that Jonson's eponymous fountain was revealed in the play's first scene, when Mercurie and Cupid enter, although 1.2 is certainly the first point at which attention is drawn to it. When the two gods appear, there is an abrupt change of tone from the light-hearted social realism of the Induction and the loftiness of the Prologue to their witty banter and casting of aspersions upon the (Olympian) court. This change of tone, as well as the implied transformation of the playhouse to 'Gargaphy', also signals to the audience that it is from this point onwards that their interpretative task properly begins. The scene allows for a quick recapitulation of the occasion of the play's action

> The Huntresse and queene of these groues, *Diana* (in regarde of some black and enuious slaunders howerly breathd against her for her deuine iustice on *Acteon* as shee pretends) hath here in the vale of *Gargaphy* proclaimd a solemne reuels, which she will grace with the full and royall expence of one of her cleerest moones (B2)

which again reinforces the parallel being drawn between Cynthia and Elizabeth.

The scene to which the fountain is most central is 1.2, the meeting between Mercurie and Echo.[49] Here, most of the remaining associations of the fountain are introduced, as the aesthetic and ethical environment of the play becomes progressively richer and more syncretic, coalescing around this one device. Most obviously, Echo makes explicit the connection with Narcissus implicit in the title of the play, especially in its quarto version. But she also makes more subtle points. She asserts, for example, a connection between self-love and flattery: 'But *Selfe loue* neuer yet could looke on trueth, | but with blear'd beames; Slicke flatterie and she: | Are twin-borne sisters' (1.2, B3ᵛ). The implication is, of course, that those who welcome or accept flattery unquestioningly are as guilty of self-love as those who demonstrate it more directly: an implicit allusion to the behaviour of Elizabeth and her courtiers? After the song 'Slow, slow fresh fount', Echo continues to discuss the physical fountain, which she no longer associates simply with Narcissus. It is not just his, but Actaeon's, and Niobe's; it is also 'the *Fountaine of selfe loue*: | In which *Latona*, and her carelesse *Nimphes* | (Regardles of my sorrowes) bath themselues' (1.2, B4ᵛ). Commentators assume that Jonson uses the name 'Latona' to refer in fact to her daughter Diana,[50] in which case this is a not particularly flattering reference to the self-absorption of Cynthia/Elizabeth and her court. It also makes explicit for the first time in the quarto text the connection between the court and the fountain that underpins the entire play,

---

[49] There is a useful discussion of the play's investigation of myth and morality, and in particular of the role of Echo, by Cécile Mauré, 'Mythe et moralité dans *Cynthia's Revels* de Ben Jonson (1600)', *Anglophonia*, 13 (2003), 113–24.

[50] Herford and Simpson, 494.

and which was finally made overt in the dedication added to the play in the 1616 Folio. The seriousness of what Echo has ultimately said is emphasized by Mercurie's swiftly condemnatory reaction: 'Stint thy babling tongue; | Fond *Echo*, thou prophanst the grace is done thee.' All the examples cited by Echo exhibit self-love in some way—presumption, pride, solipsism: her cursing of the fountain is therefore a formal confirmation of its qualities rather than a naming *per se*.[51] But she also presents Narcissus, Actaeon, and Niobe as luckless, if not entirely innocent, victims of punishments disproportionately severe to their crimes, inflicted (in the case of the latter two) by a thoughtless and self-absorbed goddess who herself displays moral failings not entirely unrelated to those which have proved the downfall of those she so harshly punishes. One is reminded of Sir John Harington's roughly contemporaneous epigram 'Of King David', and his partial excusing of the faults of Actaeon.[52]

The transition from the scene between Echo and Mercurie to that of Amorphus at the fountain is one of the neatest in the play, introducing the 'action' which will occupy most of its remainder, the satire of the false and foolish courtiers. As Mercurie once again deprives Echo of the powers of normal speech and prepares to leave, the ridiculous traveller Amorphus attempts to engage her in conversation. Failing, he tastes the water, and immediately falls to praising himself as a paragon of taste. The next scene, between Amorphus, Asotus, and Criticus, establishes the final associations of the fountain, with Helicon and the Muses, and so with poetry and poetic inspiration:

Criticus. What? the well-dieted *Amorphus* become a Water-drinker? I see he meanes not to write verses then.
Asotus. No *Criticus*? why?
Criticus. Quia nulla placere diu, nec viuere carmina possunt, quae scribuntur aquae poteribus.
Amorphus. What say you to your *Helicon*?
Criticus. O, the *Muses*, well! that's euer excepted.
Amorphus. Sir, your *Muses* haue no such water I assure you; your *Nectar*, or the Iuice of your *Nepenthe* is nothing to it; tis aboue your *Metheglin*. (1.4, C1ᵛ)

The superficiality of Amorphus' character is thus established, as well as his pretension and stupidity: he avers that metheglin is 'A kinde of Greeke wine I haue met with Sir in my Trauailes: it is the same that *Demosthenes* vsually drunke, in the composure of all his exquisite and Mellifluous Orations' (1.4,

---

[51] In mythographic terms, Echo herself is an example of self-love. 'Eccho *noteth bragging and vaunting, which being contemned and despised, turneth to a bare voyce, a winde, a blast, a thing of nothing. Narcissus is a louer of himselfe, and so it falleth out, that vaunting and bragging loues self-loue.' Abraham Fraunce, The Third Part of the Countesse of Pembrokes Yuichurch* (London, 1592), sig. E2.

[52] Discussed in Chapters 9 and 12.

C2^v), when it is in fact Welsh mead of a vaguely medicinal quality. At the same time, a distinction is drawn between good and bad poets, and the distinction is as much moral as it is aesthetic.

Thus, by this early point in the play, the symbolic and syncretic importance of the fountain is fully established. The invocation of Helicon establishes a nexus of literary and cultural inheritance, good and bad poetry, good and bad language and discourse (the meeting that follows between Amorphus and Asotus is one of the play's most cruelly observed examples of utterly meaningless conversation), and, especially, the revelation of moral character through language. Echo's lament for Narcissus and his beauty, together with her emphasis on the fountain as a mirror, introduces the importance of physical appearance and attitudes towards it for the play, a theme subsequently explored through the courtiers' obsession with clothes. Her speech and curse therefore associate the fountain not only with self-love and with flattery, but with distorted perceptions, self-delusion, and solipsism also. The twin figures of Narcissus and Echo, emblematically united at and through the fountain, figure the intertwined relationship of the visual and the oral, doomed as they are respectively to the endless self-reflexivity of face and voice. Framing all this, and ultimately inseparable from it, the strongest association of the fountain figure, which is the moral relationship between monarch and court, and court and state, is subtly implied by the play's very title, by its court setting, and primarily invoked by the physical 'prop' fountain that is present on stage.

11

The Fountain of Salmacis: Self-Love and Satire

In the mid-1950s, the Walker Art Gallery in Liverpool acquired a battered, full-length Elizabethan portrait in urgent need of conservation. Now restored, it hangs among the Renaissance portraits, a worthy companion piece to the better-known portrait of Henry VIII after Holbein and the 'Pelican' portrait of Elizabeth I by Nicholas Hilliard also on display there. The portrait depicts a man now identified as George Delves (Fig. 14),[1] it is dated 1577, and its symbolism is complex. Delves is elaborately and fashionably dressed, but the portrait as a whole speaks of mourning, renunciation, and disaffection. On his right is a mysterious woman, dressed in black, her face obscured by the myrtle branch she holds; she may represent Delves' first wife Christian Wingfield, née Fitzwilliam, but she also appears to personify love.[2] On his left is a laurel tree, representing fame, but also a pile of discarded armour; although armour frequently appears in portraits of the period to attest to the military prowess of the sitter, the broken lance included here suggests the abandonment of a military career. Delves had served in Ireland for extended periods from the late 1550s on, and was knighted there in 1591; he was one of the Queen's Gentleman Pensioners from 1561. The portrait shows him caught between the competing claims of love and fame, but both have apparently proved

---

[1] The Delves family had their seat at Doddington Hall, Cheshire, although George Delves, as a younger son, did not himself live there; it was at one time thought that the portrait was of his uncle Henry Delves, of the senior branch of the family, who did have his seat at Doddington. The portrait remained at Doddington Hall, and in the possession of the Delves family, until its purchase by a dealer, and subsequently by the Walker, in the 1950s. It is unattributed, although it has been tentatively suggested that it could be by Quentin Massys the Younger, best known for his 'Sieve' portrait of Elizabeth, which dates from roughly the same period. The density of allegorical symbolism in the picture could support this attribution. Information is taken from the catalogue entry in Hearn, *Dynasties*, 105–6, and from the dossier on the painting in the Walker Art Gallery, Liverpool.

[2] Her first husband Sir Richard Wingfield had died by June 1559, and Delves himself remarried in March 1583. The jewels she wears depict Cupid and Psyche, and myrtle is associated with Venus'.

unsatisfactory: love is coloured by the experience of bereavement, and fame without proper reward is hollow. This is underlined by its background, the two poems, and by the various mottoes which appear on the portrait—across the top is painted, presumably ironically, 'ALTRO NO[N] MI VAGLIA. CHE, A[MOR], [E] FAMA', (I prize only love and fame).³

The background of the portrait depicts an elaborate, and almost certainly wholly imaginary, Italianate garden.⁴ As with Leicester's tapestry, discussed in Chapter 9, the visual source is probably to be found in Dutch engravings.⁵ The rear section of the garden is dominated by a labyrinth, and the front section by an elaborate fountain, and conservation reports suggest that, because of the lack of under-drawing of these figures (in contrast to the rest of the garden), they were added at the same time as the poems and mottoes; they very much reflect and reinforce the subject matter and imagery of the poems:

TH[E].COVRT.WHOES.OVTWRD.SHOES
SET[S].FORTH.A.WORLD.OF.IOYES
HA[E]TH.FLATTRED.ME.TO.LONG
TH[A]T.WANDRED.IN.HER.TOYES
W[H]EAR.SHOVLD.THE.THIRSTI.DRINK
BVT.WHEAR.THE.FOVNTAIN.RON
THE HOEP OF SVCH RELEEF

HA[E]TH ALMOST ME VNDON
THE.WARS.HAETH.WAST.MI.WELT[H]
AND.BROGH.MI.YOVTH.IN.CAER
AND.TIME.CONSVMED.BY.STEALTH
AS.TROETH.CAN.WEL.DECLAER
WHEARIN.I.SOGHT.FOR.FAEM
OR.AT.THE LEAST.SOM.GAYN
IN.FINE.MY.HOEL.REWARD
WAS NOGHT BVT WOE AND PA[IN]⁶

The phrase 'wandred in her toyes' certainly suggests the labyrinth, and the significance of the fountain is obvious: far from representing (as has been suggested) either a real garden or one to which Delves aspired, as an extension of the high fashion and good taste with which he presented himself in his portrait, the garden and above all its fountain stand for the snares of court life,

---

³ The inscription has been reconstructed during restoration, as shown.

⁴ There are no traces of any comparable garden at Doddington. See Sarah Bird, John Edmondson, Susan Nicholson, Katherine Stainer-Hutchins, and Christopher Taylor, 'A Late Sixteenth-Century Garden: Fact or Fantasy? The Portrait of Sir George Delves in the Walker Art Gallery, Liverpool', *Garden History*, 24 (1996), 167–83.

⁵ Wells-Cole, *Art and Decoration in Elizabethan and Jacobean England*, 82–3.

⁶ The first poem is inscribed above Delves's left shoulder, and the second in front of Delves's feet, in the painting's foreground.

for hopes raised only to be disappointed, and for the ultimate futility of the pursuit of military glory, honour, and fame. As in Jonson's play, the court and implicitly the ultimate source of patronage within it, the Queen herself, are represented as an alluring fountain, but one that does not give proper reward or recompense. Behind the gorgeous clothes, the mysterious woman, and the diverting layers of symbolism in the jewels, mottoes, armour, and setting, this is a profoundly disillusioned, even bitter, portrait. It is, however, a fascinating 'missing piece', a stunning illustration of the fountain figure as an image for the court in both visual and textual terms, and, most importantly, one that draws on the positive humanistic associations of court and monarch as fountain of patronage to make a bitterly negative point about thwarted ambition and lack of advancement. The making of that point is left, ultimately, up to the viewer, who must decode and interpret the image's symbolic content in an associative way, inferring meaning and even narrative. As previous chapters have shown in aesthetic, spiritual, and political contexts, and as the Delves portrait attests, the fountain could be a capacious and ambiguous as well as a dense signifier in early modern England, and it is as such that it functions in Ben Jonson's *The Fountaine of Selfe-Love*.

The Fountaine of Selfe-Love, as it appeared in the quarto edition of 1601 (and, presumably, as it was first performed at the Blackfriars the previous year), can be divided into several sections. The largest of these is the satire of the false courtiers, which occupies most of Act 1 and all of Acts 2–4. Before this 'action' begins, however, there are three scenes: the boys' Praeludium (or Induction, as I will refer to it here), the Prologue, and the initial encounter between Mercurie, Cupid, and Echo, at the soon-to-be eponymous fountain. Act 5, distinguished as it is by the presence of Cynthia and by the masques, marks a departure, in tone and ethos, if not in action, from the main plot, and the play is concluded by the Palinode and the Epilogue. The plot of *The Fountaine of Selfe-Love* as a whole is not consistently well integrated, but there is a strong and obvious relationship between Acts 1–4 and Act 5, and the importance of the Echo episode is on some levels at least relatively easy to discover. The opening and concluding scenes are all fairly conventional in their nature and function, but the Induction and Prologue in particular do repay some closer examination. As in the Delves portrait, it is left to the audience to infer meaning, to read and interpret the juxtaposition of verbal and visual elements in Jonson's dramaturgy.

The main purpose of the Induction as regards the rest of the play seems to be to reveal the plot when, in the squabbling between the three boy actors as to who will speak the Prologue, the third boy decides that he will '*reuenge my selfe of the Author; since I speake not his Prologue. Ile goe tell all the Arguement of his Play aforehand, and so stale his Inuention to the Auditory before it come foorth'* (A2ᵛ). The most obvious joke here, although admittedly only with the benefit of hindsight, is that there is very little plot to give away. George Parfitt has suggested a further function of the Induction is to establish an implicit comparison between the petty behaviour of the boys and the subsequent childishness of the courtiers.[7] Perhaps more importantly, however, the Induction establishes a context of role-playing and counterfeiting that remains a constant touchstone throughout the play. The children first squabble over the speaking of the Prologue, given a physical presence by the cloak traditional to that role, and this scuffle over the cloak anticipates the fetishization of clothing and its relationship with language—in this case, the proper delivery of the Prologue—that is one of the play's recurrent motifs. After the relation of the plot, however, the boys' quarrelling gives way to a series of virtuoso imitations of theatrical personalities, such as the *'Ignorant* Critique', who smokes tobacco and complains about the play, and the 'Friend, *or Well-Wisher to the House'*, in conversation with the second boy (who *'step[s] foorth like one of the* Children'), who wants to speak to the author. Even before the play begins, therefore, the audience see themselves played upon the stage, and the boy actors play at being the audience and the actors. Thus the Induction at once establishes both the extreme artificiality of the theatre and the rupture of the 'fourth wall', the closeness and complexity of the mimetic relationship between actors and audience. What appears, therefore, to be only a clever theatrical game in fact announces the play's moral didacticism, and anticipates the figure of Narcissus (who, like Actaeon, haunts the play) in its playful depiction of the nature of reflection and imitation. Jonson's *Fountaine* holds a mirror up—*is* a mirror—not only to nature, but for the audience.

The ensuing Prologue is more conventional, in its inevitable compliments to the discerning nature of the audience and perhaps specifically of Elizabeth herself. Jonson draws attention to the exclusiveness of his project and its appeal, and in particular the obviously superior judgement and taste of those who will properly be able to appreciate it: 'The garments that she [the author's Muse] weares, their hands must twine, | Who can both censure, understand, define | What Merrit is' (B1). Judgement, the ability to distinguish between true and false, the valuable and the worthless, is another recurrent theme in the play. It is closely aligned to the idea of justice, central to the portrayal of Cynthia in Act 5 (as Chapter 12 will show). In the Prologue, Jonson asserts the connection—conventional but a vital animating principle for this play—between the ability to understand and appreciate good poetry, and moral worth and integrity, and social status. At the end of the Prologue he asserts that his 'Poesie . . . affords, | Words aboue Action: matter, aboue

---

[7] Parfitt, *Ben Jonson*, 49.

wordes' (B1). The first part of this statement reinforces the implicit significance of the third boy's giving away of the plot, that is, that the action of the play is not its point. More significantly, the second half of the maxim directs the audience to look beyond the linguistic virtuosity, superficiality, and excess of what is to follow, to the play's deeper subjects and themes, its proper argument and invention, and even to consider that 'matter' may be capable of being expressed visually, rather than verbally. Contemporary usage consistently opposed 'matter' to 'words', as in Bacon's *Advancement of Learning* (1605), where it is observed that 'Here, therefore, is the first distemper of learning, when men studie words and not matter'.[8] Like the topos of the political fountain, this was a principle seized upon by a number of Renaissance humanists, and as Martin Elsky has observed, '[e]ven as English Humanists emphasized the imitative nature of language transmitted through prior acts of speech culturally fixed in literary conventions, they warned against empty eloquence, words devoid of matter. This topos recurs throughout Cicero and was forcefully proclaimed by Erasmus', Thomas Elyot, and Gabriel Harvey'.[9] The poet worthy of royal praise is one skilful in both matter and words. The way in which Jonson begins the play, which can seem disjointed on the page, is therefore carefully structured to frame the play as a whole with this central principle and to announce some of the strategies of interpretation that will be required of the audience, as well as subtly and economically to begin to establish the multiple and nuanced associations of the fountain figure.

After its prominence in the action of the first act of *The Fountaine of Selfe-Love*, outlined in the previous chapter, the fountain recedes in importance for most of the rest of the play. But its influence continues, in various subtle ways, to permeate it throughout. For example, while the fountain functions as a symbol of the virtuous and morally exemplary court, it also stands for the utter triviality of the courtiers as they idly wait to sample the allegedly delicious waters of the fountain of self-love. While Criticus the scholar poet establishes himself as a potential reformer of the court through poetry which is presented as being in the true spirit of Helicon, the courtiers play silly word games and listen to foolish songs. Recalling Narcissus, the courtiers have a distorted image of themselves at the same time as they are obsessed with appearance and with clothes in particular. This explication of the distortion of the proper use of language and the proper attitude to physical appearance (that is, that both should manifest the true moral nature and worth of a

[8] Herford and Simpson, 492.

[9] Martin Elsky, *Authorizing Words: Speech, Writing, and Print in the English Renaissance* (London: Cornell University Press, 1989), 57.

person—and one recalls here the loaded gifts of clothing and jewellery to the Queen at around this time) continues the fountain motif throughout the entire play. It gives rise to the masque of opposites and unmasking that is the play's climax, and implies, above all, the proper moral relationship between court and state (and, more problematically, between monarch and court) of which the play demonstrates the distortion and disruption. At the end of Act 2, the fountain is invoked again, as Mercurie and Cupid interrogate the pages who have been elevated into 'Yeomen of the Bottles' (2.5, E3ᵛ). This return to the literal device of the fountain to round off the act functions as a reminder of the figure's status as the play's controlling ethical and aesthetic symbol by implying a contrast between the courtiers, whose initial introductions and exposures have taken up most of the act, and what they ought to be. Their behaviour is the antithesis of exemplary, and their all-consuming longing for the waters of the fountain of self-love neatly summarizes both their individual triviality and the moral travesty of the court as a corporate entity.

The nexus that I trace throughout *The Fountaine of Selfe-Love*, whereby the degeneracy of the courtiers is expressed in their fetishization of the physical and their trivialization of language (the two being in practice often indistinguishable, as in Moria's declaration that when her lips peel she is 'sure to haue some delicious good drinke or other approaching', 4.1, G1ᵛ)[10] is anticipated in the play's Induction. When the third boy decides to '*tell all the Argument of* [the] *Play aforehand*', he announces that '*the Scene, [is] GARGAPHIA: which I do vehemently suspect for some Fustian Countrey; but let that vanish*' (A2ᵛ). Citing *The Fountaine of Selfe-Love* as the earliest (and apparently only) occurrence, *OED* gives the meaning of 'fustian' as ' "Made up", imaginary'.[11] This is too literal and narrow an interpretation. 'Gargaphia' is not 'made up' or imaginary: it is the perfectly well-known Ovidian vale of the goddess Diana, more especially identified with the spring sacred to her there. It appears in the *Metamorphoses* specifically as the site of Actaeon's fall and might well, therefore, be evoked simply by a fountain. As the particular preserve of the goddess Diana, *The Fountaine of Selfe-Love*'s setting in 'Gargaphia' would surely have invited immediate comparison with the English realm of the other Cynthia, Queen Elizabeth. Jonson's use of 'fustian' to describe it is a clever and anticipatory combination of the two primary meanings of the word in the early seventeenth century. The first of these refers to 'a kind of coarse cloth made of cotton and flax', the second to 'Inflated, turgid, or inappropriately

---

[10] There is a close analogue to Moria's combined oral and visual fetish in Jonson's scathing 'Epigram on the Court Pucell'.

[11] 3† b.

lofty language; speech or writing composed of high-sounding words and phrases; bombast; rant'.[12] For both senses, the implication is of presumption, pretension, and misplaced aspiration; the overweening pride associated with Actaeon and Narcissus and demonstrated by Cynthia's courtiers. As the courtiers are introduced into the play, this interrelationship of words and appearance, specifically clothing, as an index of moral character is a constant touchstone.[13] In Amorphus' virtuoso soliloquy in 1.3, for example, he observes of himself that '[i]f my behauiours had beene of a cheape, or customary garbe; my Accent, or phrase, vulgar; my Garments trite; my Countenance illiterate; or vnpracticed in the encounter of a beautifull and braue-attirde Peice, then I might (with some change of coullor) haue suspected my faculties' (1.3, C1).

When Jonson especially constructs the courtiers as negative (or cautionary) exempla by lavishing particular attention on their trivial fetishization of clothes and language, he invokes sentiments which were eventually to appear as part of his *Discoveries*. It is not possible to date their specific appearance in what was essentially Jonson's commonplace book, which remained unpublished until 1640; dating is further complicated by the fact that some of his books and manuscripts were lost in the 1623 fire, although far from all, as was once supposed. They express, however, principles which are certainly very pertinent to a discussion of *The Fountaine of Selfe-Love*, and there are (as will shortly be seen) some compelling reasons for deducing that Jonson was compiling some version of the *Discoveries* at the same time as he was writing *The Fountaine of Selfe-Love*. In the *Discoveries*, as in that play, language is inextricably linked to both morality and physical appearance: 'Language most shows a man: speak that I may see thee. It springs out of the most retired, and inmost parts of us, and is the image of the parent of it, the mind. No glass renders a man's form, or likeness, so true as his speech'.[14] Citing Plutarch's *Moralia*, the Jesuit Thomas Wright had similarly commented that 'if the fruit or flowers be corrupted or vitious, we know the root must be infected: so if mens words or actions be disconsorted, doubtlesse the soule cannot be well disposed; for, as one said well, A troubled Fountaine yeedeth vnpure water, & an infected soule, vitious

---

[12] *OED*. Jonson himself had used 'fustian' in the sense of pretentious language in *Every Man out* (1600): 'let's talke Fustian a little and gull 'hem: make 'hem beleeue we are great Schollers' (3, sig. H4ᵛ). The pun on both senses was a current one, as in Marston's *The Scourge of Villanie*, reprinted three times in 1598–9: 'Here's one, to get an undeseru'd repute | Of deepe deepe learning, all in fustian sute | Of ill-plac'd farre-fetch'd words attiereth | His period, that all sence forsweareth,' Satire 6, 1598, sig. E7ᵛ.

[13] 'Courtiers' is used for the sake of convenience throughout my discussion, although it is not strictly applicable to Amorphus, for example. See also Mercurie's caveat in 2.4.

[14] 'Oratio imago animi', *Discoveries*, lines 2515–19. Quotations from the *Discoveries* are taken from *Ben Jonson: The Complete Poems*, ed. George Parfitt (rev. edn. London: Penguin, 1996).

actions'.[15] It is generally believed that it was Wright who converted Jonson to Catholicism during the latter's imprisonment for the murder of Gabriel Spencer in 1598, and Wright's work *The Passions of the minde* appears to have been a source for *The Fountaine of Selfe-Love*; its third chapter is 'Of Self Love'.[16] Elsewhere in the *Discoveries*, Jonson expands this principle to include its implications for the state as well as for the individual:

There cannot be one colour of the mind; another of the wit. If the mind be staid, grave, and composed, the wit is so; that vitiated, the other is blown, and deflowered. Do we not see, if the mind languish, the members are dull? Look upon an effeminate person: his very gait confesseth him. If a man be fiery, his motion is so: if angry, 'tis troubled, and violent. So that we may conclude: wheresoever manners, and fashions are corrupted, language is. It imitates the public riot. The excess of feasts, and apparel, are the notes of a sick state; and the wantonness of language, of a sick mind.[17]

In *The Fountaine of Selfe-Love*, Jonson demonstrates the moral corruption of the courtiers and, implicitly, the moral crisis of the court as it is embodied in the person of the Queen, through the interrelationship of the elements in this last maxim: the 'excess of feasts and apparel' and the 'wantonness of language'; the 'sick mind' and the 'sick state'. Discussing *The Fountaine of Selfe-Love* in the context of contemporary anti-court satire, Oscar Campbell used as an example the satire on court poetry in Joseph Hall's *Virgidemiarium* (1597):

Now is *Pernassus* turned to a stewes:
And on Bay-Stocks the wanton Myrtle grewes.
Cythêron hill's become a Brothel-bed,
And *Pyrene* sweet turned to a poysoned head
Of cole-black puddle: whose infectuous staine
Corrupteth all the lowly fruitfull plaine . . . [18]

but he did not go on to comment on the particular pertinence of this example to Jonson's treatment of language in the play. The similar nexus that Jonson himself constructed in the *Discoveries* between moral and poetic or more broadly linguistic corruption in turn bears out the connections made by Echo, through the fountain of self-love, between the verbal and the visual expressions of self-love. These turn on the central idea of 'flatterie' (1.2, B3ᵛ), meaning both misleading, distorting reflection and unwarrantedly extravagant compliment.

---

[15] Thomas Wright, *The Passions of the minde in generall* (London, 1604), sig. I7. See Peter Milward, 'Wright, Thomas (*c*.1561–1623)', *Oxford Dictionary of National Biography* (www.oxforddnb.com/view/article/30059, accessed 22 Mar. 2006). Wright was a close associate of Anthony Bacon, and through him involved in the 'Essex circle'. Jonson contributed a commendatory poem to the second edition in 1604, but the first edition had appeared in 1600, and Wright had apparently finished the book by 1598.
[16] Wright, *The Passions of the minde*, sig. B6.
[17] 'De corruptela morum', *Discoveries*, lines 1172–84.   [18] Sig. B3ᵛ.

The decadent Hedon, Amorphus, and Asotus are contrasted with Criticus, who is, according to Mercurie, 'A creature of a most perfect and diuine temper; One, in whom the Humors & Elements are peaceably met, without aemulation of Precedencie . . . His discourse is like his behauiour, vncommon, but not vnpleasing; he is prodigall of neither' (2.3, D4^v–E1). Criticus is presented as a man not only of temperance, but of consistency. He is the author-figure, the poet, and, it will transpire, the reformer of the court in the terms set out by Jonson himself, in the *Discoveries*:

I could never think the study of wisdom confined only to the philosopher: or of piety to the divine: or of state to the politic. But that he which can feign a commonwealth (which is the poet) can govern it with councils,[19] strengthen it with laws, correct it with judgements, inform it with religion, and morals; is all these. We do not require in him mere elocution; or an excellent faculty in verse; but the exact knowledge of all virtues, and their contraries; with ability to render the one loved, the other hated, by his proper embattling them.[20]

As early as the Prologue, Jonson asserts the poet's superior moral status, announcing the critical and ultimately reforming role that he will claim for Criticus. In this he recalls Sidney's reinterpretation of Plato's banishment of poets from the ideal republic, and his eulogy of the true poet in his *Defence*:

Let us rather plant more Laurels for to engarland the poets' heads (which honour of being laureate, as besides them only triumphant captains were, is a sufficient authority to show the price they ought to be held in) than suffer the ill-savoured breath of such wrong speakers once to blow upon the clear springs of poesy.[21]

For Jonson, as for Sidney, the bad poet is an object of contempt, not worthy of the name, while the good poet is a worthy asset to the commonwealth, and should be treated accordingly. It is a contrast implied, and a role claimed for the poet, in the initial discussion of the fountain's water, and the invocation of Helicon, at the beginning of the play's main action. As James Bednarz has observed, '[t]hrough [the] coupling of poet and sovereign—Asper and Queen Elizabeth in *Every Man Out*, Criticus and Cynthia in *The Fountaine of Selfe-Love*, and Horace and Augustus Caesar in *Poetaster*—Jonson asserted that literary and political power were equal sources of moral authority'.[22] Jonson's use of the fountain figure as a framing device for *The Fountaine of Selfe-Love* allowed him to show the complex interrelationship of these various concerns and forms of authority. In the humanist terms discussed in Chapter 9, it is the

---

[19] The original text gives 'Counsels', which seems more appropriate in the context.
[20] 'De malign. studentium', *Discoveries*, lines 1273–85.
[21] Alexander, *Sidney's 'The Defence of Poesy'*, 41.
[22] Bednarz, *Shakespeare and the Poets' War*, 62.

poet who is best equipped to act as a moral adviser to the prince, protecting the fountain of his mind, and hence his people, from moral corruption.

Some twenty-five years ago. Margaret Tudeau-Clayton demonstrated Ben Jonson's borrowing from the twelfth-century *Policraticus*, by John of Salisbury, in his *Timber, or Discoveries*.[23] Tudeau-Clayton considered a passage of some fifty-five lines, just over a third of the way through the *Discoveries*,[24] organized by Jonson under the headings 'Adulatio', 'De vita humana', 'De piis & probis', and 'Mores Aulici' ('flattery', 'of human life', 'of the upright and the good', and 'of the ways of courtiers'), showing that in this section, Jonson had drawn heavily on passages in the third book of the *Policraticus*. Editions of the *Policraticus* were printed in Lyons and Paris in 1513, and in Leiden in 1595. There was no English edition, let alone a translation, available to Jonson, but there are many copies of all three editions in English libraries, and several of the eight copies in the Cambridge University Library alone appear to have early modern English provenance. Tudeau-Clayton also suggested that Jonson had made good use of the lengthy (sixty page) 'tabula materiarum' and the marginal notes which appeared in the 1513 editions, and speculated that he could perhaps have had access to a copy through Camden, who was the friend of a known owner of a 1513 edition, Dr Francis Godwin.[25] The 'tabula materiarum' is both index and thematic guide to the contents of the *Policraticus*, which provides (through the repetition of key phrases from the chapters themselves) 'a summary version of the topics treated',[26] and Tudeau-Clayton suggests that Jonson may have begun by using the 'tabula', looking perhaps for 'adulatio' or 'adulatores', but then read on through the text itself,[27] as the passages that he draws on in this section of the *Discoveries* are located in the vicinity of, but both before and after, the passage that he uses for 'Adulatio'. Despite Tudeau-Clayton's identification of this important source for Ben Jonson, little further work has apparently been done in assessing whether others of his works might also reveal traces of the *Policraticus*. There is one very striking example in particular, which dovetails neatly into the passage in *Discoveries* discussed by Tudeau-Clayton, and which in turn perhaps suggests that Jonson was writing the *Discoveries* in some form as early as 1600. That example is, of course, *The Fountaine of Selfe-Love*, for in addition to drawing dramaturgically upon Peele's use of the fountain in *David and Bethsabe*, it seems that Jonson drew more thematic aspects of the device of the play's eponymous fountain, its central and controlling metaphor, from chapter 10 of Book 5 of the *Policraticus*.

[23] Margaret Tudeau-Clayton, 'Ben Jonson, "In Travaile with Expression of Another": His Use of John of Salisbury's *Policraticus* in *Timber*', *Review of English Studies*, 30 (1979), 397–408.
[24] *Discoveries*, lines 1320–76.   [25] Tudeau-Clayton, 'Ben Jonson', 400.
[26] Ibid. 401.   [27] Ibid. 402.

Book 5 of the *Policraticus* is concerned with the 'commonwealth', and with the proper relationship between prince and subjects. Chapter 10 is entitled 'Of the flanks of the powerful, whose needs are to be satisfied, and whose malice is to be restrained'.[28] By the end of the chapter, however, the focus is less on rulers' potential for viciousness than on the capacity of courtiers to corrupt:

For who is it whose virtue is not cast aside by the frivolities of courtiers? Who is so great, who is so resolute, that he cannot be corrupted? He is best who resists for the longest time, who is strongest, who is corrupted least. For in order that virtue be unharmed, one must turn aside from the life of the courtier. He who said the following providently and prudently expressed the nature of the court: 'He departs from the court who wishes to be pious'.[29] For this reason, the court has been compared to the infamous fountain of Salmacis, which is notorious for weakening virility . . .

This obscure poetic fiction represents the likeness of the frivolities of the courtiers, which weaken men by the debasement of their virility or pervert a retained likeness of virility. He who engages in the trifles of the courtier and undertakes the obligations of the philosopher or the good man is an hermaphrodite, whose harsh and prickly face disfigures the beauty of women and who pollutes and dishonours virility with effeminacy. For indeed the philosopher-courtier is a monstrous thing; and, while he affects to be both, he is neither one, for the court excludes philosophy and the philosopher at no time engages in the trifles of the courtier. Yet the comparison does not apply to all courts, but merely those which are mismanaged by a foolish will. For whoever is wise drives away frivolities, orders his house, and subjects everything to reason.[30]

The image of the court as an enervating fountain is here a central and potent one, and attention is drawn to it in the 1513 editions by the marginal note, 'Curia comparatur fonti salmacis' (the court compared to the fountain of Salmacis).[31]

The fountain of Salmacis and the story of Salmacis and Hermaphroditus[32] are not directly invoked by Jonson in *The Fountaine of Selfe-Love* in the same way that Narcissus and Actaeon are, but the effects of the play's fountain are very similar. By the end of Act 2, when Amorphus the courtier has reported the deliciousness of the fountain's water to the rest of the court, there is

such a drought i'the Presence, wi[t]h reporting the wonders of this new water; that all the Ladies and Gallants lie languishing vpon the Rushes, like so many pounded Cattle

---

[28] *John of Salisbury: Policraticus*, ed. and trans. Cary J. Nederman, Cambridge Texts in the History of Political Thought (Cambridge: Cambridge University Press, 1990), 85. All quotations from the *Policraticus* are taken from this edition; it is not a complete translation, but it has the advantage over all other translations of being in print and widely available.

[29] Lucan, *Pharsalia*, trans. J. D. Duff (Cambridge, Mass.: Harvard University Press, 1928), 8.493–4.

[30] *Policraticus*, ed. Nederman, 90–1.   [31] 157^v in the 1513 Lyons edition.

[32] Ovid, *Metamorphoses*, 4.288–388.

i'the midst of Haruest, sighing one to another, and gasping, as if each of them expected a Cock from the Fountaine, to be brought into his mouth: and (without we returne quickly) they are all (as a youth would say) no better than a few Trowts cast a shore, or a dish of Eeles in a Sand-bag (E3ᵛ–E4)

and by the beginning of Act 4, the water having still not been brought, the situation has not improved:

Phantaste: I would this water would arriue once our trauayling friend so commended
    to vs.
Argurion: So would I, for he has left all vs in trauaile, with expectation of it.
Phantaste: Pray *Ioue*, I neuer rise from this Couch, if euer I thirsted more for a thing,
    in my whole time of being a Courtier.
Philautia: Nor I, Ile be sworne; the very mention of it sets my lippes in a worse heate,
    then if he had sprinkled them with *Mercury*. (G1ᵛ)

While the water here is to be drunk, rather than bathed in (as in the *Policraticus* and, indeed, in the *Metamorphoses*), the names of the courtiers themselves suggest decadence, degeneracy, and enervation: in addition to Phantaste ('Boaster'), Argurion ('Silver', as in money), and Philautia ('Self Love') in the passage just quoted, the others are named as Amorphus ('Deformed'), Asotus ('Debauchee' or 'Prodigal'), Hedon ('Pleasure'), Anaides ('Impudence'), Moria ('Folly'), Prosaites ('Beggar', or 'one who importunes'), Cos ('Whetstone'), Morus ('Fool'), and Gelaia ('Laughter'). Of these, Amorphus is the central figure, and his name surely recalls the fate of Salmacis and Hermaphroditus, as it can also be translated as 'shapeless' or even 'one who changes shape'. The male courtiers in *The Fountaine of Selfe-Love* are certainly stereotypically effeminate in their obsessions with clothes and their garrulousness, and it is implied that they have been corrupted by too much contact with women; they are therefore effeminate in the now obsolete sense of 'devoted to women'.[33]

It is of course significant for Jonson's play as a whole, therefore, that the first part of the *Policraticus'* alternative title, or subtitle, is 'De Nugis Curialium' (Concerning the frivolities of courtiers) for it is the corruptions and frivolities of courtiers that are exposed and satirized by Jonson. The other part of this alternative title is 'et Vestigiis Philosophorum', 'and the Footprints of Philosophers': Criticus, not surprisingly the voice of reason and virtue in the play, who is described in the Induction as '*a retir'd* Scholler'

---

[33] There is a persuasive account of the play's investigation of narcissism by Mario Digangi, ' "Male Deformities": Narcissus and the Reformation of Courtly Manners in *Cynthia's Revels*', in Goran V. Stanivukovic (eds.), *Ovid and the Renaissance Body* (Toronto: University of Toronto Press, 2001), 94–110, although he bases his discussion on the Folio text and does not specifically consider the turn-of-the-century context.

and later dismissed by Hedon and Anaides as 'a whoore-sonne *Book-worme*, a *Candle-waster*... poore *Grogran* Rascall... *Dormouse*' (A3, E4ᵛ), is surely the philosopher whom John discusses, who is of the court yet apart from it in his comportment and concerns. If Jonson is indeed recalling this passage from the *Policraticus* in its entirety, he is treading on dangerous ground: it would not do for Queen Elizabeth to have been invited to identify too closely with John's statement that 'the court excludes philosophy and the philosopher at no time engages in the trifles of the courtier. Yet the comparison does not apply to all courts, but merely those which are mismanaged by a foolish will. For whoever is wise drives away frivolities, orders his house, and subjects everything to reason.' Cynthia's loss of control over her court and its denizens is particularly shown in the way in which the false courtiers use language, and in the fact that it is a poet who is to be the agent of reform. Whatever part the courtiers' linguistic excesses may have played in the 'Poets' War', they, together with their trivial word games, riddles, and foolish songs, show the corruption of nothing less than the 'Queen's English', a concept far less abstract in Jonson's day than current usage might suggest. There was a close association in the Renaissance between the person of the monarch and the language of his or her realm, of which he or she was the patron. The vernacular identification of King James with the Authorized Version of the Bible is the best example of this habit of mind, but Elizabeth herself was similarly identified with (and visually inscribed into, through illuminated capitals and frontispieces) the biblical translations produced in her reign.[34] As previous chapters have shown, her acceptance of the gift of the English Bible during the pageant of *Veritas Temporis Filia* in her coronation entry was a defining moment in her cultural memory, and one significantly revisited and reinvented throughout her reign. According to Martin Elsky, 'the linguistic responsibility asked of English Renaissance monarchs is well documented'. He has argued that

the force responsible for creating a society in which it is possible for a speaker to unite word and thing is the monarch, who is responsible for the political fortunes of his kingdom. The connection between morally disposed political power and the verbal health of a nation may have its origins among the Stoics, who held that the initial

---

[34] Discussing Robert Cawdrey's *A Table Alphabeticall* (1604), which she describes as 'arguably the first dictionary of vernacular English', Juliet Fleming has cited his recommendation of 'recourse to the protection of the monarch when he activates the traditional claim that "the king... is lord of this language". Published in 1604, Cawdrey's assertion that English is the king's is at least topical, for the accession of James I had brought to an end a half century of female rule during which English had been under the nominal aegis of the queen.' She notes that this concept was 'first recorded in the preface to Chaucer's *Treatise on the Astrolabe* (1391)'. Juliet Fleming, 'Dictionary English and the Female Tongue', in Richard Burt and John Michael Archer (eds.), *Enclosure Acts: Sexuality, Property and Culture in Early Modern England* (Ithaca, NY: Cornell University Press, 1994), 290, 305, 23 n. 46.

imposition of a name or thing occurs under a good king, and deteriorates as the moral virtue of the kings declines.[35]

In *The Fountaine of Selfe-Love*, Jonson figures the dislocation between court and state and monarch and court, and the disjunction between the false court and the ideal, exemplary one, through a debased, trivial, artificial language, which in turn reflects badly on the monarch. As Peter Womack has economically observed (à propos the courtiers' word games in Act 4) 'Language is supposed to do honour to the mind it represents, as a royal court is supposed to do honour to the monarch it expresses: these courtiers profane both dignities, and each sacrilege is a metaphor for the other'.[36] Jonson offers a solution in the person of the scholar-poet-author. Perhaps, in the authorial figure of Criticus, he even questions the monarch's right to control language as his play demonstrates the loss of that control.

The play in general, even without its apparent pro-Essex agenda (which is the subject of the next, and final, chapter) *does* tread on dangerous ground. The corruption and decadence of the courtiers is shown primarily in their languishing after the waters of the fountain of self-love, but also (and far more pervasively) in their trivial and decadent language; they debase the very 'Queen's English', and themselves pollute the waters of Helicon. Those passages in the *Discoveries* in which Jonson explores the morality of language, discussed above, are not especially distant from those which Tudeau-Clayton demonstrated were drawn from the *Policraticus*, and the intervening sections address, like both the *Policraticus* and *The Fountaine of Selfe-Love*, questions of the nature of the prince, the purpose and nature of study, and the function of poets and philosophers in the commonwealth. It may well be that further examination of the *Policraticus* could reveal other passages upon which Jonson was drawing here, and it is perhaps telling that the last passage from the *Discoveries* identified by Tudeau-Clayton as owing a debt to John of Salisbury is 'Mores Aulici' ('of the ways of courtiers'), a theme obviously relevant to *The Fountaine of Selfe-Love*. Tudeau-Clayton herself suggested parallels between the passages from the *Policraticus* drawn on in the *Discoveries* and the concerns of Jonson in *Poetaster* (1602);[37] the closeness of this in date to the composition of *The Fountaine of Selfe-Love*, and indeed the overlap in material and concerns (especially with the morality of language) between the two plays, is further evidence that Jonson was indeed reading the *Policraticus* around this time.

---

[35] Elsky, *Authorizing Words*, 75.
[36] Peter Womack, *Ben Jonson* (Oxford: Basil Blackwell, 1986), 100. He cites the *Discoveries*, but does not explore their specific relevance to *The Fountaine of Selfe-Love*.
[37] Tudeau-Clayton, 'Ben Jonson', 406.

In *The Fountaine of Selfe-Love*, Jonson's false courtiers pursue a life that is not merely shallow and trivial, but false, dissembling, and second-hand. As Act 4 opens, the women of the court are still awaiting the delivery of the water from the Fountain of Selfe-Love, its mention at the beginning of 4.1 once again deftly touching in the importance of the fountain figure to the play's moral agenda. They discuss the court gallants, and when Hedon appears (4.2), followed by Amorphus and Asotus (4.3), the flirtatious banter continues. As the culmination of the play's demonstration of the immorality and degeneracy of the court through the twin strands of the courtiers' simultaneous obsession with clothes and debasement of language, the courtiers play the game of 'substantives and adjectives', in which the adjectives '*Odoriferous. Popular. Humble. White-liuer'd. Barbarous. Pythagoricall*', and finally '*Well-spoken*' (4.3, H–H^v) end up being applied to the substantive 'Breeches', thus bringing together the two themes in the final pairing '*Well-spoken* Breeches' (H2). The much-anticipated fountain water finally arrives at the beginning of 4.4. But almost as soon as the foolish courtiers have drunk, 'the virtuous' Arete appears, refuses the water and announces that the courtiers must prepare an entertainment: 'Gallants, you must prouide for some solemne Reuels to night, *Cynthia* is minded to come foorth, and grace your sports with her presence' (4.5, I2^v). (It is a slight deficiency in Jonson's plotting that the false courtiers are not so much transformed as confirmed in their moral characters by their drinking from the fountain of self-love: they are already thoroughly enamoured of themselves.) Arete is mocked after her exit as 'good Lady *Sobriety*' (I3), but this is the last time the courtiers mention the fountain and its qualities even implicitly. It has served its purpose as a unifying plot device, and its associations and implications have been so thoroughly woven into the fabric of the play that from this point onwards it functions in a purely thematic, symbolic sense only, via the nexus of associations established around it.

At the beginning of Act 5, therefore, the tone of the play shifts abruptly, with the appearance of Cynthia and the Hymn to her sung by Hesperus.[38] The Hymn and the speech by Cynthia which follows it concern the goddess's powers of illumination. There is a recollection here of the play's implicit condemnation of the closed circle of self-reflexiveness exemplified by Echo and Narcissus in her first, perhaps rather defensive, statement: 'When hath *Diana*, like an enuious wretch, | That glitters only to his soothed selfe, | Denying to the world the precious vse | Of hoorded wealth, with-held her friendly ayde? (5.1, K1–K2). 'Hesperus *intreats thy light*': Cynthia however denies that she has ever kept her light from the world, even though it is undeserved by humanity. In an obvious

---

[38] Discussed in Chapter 12.

contrast with the verbal dissemblings and manipulations of the courtiers, Arete observes of Cynthia 'How *Cynthianly* (that is how worthely | And like her selfe) the matchlesse *Cynthia* speakes . . . Thy Presence broad-seales our delights for pure, | What's done in *Cynthias* sight, is done secure' (5.1, K2ᵛ). Cynthia is therefore, potentially, the positive embodiment of Jonson's principle of the consistency of utterance and moral character, as the courtiers have been its negative embodiment; furthermore, her presence is a guarantee of truth and undistorted vision. Her first just action is to recognize the moral worth of Criticus, and promise him reward: '*Cynthia* shall brighten what the World made dim' (5.1, K3).

Cynthia's appearance at this point and the terms in which she is introduced closely recall the notorious and swiftly suppressed representation of Queen Elizabeth in the final scene of *Every Man out of his Humor* in 1599. In the original version of that play (1600), confronted with a vision of the Queen, Macilente eulogizes her graces and explains that her presence has transformed his character:

> *Enuie* is fled my Soule at sight of her,
> And shee hath chac'd all blacke thoughts from my bosome,
> Like as the *Sunne* doth darknesse from the world.
> My streame of *Humor* is run out of me:
> And our Citties *Torrent* (bent t'infect
> The hallow'd bowels of the siluer *Thames*)
> Is checkt by strength and clearenesse of the Riuers,
> Till it hath spent it selfe e'ene at the Shore?
> So in the ample and vnmeasur'd Flood
> Of her *Perfections*, are my *Passions* drown'd:
> And I haue now a *spirit* as sweet and cleere,
> As the most rarefi'd and subtill Aire. (Q3ᵛ–Q4)

Elizabeth's power to transform moral character is figured first like that of the sun, in a way analogous to the plea for the moon's illumination in the Hymn sung by Hesperus.[39] More pertinent, however, is Macilente's speaking of 'the ample and vnmeasur'd Flood | Of her *Perfections*'. The imagery here is of rivers rather than fountains, but it all the same envisages Elizabeth in terms of a purifying rush of water, curing the moral flaws of her subjects as the Thames cleanses her capital. It is therefore an anticipatory gesture towards the same metaphorical tradition in humanist political theory that Jonson was, in his next play, to explore more fully.

[39] Karl F. Zender discusses the light imagery common to these passages, but not the water imagery. 'The Unveiling of the Goddess in *Cynthia's Revels*', *Journal of English and Germanic Philology*, 77 (1978), 45 f.

For all his explanatory protestations, Jonson learned his lesson: when he represented Elizabeth again in *The Fountaine of Selfe-Love*, it was in the familiar but acceptable guise of the moon goddess, and there is at least no surviving indication that it was his thinly veiled representation of the monarch in particular that caused the play to be (as Dekker snidely remarked) 'misse-likt at Court'.[40] The structural similarities between the appearances of Elizabeth and Cynthia—both almost at the end of the play—suggest further points of comparison between them. Most obviously, each has an effect upon the characters and action of her respective play that is catalytic and transformative. In *Every Man out*, Elizabeth transforms Macilente from a creature of 'blacke thoughts', dull earth, and dirty water to one of fire and air. But Cynthia's appearance at the climax of *The Fountaine of Selfe-Love* is much more problematic, although still an elaborate compliment to the Queen. In the first place, it occupies the entire fifth act of the play. Furthermore, freed (one assumes) from the risks inherent in an uncoded representation of Elizabeth, Jonson gives Cynthia long speeches, which include some of the play's most pointed topical allusions and which, together with the dialogue with Criticus and Arete, in the context of the two 'unmasking' masques, carry much of the play's didactic and moral weight. Jonson's Cynthia is a complex character who does not entirely escape implication in her own elucidation of the problems of her court. She may have the power to illuminate, transform, and reform, but Jonson makes little attempt to disguise the implication that the degeneracy of the false courtiers is ultimately her responsibility in the first place. The connections made in the play between language, morality, and power, as they are signalled and worked out through the figure of the fountain, in fact subtly question and even undermine the simple eulogy of the Queen that appears to have hitherto been the most widespread, if not the universal, interpretation of the play.

The first masque (5.2), in which the court women appear, presented by Cupid 'like *Anteros*' (K3), turns on the device of true reflection, and thus harks back to Echo's invocation of the fountain as the 'flattering mirror' and the 'truer glasse' (1.2, B3ᵛ), and even beyond to the play's Induction and Prologue. In the masque, the *'foure faire Virgins from the Pallace of their Queene Perfection'* have been sent to Cynthia *'wholy to consecrate themselues to thy Coelestiall seruice, as in whose cleare Spirit (the proper Element, and Sphaere of vertues) they should behould not her alone, (their euer honor'd*

---

[40] Thomas Dekker, *Satiromastix*, 5.2.324–5, in *The Dramatic Works of Thomas Dekker*, vol. i, ed. Fredson Bowers (Cambridge: Cambridge University Press, 1962). *Satiromastix* was entered into the Stationers' Register in 1601, having been first performed that year, and published in 1602.

Mistresse) but themselues (more truely themselues)' (K3). Their gift is a *'Christall Mound*[41] *... to shew whatsoeuer the World hath excellent, howsoeuer remote and various'* (5.2, K3ᵛ). After the presentation of the masquers, Cynthia examines the orb and (in an obvious compliment to Elizabeth) discerns 'On Sea-girt Rocke like to a *Goddesse...* | Another *Cynthia*, and another Queene, | Whose glory (like a lasting *Plenilune*) | Seems ignorant of what it is to wane' (5.3, K4). The crystal globe—which is implicitly also a mirror, as much as it is a symbol of monarchy—shows a queen who is 'semper eadem' but also, in Spenser's phrase, 'eterne in mutabilitie',[42] as the paradoxical 'lasting *Plenilune*'. She begins her response by averring that 'Not without wounder, nor with out delight, | Mine eyes haue veiwd in Contemplations depth, | This worke of wit, diuine, and excellent'. Although her comments specifically concern the crystal globe, they also apply to the masque as a whole and, by extension, the play. Judith Dundas has observed that '[a]rt, in this familiar Neo-Platonic language, becomes an immortal mirror into which the soul gazes and discovers itself'.[43] It is not simply 'art' in its purely visual or plastic sense that has become Echo's 'truer glasse', however, but the facility of Criticus' poetic invention and the medium of language itself. In the paradox of the fountain that is at once Narcissus' and Echo's, the fluency of discourse from a morally pure source yet retains the capacity for clear and true reflection no real fountain or mirror can ever display. Cynthia praises Criticus in terms similar to those he has applied to herself and takes him into her service: 'Hence forth be ours, the more thy selfe to be' (K4ᵛ). Criticus is rewarded for his perception, in moral and poetic terms, by the freedom to be himself.

In the second masque (5.4), Mercurie presents the men of the court as *'the foure Cardinall properties without which the Body of Complement mooueth not'*, analogous to the *'foure Cardinall vertues vpon which the whole Frame of the Court dooth mooue'* (L1). The courtiers appear as Virginity, Goodness, Courage, and Good Nature, and the two masques together present the ideal court, joining these qualities with the 'naturall Affection... delectable and pleasant Conuersation... well conceited Wittinesse... Symplicity' represented by the women, with the addition of the order and harmony symbolized in the dance itself. Once again, the idea of the distorted reflection is being played with: in a neat reversal of reality, the masque represents the ideal of which the false courtiers are but a travesty. The satire of the false courtiers in the first

---

[41] A globe or orb. [42] *The Faerie Queene*, 3.6.47.
[43] Judith Dundas, ' "Those Beautiful Characters of Sense": Classical Deities and the Court Masque', *Comparative Drama*, 16 (1982), 176. L. A. Beaurline discusses the mirror as a Platonic and Augustinian image in *Jonson and Elizabethan Comedy: Essays in Dramatic Rhetoric* (San Marino, Calif.: Huntington Library, 1978), 45 f.

four acts of the play therefore anticipates Jonson's later anti-masques, in its relationship to the final masque.[44] The nature of the virtues represented in the masques, particularly by the women, shows how closely related they are to their respective vices or moral failings, a mere question of emphasis, a false interpretation, a failure of perception and application. The courtiers are not so much inherently wicked as utterly self-obsessed, a flaw enhanced by their drinking from the fountain, which is borne out by the failure of Cupid's arrows to have any effect in 5.5.

In Cynthia's long speech which leads to the unmasking of the courtiers, she again examines the issue of her justice, in a passage which has universally been interpreted as referring to the situation of the Earl of Essex.[45] Actaeon's crime is represented as pride and presumption, as is Niobe's, the typical failings of the courtier. Actaeon looked at what he ought not to have, and in the wrong way. This is the first mention of Actaeon since Echo's lament in 1.2, but to Echo he was 'pursu'd, and torne, | By *Cynthias* wrath', while Niobe was the victim of Diana's 'sharpe reuenge' (B4). With this background, Cynthia's assertion that 'A Goddesse did it; therefore it was good: | We are not cruell, nor delight in blood' (L3^v) perhaps rings a little hollow. It is of presumption that Cynthia accuses the false courtiers when they unmask: 'Is there so little awe of our Disdeigne, | That any (vnder trust of their disguise) | Should mixe themselues with others of the Court?' (L3^v). This is the same crime for which Actaeon was punished. But instead of punishing them herself, after banishing Cupid, she delegates to Arete and Criticus the task of the courtiers' reformation.

It is specifically as a poet that Criticus undertakes the task of reformation, as he has also been responsible, as author, for engineering the false courtiers' exposure. The penance that he devises returns the play neatly, in its conclusion, to the fountain once again, as the courtiers are ordered first to '*Niobes* stone, | [To] offer vp two teares a piece thereon; | That it may change the name, as you must change, | And of a stone be called *Weeping Crosse*' and then 'to the Well of Knowledge, *Helicon*' (5.5, M1). The antidote to the waters of the fountain of self-love, the corrective to the enervating waters of the fountain of Salmacis, the court, is therefore in the hands of the poet: he alone, as Jonson observed in the *Discoveries*, is properly equipped to reform both court and commonwealth. The play's final palinode is a return to the arch, satiric tone of Acts 1–4, as the courtiers, led by Amorphus and Phantaste, forswear their

---

[44] This is a point made by K. W. Evans, with particular reference to the Folio version of the play: 'The broad irony of Jonson's dedication is enough to show his emphasis, for the play as a whole serves as one long antimasque of the "fountain of self-love", the real court, to "The Special Fountain of Manners", the ideal court.' K. W. Evans, 'The Political Philosophy of Jonson's Masques', *Work in Progress*, 1 (1972), 76.

[45] See the discussion of the Essex allusions in Chapter 12.

trivial preoccupations and vow themselves to a better life, and the closing song is a neat summation of the process of reformation:

> Now each one dry his weeping eyes,
> and to the *Well of Knowledge* hast;
> Where purged of your Maladies,
> We may of sweeter waters taste:
> And with refined voice report
> The Grace of *Cynthia*, and her Court. (5.5, M2)

But prior to this more light-hearted ensemble ending, Cynthia has had the last word in the play proper:

> Princes that would their People should do well
> Must at themselues begin, as at the heads;
> For men by their example patterne out
> Their Imitations, and reguard of Lawes:
> A vertuous Court, a world to vertue drawes. (5.5, M1^v)

This is as close as Jonson comes in the 1601 quarto (and, one assumes, in performance) to articulating the implied criticism of Elizabeth herself that underlies the entire play. The degeneracy of her courtiers, and so her court's failure to be a virtuous example to the world, is ultimately her responsibility.

To read *Cynthia's Revels* once again as *The Fountaine of Selfe-Love* recovers the urgency of its project as a daring attempt by a poet, at the beginning of his court career, to stake his claim to a role the nature of which he himself seeks simultaneously to determine. Focusing on the fountain, so prominent in the play's title and staging, and using it as a starting point, in addition to recovering its debt to John of Salisbury's *Policraticus*, makes sense of this difficult and neglected play and reveals the interests and concerns that hold it together. The linguistic and literary associations of the fountain in the classical tradition, and in humanist discourse, allowed Jonson to use it as the matrix for an Erasmian elision of language and power, and to explore both the threats to royal power and control and the possible role of the poet in thwarting or ameliorating them. The way in which the device of the fountain frames the play, whether visually in the theatre or textually in the Folio, together with this symbolic density and complexity, announces the syncretic strategies of interpretation, going beyond the merely intertextual, that Jonson elicits. Jonson's fountain is both visual and material, at the same time as it is textual and metaphorical. It points at once to a theatrical precedent (the fountain in Peele's *David and Bethsabe*) and a political text, the *Policraticus*. The action and concerns of his play encourage the elision of all these media, the modes in which they are experienced, and the ways in which they might be read. In the terms of the Prologue, matter can be contained in images, things, and metaphors, as well as in words. As Jonson's play makes its controlling metaphor visible and tangible, it becomes a matrix for the elucidation and exploration of some of the features of the cultural, and the real, landscape of England—the gardens of Nonsuch, the fall of Essex—that shaped its first production, and it is these that are the subject of the next, and final, chapter.

12

Diana's Justice: Essex, Nonsuch, and Hampton Court

At about the same time as George Delves had himself portrayed in front of an elaborate imaginary garden, himself composing (one can only assume) the jaded little verses which were among its finishing touches, the most elaborate real garden in early modern England was being completed, a garden which similarly integrated texts and symbols into its design. This was the great garden at Nonsuch (Fig. 15), the fountains of which I will consider here in relation to *The Fountaine of Selfe-Love*, showing how Jonson used coterie knowledge of those fountains, and of another at Hampton Court, to enhance and reinforce his pleas for the Earl of Essex. Virtually nothing of Nonsuch remains above ground level, although for a period of almost 150 years it was probably the most spectacular of all the royal palaces in England.[1] Despite its almost complete obliteration, it is also (fortunately) one of the best documented of all the palaces, and there are particularly good descriptions of its grounds and its elaborate fountains in their heyday.[2]

---

[1] Nonsuch was extensively excavated and then reburied in 1959–60: before then even its location had become uncertain. For the history of the palace and of the excavation see John Dent, *The Quest for Nonsuch* (2nd edn., Sutton: London Borough of Sutton Leisure Services, 1970; repr. 1981, 1988), from which much of the information here is drawn; there are more illustrations in Lalage Lister, *Nonsuch: Pearl of the Realm* (Sutton: Sutton Leisure Services, 1992). The full account of the excavation's architectural discoveries has yet to appear, but the second volume of a planned two-volume set has recently appeared: Martin Biddle (ed.), *Nonsuch Palace: The Material Culture of a Noble Restoration Household* (Oxford: Oxbow Books, 2005).

[2] The best is that written by Anthony Watson, entitled *Magnificae et plane regiae domus quae vulgo vocatur Nonesuch brevis et vera descriptio* (c.1582). The account (Trinity College MS R.7.22) has never been published or translated in its entirety; text quoted here is from Martin Biddle, 'The Gardens of Nonsuch: Sources and Dating', *Garden History*, 27 (1999), 145–83. Biddle suggests the 1582 date because the *Descriptio* was written for John, Lord Lumley, who in 1581 had 'appointed Watson to the rectory of Cheam, and in 1582 . . . married for the second time, settling the Nonsuch estate on his new wife. This seems an obvious moment for the new rector to have written a description of Nonsuch for his patron, in gratitude for his preferment and in celebration of the new marriage,' 158–9. The only drawback of Watson's account (apart from the practical limitations noted below) is that it appears to describe work in progress: he fails to mention several features commented on by later visitors to the garden.

Before embarking upon a discussion of the palace's gardens and fountains, something needs to be said about the ownership and history of Nonsuch, which is complex. Henry VIII began to build his palace in 1538 on the site then occupied by the manor (and parish church) of Cuddington, displacing (but compensating) Elizabeth and Richard Codington. The building cannibalized stone from the manor and church as well as from the nearby Merton Priory: the 1959 excavations uncovered carved stone from both, used as rubble and in the foundations, as well as revealing that the palace had been built directly over the church, including the graves in the chancel. Nonsuch was unfinished (although habitable) at the time of the King's death in 1547, and Queen Mary gave (or sold) it to Henry Fitzalan, Earl of Arundel, in a complex transaction in 1556. When he died in 1580, it passed to his son-in-law and close friend John, Lord Lumley, who in 1592 gave it to the Queen (a regular, indeed constant, visitor) as a means of discharging the massive debts to the Crown that he had also inherited from Arundel. Lumley remained in the palace as Keeper until his death in 1609, but James I settled it on Anne of Denmark in 1603. The King and his sons seem to have made more use of it than the Queen, as the hunting was excellent. Nonsuch became part of the jointure of Henrietta Maria in 1625 and had various tenants during the Interregnum. It was used for temporary accommodation for government offices after the Fire of London, and in 1670 was given by Charles II to his mistress Barbara Villiers (Baroness Nonsuch), his mother having died the previous year. Increasingly derelict, it was demolished in 1682.[3] Nonsuch is unique in that not only written descriptions survive but also a detailed visual record of many of its finest ornaments. This is the so-called 'Red Velvet Book', otherwise known as the Lumley Inventory of 1590, which was probably drawn up as part of the lengthy process of negotiating the 'sale' of the palace to the Crown. It combines a written inventory of the palace's contents (paintings, furnishings, statuary, books) with illustrations of some of the most notable; it has been described as 'probably the single most important document for the study of the cultural history of the Elizabethan era'.[4] Included in the illustrations are six fountains.

The fountains of Nonsuch, as they are known through these illustrations and Watson's and others' descriptions, combine with extraordinary density classical mythology, the personal history (or mythology) of Arundel and Lumley, the flattery of Queen Elizabeth, and, naturally, the magnificent display of wealth and prestige for its own sake. The tourist Thomas Platter, for example, noted in the Inner Court a 'very handsome and elaborate snow white

---

[3] The history of Nonsuch is summarized from Dent, *Quest for Nonsuch*, 30, 52, 147, 163–74, 185–6, 190, 207.

[4] See Hearn, *Dynasties*, 158–9. The illustrations may have been added in 1597.

stone fountain, showing a griffin angrily spewing water with great violence',[5] which was more prosaically described in the Parliamentary Survey of 1650 as 'one fayer fountayne of whyte marble supported with two brass dragons vnder which is a large square cesterne of lead sett within a frame of whyte marble, vnto which cesterne is an assent of three stepps'.[6] Watson's description[7] is the fullest:

At the top is a noble horse (emblem of the Arundels) holding a graven stone with one hoof.[8] The bowl over which the horse stands is supported by a stone held by three slender maidens with milk-white bodies; in this stone are little water-pipes which produce a pleasing murmur. The bowl below the maidens is held by two golden griffins, and a great force of water pours from their mouths into the lead cistern, which is surrounded by ivory marble.[9]

The personal heraldry of Henry Fitzalan, Earl of Arundel, was thus combined with more conventional classical figures, presumably the Three Graces and (judging from the illustration) Italianate mascarons and swags of foliage. This particular fountain was at the centre of the palace, a natural point of rest for visitors before they penetrated further into the larger and more symbolically dense arena of the garden. It hinted at the garden's emphasis on transformation, through both the hybrid form of the griffins and the metamorphic associations of the fountain form itself.

In the Privy Garden at Nonsuch one of the features closest to the house was another fountain, which in fact appears in Speed's engraving of Nonsuch (from his *Map of Surrey*, 1610) albeit inaccurately and in a misleading perspective, as well as in the Lumley Inventory. Watson describes it thus:

In the biggest open part of the grounds three equidistant mounds stand out, in the centre of which everyone admires the beauty of a striking fountain. That addition of beauty (for which the heroic Lumley is responsible) is set inside two circles of grass, of which the one is reached from the other by the means of three steps, and similarly the whole plot itself from the lower part. On the top of this tiny mound is set a shining column which carries a high-standing statue of a snow-white nymph, perhaps Venus, from whose tender breasts flow jets of water into the ivory-coloured marble, and from there the water falls down through narrow pipes into marble basins.[10]

---

[5] Dent, *Quest for Nonsuch*, 113. [6] Ibid. 289.

[7] Here in Dent's paraphrase. Biddle includes only translations of the portions of Watson's text relating to the garden in his article, and this, being in the Inner Court of the palace proper, is unfortunately not included. As far as I can gather, the Watson text was only ever translated in full as a working document to provide practical assistance during the 1959 dig, during the evenings on site and largely by Cambridge undergraduates.

[8] As the horse is not mentioned by either Platter or the 1650 Survey it may have been removed at some point. It is, however, clearly visible in the Inventory drawing.

[9] Dent, *Quest for Nonsuch*, 98, 99. [10] Biddle, 'Gardens of Nonsuch', 174.

As the Inventory illustration clearly shows (Fig. 16), the figure in the fountain is indubitably Diana, her hair crowned with a crescent moon. That this was a tribute and demonstration of loyalty to Queen Elizabeth is shown in the way in which the fountain was flanked on either side by two of the so-called 'Falcon Perches', columns surmounted by Lord Lumley's device (which was in fact a popinjay). Lumley's crest with three of the birds[11] also appeared on the base of the Diana fountain, and in many other places (and guises) throughout the garden and house.[12] A second Diana fountain is also illustrated in the Inventory, although its location is less certain and it may have been at one of the other Lumley residences.[13] It consists of a scalloped basin on a base carved with what appear to be mermen, in which stands (caryatid-like) a half-length nymph on a column with spitting mascarons at many levels. From her head rises a jet upon which 'balances' an imperial crown surmounted by a crescent moon (Fig. 17). The combination of crown and crescent moon makes it clear that this fountain, too, was a tribute to Queen Elizabeth.

These Diana fountains at Nonsuch, and especially that at the centre of the Privy Garden, are perhaps disconcerting to a modern audience potentially ill at ease with the symbolic representation—and celebration—of a Queen as a naked goddess with water streaming from her breasts, especially given the erotic associations of similar fountains in texts such as the *Hypnerotomachia*. As the vandalism of the Cheapside Cross in the late 1590s revealed, however, context was all: while it might be inappropriate or even contentious to set up the Queen's most familiar avatar, Diana, as a naked fountain in a public space such as Cheapside, to do so in the elite environs of a royal palace or great house, where access could be controlled and a reasonably sophisticated audience could be assumed, was another matter altogether. A privy garden, such as the one in which Nonsuch's first Diana fountain was displayed (or that

---

[11] Properly 'a red fess between three green parrots on a white field', Dent, *Quest for Nonsuch*, 170.

[12] Several other fountains, illustrated in the Inventory, featured parrots. Lumley was obsessed with his family heritage, and the Red Book traces his family tree back to the Norman Conquest (and that of the royal family back to Adam). The Lumley arms were originally 'six silver popinjays, or parrots, on a red field, with a silver pelican as a crest', ibid. 170. A pelican fountain appears in both the Inventory and the 1650 Survey, and in fact survives at Sandbeck Hall, the home of the present Earl of Scarborough; it is illustrated in Henderson, *The Tudor House and Garden*, fig. 218.

[13] A drawback of the Lumley Inventory (Fig. 18) is that it lists all Lumley's property without distinction of location. 'The inventory was compiled from separate books listing the contents of each house and signed by the "severall wardropers", but unfortunately John Lambton, Steward of Household to Lumley, was too efficient and amalgamated all the books into one . . . In examining the inventory, then, allowance must be made for the fact that many of the articles were at other Lumley residences, notably at the town house on Tower Hill, at Stansted in Sussex and at Lumley Castle,' Dent, *Quest for Nonsuch*, 171.

at Kenilworth, to which Robert Langham had to gain access semi-illicitly, in order to describe its great fountain), was just that; it was walled, and designed in part to be seen and appreciated from the 'privy gallery' on the first floor. Travellers' descriptions of the gardens, as well as Watson's fuller account, make it clear that visitors to Nonsuch and its gardens had their wanderings strictly controlled, with prescribed routes to follow; they were told what to look at and had their special attention drawn to particular features. The Diana fountain at the centre of the Privy Garden was publicly located, but in a nominally private space, erected as that space's tutelary deity and placed on a literal pedestal as an elevated and remote figure and thus encoding, defining and legitimizing its own specularity.

In stark and perhaps deliberate contrast, the most interesting—and famous—feature of the gardens of Nonsuch was the Grove of Diana, which employed mottoes and poems (like the Delves portrait) to direct the visitor to consider issues of majesty and courtiership, and in which the question of how to look at the naked goddess was central. The Grove of Diana has been conjecturally situated to the west of the palace, and would have been reached by passing through the Privy Garden[14] and then through the Wilderness. No visual record survives, and Watson's account omits some of its known components; it is, nevertheless, the fullest description, and deserves to be quoted at length:

Diana her woodde.[15] In the woodland walk near to the Piper an ancient oak rises up into the sky with its propitious branches and shows the way straight into the shady Grove of Diana. There, throughout almost the whole copse and the glade, are places arched over by the skill of topiary, walls erected and sandy walks which lend an air of majesty worthy of the chaste virgin and most powerful goddess. So that I am not surprised that Diana herself, guardian of the groves, lurks in the shadows, satisfied with the service of nymphs alone; she flees the sun, and the sight of men; she resorts but rarely to the plain that lies open to the eyes of all; she fears the ceaseless dins of earthly affairs, and stays fast in the leafy woods, as in a well-fortified kingdom. If she is melancholy, the harmless symphony of the birds consoles her with its healing art; if alone, the trembling fawns will give her occupation, and the curved bow will relieve boredom.

The Vaile of Gargaphy. If the goddess should be faint from the chase, weary of effort, the Vale of Gargaphy will provide her with its icy spring. Actaeon's misfortune is well-known, the just punishment of a base life and the preservation of the armour of virtuous fear. But when the keen sense of the eyes forgets the sharper pangs of affliction, and tends more to leniency of judgement, then I should like witnesses and judges of

---

[14] The Orchard and the Kitchen Garden lay to the west and east of the Outer Court, while there was a bowling green on the palace's northern approach.

[15] This is Biddle's translation. The section headings are in English in the original text.

this sad sight to come forward as severe critics, either of the virgin's punishment or of the young man's rashness. Whatever opinion they hold, they will attain the easy indulgence of Diana, and the due gratitude of Actaeon. Only let them restrain the licence of their eyes, and rein in their hasty desire, for fear lest the hand of the avenging spirit should strike them down. It would indeed have been a daring crime to spy on the modesty of others, but to defile the most chaste of virgins with such dishonour, was the height of wickedness, and an extreme irreverence. If he had rushed unaware on the sacred spring of the Nymphs, not knowing the place, could the merciful virgin have taken vengeance? But if he approached stirred by the flames of desire, could the powerful goddess have pardoned him?

Actaeon transformde. Diana saw the daring of the youth, but she did not, as she could have done, put out the light of his reason; instead she changed the fashion of his mouth and tongue; meaning to put aside her mood of vengeance, if unknowing Actaeon should change his mind. But though impaired alike in tongue and mind, to satisfy his desire he moved hand and foot that he might catch the virgin herself, or one of the nymphs. Diana was incensed against such madness in a man; she put out the flames of unlawful love with sprinkled water, remade the fashion of his body; from a man she created a beast, from Actaeon a stag, from the noble hunter a wretched prey to dogs.

The rocke welle. Now the divine virgin enjoys the pleasures of the rock-well in peace, washes her limbs in the icy liquid, regards the absurd shade of her foe, and listens to the wily hounds pursuing with pleasing barks the new stag through all the wood. Whether the rock is more of an embellishment to the well, or the well to the rock, is a problem full of hazards, and the case is still before the court. Of no matter what art, nature or divinity it may be, who is there who does not admire in this hard rock, the skilful arrangement of stones, the plentiful variety of blossoms and fruits, but especially how the rush of spraying water now subsides with gentle murmur, now bubbles up on high in full force?

A statelye bower for Diana. Where the most renowned goddess bathes the snowy parts of her virgin body, the way leads through the middle of the vale to a stately bower—some woodland palace. Here one neither should ask after nor may pursue further the virgin's affairs. But one must hope, that reports of the charm and great extent of the place are made without trace of calumny or ill-will; among them is to be seen the manifest glory of honour, or nobility, or some divine power. From a form of lofty arch the king of birds, the winged Eagle, sits watching for poisonous snakes, for fear that they should beset the solitary steps of Diana. On one pinnacle the Pelican sits, a bird all too tender to its chicks; it draws its blood for its children's food with the harsh stroke of its steely bill, looks to the insignia of Lumley and provides a sure token of a guardian's faith and love. On the other pinnacle stands the Phoenix, another Diana among birds; the laws of love she never knew nor hoped to know; she made her nest with cinnamon and young sprigs of frankincense; they caught light with the heat of the sun, and willingly she loosed the bonds of nature, to leave in the ashes an heir of the same race. In the grassy space of an orchard a handsome pyramid rises, set off with divers heads, which counterfeit dryness in the mouth, but for delight disgorge small streams of clear water. Most powerful Diana claims all the magnificence and glory of the place as her own; let us pray to her for that enjoyment of everlasting honour and service to the state, and most happy memory, on which the far-seeing hero, Lumley, in the course of another history to this, set his heart.[16]

This description—and it can probably be assumed, the Grove of Diana itself—is conspicuously Ovidian, in particular in the way in which it draws attention to the relationship between art and nature in the Grove, for Ovid's text does the same: 'In its most secret nook there was a well-shaded grotto, wrought by no artist's hand. But Nature by her own cunning had imitated art; for she had shaped a native arch of the living rock and soft tufa'.[17] As Leonard Barkan puts it, Ovid's description 'confounds real-life categories by transforming nature into art';[18] the same was true of its 'real-life' re-creation at Nonsuch, which additionally transformed politics into art and Ovid into ideology.

Baron Waldstein's description of the Grove in 1600 is far shorter than Watson's, but it shares the awareness of the theatricality of the setting apparent in the longer Watson version:

From here, by going along various paths between the growing shrubs, with trees shading us from the summer heat, we entered the famous Grove of Diana where Nature is imitated with so much skill that you would dare to swear that the original Grove of the real Diana herself was hardly more delightful or of greater beauty. This Grove is approached by a gentle slope leading down from the garden by a path half hidden in the shade of trees . . . The source was from a number of pipes hidden in the rock and from them a gentle flow of water bathed Diana and her two nymphs; Actaeon had approached; he was leaning against a nearby tree to hide himself and gazing lecherously at Diana; she, with a slight gesture of her hand towards him, was slowly changing his head to that of a stag; his three hounds were in close pursuit.[19]

Michael Leslie describes Waldstein's version as 'wonderful . . . for the way it sees the impossible: the head of a static statue *slowly* changing into that of a stag',[20] and John Dixon Hunt observes that 'despite the lack of hydraulic equipment to start the figures into motion as happened at Pratolino, the visitors all seem to have responded to the groups of statues and their theatrical setting as if they actually saw the scene enacted before their eyes'.[21] The statues, including the dogs, were all painted,[22] and Watson emphasizes the verisimilitude of 'the rocke welle' where Diana bathed, presumably a grotto-like fountain setting. Thomas Platter gave a brief and pedestrian account of the Grove but, interestingly, described it as being at the entrance of the

[16] Biddle, 'Gardens of Nonsuch', 176–7.   [17] Ovid, *Metamorphoses*, 3.157–60.
[18] Barkan, 'Diana and Actaeon', 321.
[19] Leslie, 'Spenser, Sidney and the Renaissance Garden', 26–8.
[20] Ibid. 28.   [21] Dixon Hunt, *Garden and Grove*, 106.
[22] Strong, *The Renaissance Garden in England*, 226 n. 44.

garden,[23] which, according to the reconstructions of the garden's layout, is not possible. Perhaps, despite his rather dull account, Platter picked up the liminal, transformative nature of the grove, 'as though it is a gateway through which we must pass in order to be initiated into the garden's mythic content and into the necessary ways of reading'.[24] It may have been the case that the standard tour of the palace's gardens given to tourists like Platter was ordered in this way. Spectators, as they moved through this landscape infused with mythological and royal symbolism, were not passive, as Watson's account in particular demonstrates. As they read the poems and mottoes (discussed below), looked at the sculpture and architecture, and moved through the landscape itself, they were participants in it by virtue of their own interpretative acts and even, as the *giocchi d'acqua* they unwittingly activated sprinkled them in turn with the fountain's water, implicated in Actaeon's fate.

A vital aspect of the Grove of Diana which emphasized this interactive aspect, as well as its narrative and ideological dimensions, was its mottoes and poems. In a small building adjacent to the 'bower', which contained a black marble table,[25] there were three Latin maxims:

> Nil impudicum pudicitiae Dea
> Nil turpe suadet sceleris vindicta,
> Sed mala mens malus animus.
>
> Impuri fontis
> Ingrati rivuli,
> Ingratae mentis
> Impuri oculi.
>
> Aestuanti umbra,
> Languenti sedes.
> Noli in umbra umbratilis esse,
> Nec sint sedenti serpentis oculi.

Nothing immodest does the Goddess of Modesty advise, nothing base to punish sin, but an evil mind advises with an evil soul.

Of an impure spring, unpleasant are the streams; of an unpleasant mind, impure are the eyes.

To the hot a shade, to the weary a seat; do not be overshadowed in the shade, nor let the seated have a serpent's eyes.[26]

---

[23] Quoted and discussed in Michael Leslie, 'Gardens of Eloquence: Rhetoric, Landscape, and Literature in the English Renaissance', in Lynette Hunter (ed.), *Toward a Definition of Topos: Approaches to Analogical Reasoning* (London: Macmillan, 1991). Leslie's account of the Grove has informed my own discussion.

[24] Ibid. 25–6.

[25] This was presumably a small banqueting or summerhouse. It does not appear in Watson's account, although Waldstein noted it.

[26] Biddle, 'Gardens of Nonsuch', 172, 178.

These mottoes forced a choice, in the form of the necessity of interpretation, upon those who read them. This might have even involved a choice of path: Platter's description noted that the mottoes were on three different walls of the 'small vaulted temple', each of which (although it is nowhere stated) could well have contained a door or gate.[27] They all address the fraught nature of looking. To look in the wrong way implies a catastrophic moral failing, and the parallel construction of the second motto in particular makes a specific connection between the familiar humanist depiction of the prince as fountain—it is interesting to note in this context that Lumley had made a translation of Erasmus' *Education of a Christian Prince* in about 1550[28]—and acts of visual transgression; the parallelism almost suggests that the unpleasant mind, looking with impure eyes, will see only an impure spring, and will suffer the consequences accordingly. These mottoes, however, were only the start, for elsewhere in the Grove there were other Latin poems:

O Dea quae silvas, fontes, umbram, atque venatum
Experis, et Nymphas, et rustica numina, casto
Dirigis imperio, cur te commertia mundi
Non tangunt? Hominum cur non amplexibus haeres?
Cur hymenaea fugis niveo perfusa decore?
Scilicet humanae divina monilia sorti,
Vix bene conveniunt. Sic stat sententia Divum.

Quisquis ut Actaeon grassanti libidini nullos
Imponit fraenos oculis animique furori,
Bellua fit monstrumque hominum semetque vorandum.
Dat canibus propriis, dum amens affectibus ignes
Subjicit, et nullo retinet moderamine sensus.

Thou Goddesse which delightst to hunte, and lov'st the fountaines cleare,
The woods, the shade, which rulst eche nymphe and everie rurall peere,
Why dost thou shunne this world's delight and Venus sporte defie?
The glorie of the maried state why dothe Diana flye?

---

[27] The garden which demanded a choice of its visitors, which then determined their subsequent experience of it, was familiar in Italy, for example at the Villa d'Este. See David R. Coffin, *The Villa d'Este at Tivoli* (Princeton: Princeton University Press, 1960).

[28] British Library, Royal MS 17 A.xlix. This is noted in Lumley's entry in the *ODNB*, Kathryn Barron, 'Lumley, John, First Baron Lumley (*c.*1533–1609)', *Oxford Dictionary of National Biography* (www.oxforddnb.com/view/article/17179, accessed 22 Feb. 2006). Suggestively, too, Lumley had (although at Lumley Castle, not at Nonsuch) four portrait busts of Henry VIII and his children which are demonstrably based on medals: the source for the bust of Elizabeth is the van Herwijk medal of Elizabeth as Divine Fountain of the Realm (discussed in Chapter 9). There is no indication, however, that Lumley owned a copy of the medal, and there may have been an intermediate source, such as a portrait. See Hearn, *Dynasties*, 84. A version of the bust, together with a matching bust of Leicester, is now in the National Portrait Gallery.

The cause is this as all the Godd's decree,
Such pearles and man's estate cannot agree.

Who so doth runne Actaeon's race when raging luste constraines,
Who bridleth not his wandringe eyes, nor furious minde restraines,
Is made a beaste and monstrous man, and makes him self a praye,
To be devoured by cruell doggs, whiles fancie beares the swaye;
Whiles fonde affections are inflam'd,
Whiles dotinge senses are untam'de.[29]

The first poem therefore emphasized Diana/Elizabeth's uniqueness as the Virgin Queen, while the second drew attention to Actaeon's 'wandringe eyes'—the same phrase applied by the Palmer to Guyon's gazing on the bathers in the fountain in Spenser's Bowre of Bliss—associating ill-advised looking with general intemperance and folly.[30] A further pair of verses appeared in the same place as 'Quisquis ut Actaeon':

Actaeon
Splene opus humano capiti si pictor equinas
Iungere cervices aut canis ora velit.
Cervinam Diana caput cervicibus istis
Addit. In injustam viscera justa rogo.

Diana
Mente opus humana, ne feros in corpore mores
Parrhasius pingat Praxitilesve dolet.
Cervina Actaeon tua sunt praecordia. Quidni
Cornua sint? Prudens pectora stulta queror.

Actaeon: It would cause resentment if a painter should choose to join a horse's neck or a dog's face to a human head. Diana lays a stag's head on my neck. I demand against the unjust one my proper flesh.

Diana: There must be humanity if Parrhasius is not to paint nor Praxiteles carve the morals of a beast in human frame. Your inclinations are a stag's, Actaeon. Why should there not be horns? Prudent myself, I lament foolish affections.[31]

Their dialogic quality added to the theatricality of the scene, and again emphasized Actaeon's folly. An important addition, however, was the suggestion

---

[29] The English translations are those included in the Watson manuscript, and are quoted from Biddle, 'Gardens of Nonsuch', 172–3.

[30] Guyon's wandering eyes are discussed in Chapter 8. The emphasis on marriage in the Diana poem suggests that the poems had been set up in the Grove not long before the assumed 1582 date of composition of Watson's description, as praises of Elizabeth as Diana and as perpetually Virgin Queen are rare before the late 1570s, when they appear for the first time in the context of the French marriage controversy.

[31] Biddle, 'Gardens of Nonsuch', 173, 178. This poem, and the Grove of Diana, are briefly discussed by Montrose, 'Spenser and the Elizabethan Political Imaginary', 920–1. In passing, he also notes *Cynthia's Revels* (p. 930), although not in relation to Nonsuch.

by Actaeon that Diana had been 'unjust', and Diana's rejoinder that she had simply been 'prudent'; these are important aspects of the Ovidian account of Actaeon's metamorphosis and, as will shortly be seen, they also inform Jonson's adaptation of it in *The Fountaine of Selfe-Love*.[32]

A final poem was fixed on the 'bower' (the arch surmounted by eagle, pelican, and phoenix, next to the water-spouting obelisk) 'in letters of gold':

> Ictus Piscator tandem sapit,
> sed infelix Actaeon semper praeceps.
> Casta virgo facile miseretur,
> sed potens Dea scelus ulciscitur.
> Praeda canibus, exemplum iuvenibus,
> suis dedecus pereat Actaeon.
> Cura coelitibus, chara mortalibus,
> suis securitas vivat Diana.

The smitten fisherman at length grows wise, but unhappy Actaeon is ever rash; the chaste virgin may easily feel compassion, but the powerful goddess punishes the crime. Let Actaeon die, a prey to dogs, a warning to youths, to his own a shame; long live Diana, a care to the gods, beloved of mortals, the security of her own.[33]

John Dixon Hunt describes the poems and mottoes in general as having been added to the statues, fountains, and buildings of the Grove 'to underline the [Ovidian] narrative',[34] but their function was surely far more complex and multi-layered. They first added emphasis to the Diana-Elizabeth identification. But they also involved the spectator/reader in a series of interpretative transactions. That these acts of choice and interpretation were often centred on fountains made them physically, as well as intellectually, interactive and consequential, through the *giocchi d'acqua*, so often dismissed as puerile and evidence only of Italian luxury and superficiality. In Nonsuch's Grove of Diana, praise of the Queen and, implicitly, declarations of fealty to her could not be separated from the deeper moral content of their depiction of ill-advised and inappropriate looking and folly; in turn, neither could these aspects be divorced from John, Lord Lumley, as he sought to fashion himself. Even if it seems (from the extant descriptions) that the Grove was relatively free of parrots, it was 'about' Lumley as much as Diana–Elizabeth, and in a quite specific way. Martin Biddle has persuasively linked the Grove of Diana (with the possible exception of the more marriage-focused poem) to Lumley's involvement, with his father-in-law the Earl of Arundel, in the Ridolfi Plot in

---

[32] See also the discussion by John Heath, *Actaeon, the Unmannerly Intruder: The Myth and its Meaning in Classical Literature* (New York: Peter Lang, 1992), 4, 60, 64.

[33] Biddle, 'Gardens of Nonsuch', 172, 177. [34] Dixon Hunt, *Garden and Grove*, 106.

1571,[35] which led to his imprisonment for two years, for some of that time in the Tower of London. It is to this that Watson refers as '*alienae historiae misterio*' (the course of another history than this). As Biddle puts it, ' "The smitten fisher at length grows wise" was Lumley's *apologia*, and the Grove his personal statement of loyalty'.[36] Actaeon was his alter ego, and in the Grove of Diana and its poems he drew attention to both his own folly and the Queen's justice, in his case tempered by clemency, as Diana's was not. The Ovidian motif of transgression and transformation was enacted (as so often in the *Metamorphoses*) in water and stone. Thus mediated, the narratives of Diana and Actaeon, Lumley and the Queen, and the visitor in the garden coalesced and were brought to bear upon one another, to delight, to divert, to involve, to instruct—and to warn.

If Ben Jonson had merely drawn out the underlying parallels between the situation of the Earl of Essex in 1600 and the story of Diana and Actaeon in *The Fountaine of Selfe-Love*, it would have been enough. But, in a case of life imitating art, it was at Nonsuch that Essex paid an Actaeon-like visit to the Queen, which symbolically began the train of events which led to his fall from favour, rebellion, and eventual execution in 1601. For some time before this disastrous encounter, his place in Elizabeth's favour had been becoming precarious. The expedition which he had led to Cadiz in 1596 was only a qualified success, he had consistently failed to persuade the Queen to make a definite commitment to sustained military intervention on the continent in the Protestant cause, his pet project of the Azores expedition in the autumn of 1597 had failed (as had its secondary objective, the interception of the Spanish treasure fleet), he had continually intrigued against the Cecils, and, at a Privy Council meeting in the summer of 1598, he had turned his back on the Queen and then laid his hand on his sword when she boxed his ears by way of rebuke. A short period of exile had been followed by a rapprochement, and Elizabeth appointed him Lord Lieutenant of Ireland that December. He went to Ireland at the end of March 1599, but the campaign went badly and looked to be a long one, and Essex again angered the Queen by creating large numbers of knights (among them John Harington), and by treating with Tyrone. Convinced that he was being plotted against and undermined in England, he appears to have decided that the only possible course was to speak with the Queen in person, and accordingly he took a ship with a few companions (Harington

---

[35] The plot had as its objective the marriage of Mary Stuart to the Duke of Norfolk, and the deposition of Elizabeth in her favour. Despite his involvement in this, and indeed in earlier recusant plots, Lumley apparently repented sufficiently to act as one of the commissioners for the eventual trial of Mary Stuart in 1586.

[36] Biddle, 'Gardens of Nonsuch', 166.

again among them) on 24 September 1599, subsequently riding through the
night to Nonsuch to arrive early on the morning of 28 September.[37] When
he arrived, covered with mud, he burst into the Queen's bedroom, finding
her not yet dressed (and presumably without her wig as well as her make-up).
It was indeed a case of Diana and Actaeon, life imitating art, that would be
unbelievable were it not true. Ten days later, and with some understatement,
Robert Cecil wrote to Sir Henry Neville that Essex '*was in the Court before
ever her Majestie knew yt.* A matter that did displease her *in the Forme* very
much'.[38] Essex and the Queen never met again in person after that day,[39]
and thenceforth he was effectively under various degrees of house arrest until
his disastrous rebellion on 8 February 1601 and subsequent execution on 25
February.[40]

Essex's condition had temporarily improved, however, in the summer and
autumn of 1600, and it was in this context that Jonson wrote his play, when
it seems to have been widely believed, at least among Londoners, that Essex
might soon return to favour. While Elizabeth's failure to renew his monopoly
on sweet wines (which fell due at Michaelmas) should have signalled otherwise,
there was significant popular feeling that she was growing more kindly disposed
towards him: she did not formally announce the reservation of the monopoly
to the Crown until late October. Although those in court circles perhaps knew
better, there were rumours that he would make a symbolic return to court and
the Queen's service as the Unknown Knight in the Accession Day Tilts on 17
November: on 10 October Chamberlain wrote to Carleton, 'The Earl of Essex
is here, and at Barn-Elms;[41] his friends make great means for him to run on
the Queen's Day, and hope soon to see him in favour; I do not expect it, for
his licence for sweet wines, expired at Michaelmas, is not renewed.' Even as
late as 2 November Neville wrote to Winwood that 'there is an Expectation
of his *running* at the *Coronation-Day*, and that it shall be the first step of his
Grace and Access to the Court; But I am not very prone to beeleeve it.' The
use of imprese in the masques of the fifth act of *The Fountaine of Selfe-Love*,
and the setting of the 'Revels' themselves, perhaps imply a reference to the
conventions of the Accession Day festivities. But on 15 November Neville duly
confirmed that '*The Earl of* Essex is no Actor in our Triumphs, as I wrote was

---

[37] This was only five days after the Swiss tourist Thomas Platter had paid his visit.

[38] *Cal. S.P. Dom.*, 8 October 1599, p. 118.

[39] They did have two further, more formal, meetings on 28 September.

[40] Details of Essex's biography are taken from the *ODNB* essay, Paul E. J. Hammer,
'Devereux, Robert, Second Earl of Essex (1565–1601)', *Oxford Dictionary of National Biography*
(www.oxforddnb.com/view/article/7565, accessed 22 Feb. 2006).

[41] His wife's country house.

conceaved, but yet is not out of hope of some Melioration of Fortune'.[42] It seems not unlikely that Jonson was cautiously responding to this climate of popular opinion.

It has long been assumed, however, that the allusions in *The Fountaine of Selfe-Love* to Essex's situation must express approval of his treatment by Elizabeth as just and condemn his crimes. Little attempt has been made to link these allusions to the project of the play as a whole, the reformation of the culture of the court, and doing so reveals a far more ambivalent attitude towards both the perceived agenda of the Earl and the actions of the Queen than has hitherto been assumed. There are also more allusions to Essex in *The Fountaine of Selfe-Love* than previously realized, including one of some moment. Reading the play as not entirely unsympathetic towards Essex allows sense to be made of the issues it presents, as well as allowing a more precise historical context to be inferred for its first performances. *The Fountaine of Selfe-Love* is 'about' far more than Essex and the Queen but, as Ian Donaldson has observed, Jonson's work, 'more densely topical and allusive than that of Shakespeare, is particularly seductive to interpretation of this kind'.[43] The fountain which is the play's controlling metaphor allows it to explore the plight of Essex, via the Actaeon motif (and, specifically, the Nonsuch connection), but, as previous chapters have shown, the same fountain image makes the play not only topical, but also radical and polemical, engaged with important contemporary issues and concepts as well as with the more ephemeral business of comment and satire.

The character of Philautia forms a further underlying connection between Essex and Jonson's play. One of Essex's most talked-of acts at court was the entertainment devised by him (or by Francis Bacon on his behalf) for the Accession Day Tilt on 17 November 1595. This, referred to many years later by Sir Henry Wotton as 'his darling piece of love, and selfe love',[44] seems not to have been a particular success with the Queen, but to have been well regarded by others. Jonson himself discussed it with Drummond, especially mentioning Essex's impresa, which was 'the device of a diamond and the legend *Dum formas minuis*, ("While you form me, you deform me"), suggesting that—as in the cutting of a diamond—he could not be made to act against his own nature without being destroyed'.[45] In this entertainment, the knight Erophilus

[42] *Cal. SP Dom.*, *1598–1601*, 477; Ralph Winwood, *Memorials of Affairs of State in the Reigns of Q. Elizabeth and K. James I*, 2 vols. (London, 1725), i. 271, 274.

[43] Ian Donaldson, *Jonson's Magic Houses: Essays in Interpretation* (Oxford: Clarendon Press, 1997), 126.

[44] Sir Henry Wotton, *A Parallell Betweene Robert Late Earle of Essex, and George Late Duke of Buckingham* (London, 1641), sig. B1ᵛ.

[45] Paul E. J. Hammer, *The Polarisation of Elizabethan Politics: The Political Career of Robert Devereux, 2nd Earl of Essex, 1585–1597* (Cambridge: Cambridge University Press, 1999), 233.

was petitioned by three emissaries from Lady Philautia, a hermit, a soldier, and a statesman, each of whom advanced his own way of life as offering the best possible service to Philautia. Erophilus' Squire, speaking on his master's behalf, rejected all three and Philautia herself as well. Instead, the Knight vowed his service to the Queen, in any or all of these capacities. The personification of 'Philautia' is not especially radical, either in Essex's device or in Jonson's play, and there is not necessarily a connection between the two. But it is not impossible that Jonson's elucidation and exposure of self-love, especially in court circles, might intentionally have encompassed such a gesture towards Essex's own past identification of himself as a spurner of Philautia in the Queen's service.

The universally recognized Essex allusions in *The Fountaine of Selfe-Love* are those to Actaeon, the first of which is clearly spelled out by Cupid in 1.1: 'The Huntresse and queene of these groues, *Diana* (in regarde of some black and enuious slaunders howerly breathd against her for her deuine iustice on *Acteon* as she pretends) hath here in the vale of *Gargaphy* proclaimd a solemne reuels' (B2^v). The play's occasion is therefore an exercise in royal public relations: it is acknowledged at the outset that there is a situation in need of redress. But what is to be made of the qualifier 'as she pretends'? The many shades of this verb are generally negative; it carries the implication of making excuses.[46] Furthermore, the avowed intention of the Queen is apparently not to justify her treatment of Actaeon *per se*, but to demonstrate that she is also capable of magnanimity. Thus dissected, it is a curiously ambivalent pretext. The next mention of Actaeon, in Echo's lament, is a passing one, but nevertheless casts him as the victim of '*Cynthias* wrath (more egar than his houndes)' (1.2, B4).

The third and final allusion to Actaeon, made by Cynthia herself, is the fullest and also the most defensive. Addressing the courtiers at the end of the masque, before their unmasking, she states

> For you are they, that not (as some haue done)
> Do censure vs, as too *seuere*, and *sower*,
> But as (more rightly) *Gratious* to the good;
> Although we not deny, vnto the Proud,
> Or the Prophane, perhaps indeed austere:
> For so *Actaeon* by presuming farre,

Conversations, 582–4. Quotations from the *Conversations* are taken from *Ben Jonson: The Complete Poems*, ed. George Parfitt (rev. edn., London: Penguin, 1996).

[46] This is noted by Brown, 'Arachne's Web', 129. The most comprehensive discussion of the Actaeon myth and motif in Renaissance mythography, literature, and art is Barkan, 'Diana and Actaeon', 317–59. He emphasizes the syncretism of the motif, and comments on *The Fountaine of Selfe-Love*, 333.

> Did (to our griefe) incurre a fatall doome;
>
> .   .   .   .
>
> But are we therefore iudged too extreame?
> Seemes it no Crime to enter sacred Bowers,
> And hallowed Places with impure aspect
> Most lewdly to pollute? Seemes it no crime,
> To braue a Deity?.   (5.5, L3–L3ᵛ)

This passage can be read as a specific allusion to Essex's precipitate arrival at Nonsuch on 28 September 1599, and his entering, unannounced, uninvited, and still muddied from riding through the night, into the Queen's bedchamber.[47] The event was old news by the time *The Fountaine of Selfe-Love* was first performed, although some historians[48] cite it as the irreversible beginning of Essex's declining fortunes. Jonson, however, took this lapse of protocol and judgement and used it metonymically to stand for the ultimate—but unwitting—crime of the overweening courtier. No critic seems to have noticed quite how oddly specific the allusion to this particular incident via the figure of Actaeon is. It seems not unlikely, however, that it was Jonson's intention: Essex committed his crime at Nonsuch, which was famous above all for its celebration of Elizabeth as Diana through its elaborate fountains and the Grove of Diana which had, in addition, been erected in the first place as an apology for a different, but analogous, act of *lèse-majesté*. A curious case of art imitating life imitating art indeed—and perhaps one more reason why Jonson chose the device of the fountain to underpin his play's moral and thematic agenda. Actaeon's transgression is by no means depicted as trivial, but the defensiveness of Cynthia's justification of her response begs the question of whether the punishment has been disproportionate to the crime.

It is therefore worth noting a reference to Actaeon in another Ovidian text. In the *Tristia*, the poet's lament of his exile, he castigates himself thus:

Why did I see anything? Why did I make my eyes guilty? Why was I so thoughtless as to harbour the knowledge of a fault? Unwitting was Actaeon when he beheld Diana unclothed; none the less he became the prey of his own hounds. Clearly, among the

---

[47] Janet Clare, 'Jonson's "Comical Satires" and the Art of Courtly Compliment', in Julie Sanders, Kate Chedgzoy, and Susan Wiseman (eds.), *Refashioning Ben Jonson: Gender, Politics and the Jonsonian Canon* (London: Macmillan, 1998), 37; David Riggs, *Ben Jonson: A Life* (Cambridge, Mass.: Harvard University Press, 1989), 69; Bate, *Shakespeare and Ovid*, 162–4.

[48] 'His most flagrant offence was . . . to burst unannounced into her presence at ten o'clock in the morning before she had applied cosmetics. By his recklessness he became the only courtier (other than the bedchamber servants) to have seen the "imperial" Virgin stripped of the veil of state. This was *lèse-majesté* and condemned him to disgrace,' Guy, 'The 1590s: The Second Reign of Elizabeth I?', 4.

gods, even ill-fortune must be atoned for, nor is mischance an excuse when a deity is wronged.[49]

The passage is an extended lament for the loss of imperial favour and, as Jonathan Bate notes, in his discussion of *The Fountaine of Selfe-Love*, it was later inserted by George Sandys into his commentary on the *Metamorphoses*, together with the comment that 'this fable was invented to shew vs how dangerous a curiosity it is to search into the secrets of Princes, or by chance to discover their nakednesse: who thereby incurring their hatred, ever after liue the life of a Hart, full of feare and suspicion'.[50] 'Guard we therefore our eyes,' Sandys adds, in a phrase reminiscent of both the mottoes in the Nonsuch garden and Spenser's Palmer in the Bowre of Bliss. Perhaps particularly indicating that Jonson might have had the *Tristia* in mind when thinking of Essex as an Actaeon-figure (its general subject and tenor are, after all, very apt to Essex's situation) is a statement in the *Tristia* fifteen lines before the reference to Actaeon: 'And yet, I remember, thou wert wont to approve my life and my ways when I passed before thee with the steed thou hast granted me'.[51] Like his stepfather the Earl of Leicester before him, Essex was Elizabeth's Master of the Horse and when, following a hearing before a special commission on 5 June 1600, he was stripped of his other offices (Privy Councillor, Earl Marshal, Master of the Ordnance) this was the one title he was allowed to retain.

In addition to *The Fountaine of Selfe-Love*'s barely lukewarm endorsement of Cynthia's treatment of Actaeon, there is a further allusion to Essex which amounts to a direct plea for clemency on his behalf. This is the 'Hymn to Cynthia', which begins the play's fifth act and occasions Cynthia's most defensive speeches. It is sung by Hesperus, the evening star, sometimes Latinized as 'Vesper' and described as Cynthia's page (for example by Spenser in the *Mutabilitie Cantos*).[52] The scene is a puzzle: it is its singer's only appearance in the play, and he exits immediately following the Hymn's end. Yet in the cast-list at the beginning of the play (A1ᵛ), which appears to be in order of precedence, Hesperus is listed in fourth place out of twenty-two, ahead of Echo, Criticus, Arete, Amorphus, and the rest, and following only Cynthia, Mercurie and Cupid. He is obviously meant to be a character of some note. The Hymn itself is a plea for favour and clemency. After eulogizing

---

[49] Ovid, *Tristia; Ex Ponto*, trans. Arthur Leslie Wheeler, rev. G. P. Goold (Cambridge, Mass.: Harvard University Press, 1988), 2.103 f.

[50] Bate, *Shakespeare and Ovid*, 163, and George Sandys, *Ouids Metamorphosis Englished, mythologiz'd, and represented in figures* (Oxford, 1632), 100. Sandys's translation and commentary clearly post-dates Jonson's play, but his interpretation of the Actaeon episode, and his citation of the *Tristia*, reflects the mythographic tradition.

[51] Ovid, *Tristia*, 2.89.   [52] *The Faerie Queene*, 6.9.

Cynthia in conventional terms, the first stanza ends 'Hesperus *intreats thy light,* | *Goddesse excellently bright*'. The second stanza is a general plea for the goddess's insight-granting illumination, and this imagery in particular recalls Jonson's 'First Ode', which, according to Mark Bland, may have had Essex as its original addressee.[53] The Ode's final stanza refers to the hope that

> our drad *Cynthias* shine
> shall light those places
> w^{t}h lustrous graces
> Where Darknesse w^{t}h her gloomy=sceptred hand
> doth now command

Bland has suggested a very similar date of composition for the Ode (autumn 1600) to that suggested for *The Fountaine of Selfe-Love*.[54] The Hymn's third stanza is the most specific:

> *Lay thy Bowe of Pearle apart,*
> *And thy Christall-shining Quiver;*
> *Giue vnto the flying Hart,*
> *Space to breath, how short soeuer.*
> *Thou, that makst a day of night,*
> *Goddesse excellently Bright.*   (5.1, K1^v)

The imagery of hunting suggests a return to the Actaeon motif, asking for clemency and understanding. The beauty of the lyric has perhaps obscured the fact that Jonson's Hymn is not unalloyed in its eulogy; that it has a specific purpose which itself implies a criticism of the Queen. In his epigrams on a 'naked image', perhaps specifically of Diana and Actaeon, Sir John Harington similarly transferred some blame to the female party, as he had in his epigram on King David:[55]

> *Of the naked Image that was to stand in my Lo: Chamberlaines Gallery.*
> Actaeon, guiltelesse, unawares espying
> Naked *Diana*, bathing in her bowre,
> Was plagu'd with horns, his dogs did him deuoure.
> Wherefore take heede, ye that are curious prying,
> With some such forked plague you be not smitten,
> And in your foreheads so your faults be written.

---

[53] Mark Bland, ' "As Far from All Reuolt": Sir John Salusbury, Christ Church MS 184, and Ben Jonson's First Ode', *English Manuscript Studies*, 8 (2000), 43–78. The quotation is taken from Bland's transcription.

[54] See also Richard C. McCoy, *The Rites of Knighthood: The Literature and Politics of Elizabethan Chivalry* (Berkeley and Los Angeles: University of California Press, 1989), 98–9. He quotes a letter from Essex to the Queen comparing his own situation at the time to those who 'feel the comfortable influence of your favour or stand in the bright beams of your presence'.

[55] See the discussion in Chapter 9.

Of the same to the Ladies.
Her face vnmask't, I saw, her corps vnclad,
No vaile, no couer, her and me betweene:
No ornament was hid, that beauty had,
I blusht that saw, she blusht not that was seene.
With that I vow'd neuer to care a rush,
For such a beauty, as doth neuer blush.

For Harington, Actaeon was 'guiltelesse', and his friendship with Essex was perhaps not insignificant in this regard.[56] Even the *Metamorphoses* records that there was no unanimous reaction to Diana's treatment of Actaeon: 'Common talk wavered this way and that: to some the goddess seemed more cruel than was just; others called her act worthy of her austere virginity; both sides found good reasons for their judgement'.[57] The question of Actaeon's guilt and Diana's culpability, not to mention the justice of her punishment of his transgression, is similarly addressed in *The Fountaine of Selfe-Love*. Jonson could merely be recording the ambivalent response to the goddess in what was presumably his source text, but it is certainly an ambivalence that he does not attempt to gloss over.

Most specifically, the singing of the Hymn by Hesperus appears to be a direct allusion to another poem, in which Essex himself was eulogized as Hesperus: Spenser's *Prothalamion* (1596). It was written to mark the betrothal of Katherine and Elizabeth Somerset, the two elder daughters of the Earl of Worcester, one of Essex's friends and supporters.[58] Having first lamented the death of his sometime patron Leicester, Spenser devoted most of the poem's final two stanzas to the praise of Essex, the new occupant of Leicester House, whose patronage Spenser was seeking at the time:

Yet therein now doth lodge a noble Peer,
Great *Englands* glory and the Worlds wide wonder,
Whose dreadfull name, late through all *Spaine* did thunder.
And *Hercules* two pillors standing neere,
Did make to quake and feare:
Faire branch of Honor, flower of Cheualrie,

[56] Harington compiled the presentation manuscripts of his epigrams on 19 December 1600. See Jason Scott-Warren, 'Harington, Sir John (bap. 1560, d. 1612)', *Oxford Dictionary of National Biography* (www.oxforddnb.com/view/article/12326, accessed 22 Feb. 2006).

[57] Ovid, *Metamorphoses*, 3.253–5. Barkan points out that 'Ovid's stress on Actaeon's victimized innocence is virtually unique in the myth's history, and all subsequent versions which dramatize the young man's crime and justify his punishment derive in part from the exegesis of non-Ovidian versions', 'Diana and Actaeon', 323. This is also discussed by Brown, 'Arachne's Web', 122.

[58] The ceremony took place at Essex House, and Essex was additionally related by marriage to the two bridegrooms.

> That fillest *England* with thy triumphes fame
>
> .   .   .   .
>
> From those high Towers, this noble Lord issuing,
> Like radiant *Hesper* when his golden hayre
> In th'*Ocean* billowes he hath Bathed fayre,
> Descended to the Riuers open vewing,
> With a great traine ensuing . . . [59]

'Hesperus' was not a common epithet in the literature of the period.[60] In addition, at the time of *The Fountaine of Selfe-Love* Jonson was seeking to position himself in some respects as Spenser's literary heir,[61] and '[Spenser's] funeral, according to Camden's *Annales*, was held in the south transept of Westminster Abbey, "neere *Chawcer*, at the charges of the Earle of *Essex*, all Poets carrying his body to the Church, and casting their dolefull Verses, and Pens too into his grave" '. Jonson himself is the source for the much-cited, but doubtful, tradition that Spenser had 'refused 20 pieces sent to him by my Lord of Essex & said he was sorrie he had no time to spend them'.[62] It seems likely that Jonson was employing a subtle allusion to the elaborate compliments paid to Essex by his predecessor as would-be laureate of the Elizabethan court to advance Essex's cause, or at the very least petition for a more sympathetic consideration of his plight.

If the famous Nonsuch fountains are being evoked through the references to Actaeon, there is perhaps also, in Jonson's plea for clemency for Essex, an implied comparison with a great fountain at another of Elizabeth's palaces. John Norden had written in his *Speculum Britanniae* (1593) that at Hampton Court 'Queene ELIZABETH hath of late caused a very bewtifull fountaine, there to be erected, in the second court which graceth the pallace, and serueth to great and necessarie vse, the fountaine was finished in *Anno* 1590. not without great charge' (Fig. 19).[63] The fountain was the only physical detail of Hampton Court that Norden included, other than that it had two parks with brick walls. The *Speculum Britanniae* is a brief and rather idiosyncratic gazetteer, but Norden's dwelling on Hampton Court's fountain, to the exclusion of almost every other feature of the great palace, surely suggests that it was regarded at the time as either a novelty or a particular marvel, and one that was especially associated with the Queen herself. More details are supplied

[59] Edmund Spenser, *Prothalamion* (London, 1596), sig. B2–B2^v.

[60] Although, intriguingly, Narcissus is addressed as 'brightest Hasparus' in the university play discussed in Chapter 10, which may have been referencing Jonson's *Fountaine of Selfe-Love*. *Narcissus*, ed. Lee, 14.

[61] Spenser had died in January 1599.

[62] Ruth Mohl, 'Edmund Spenser', in Hamilton (ed.), *Spenser Encyclopedia*, 671. *Conversations*, 174–6.

[63] John Norden, *Speculum Britanniae: Description of Middlesex* (London, 1593), sigs. E1–E1^v.

by the traveller Paul Hentzner, who visited the palace in 1598: 'The cheif [*sic*] area is paved with square stone, in it's [*sic*] center is a fountain that throws up water, covered with a gilt crown, on the top of which is a statue of Justice, supported by columns of black and white marble.'[64] The fountain was located in what is now the Clock Court of the palace, and replaced an earlier Henrician fountain.[65] Although the fountain no longer exists, a design for it does,[66] as do the accounts for its construction: the eventual cost was £1,000, which makes Norden's note that it was set up 'not without great charge' something of an understatement;[67] it must have been both enormous (Thomas Platter described it as being 'of great height')[68] and spectacular. Royal justice could also, therefore, be conceived of as a fountain, and it seems, from this example at Hampton Court, that this was a metaphor endorsed and encouraged by the Queen herself. In his (admittedly partisan and retrospective) account of Essex's fall, and in particular the hope in the autumn of 1600, when Jonson was writing his play, that he would return to favour, William Camden described the grounds for that hope thus:

That the Queene was borne to clemency and quietnesse. That in her wisedome she knew that mercy was the pillar of her Kingdome. That she both would and could shew mercy, & yet with discretion. That she would not driue so great a man into despaire. That she would not, that any one should perish, that was any commodity to the Common-wealth. That she had squared all her actions hitherto to the rule of iustice. That she intended not the ouerthrow, but the amendment of the Earle.[69]

But in *The Fountaine of Selfe-Love*, Cynthia is exhorted to return to her true nature as a merciful prince. Elizabeth's lack of clemency is exposed; her justice is found wanting.

[64] Paul Hentzner, *Paul Hentzner's Travels in England, During the Reign of Queen Elizabeth*, trans. Horace Walpole (London, 1797), sig. Y4. Black and white were, of course, the Queen's personal colours.

[65] Confusingly, there is also a 'Fountain Court' in the present-day palace. The Henrician fountain appears in a drawing by Anthonis van den Wyngaerde; see Simon Thurley, *Hampton Court: A Social and Architectural History* (New Haven: Yale University Press, 2003), 26.

[66] The design has been attributed to Cornelius Cure, a mason who also worked for Lord Burghley and is known to have designed other fountains; it is preserved at Hatfield House. The coloured stone came from quarries in Kent, but the white marble was taken from some of the stocks intended for Henry VIII's tomb, and the figure of Justice was made from bronze and copper. See Henderson, *The Tudor House and Garden*, 172, 185–6, and also H. M. Colvin et al., *The History of the King's Works*, iv: *1485–1660 (Part 2)* (London: HMSO, 1982), 143–4.

[67] It may be recalled that Leicester's spectacular fountain at Kenilworth was valued at less than £50 in an inventory early in the next century. See Chapter 8.

[68] Williams, *Thomas Platter's Travels in England*, 116.

[69] William Camden, *The historie of the life and reigne of that famous princesse Elizabeth* (London, 1634), Nn1ᵛ.

The Fountaine of Selfe-Love is far more than an allegory of the Earl of Essex. But to read it also as Jonson's apparently sympathetic response to the Earl's situation in the autumn of 1600 brings into a sharper, topical focus Jonson's concern with courtiership and the ways in which monarchs should govern and be advised. As Blair Worden has pointed out, early seventeenth-century dramatists saw Essex 'not as an instrument of courtly wickedness, but as a victim of it . . . Essex, as William Camden said, "seemed not to be made for the court": his enemies, as dramatists portrayed them, were arch-courtiers'.[70] This aspect of the play can be read almost as a play within a play, in which the fountain of self-love of the court (which Essex, according to his apologists and recent biographers, was attempting to reform by his example, as in his 1595 Accession Day pageant)[71] is opposed not only to the Well of Knowledge, invoked in the play's conclusion, but also to the Fountain of Justice. Jonson implicitly invokes Astraea, goddess of justice and another familiar persona of the Queen, who stands for both just punishment and mercy, at the same time as he does Diana or Cynthia. He does not deny or even excuse the behaviour of Actaeon/Essex, but solicits on his behalf a response from Cynthia/Elizabeth that is both just and merciful; he seeks to shift the Queen, as much as the concerns of his play and the court, from the Grove of Diana at Nonsuch to the Fountain of Imperial Justice at Hampton Court.

When James VI and I was officially welcomed into London on 15 March 1604 he was, like Elizabeth half a century before him, greeted by a series of elaborate pageants, several of which employed fountains to portray the revivifying, transformative power of James as England's, and specifically London's, new monarch.[72] At the Great Conduit, James's mere presence caused the Fountain

---

[70] Early Jacobean plays which addressed the fall of Essex included Samuel Daniel's *Philotas* (1604) and George Chapman's *The Conspiracy and Tragedy of Byron* (1607–8) and *Charles Duke of Byron* (1608). Blair Worden, 'Favourites on the English Stage', in J. H. Elliott and L. W. B. Brockliss (eds.), *The World of the Favourite* (New Haven: Yale University Press, 1999), 168, 169. Camden's influential description of Essex as the antithesis of Leicester, 'a most accomplished Courtiour', appeared in his *Historie* (1630), a translation of his Latin *Annales* (1615), 145–6. See also Simon Adams, *Leicester and the Court: Essays on Elizabethan Politics* (Manchester: Manchester University Press), 46–67.

[71] See Robert Devereux, *An Apologie of the Earle of Essex . . . Penned by Himselfe in Anno 1598* (London, 1603), Wotton, *A Parallell*, and Hammer, *The Polarisation of Elizabethan Politics*.

[72] Although James was crowned according to plan in the summer of 1603, his official coronation entry was delayed until the following March because of plague. His coronation entry eventually featured speeches by Ben Jonson, Thomas Dekker, and Thomas Middleton. See Stephen Harrison, *The Arch's of Triumph* (London, 1604) (which includes engravings of the arches by William Kip); Thomas Dekker, *The VVhole Magnificent Entertainment Giuen to King Iames* (London, 1604); Ben Jonson, *B. Ion: His Part of King Iames His Royall and Magnificent Entertainement* (London, 1604).

of Virtue to run with milk, wine, and balm,[73] and at the Little Conduit there was erected 'a sommer Arbor, [which] seemed to growe close to the little *Conduit in Cheape*, which ioyning to the backe of it, serued (or might bee supposed to haue bene) as a Fountaine to water the fruits of this *Garden* of *Plenty*'.[74] As the Little Conduit was the fountain that physically 'watered' the bower so, metaphorically, James was to be a fountain, ensuring peace and plenty in his realm; a final song likened his presence to 'nourishing siluer streames'.[75] Yet this pageant and its fountain, and the hopes that it expressed for the forthcoming reign, had little of the ideological density and tension of its exact equivalent half a century before. James was being greeted not as a Protestant hero, but as a new Apollo, who was specifically to restore the fountain of the Muses:

The nine Muses that could expect no better entertainement than sad banishment, hauing now louely and amiable faces: Arts that were threatned to be trod vnder foot by Barbarisme, now (euen at the sight of his Maiestie, who is the Delian Patron[76] both of the Muses & Arts) being likewise aduanced to most high preferment.[77]

In *The Wonderfull Yeare* (1603) Dekker had used a similar image to draw attention to James's skill as a poet: 'the Scholler sings Hymnes in honor of the Muses, assuring himselfe now that *Helicon* will be kept pure, because *Apollo* himselfe drinkes of it'.[78] In his 'Pangyre' to the new king, which he published in tandem with his part in the coronation entry, however, Jonson went further, using as an epigraph a line from Martial's twelfth epigram: '*Licet toto nunc Helicone frui*' (Now we may enjoy Helicon in safety). Martial's epigram praises Nerva, and the vein in which it continues suggests that Jonson's choice levels implicit and subtle criticism at James's predecessor: '*recta fides, hilaris clementia, cauta potestas iam redeunt; longi terga dedere metus*' (Unswerving honor, cheerful clemency, circumspect power now return. The terrors that were with us so long have taken flight). In his choice of epigraph, Jonson's flattery of the new monarch was inseparable from his implicit censure of the old.[79] Jonson's praises of James in 1604 were as loaded as his commendations

---

[73] The thought of a fountain running with milk is extremely unpleasant. One hopes that 15 March 1604 was not too mild.

[74] Harrison, *Arch's*, F1, G1.   [75] Ibid., G4[v].   [76] Apollo.

[77] The speech survives only in Dekker's paraphrase. Dekker, *VVhole Magnificent Entertainment*, G3[v].

[78] Thomas Dekker, *The VVonderfull Yeare. 1603* (London, 1603), sig. C2.

[79] He perhaps also made a specific plea for toleration for Catholics, widely hoped for upon James's accession. Of lines 101–2 of the 'Panegyre' ('Where Acts gaue Licence to impetuous lust | To bury Churches, in forgotten dust') Herford and Simpson note that the poem was 'Written in Jonson's Catholic days', 10.393. The circles in which Jonson was moving in 1603–4 included many who had risen with Essex in 1601 (the Essex Rebellion being notable for the diversity of religious allegiances among those who participated), some of whom went on to be

of Cynthia's virtues in *The Fountaine of Selfe-Love*; their full impact was perhaps as dependent upon a knowledge of the latter as that play had in turn been upon the misfortunes of the Earl of Essex and the fountains of Nonsuch.

involved in the Gunpowder Plot the following year. On about 9 October 1605 Jonson had supper with many of the leading conspirators, including Francis Tresham, who had guarded Egerton at Essex House and had been imprisoned and heavily fined for his part in the Rebellion, and the Plot's chief originator, Robert Catesby, who had been wounded in the Rebellion and was also imprisoned and fined £3,000.

Conclusion

England's Helicon has at several points employed the metaphor of the palimpsest to describe the textuality of landscape, an image used by Thomas Greene to describe the way in which Petrarch apprehended the ruins of Rome:

Petrarch essentially *read* an order into the Roman wilderness, intuited a plan beneath the shattered temples and grazing sheep whose overwhelming human drama rendered the surface accidents of the city merely evocative pretexts... [he] might be said to have divined the subterranean plan of a living city in the way a scholar might puzzle out conjecturally the precious and nearly obliterated text of a palimpsest whereon a debased modern text had been superimposed.[1]

Greene goes on to develop this into a discussion of what he terms 'this necromantic superstition at the heart of the humanist enlightenment', which produced 'buildings and statues and poems that have to be scrutinized for subterranean outlines or emergent presences or ghostly reverberations'.[2] In Greene's account, the humanist hermeneutic is simultaneously and inseparably textual and material. The image of the palimpsest suggests the intertextuality of landscape, the intersection and overlapping of various signifying practices, such as might be applied to the interpretation of an ancient landscape, or the ruins within it, from and through visual, material, and textual evidence as well as the reading of a past 'reality' into (or onto) existing terrain; it also imagines the quasi-archaeological embeddedness of texts within that landscape (as English travellers were to embed fragments of Livy and Ovid in their travel

---

[1] Thomas Greene, 'Petrarch and the Humanist Hermeneutic', in Giose Rimanelli and Kenneth John Atchity (eds.), *Italian Literature: Roots and Branches: Essays in Honor of Thomas Goddard Bergin* (New Haven: Yale University Press, 1976), 201–2.

[2] Ibid. 208. Greene's ideas are developed with further and particular reference to the poetic landscape of Petrarch and Scève by Kenneth E. Cool, 'The Petrarchan Landscape as Palimpsest', *Journal of Medieval and Renaissance Studies*, 11 (1981), 83–100. As Cool observes, 'even more important than the issue of the accuracy of Petrarch's historical projections is the paradigm of the reading process and its relation to the texts to be deciphered that his hermeneutic strategy in fact fostered. For as a kind of visual scanning of the superimposed layers of the archeological site, his humanist version of cultural recovery required an imaginative extrapolation of present meaning where only dim fragments of past significance lingered on in the actual terrain' (84). In Cool's account the urban, monumental landscape described by Petrarch and specifically discussed by Greene is silently transmuted into a rural, natural one.

diaries) in terms that are more or less material. Petrarch's Roman *modus legendi* can also be applied to the real mottoes, poems, and inscriptions set up in early modern English gardens and the narratives that structured them; it additionally suggests the multiple meanings which attach to both 'remains' and 'monument'/'muniment' in early modern English usage.

Poliphilus' love of ruins and his obsessive recording of the fragmentary inscriptions of the Polyandrion in the *Hypnerotomachia* are, in this sense, Petrarchan. It is above all Poliphilus' journey *through a landscape* that expresses his philosophical, spiritual, and erotic development, a landscape in which fantastic fountains are strong points, super-signifiers, artistic (and literary) *tours de force*, and the literal manifestation of Poliphilus' erotic desires as thirst. The reader is involved and implicated in this continuing encounter through his or her own experience of the book as a visual and material object, the sculptural and scopophiliac qualities of its illustrations, the lingering eroticism of its passages of description (more so than of its plot), and the compulsion to turn its pages and possess it. Its illustrations, not least of fountains, are central to this. Like an early modern garden, the *Hypnerotomachia*—as it is epitomized in the surfaces of the fountains of Venus and Adonis—is an arena for the exploration and experience of ideas and sensations; it exists as a space as much as a text.

In rewriting the *Hypnerotomachia*'s Fountain of Adonis at the beginning of his revised *Arcadia*, Sidney reorients the space of the fountain in moral terms, drawing attention to the dangers of narcissism in love and art. In the Bowre of Bliss, Spenser too creates an environment—epitomized by its central fountain—which warns at the same time as it allures. Yet in Books 2 and 3 of *The Faerie Queene* he also continues the process begun in Book 1 of creating a careful and discerning reader, one able to read not only texts and landscapes but the relationships between them also. The landscape of Protestant England was also a palimpsestic one, its old landmarks rewritten and so re-experienced in new ways as signs of God's favour to the English people. In the writings of humanists and Protestant apologists, the return *ad fontes* is frequently literalized, and in the gift of the English Bible to Elizabeth at the Little Conduit in 1559, it was made material. Spenser's landscapes and their fountains do not need to be illustrated; they occupy the country and the city, the mind and the soul.

No discussion of gardens in early modern England would be complete without at least a mention of Francis Bacon's essay 'On Gardens', for Bacon's declaration that 'God Almighty first planted a garden; and, indeed, it is the purest of human pleasures' remains perhaps the best-known statement on the early modern garden. To encounter Bacon's description of fountains in particular at the end of such a discussion, however, is very different from using it as a starting point, as so many writers on the early modern garden have done, for it shows the way in which his essay depends upon and articulates the interconnectedness of literary, ideal, and real gardens and fountains in early modern England:

For fountains, they are a great beauty and refreshment; but pools mar all and make the garden unwholesome and full of flies and frogs. Fountains I intend to be of two natures; the one that sprinkleth or spouteth water: the other a fair receipt of water, of some thirty or forty foot square, but without fish or slime or mud. For the first, the ornaments of images gilt or of marble which are in use do well: but the main matter is so to convey the water as it never stay, either in the bowls or in the cistern, that the water be never by rest discoloured, green, or red, or the like, or gather any mossiness or putrefaction; besides that, it is to be cleansed every day by the hand: also some steps up to it, and some fine pavement about it doth well. As for the other kind of fountain, which we may call a bathing pool, it may admit much curiosity and beauty, wherewith we will not trouble ourselves: as that the bottom be finely paved, and with images; the sides likewise; and withal embellished with coloured glass and such things of lustre; encompassed also with fine rails of low statuas; but the main point is the same which we mentioned in the former kind of fountain; which is that the water be in perpetual motion, fed by a water higher than the pool, and delivered into it by fair spouts and then discharged away under ground by some equality of bores, that it stay little; and for fine devices, of arching water without spilling, and making it rise in several forms (of features, drinking-glasses, canopies, and the like), they be pretty things to look on but nothing to health and sweetness.[3]

Bacon's description draws extensively on his own water gardens at Gorhambury.[4] When John Aubrey visited the estate in 1656 he described the mosaics on the bottoms of the ponds as 'now over-grown with flagges and rushes',[5] and it seems likely that the ambitious design of the ponds had proved difficult to maintain even in Bacon's time, which would account for his precise direction that 'the main matter is so to convey the water as it never stay, either in the bowls or in the cistern, that the water be never by rest discoloured, green, or red, or the like, or gather any mossiness or putrefaction' and, indeed, his negative attitude towards ponds and pools.[6]

To come to these pronouncements having explored the moral, political, and religious associations of fountains in early modern literature and culture is to see them in a new way: there is surely a political undertone here, a comment on the stagnant nature of public life and a disparagement of ostentation of

---

[3] Francis Bacon, *The Major Works*, ed. Brian Vickers (Oxford: Oxford University Press, 1996), 430, 433.
[4] The main source here is Paula Henderson, 'Sir Francis Bacon's Water Gardens at Gorhambury', *Garden History*, 20 (1992), 116–31.
[5] Ibid. 122. [6] This suggestion is made by Henderson.

all kinds, at the same time as there is an entirely practical prescription for a healthy garden pond. Just as the decoration of a fountain can distract with artifice or even entice with erotic imagery, its surfaces can distort rather than truly reflect, and its clear waters are dangerously vulnerable to corruption. Fountains are powerful literary devices because of their capaciousness as signifiers, but their very multivalence frequently makes them ambivalent also. Whereas Colonna illustrates his fountains as well as describing them, and Spenser creates readers who can interpret both landscapes and texts, Jonson stages a fountain that stands for fountains both real and imagined. His Well of Knowledge is apparently not far from his Fountain of Self-Love: the court-fountain has all too easily become a source of moral lassitude, self-indulgence, and impropriety, rather than a true reflecting glass and an agent of moral edification. Cynthia, its Queen and tutelary deity, has lost both control and perspective, and not long after her *Revels* were first staged, the game-playing of her Grove at Nonsuch was relived in deadly earnest.

In its discussion of fountains in the literature of Renaissance England, and in their wider cultural and material context, *England's Helicon* has shown the profound and complex interconnectedness of the textual, visual, material, and experiential in early modern literature and culture. It has demonstrated that to focus on a material entity that is simultaneously such a salient feature of the literary, the aesthetic, the real, and the ideal landscape reveals this inextricability. This elaborate and integrated visual, spatial, and material environment, in which fountains featured in many ways, both informed their literary appearances and revealed their tensions: to look at 'Diana in the fountain', whether at Nonsuch or in Cheapside, or, more allusively, in the *Hypnerotomachia*, the *Arcadia*, *The Faerie Queene*, or *The Fountaine of Selfe-Love*, was—and remains—a complex and ambivalent act. To read other fountains, alluded to or described by Colonna and Dallington, Sidney, Spenser, Shakespeare, Jonson, Peele, Stow, and Mulcaster, Dekker, Heywood, and many others, is therefore to be aware of these and other, related tensions and pluralities, contexts and intertexts, of which Actaeon's fate is only the most sharply focused and extreme outcome. It is also to realize and read the interconnectedness of these and other texts and the material contexts to which they refer or respond, directly or indirectly, which they invoke, or with which they implicitly interact.

Nearly a century after Thomas Hoby's travels in Italy,[7] another Englishman set off on a 'grand tour'. The young John Evelyn, after Oxford, the Middle Temple, and an earlier visit to the Low Countries as part of a diplomatic mission, began his travels in 1643, having sought the advice of Thomas

---

[7] Discussed in the Introduction.

Howard, Earl of Arundel, England's first great collector of classical antiquities and Italian paintings, bibliophile, antiquary, and patron of Van Dyck. Evelyn's tour, chiefly of France and Italy, lasted for four years. Within five years of his return in 1647, he had begun to remodel the garden at Sayes Court, his home in Deptford, and at the same time he embarked upon a project on which he was to work sporadically for the rest of his life, the *Elysium Britannicum*, an encyclopedic work encompassing garden history and design, horticulture, forestry, and botany.[8] It is not, however, the *Elysium Britannicum* with which *England's Helicon*'s discussion of fountains in early modern literature and culture concludes, but rather with one of the purchases Evelyn made on his Italian travels in the 1640s. Evelyn is now best known for his diary, which he began in a rudimentary form as an 11-year-old schoolboy, and which in 1813 was discovered in an ebony cabinet at Wotton House in Surrey.

This ebony cabinet has been identified as one now in the British Galleries of the Victoria and Albert Museum. The cabinet proper was made for Evelyn in Florence *c.*1644–6 and, on his return to England, its drawers and front were further ornamented with nineteen *pietra dura* plaques which Evelyn had ordered from Domenico Benotti, also in Florence.[9] Ten of the plaques depict flowers, and a further eight birds, but the door of the cabinet's central cupboard, more than twice the size of the smaller plaques, is decorated with a fountain and the overall effect—the central fountain surrounded by birds and flowers, and indeed by the gilded mythological figures and plaques of animals—is of a garden. Evelyn no doubt had many cupboards and cabinets. But the image of the passionate gardener and writer of the *Elysium Britannicum* choosing to organize his writings or most personal possessions—perhaps even in the manner of a 'cabinet of curiosities'—in a cabinet decorated with a fountain in the middle of a garden is an immensely pleasing one, in the material and immediate connection that it forges between Evelyn's travels, his writing, his passion for gardening, and the environment in which he lived.

As I observed in the Introduction, a hat badge is not a fountain; neither is an ebony cabinet. Evelyn's travels were in part a reaction to the Civil War, his cabinet and its decoration were the products of a *seicento* Florentine aesthetic, and his gardens and the ways in which he wrote about them recorded and

---

[8] The *Elysium Britannicum* remained unpublished until 2001, although various portions of it were 'spun off' and appeared as, for example, *Sylva* (1664) (on trees) and *A Philosophical Discourse of Earth* (1676) (on soil). See *Elysium Britannicum, or The Royal Gardens*, ed. John E. Ingram (Philadelphia: University of Pennsylvania Press, 2001).

[9] The work was done in the London workshop of Francesco Fanelli, who had died in 1641. A similar cabinet in the Gilbert Collection at Somerset House in London has an almost identical central fountain.

responded to a different age from the one of the gardens and texts that have been the subject of *England's Helicon*. To walk around a museum or gallery is not to walk around a garden any more than to visit even a great house restored to its Elizabethan state or a recreated early modern garden is to experience that house or that garden as those who designed, lived in, wrote, and read in and about them did. Yet it is in such experiences that there is the possibility of recovering something of the material and experiential immediacy which colours their literary counterparts and, more, it is perhaps in the calm, dissociated, even sterile environs of the museum or gallery that such immediacy is most recoverable. A hat badge, an embroidered book-binding, a tapestry, a sweetmeat box, or a portrait—even as we struggle to read them—can perhaps reveal far more than any recreated garden about what early modern writers and readers thought about fountains and gardens (or indeed royal power and patronage, or the Word of God). In a museum or gallery (as in an early modern garden) ideas are organized and apprehended in visual, spatial, and experiential terms, through a labour of the imagination. In the previous chapters, therefore, I have sought to make productive juxtapositions between objects, images, and texts as well as between texts and what can be known of early modern English gardens and their fountains, because such juxtapositions solicit strategies of apprehension and interpretation that must necessarily go beyond the merely textual.

It is, of course, vital to recognize (as previous chapters have) that early modern literary gardens and their fountains were influenced by other gardens and fountains in literature, classical, biblical, and medieval, as well as Renaissance. Yet those literary influences on writers and readers cannot be separated from visual, material, and experiential influences, and the ways in which the literary intertext can be discerned and read must in turn be informed by inter- and multidisciplinary strategies of interpretation. Modern readers and critics, especially of Renaissance texts, have become accustomed to reading texts with reference above all to other texts, identifying an allusion here, an unacknowledged borrowing there; it is still necessary (and frequently still exciting) to read in this way, and some of what *England's Helicon* has sought to do, especially with respect to the *Hypnerotomachia*, has continued in this approach. Such a *modus legendi*, however, risks becoming the critical equivalent of the Sunday afternoon stroll around a stately home, an experience that is essentially passive, emphasizing consumption rather than participation. At the very least, a text can itself be thought of as an object, as in the case of the *Hypnerotomachia*, as a landscape to be experienced by protagonist and reader alike, as in Book 1 of *The Faerie Queene*; the features of a landscape (like the Grove of Diana, the Theobalds summerhouse, or the privy garden at Kenilworth) can be thought of as a text, and as both coexistent and coextensive with the texts and objects produced and consumed by those who knew and experienced such landscapes.

To consider what—and how—an image, an object, or a landscape might do or mean to a literary text, and vice versa, requires an effort that is imaginative as much as it is intellectual, a way of reading that is active and participatory. Such a strategy of interpretation begins to approach that solicited by gardens (and houses) like Theobalds, Kenilworth, and Nonsuch, and texts such as the *Hypnerotomachia Poliphili*, the *Arcadia*, *The Faerie Queene*, and *The Fountaine of Selfe-Love*. To focus on the fountains as a point of access to these texts itself suggests that other features of the early modern symbolic vocabulary, landscape, and experience might be employed in a similar way. The fountains of early modern England and the gardens in which they once stood solicit strategies of interpretation, modes of apprehension, and simple ways of reading similar or analogous to other cultural productions such as textiles, jewellery, and portraits, and literary texts. One of the few differences between them in this respect is that the gardens and their fountains are lost, while texts and objects survive: to generate a conversation between texts and objects, therefore, is to reimagine and reanimate those gardens and their fountains once again.

Bibliography

Primary Sources

A direction for trauailers Taken out of Iustus Lipsius, and enlarged for the behoofe of the right honorable Lord, the yong Earle of Bedford, being now ready to trauell (London, 1592).

Alberti, Leon Battista, *On the Art of Building in Ten Books*, trans. Joseph Rykwert, Neil Leach, and Robert Tavernor (Cambridge, Mass.: MIT Press, 1988).

—— *On Painting*, trans. Cecil Grayson, ed. Martin Kemp (London: Penguin, 1991).

Alciati, Andrea, *Emblemata cum commentariis* (Padua, 1621).

Apuleius, *The Golden Ass*, trans. E. J. Kenny (London: Penguin, 1998).

Ascham, Roger, *The Scholemaster* (London, 1570).

Bacon, Francis, *The Major Works*, ed. Brian Vickers (Oxford: Oxford University Press, 1996).

Bale, John, *The Image of Both Churches* (London, 1548).

Baley, Walter, *A Briefe Discours of certain Bathes or medicinall Waters in the Countie of Warwicke neere vnto a village called Newnham Regis* (London, 1587).

Barnes, Barnabe, *A Centurie of Divine Sonnets* (London, 1595).

Batman, Stephen, *The Golden Book of the Leaden Gods* (London, 1577).

Boccaccio, Giovanni, *The Decameron*, trans. G. H. McWilliam (Harmondsworth: Penguin, 1995).

Camden, William, *Britain, or a Chorographicall Description*, trans. Philemon Holland (London, 1610).

—— *The historie of the life and reigne of that famous princesse Elizabeth* (London, 1634).

Castiglione, Baldassare, *The Book of the Courtier*, trans. Thomas Hoby, ed. Virginia Cox (London: J. M. Dent, 1994).

Certayne sermons, or Homelies appoynted by the Kynges Maiestie, to bee declared and redde, by all persons, vicares, or curates, euery Sondaye in their churches, where they haue cure (London, 1547).

Chaucer, Geoffrey, *The Riverside Chaucer*, ed. Larry D. Benson (Oxford: Oxford University Press, 1987).

Colonna, Francesco, *Hypnerotomachia Poliphili* (Venice, 1499, 1545).

—— *Hypnerotomachia Poliphili*, trans. Joscelyn Godwin (London: Thames and Hudson, 1999).

—— *Hypnerotomachia Poliphili*, ed. Giovanni Pozzi and Lucia A. Ciapponi (Padua: Editrice Antenore, 1964).

—— *Hypnerotomachia: The Strife of Love in a Dreame*, trans. R.D., ed. Lucy Gent (New York: Scholars' Reprints and Facsimiles, 1973).

—— *Le Songe de Poliphile*, ed. Gilles Polizzi (Paris: Imprimerie Nationale, 1994).

Dallington, Robert, *A Survey of the great dukes state of Tuscany: In the yeare of our Lord 1596* (London, 1605).

Davies, Sir John, 'A Contention betwixt a Wife, a Widdow, and a Maide', in Francis Davison, *A poetical rapsodie* (London, 1611).

Dekker, Thomas, *The VVhole Magnificent Entertainment Giuen to King Iames* (London, 1604).

—— *The Dramatic Works of Thomas Dekker*, vol. i, ed. Fredson Bowers (Cambridge: Cambridge University Press, 1962).

—— *The VVonderfull Yeare. 1603* (London, 1603).

Deloney, Thomas, *Strange Histories* (London, 1602).

Devereux, Robert, *An Apologie of the Earle of Essex . . . Penned by Himselfe in Anno 1598* (London, 1603).

Donne, John, *The Major Works*, ed. John Carey (Oxford: Oxford University Press, 1990).

Drue, Thomas, *The life of the dutches of Suffolke* (London, 1631).

Elyot, Sir Thomas, *The Image of Governaunce* (London, 1556).

Englands Helicon (London, 1600).

Erasmus, Desiderius, *Colloquies*, trans. Craig R. Thompson (Toronto: University of Toronto Press, 1997).

—— *De Copia; De Ratione Studii*, trans. Betty I. Knott and Brian McGregor, ed. Craig R. Thompson (Toronto: University of Toronto Press, 1978).

—— *The Correspondence of Erasmus: Letters 298 to 445, 1514 to 1516*, trans. R. A. B. Mynors and D. F. S. Thomson (Toronto: University of Toronto Press, 1976).

—— *A dialoge or communication of two persons deuysyd and set forthe in the laten tonge, by the noble and famose clarke. Desiderius Erasmus intituled [the] pylgremage of pure deuotyon. Newly translatyd into Englishe* (London?, 1540).

—— *The Education of a Christian Prince*, trans. Neil M. Cheshire and Michael J. Heath (Toronto: Toronto University Press, 1986).

—— *The Manuell of the Christen Knyght*, trans. William Tyndale (?) (London, 1533).

—— *Paraphrase on Mark*, trans. Erika Rummel (Toronto: University of Toronto Press, 1988).

—— *Paraphrases on Romans and Galatians*, ed. Robert D. Sider, trans. John B. Payne, Albert Rabil, and Warren S. Smith (Toronto: University of Toronto Press, 1984).

Evelyn, John, *Elysium Britannicum, or The Royal Gardens*, ed. John E. Ingram (Philadelphia: University of Pennsylvania Press, 2001).

Fletcher, Anthony, *Certaine Very Proper, and Most Profitable Similies* (London, 1595).

The Fountayne or well of lyfe, out of which doth springe most swete consolations, right necessary for troubled consciences, to thentent that they shall nat despayre in aduersite and trouble. Translated out of latyn in to Englysshe (London, 1532).

Foxe, John, *Actes and monuments of matters most speciall and memorable, happenyng in the Church with an vniuersall history of the same, wherein is set forth at large the whole race and course of the Church, from the primitiue age to these latter tymes of ours, with the bloudy times, horrible troubles, and great persecutions agaynst the true martyrs of Christ, sought and wrought as well by heathen emperours, as nowe lately practised by Romish prelates, especially in this realme of England and Scotland* (London, 1583).

Fraunce, Abraham, *The Third Part of the Countesse of Pembrokes Yuichurch* (London, 1592).

Fulke, William, *A defense of the sincere and true translation of the Holy Scriptures into the English tongve* (London, 1583, 1617).

Grafton, Richard, *Graftons Abridgement of the Chronicles of Englande. Newly and diligently corrected* (London, 1570).

Groos, G. W., *The Diary of Baron Waldstein: A Traveller in Elizabethan England* (London: Thames and Hudson, 1981).

Harington, Sir John, *The Epigrams of Sir John Harington*, ed. N. E. McClure (Philadelphia: University of Pennsylvania Press, 1926).

—— *The Metamorphosis of Ajax*, ed. Elizabeth Story Donno (London: Routledge and Kegan Paul, 1962).

Harrison, Stephen, *The Arch's of Triumph* (London, 1604).

Harrison, William, *The Description of England*, ed. Georges Edelen (Ithaca, NY: Cornell University Press, 1968).

Hawes, Stephen, *The historie of graunde Amoure and la bell Pucel, called the Pastime of plesure* (London, 1554).

—— *The Minor Poems*, ed. Florence W. Gluck and Alice B. Morgan (London: Oxford University Press, 1974).

—— *The Pastime of Pleasure (1517)*, ed. William Edward Mead (London: Oxford University Press, 1928).

Hentzner, Paul, *Paul Hentzner's Travels in England, During the Reign of Queen Elizabeth*, trans. Horace Walpole (London, 1797).

Here begynneth a treatyse howthe hye fader of heven sendeth dethe to somon euery creature to come and gyue a counte of theyr lyues in this worlde and is in maner of a morall playe (London, 1535) [*Everyman*].

Hesiod, *The Homeric Hymns and Homerica*, trans. Hugh G. Evelyn-White (Cambridge, Mass.: Harvard University Press, 1967).

Hoby, Thomas, 'The Travels and Life of Sir Thomas Hoby', ed. E. Powell, *Camden Miscellany*, 10, 3rd ser. 4 (1902), 1–144.

Horace, *Odes and Epodes*, trans. Niall Rudd (Cambridge, Mass.: Harvard University Press, 2004)

Jewel, John, *An Apologie or answere in defence of the Churche of Englande*, trans. Ann Bacon (London, 1564).

Jones, John, *The Benefit of the auncient Bathes of Buckstones* (London, 1572).

Jonson, Ben, *B. Ion: His Part of King Iames His Royall and Magnificent Entertainement* (London, 1604).

—— *The Complete Poems*, ed. George Parfitt (rev. edn. London: Penguin, 1996).

—— *The Fountaine of Selfe-Love* (London, 1601).

—— *Poetaster* (London, 1601).

—— *The Workes of Beniamin Ionson* (London, 1616).

—— *Works*, ed. C. H. Herford and Evelyn and Percy Simpson (Oxford: Clarendon Press, 1925–52).

Laneham, Robert, *A LETTER: Whearin, part of the entertainment vntoo the Queenz Maiesty, at Killing woorth Castl, in warwik Sheer, in this soomerz Progress·1575. iz signified* (London, 1575).

Langland, William, *The Vision of Piers Plowman: A Critical Edition of the B-Text Based on Trinity College Cambridge MS B.15.17*, 2nd edn. ed. A. V. C. Schmidt (London: Everyman, 1995).

Lawson, William, *A nevv orchard and garden. Or The best way for planting, grafting, and to make the ground good, for a rich orchard particularly in the north parts of England: generally for the whole kingdome, as in nature, reason, scituation, and all probability, may and doth appeare* (London, 1618).

Lucan, *Pharsalia*, trans. J. D. Duff (Cambridge, Mass.: Harvard University Press, 1928).

Lyly, John, *Endimion, the Man in the Moone* (London, 1591).

—— *Endymion*, ed. David Bevington (Manchester: Manchester University Press, 1996).

—— *Loues Metamorphosis* (London, 1601).

Lynche, Richard, *The Fountaine of Ancient Fiction* (London, 1599).

Malory, Sir Thomas, *Complete Works*, ed. Eugène Vinaver (2nd edn., Oxford: Oxford University Press, 1971).

Markham, Gervase, *The English husbandman. The first part: contayning the knowledge of the true nature of euery soyle within this kingdome: how to plow it; and the manner of the plough, and other instruments belonging thereto. Together with the art of planting, grafting, and gardening after our latest and rarest fashion. A worke neuer written before by any author: and now newly compiled for the benefit of this kingdome* (London, 1613).

Marston, John, *The Scourge of Villanie* (London, 1598).

Moryson, Fynes, *An itinerary vvritten by Fynes Moryson Gent. First in the Latine tongue, and then translated by him into English: containing his ten yeeres trauell through the tvvelue dominions of Germany, Bohmerland, Sweitzerland, Netherland, Denmarke, Poland, Italy, Turky, France, England, Scotland, and Ireland* (London, 1617).

Mulcaster, Richard, *Positions Concerning the Training Up of Children*, ed. William Barker (Toronto: Toronto University Press, 1994).

Narcissus: A Twelfe Night Merriment, ed. Margaret L. Lee (London: David Nutt, 1893).

Nashe, Thomas, *Nashes Lenten stuffe containing, the description and first procreation and increase of the towne of Great Yarmouth in Norffolke: with a new play neuer played before, of the praise of the red herring* (London, 1599).

—— *Pierces supererogation or A new prayse of the old asse* (London, 1593).

—— *Strange newes, of the intercepting certaine letters, and a conuoy of verses, as they were going priuilie to victuall the Low Countries* (London, 1592).

Norden, John, *Speculum Britanniae: Description of Middlesex* (London, 1593).

Ovid, *Metamorphoses*, trans. Frank Justus Miller 3rd edn. Cambridge, Mass.: Harvard University Press, 1977).

—— *Tristia; Ex Ponto*, trans. Arthur Leslie Wheeler, rev. G. P. Goold (Cambridge, Mass.: Harvard University Press, 1988).

The passage of our most drad Soueraigne Lady Quene Elyzabeth through the citie of London to westminster the daye before her coronacion Anno 1558 (London, 1559).

Peacham, Henry, *Minerva Britanna, or a Garden of Heroical Devises* (London, 1612).

Peck, D. C., *Leicester's Commonwealth: The Copy of a Letter Written by a Master of Art of Cambridge (1584) and Related Documents* (Athens: Ohio University Press, 1985).

Peele, George, *The araygnement of Paris a pastorall. Presented before the Queenes Maiestie, by the Children of her chappell* (London, 1584).

—— *The battell of Alcazar fought in Barbarie, betweene Sebastian king of Portugall, and Abdelmelec king of Marocco. With the death of Captaine Stukeley* (London, 1594).

—— *Descensus astraeae the device of a l'ageant [sic] borne before M. William Web, lord maior of the citie of London on the day he tooke his oath, beeing the 29. of October. 1591* (London, 1591).

—— *The deuice of the pageant borne before the Woolstone Dixi Lord Maior of the citie of London. An. 1585* (London, 1585).

—— *The famous chronicle of king Edward the first, sirnamed Edward Longshankes with his returne from the holy land. Also the life of Lleuellen rebell in Wales. Lastly, the sinking of Queene Elinor, who sunck at Charingcrosse, and rose againe at Pottershith, now named Queenehith* (London, 1593).

—— *The loue of King Dauid and fair Bethsabe With the tragedie of Absalon* (London, 1599).

—— *The old wiues tale A pleasant conceited comedie* (London, 1595).

Percy, William, *The Cuck-Queanes and Cuckolds Errants, or the Bearing Down the Inne, a Comedy. The Faery Pastorall, or Forrest of Elues* (London, 1824).

Plato, *Phaedrus*, trans. Robin Waterfield (Oxford: Oxford University Press, 2002).

Pliny the Younger, *Letters and Panegyricus*, trans. Betty Radice (Cambridge, Mass.: Harvard University Press, 1969).

Plutarch, *Moralia*, trans. Harold North Fowler (Cambridge, Mass.: Harvard University Press, 1969).

Rich, Barnaby, *New Description of Ireland* (London, 1610).

Ripa, Cesare, *Iconologia* (Padua, 1611).

Salisbury, John of, *John of Salisbury: Policraticus*, ed. and trans. Cary J. Nederman, Cambridge Texts in the History of Political Thought (Cambridge: Cambridge University Press, 1990).

Sandys, George, *Ouids Metamorphosis Englished, mythologiz'd, and represented in figures* (Oxford, 1632).

—— *A relation of a iourney begun an: Dom: 1610 Foure bookes. Containing a description of the Turkish Empire, of AEgypt, of the Holy Land, of the remote parts of Italy, and ilands adioyning* (London, 1615).

Shakespeare, William, *As You Like It*, ed. Juliet Dusinberre, The Arden Shakespeare: Third Series (London: Thomson Learning, 2006).

—— *As You Like It*, ed. Michael Hattaway (Cambridge: Cambridge University Press, 2000).

—— *Cymbeline*, ed. J. M. Nosworthy, The Arden Shakespeare: Second Series (London: Methuen, 1955; repr. Routledge, 1994).

—— *Hamlet*, ed. Ann Thompson and Neil Taylor, The Arden Shakespeare: Third Series (London: Thomson Learning, 2006).

—— *Julius Caesar*, ed. David Daniell, The Arden Shakespeare: Third Series (London: Thomas Nelson and Sons, 1998).

Shakespeare, William, *King Henry IV Part I*, ed. David Scott Kastan, The Arden Shakespeare: Third Series (London: Thomson Learning, 2002).

—— *Titus Andronicus*, ed. Jonathan Bate, The Arden Shakespeare: Third Series (London: Routledge, 1995).

Sidney, Philip, *The Countess of Pembroke's Arcadia*, ed. Maurice Evans (London: Penguin, 1977).

—— *The Major Works*, ed. Katherine Duncan-Jones (Oxford: Oxford University Press, 1989).

—— *Sidney's 'The Defence of Poesy' and Selected Renaissance Literary Criticism*, ed. Gavin Alexander (London: Penguin, 2004).

Spenser, Edmund, *The Faerie Queene*, ed. A. C. Hamilton (London: Longman, 2001).

—— *Prothalamion* (London, 1596).

—— *The Shorter Poems*, ed. Richard A. McCabe (London: Penguin, 1999).

—— *A View of the Present State of Ireland*, ed. Rudolph Gottfried, in *A Variorum Edition of the Works of Edmund Spenser*, ed. Edwin Greenlaw et al. (Baltimore: Johns Hopkins University Press, 1932–49).

Stow, John, *The Annales of England* (London, 1592).

—— *The Chronicles of England* (London, 1580).

—— *The Survay of London* (London, 1598).

—— *A Svrvay of London* (London, 1603).

—— and Howes, Edmund, *Annales, or a Generall Chronicle of England* (London, 1631).

—— and Munday, Anthony, *The Svrvay of London* (London, 1618).

Tasso, Torquato, *Jerusalem Delivered: An English Prose Version*, trans. and ed. Ralph Nash (Detroit, Mich.: Wayne State University Press, 1987).

Tatius, Achilles, *Leucippe and Clitophon*, trans. Tim Whitmarsh (Oxford: Oxford University Press, 2001).

Turner, William, *A Booke of the natures and properties, as well of the bathes in England as of other bathes in Germanye and Italye, very necessarye for all suche persons that can not be healed without the helpe of natural bathes, lately ouersene and enlarged by William Turner Doctor in Physick* (London, 1568).

Tyard, Pontus de, *Douze fables des fleuves ou fontaines* (Paris, 1585).

Von Bülow, Gottfried (ed.), 'Diary of the Journey of Philip Julius, Duke of Stettin-Pomerania, through England in the Year 1602', *Transactions of the Royal Historical Society*, 6 (NS) (1892), 1–67.

Von Strassburg, Gottfried, *Tristan (with the 'Tristan' of Thomas)* (rev. edn.), ed. A. T. Hatto (London, Penguin, 2004).

Webster, John, *The Works of John Webster*, i: *The White Devil, The Duchess of Malfi*, ed. David Gunby, David Carnegie, and Antony Hammond (Cambridge: Cambridge University Press, 1995).

Whitney, Geoffrey, *A Choice of Emblemes* (London, 1586).

Williams, Clare, *Thomas Platter's Travels in England, 1599* (London: Jonathan Cape, 1937).

Winwood, Ralph, *Memorials of Affairs of State in the Reigns of Q. Elizabeth and K. James I*, 2 vols. (London, 1725).

Wotton, Sir Henry, *A Parallell Betweene Robert Late Earle of Essex, and George Late Duke of Buckingham* (London, 1641).

Wright, Thomas, *The Passions of the minde in generall* (London, 1604).

Wroth, Mary, *The First Part of the Countess of Montgomerie's Urania*, ed. Josephine A. Roberts (Binghamton, NY: Renaissance English Text Society, 1995).

Secondary Sources

Adams, H. M., *Catalogue of Books Printed on the Continent of Europe, 1501–1600, in Cambridge Libraries* (Cambridge: Cambridge University Press, 1967).

Adams, Simon, *Leicester and the Court: Essays on Elizabethan Politics* (Manchester: Manchester University Press, 2002).

Airs, Malcolm, 'Pomp or Glory: The Influence of Theobalds', in Pauline Croft (ed.), *Patronage, Culture and Power: The Early Cecils, 1558–1612* (New Haven: Yale University Press, 2002), 3–19.

Allen, Peter L., *The Art of Love: Amatory Fiction from Ovid to the Romance of the Rose* (Philadelphia: University of Pennsylvania Press, 1992).

Alpers, Paul J., *The Poetry of The Faerie Queene* (Princeton: Princeton University Press, 1967).

Alter, Robert, and Kermode, Frank (eds.), *The Literary Guide to the Bible* (London: Collins, 1987).

Anderson, Christy, 'Learning to Read Architecture in the English Renaissance', in Lucy Gent (ed.), *Albion's Classicism: The Visual Arts in Britain, 1550–1660* (New Haven: Yale University Press, 1995), 239–86.

—— 'Wild Waters: Hydraulics and the Forces of Nature', in Peter Hulme and William H. Sherman (eds.), *The Tempest and its Travels* (London: Reaktion Books, 2000), 41–7.

Andrews, Martin, 'Theobalds Palace: The Gardens and Park', *Garden History*, 21 (1993), 129–49.

Anglo, Sydney, *Images of Tudor Kingship* (London: Seaby, 1992).

—— *Spectacle, Pageantry, and Early Tudor Policy* (Oxford: Clarendon Press, 1997).

Archer, Ian, 'John Stow's *Survey of London*: The Nostalgia of John Stow', in David L. Smith, Richard Strier, and David Bevington (eds.), *The Theatrical City: Culture, Theatre and Politics in London, 1576–1649* (Cambridge: Cambridge University Press, 1995), 17–34.

Arnold, Janet, *Queen Elizabeth's Wardrobe Unlock'd: The Inventories of the Wardrobe of Robes Prepared in July 1600 Edited from Stowe MS 557 in the British Library, MS LR 2/121 in the Public Record Office, London, and MS V.b.72 in the Folger Shakespeare Library, Washington DC* (London: Maney, 1988).

Atkinson, Dorothy F., '*The Wandering Knight*, the Red Cross Knight and "Miles Dei"', *Huntington Library Quarterly*, 7 (1944), 109–34.

Auerbach, Erich, *Mimesis: The Representation of Reality in Western Literature* (Princeton: Princeton University Press, 1953; repr. 2003).

Axton, Richard, 'Spenser's "Faire hermaphrodite": Rewriting the *Faerie Queene*', in Alisoun Gardner-Medwin and Janet Hadley Williams (eds.), *A Day Estivall: Essays* on the Music, Poetry and History of Scotland and England and Poems Previously Unpublished in Honour of Helena Mennie Shire (Aberdeen: Aberdeen University Press, 1990), 35–47.

Bachelard, Gaston, *L'Eau et les rêves: essai sur l'imagination de la matière* (Paris: Librairie José Corti, 1947).

—— *Water and Dreams: An Essay on the Imagination of Matter*, trans. Edith R. Farrell (Dallas: Dallas Institute of Humanities and Culture, 1983).

Bann, Stephen, *The True Vine: On Visual Representation and the Western Tradition* (Cambridge: Cambridge University Press, 1989).

Barkan, Leonard, 'Diana and Actaeon: The Myth as Synthesis', *English Literary Renaissance*, 10 (1980), 317–59.

—— *The Gods Made Flesh: Metamorphosis and the Pursuit of Paganism* (New Haven: Yale University Press, 1986).

Barolini, Helen, *Aldus and his Dream Book* (New York: Italica Press, 1992).

Baron, Xavier, 'Medieval Traditions in the English Renaissance: John Stow's Portrayal of London in 1603', in Rhoda Schnur (ed.), *Acta Conventus Neo-Latini Hafniensis: Proceedings of the Eighth International Congress of Neo-Latin Studies* (Binghamton, NY: Medieval and Renaissance Texts and Studies, 1994), 133–41.

Barrier, Philippe, *Forêt légendaire: contes, légendes, coutumes, anecdotes sur les forêts de France* (Etrépilly: Christian de Bartillat, 1991).

Barthes, Roland, *S/Z*, trans. Richard Miller (London: Jonathan Cape, 1975).

Barton, Anne, *Ben Jonson, Dramatist* (Cambridge: Cambridge University Press, 1984).

Bate, Jonathan, *Shakespeare and Ovid* (Oxford: Clarendon Press, 1993; repr. 2001).

Bath, Michael, *Speaking Pictures: English Emblem Books and Renaissance Culture* (London: Longman, 1994).

Beaurline, L. A., *Jonson and Elizabethan Comedy: Essays in Dramatic Rhetoric* (San Marino: Huntington Library, 1978).

Beck, Thomasina, *Gardening with Silk and Gold: A History of Gardens in Embroidery* (London: David and Charles, 1997).

Bednarz, James, *Shakespeare and the Poets' War* (New York: Columbia University Press, 2001).

Beecher, Donald A., 'The Tudor Translation of Colonna's *Hypnerotomachia*', *Cahiers élisabéthains*, 15 (1979), 1–16.

Bellamy, Elizabeth J., *Translations of Power: Narcissism and the Unconscious in Epic History* (Ithaca, NY: Cornell University Press, 1992).

Bender, John B., *Spenser and Literary Pictorialism* (Princeton: Princeton University Press, 1972).

Bengtson, Jonathan, 'Saint George and the Formation of English Nationalism', *Journal of Medieval and Early Modern Studies*, 27 (1997), 317–40.

Bennett, Josephine Waters, *The Evolution of the Faerie Queene* (Chicago: University of Chicago Press, 1942).

Berger, Harry, 'Actaeon at the Hinder Gate: The Stag Party in Spenser's Garden of Adonis', in *Desire in the Renaissance: Psychoanalysis and Literature* (Princeton: Princeton University Press, 1994), 91–119.

Berger, Harry, *The Allegorical Temper: Vision and Reality in Book II of Spenser's* Faerie Queene (New Haven: Yale University Press, 1957).

—— 'Displacing Autophobia in *Faerie Queene* I: Ethics, Gender, and Oppositional Reading in the Spenserian Text', *English Literary Renaissance*, 28 (1998), 163–82.

—— *Revisionary Play: Studies in the Spenserian Dynamics* (Berkeley and Los Angeles: University of California Press, 1988).

Bergeron, David, 'The Bible in English Renaissance Civic Pageants', *Comparative Drama*, 20 (1986), 160–70.

—— *English Civic Pageantry 1558–1642* (London: Edward Arnold, 1971).

—— *Practicing Renaissance Scholarship: Plays and Pageants, Patrons and Politics* (Pittsburgh: Duquesne University Press, 2000).

—— 'Representation in English Renaissance Civic Pageants', *Theatre Journal*, 40 (1988), 319–31.

—— *Twentieth-Century Criticism of English Masques, Pageants, and Entertainments: 1558–1642* (San Antonio, Tex.: Trinity University Press, 1972).

—— 'Urban Pastoralism in English Civic Pageants', in G. R. Hibbard (ed.), *The Elizabethan Theatre* (Ontario: P. D. Meany, 1982), 129–43.

Bergvall, Åke, 'Between Eusebius and Augustine: Una and the Cult of Elizabeth', *English Literary Renaissance*, 27 (1997), 3–30.

Berlin, Michael, 'Civic Ceremony in Early Modern London', *Urban History Yearbook* (1986), 15–27.

Berringer, Ralph W., 'Jonson's *Cynthia's Revels* and the War of the Theatres', *Philological Quarterly*, 22 (1943), 1–22.

Berry, Edward, *The Making of Sir Philip Sidney* (Toronto: University of Toronto Press, 1988).

Berry, Philippa, *Of Chastity and Power: Elizabethan Literature and the Unmarried Queen* (London: Routledge, 1989).

Bevington, David, *Tudor Drama and Politics: A Critical Approach to Topical Meaning* (Cambridge, Mass.: Harvard University Press, 1968).

Biddle, Martin, 'The Gardens of Nonsuch: Sources and Dating', *Garden History*, 27 (1999), 145–83.

—— (ed.), *Nonsuch Palace: The Material Culture of a Noble Restoration Household* (Oxford: Oxbow Books, 2005).

Bieman, Elizabeth, *Plato Baptized: Towards the Interpretation of Spenser's Mimetic Fictions* (Toronto: University of Toronto Press, 1988).

Bird, Sarah, Edmondson, John, Nicholson, Susan, Stainer-Hutchins, Katherine, and Taylor, Christopher, 'A Late Sixteenth-Century Garden: Fact or Fantasy? The Portrait of Sir George Delves in the Walker Art Gallery, Liverpool', *Garden History*, 24 (1996), 167–83.

Black, Lynette C., 'Prudence in Book II of *The Faerie Queene*', *Spenser Studies*, 13 (1999), 65–88.

Bland, Mark, ' "As Far from All Reuolt": Sir John Salusbury, Christ Church MS 184, and Ben Jonson's First Ode', *English Manuscript Studies*, 8 (2000), 43–78.

Block, Alexandra, and Rothstein, Eric, 'Argument and "Representation" in *The Faerie Queene*, Book III', *Spenser Studies*, 19 (2004), 177–207.

Blomefield, Francis, *An Essay Towards a Topographical History of the County of Norfolk* (London: William Miller, 1807).

Bonahue, Edward T., 'Citizen History: Stow's *Survey of London*', *Studies in English Literature*, 38 (1998), 61–85.

Braunmuller, A. R., *George Peele* (Boston: Twayne Publishers, 1983).

Breitenberg, Mark, 'Reading Elizabethan Iconicity: *Gorboduc* and the Semiotics of Reform', *English Literary Renaissance*, 18 (1988), 194–217.

Bresc-Boutier, Geneviève, 'Fontaines laïques de la première Renaissance française: les marbres de Tours, de Blois et de Gaillon', in *Sources et fontaines du Moyen Âge à l'Âge Baroque: actes du colloque tenu à l'Université Paul Valéry, Montpellier III, les 28, 29 et 30 novembre 1996* (Paris: Honoré Champion Éditeur, 1998), 185–201.

Brighton, Trevor, 'Chatsworth's Sixteenth-Century Parks and Gardens', *Garden History*, 23 (1995), 29–55.

Britland, Karen, 'Circe's Cup: Wine and Women in Early Modern Drama', in Adam Smyth (ed.), *A Pleasing Sinne: Drink and Conviviality in Seventeenth-Century England*, Studies in Renaissance Literature (Woodbridge: D. S. Brewer, 2004), 109–25.

Brooke, N. S., 'C. S. Lewis and Spenser: Nature, Art and the Bower of Bliss', in *Essential Articles for the Study of Edmund Spenser* (Hamden, Conn.: Archon Books, 1972), 13–28.

Brooks-Davies, Douglas, *Spenser's Faerie Queene: A Critical Commentary on Books I and II* (Manchester: Manchester University Press, 1977).

Brown, Patricia Fortini, *Venice & Antiquity: The Venetian Sense of the Past* (New Haven: Yale University Press, 1996).

Brown, Sarah Annes, 'Arachne's Web: Intertextual Mythography and the Renaissance Actaeon', in Neil Rhodes and Jonathan Sawday (eds.), *The Renaissance Computer: Knowledge Technology in the First Age of Print* (London: Routledge, 2000), 120–34.

Bryant, J. A., *The Compassionate Satirist: Ben Jonson and his Imperfect World* (Athens: University of Georgia Press, 1972).

Bulger, Thomas Francis, *The Historical Changes and Exchanges as Depicted by Spenser in* The Faerie Queene (Lewiston, NY: Edwin Mellen Press, 1993).

Burke, Peter, 'Popular Culture in Seventeenth-Century London', *London Journal*, 3 (1977), 143–60.

Burrow, Colin, *Edmund Spenser*, Writers and their Work (Plymouth: Northcote House, 1996).

—— *Epic Romance: Homer to Milton* (Oxford: Clarendon Press, 1993).

—— 'Original Fictions: Metamorphoses in *The Faerie Queene*', in Charles Martindale (ed.), *Ovid Renewed: Ovidian Influences on Literature and Art from the Middle Ages to the Twentieth Century* (Cambridge: Cambridge University Press, 1988), 99–119.

Bushnell, Rebecca, *Green Desire: Imagining Early Modern English Gardens* (Ithaca, NY: Cornell University Press, 2003).

Butler, Todd, 'That "Saluage Nation": Contextualising the Multitudes in Edmund Spenser's *The Faerie Queene*', *Spenser Studies*, 19 (2004), 93–124.

Buxton, John, *Elizabethan Taste* (London: Macmillan, 1963).

—— *Sir Philip Sidney and the English Renaissance* (London: Macmillan, 1964).

Cain, Tom, '"Satyres, That Girde and Fart at the Time": *Poetaster* and the Essex Rebellion', in Julie Sanders, Kate Chedgzoy, and Susan Wiseman (eds.), *Refashioning Ben Jonson: Gender, Politics and the Jonsonian Canon* (London: Macmillan, 1998), 48–70.

Campbell, Oscar, *Comicall Satyre and Shakespeare's Troilus and Cressida* (San Marino, Calif.: Huntington Library, 1938).

Carroll, Michael, *Irish Pilgrimage: Holy Wells and Popular Catholic Devotion* (Baltimore: Johns Hopkins University Press, 1999).

Casanova-Robin, Hélène, *Diane et Actéon: éclats et reflets d'un mythe à la Renaissance et à l'Âge Baroque* (Paris: Honoré Champion Éditeur, 2003).

Cavanagh, Sheila T., *Wanton Eyes and Chaste Desires: Female Sexuality in The Faerie Queene* (Bloomington: Indiana University Press, 1994).

Cave, Richard Allen, *Ben Jonson*, English Dramatists (London: Macmillan, 1991).

Chambers, E. K., *The Elizabethan Stage* (Oxford: Clarendon Press, 1923).

Chan, Mary, *Music in the Theatre of Ben Jonson* (Oxford: Clarendon Press, 1980).

Charlesworth, Michael (ed.), *The English Garden: Literary Sources and Documents* (Mountfield: Helm Information Ltd., 1993).

—— 'Movement, Intersubjectivity, and Mercantile Morality at Stourhead', in Michel Conan (ed.), *Landscape Design and the Experience of Motion* (Washington, DC: Dumbarton Oaks Research Library and Collection, 2003), 263–85.

Cheney, Donald, 'Spenser's Hermaphrodite and the 1590 *Faerie Queene*', *PMLA* 87 (1972), 192–200.

—— *Spenser's Image of Nature: Wild Man and Shepherd in* The Faerie Queene (New Haven: Yale University Press, 1966).

Cheney, Liana de Girolami, 'Francesco Colonna's *Hypnerotomachia Poliphili*: A Garden of Neoplatonic Love', *Discoveries*, 21 (2004), 3–4, 12–17.

Cheney, Patrick, *Marlowe's Counterfeit Profession: Ovid, Spenser, Counter-Nationhood* (Toronto: University of Toronto Press, 1997).

Cirillo, A. R., 'The Fair Hermaphrodite: Love-Union in the Poetry of Donne and Spenser', *Studies in English Literature*, 9 (1969), 81–95.

Clare, Janet, *Art Made Tongue-Tied by Authority: Elizabethan and Jacobean Dramatic Censorship* (Manchester: Manchester University Press, 1999).

—— 'Jonson's "Comical Satires" and the Art of Courtly Compliment', in Julie Sanders, Kate Chedgzoy, and Susan Wiseman (eds.), *Refashioning Ben Jonson: Gender, Politics and the Jonsonian Canon* (London: Macmillan, 1998), 28–48.

Coffin, David R., *The Villa d'Este at Tivoli* (Princeton: Princeton University Press, 1960).

Cole, Mary Hill, 'Ceremonial Dialogue Between Elizabeth I and her Civic Hosts', in Douglas F. Rutledge (ed.), *Ceremony and Text in the Renaissance* (Newark, NJ: University of Delaware Press, 1996), 84–100.

Colvin, Howard M., 'Royal Gardens in Medieval England', in Elisabeth B. MacDougall (ed.), *Medieval Gardens* (Washington, DC: Dumbarton Oaks, 1986), 7–22.

—— et al., *The History of the King's Works*, iv: *1485–1660 (Part 2)* (London: HMSO, 1982).

Comito, Terry, 'Beauty Bare: Speaking Waters and Fountains in Renaissance Literature', in Elisabeth MacDougall (ed.), *Fons Sapientiae: Renaissance Garden Fountains* (Washington, DC: Dumbarton Oaks, 1978), 15–58.

—— 'Caliban's Dream: The Topography of Some Shakespeare Gardens', *Shakespeare Studies*, 14 (1981), 23–54.

Conan, Michel, 'Landscape Metaphors and Metamorphosis of Time', in Michel Conan (ed.), *Landscape Design and the Experience of Motion* (Washington, DC: Dumbarton Oaks Research Library and Collection, 2003), 287–317.

Conelli, Maria Ann, 'Boboli Gardens: Fountains and Propaganda in Sixteenth-Century Florence', *Studies in the History of Gardens and Designed Landscapes*, 18 (1998), 300–15.

Cook, Patrick J., *Milton, Spenser and the Epic Tradition* (Aldershot: Scolar Press, 1996).

Cool, Kenneth E., 'The Petrarchan Landscape as Palimpsest', *Journal of Medieval and Renaissance Studies*, 11 (1981), 83–100.

Cooney, Helen, 'Guyon and his Palmer: Spenser's Emblem of Temperance', *Review of English Studies*, 51 (2000), 169–92.

Cooper, Helen, *The English Romance in Time: Transforming Motifs from Geoffrey of Monmouth to the Death of Shakespeare* (Oxford: Oxford University Press, 2004).

—— 'Location and Meaning in Masque, Morality and Royal Entertainment', in David Lindley (ed.), *The Court Masque* (Manchester: Manchester University Press, 1984), 135–48.

Cosgrove, Denis E., *Social Formation and Symbolic Landscape* (London: Croom Helm, 1984).

Costley, Clare L., 'David, Bathsheba, and the Penitential Psalms', *Renaissance Quarterly*, 57 (2004), 1235–77.

Craft, William, *Labyrinth of Desire: Invention and Culture in the Work of Sir Philip Sidney* (Newark, NJ: University of Delaware Press, 1994).

Craig, Joanne, ' "All Flesh Doth Frailtie Breed": Mothers and Children in *The Faerie Queene*', *Texas Studies in Literature and Language*, 42 (2000), 16–32.

Crane, Mary Thomas, *Framing Authority: Sayings, Self, and Society in Sixteenth-Century England* (Princeton: Princeton University Press, 1993).

Crowley, James P., ' "He Took his Religion by Trust": The Matter of Ben Jonson's Conversion', *Renaissance and Reformation/Renaissance et réforme*, 22 (1998), 53–70.

Cullen, Patrick, *Infernal Triad: The Flesh, the World, and the Devil in Spenser and Milton* (Princeton: Princeton University Press, 1974).

Curtius, Ernst Robert, *European Literature and the Latin Middle Ages*, trans. Willard R. Trask (Princeton: Princeton University Press, 1983).

Daly, Peter M., *Literature in the Light of the Emblem: Structural Parallels between the Emblem and Literature in the Sixteenth and Seventeenth Centuries* (Toronto: University of Toronto Press, 1979).

Dasenbrock, Reed Way, *Imitating the Italians: Wyatt, Spenser, Synge, Pound, Joyce* (Baltimore: Johns Hopkins University Press, 1991).

Dauber, Antoinette, 'The Art of Veiling in the Bower of Bliss', *Spenser Studies*, 1 (1980), 163–75.

Davenport, Cyril, 'Embroidered Bindings of Bibles in the Possession of the British and Foreign Bible Society', *Burlington Magazine*, 4 (1904), 267–80.

Davidson, Clifford, 'Repentance and the Fountain: The Transformation of Symbols in English Emblem Books', in Michael Bath, John Manning, and Alan R. Young (eds.), *The Art of the Emblem: Essays in Honor of Karl Josef Höltgen* (New York: AMS Press, 1993), 5–37.

Davies, Douglas, 'The Evocative Symbolism of Trees', in Denis Cosgrove and Stephen Daniels (eds.), *The Iconography of Landscape: Essays on the Symbolic Representation, Design and Use of Past Environments* (Cambridge: Cambridge University Press, 1988), 32–42.

Dent, John, *The Quest for Nonsuch* (2nd edn. Sutton: London Borough of Sutton Leisure Services, 1970; repr. 1981, 1988).

Deonna, W., 'Fontaines anthropomorphes: la femme aux seins jaillissants et l'enfant "mingens" ', *Genava*, 6 (1958), 239–96.

Dessen, Alan C., and Thomson, Leslie, *A Dictionary of Stage Directions in English Drama 1580–1642* (Cambridge: Cambridge University Press, 1999).

Dickinson, J. C., *The Shrine of Our Lady at Walsingham* (Cambridge: Cambridge University Press, 1956).

Digangi, Mario, ' "Male Deformities": Narcissus and the Reformation of Courtly Manners in *Cynthia's Revels*', in Goran V. Stanivukovic (ed.), *Ovid and the Renaissance Body* (Toronto: University of Toronto Press, 2001), 94–110.

Dillon, Janette, *Theatre, Court and City, 1595–1610: Drama and Social Space in London* (Cambridge: Cambridge University Press, 2000).

Dodge, R. E. Neil, 'The Well of Life and the Tree of Life', *Modern Philology*, 6 (1908–9), 191–6.

Doebler, Bettie Anne, 'Venus-Humanitas: An Iconic Elizabeth', *Journal of European Studies*, 12 (1982), 233–48.

Donaldson, Ian, *Jonson's Magic Houses: Essays in Interpretation* (Oxford: Clarendon Press, 1997).

Dorez, Léon, 'Des origines et de la diffusion du "Songe de Poliphile" ', *Revue des bibliothèques*, 6 (1896), 239–83.

Dronke, Peter, 'Introduction', in *Hypnerotomachia Poliphili (Venetiis, Aldo Manuzio, 1499)* (Zaragoza: Ediciones del Pórtico, 1981), 1–70.

Duffy, Eamon, *The Stripping of the Altars: Traditional Religion in England c.1400–c.1580* (New Haven: Yale University Press, 1992).

Dughi, Thomas A., 'Redcrosse's "Springing Well" of Scriptural Faith', *Studies in English Literature*, 37 (1997), 21–38.

Duncan-Jones, Katherine, *Sir Philip Sidney, Courtier Poet* (London: Hamish Hamilton, 1991).

—— 'Sidney and Titian', in John Carey and Helen Peters (eds.), *English Renaissance Studies Presented to Dame Helen Gardner in Honour of her Seventieth Birthday* (Oxford: Clarendon Press, 1980), 1–11.

Dundas, Judith, *The Spider and the Bee: The Artistry of Spenser's* Faerie Queene (Urbana: University of Illinois Press, 1985).

Dundas, Judith, ' "Those Beautiful Characters of Sense": Classical Deities and the Court Masque', *Comparative Drama*, 16 (1982), 166–79.

Durling, Robert M., 'The Bower of Bliss and Armida's Palace', in A. C. Hamilton (ed.), *Essential Articles for the Study of Edmund Spenser* (Hamden, Conn.: Archon Books, 1972), 113–24.

DuRocher, Richard J., 'Guiding the Glance: Spenser, Milton, and "Venus looking glas" ', *Journal of English and Germanic Philology*, 92 (1993), 325–41.

Dutton, Richard, *Ben Jonson: Authority: Criticism* (London: Macmillan, 1996).

Eggert, Katherine, 'Spenser's Ravishment: Rape and Rapture in *The Faerie Queene*', *Representations*, 70 (2000), 1–26.

Ekeblad, Inge-Stina, '*The Love of King David and Fair Bethsabe*: A Note on George Peele's Biblical Drama', *English Studies*, 39 (1958), 57–62.

Elsky, Martin, *Authorizing Words: Speech, Writing, and Print in the English Renaissance* (London: Cornell University Press, 1989).

Engammare, Max, 'David côté jardin: Bethsabée, modèle et anti-modèle littéraire à la Renaissance', in *Cité des hommes, cité de Dieu: travaux sur la littéraire de la Renaissance en l'honneur de Daniel Ménager* (Geneva: Droz, 2003), 533–42.

—— 'La Morale ou la beauté? Illustrations des amours de David et Bethsabée (II Samuel 11–12) dans les bibles des xvᵉ–xviiᵉ siècles', in Bertram Schwarzbach (ed.), *La Bible imprimée dans l'Europe moderne* (Paris: Bibliothèque Nationale de France, 1999), 447–76.

Erickson, Wayne, *Mapping the Faerie Queene: Quest Structures and the World of the Poem* (New York: Garland Publishing, 1996).

Esolen, Anthony, 'Spenserian Allegory and the Clash of Narrative Worlds', *Thalia: Studies in Literary Humor*, 11 (1989), 3–13.

—— 'Spenser's "Alma Venus": Energy and Economics in the Bower of Bliss', *English Literary Renaissance*, 23 (1993), 267–86.

Evans, K. W., 'The Political Philosophy of Jonson's Masques', *Work in Progress*, 1 (1972), 43–95.

Evans, Robert C., *Ben Jonson and the Politics of Patronage* (London: Associated Universities Press, 1989).

Ewbank, Inga-Stina, 'The House of David in Renaissance Drama: A Comparative Study', *Renaissance Drama*, 8 (1965), 3–40.

—— ' "What Words, What Looks, What Wonders?" Language and Spectacle in the Theatre of George Peele', in G. R. Hibbard (ed.), *The Elizabethan Theatre 5* (London: Macmillan, 1975), 124–54.

Farmer, Norman K., *Poets and the Visual Arts in Renaissance England* (Austin: University of Texas Press, 1984).

—— 'The World's New Body: Spenser's *Faerie Queene* Book II, St Paul's Epistles and Reformation England', in Jean R. Brink and William F. Gentrup (eds.), *Renaissance Culture in Context: Theory and Practice* (Aldershot: Scolar Press, 1993), 75–85.

Fellows, Jennifer, 'St George as Romance Hero', *Reading Medieval Studies*, 19 (1993), 27–54.

Feuillerat, Albert, *Documents Relating to the Office of the Revels in the Time of Queen Elizabeth* (Louvain: Bang, 1908).

Fichter, Andrew, *Poets Historical: Dynastic Epic in the Renaissance* (New Haven: Yale University Press, 1982).

Fierz-David, Linda, *The Dream of Poliphilo*, trans. Mary Hottinger (New York: Pantheon, 1950).

Finaldi, Gabriele, *The Image of Christ* (London: National Gallery Company Limited, 2000).

Fitzpatrick, Joan, 'Spenser and Land: Political Conflict Resolved in Physical Topography', *Ben Jonson Journal*, 7 (2000), 365–77.

Fleming, Juliet, 'Dictionary English and the Female Tongue', in Richard Burt and John Michael Archer (eds.), *Enclosure Acts: Sexuality, Property and Culture in Early Modern England* (Ithaca, NY: Cornell University Press, 1994), 290–325.

—— *Graffiti and the Writing Arts of Early Modern England* (London: Reaktion, 2001).

Fowler, Alastair, 'The Image of Mortality: *The Faerie Queene*, II.i–ii', in A. C. Hamilton (ed.), *Essential Articles for the Study of Edmund Spenser* (Hamden, Conn.: Archon Books, 1972), 139–52.

—— 'Neoplatonic Order in *The Faerie Queene* (1973)', in Peter Bayley (ed.), *Spenser: The Faerie Queene: A Casebook* (London: Macmillan, 1977), 224–39.

—— *Spenser and the Numbers of Time* (London: Routledge and Kegan Paul, 1964).

Fragonard, Marie-Madeleine, 'L'Adieu aux fées', in *Sources et fontaines du Moyen Âge à l'Âge Baroque* (Paris: Honoré Champion Éditeur, 1998), 3–8.

Fraser, Antonia, *The Gunpowder Plot: Terror and Faith in 1605* (London: Weidenfeld and Nicolson, 1996).

Frye, Northrop, *The Great Code: The Bible and Literature* (London: Routledge and Kegan Paul, 1982).

Frye, Susan, *Elizabeth I: The Competition for Representation* (New York: Oxford University Press, 1993).

Fukuda, Shohachi, 'The Numerological Patterning of *The Faerie Queene* I–III', *Spenser Studies*, 19 (2004), 37–63.

Fumerton, Patricia, *Cultural Aesthetics: Renaissance Literature and the Practice of Social Ornament* (Chicago: University of Chicago Press, 1991).

Furno, Martine, 'Imaginary Architecture and Antiquity: The Fountain of Venus in Francesco Colonna's *Hypnerotomachia Poliphili*', in Alina Payne, Ann Kuttner, and Rebekah Smick (eds.), *Antiquity and its Interpreters* (Cambridge: Cambridge University Press, 2000), 70–82.

Gallais, Pierre, *La Fée à la fontaine et à l'arbre: un archétype du conte merveilleux et du récit courtois* (Amsterdam: Rodopi, 1992).

Gent, Lucy, '*Hypnerotomachia Poliphili*', in A. C. Hamilton (ed.), *The Spenser Encyclopedia* (Toronto: University of Toronto Press, 1990), 385–6.

—— 'Introduction', in Lucy Gent (ed.), *Albion's Classicism: The Visual Arts in Britain, 1550–1660* (New Haven: Yale University Press, 1995), 1–18.

—— *Picture and Poetry 1560–1620* (Leamington Spa: James Hall, 1981).

Gerrish, B. A., *Grace and Gratitude: The Eucharistic Theology of John Calvin* (Edinburgh: T. & T. Clark, 1993).

Giamatti, A. Bartlett, *The Earthly Paradise and the Renaissance Epic* (Princeton: Princeton University Press, 1966).

Giannetto, Raffaella Fabiani, 'Writing the Garden in the Age of Humanism: Petrarch and Boccaccio', *Studies in the History of Gardens and Designed Landscapes*, 23 (2003), 231–57.

Gilbert, Allan H., 'The Function of the Masques in *Cynthia's Revels*', *Philological Quarterly*, 22 (1943), 211–30.

Gillespie, Raymond, *Devoted People: Belief and Religion in Early Modern Ireland* (Manchester: Manchester University Press, 1997).

Gleckman, Jason, 'Providential Love and Suffering in *The Faerie Queene*, Book III', *Spenser Studies*, 19 (2004), 209–35.

Gless, Darryl J., *Interpretation and Theology in Spenser* (Cambridge: Cambridge University Press, 1994).

Goldberg, Jonathan, *Endlesse Worke: Spenser and the Structures of Discourse* (Baltimore: Johns Hopkins University Press, 1981).

—— *James I and the Politics of Literature: Jonson, Shakespeare, Donne, and their Contemporaries* (Baltimore: Johns Hopkins University Press, 1983).

Goldring, Elizabeth, ' "A Mercer Ye Wot az We Be": The Authorship of the Kenilworth *Letter* Reconsidered', *English Literary Renaissance*, forthcoming.

—— 'Portraits of Queen Elizabeth I and the Earl of Leicester for Kenilworth Castle', *Burlington Magazine*, 147 (2005), 654–60.

—— 'Portraiture, Patronage and the Progresses: Robert Dudley, Earl of Leicester and the Kenilworth Festivities of 1575', in Jayne Archer, Elizabeth Goldring, and Sarah Knight (eds.), *The Progresses, Pageants and Entertainments of Queen Elizabeth I* (Oxford: Oxford University Press, 2007), 163–88.

Grabes, Herbert, *The Mutable Glass: Mirror-Imagery in Titles and Texts of the Middle Ages and English Renaissance* (Cambridge: Cambridge University Press, 1982).

Greene, Thomas, *The Light in Troy: Imitation and Discovery in Renaissance Poetry* (New Haven: Yale University Press, 1982).

—— 'Petrarch and the Humanist Hermeneutic', in Giose Rimanelli and Kenneth John Atchity (eds.), *Italian Literature: Roots and Branches: Essays in Honor of Thomas Goddard Bergin* (New Haven: Yale University Press, 1976), 201–24.

Greenfield, Sayre N., 'Reading Love in the Geography of *The Faerie Queene*, Book III', *Philological Quarterly*, 68 (1989), 425–42.

Gregerson, Linda, *The Reformation of the Subject: Spenser, Milton, and the English Protestant Epic* (Cambridge: Cambridge University Press, 1995).

Griggs, Tamara, 'Promoting the Past: The *Hypnerotomachia Poliphili* as Antiquarian Enterprise', *Word & Image*, 14 (1998), 17–39.

Gurr, Andrew, *The Shakespearean Stage* (Cambridge: Cambridge University Press, 1992).

Guy, John (ed.), *The Reign of Elizabeth I: Court and Culture in the Last Decade* (Cambridge: Cambridge University Press, 1995).

Habicht, Werner, 'Tree Properties and Tree Scenes in Elizabethan Theatre', *Renaissance Drama*, 4 (1971), 69–92.

Hackett, Helen, *Virgin Mother, Maiden Queen: Elizabeth I and the Cult of the Virgin Mary* (London: Macmillan, 1996).

Hadfield, Andrew, *Edmund Spenser's Irish Experience: Wilde Fruit and Saluage Soyl* (Oxford: Clarendon Press, 1997).

Hall, Anne D., 'The Actaeon Myth and Allegorical Reading in Spenser's "Two Cantos of Mutabilitie"', *Sixteenth Century Journal*, 26 (1995), 561–75.

Hall, William Keith, 'A Topography of Time: Historical Narration in John Stow's *Survey of London*', *Studies in Philology*, 88 (1991), 1–15.

Hamilton, A. C., ' "Like Race to Runne": The Parallel Structure of *The Faerie Queene*, Books I and II', *PMLA* 73 (1958), 327–34.

—— (ed.), *The Spenser Encyclopedia* (Toronto: University of Toronto Press, 1990).

—— *The Structure of Allegory in The Faerie Queene* (Oxford: Clarendon Press, 1961).

—— 'A Theological Reading of *The Faerie Queene*, Book I', *English Literary History*, 25 (1958), 155–62.

Hammer, Paul E. J., ' "Absolute and Sovereign Mistress of her Grace?" Queen Elizabeth I and her Favourites, 1581–1592', in J. H. Elliott and L. W. B. Brockliss (eds.), *The World of the Favourite* (New Haven: Yale University Press, 1999), 38–53.

—— *The Polarisation of Elizabethan Politics: The Political Career of Robert Devereux, 2nd Earl of Essex, 1585–1597* (Cambridge: Cambridge University Press, 1999).

Hankins, John Erskine, *Source and Meaning in Spenser's Allegory: A Study of The Faerie Queene* (Oxford: Clarendon Press, 1971).

—— 'Spenser and the Revelation of St John', *PMLA* 60 (1945), 364–81.

Hansen, Niels Bugge, *That Pleasant Place: The Representation of Ideal Landscape in English Literature from the 14th to the 17th Century* (Copenhagen: Akademik Forlag, 1973).

Harbage, Alfred, *Annals of English Drama* (London: Routledge, 1989).

Harbison, Robert, *Eccentric Spaces* (London: André Deutsch, 1977).

Hardin, William, ' "Pipe-Pilgrimages" and "Fruitfull Rivers": Thomas Middleton's Civic Entertainments and the Water Supply of Early Stuart London', *Renaissance Papers* (1993), 63–73.

Harris, Jonathan Gil, 'This Is Not a Pipe: Water Supply, Incontinent Sources, and the Leaky Body Politic', in Richard Burt and John Michael Archer (eds.), *Enclosure Acts: Sexuality, Property and Culture in Early Modern England* (Ithaca, NY: Cornell University Press, 1994), 203–28.

Hart, Vaughan, *Art and Magic in the Court of the Stuarts* (London: Routledge, 1994).

Hayes, T. Wilson, 'Ben Jonson's Libertine Catholicism', in William P. Shaw (ed.), *Praise Disjoined: Changing Patterns of Salvation in 17th-Century English Literature* (New York: Peter Lang, 1991), 119–36.

Heale, Elizabeth, *The Faerie Queene: A Reader's Guide* (Cambridge: Cambridge University Press, 1987).

Hearn, Karen (ed.), *Dynasties: Painting in Tudor and Jacobean England 1530–1630* (London: Tate Gallery, 1995).

Heath, John, *Actaeon, the Unmannerly Intruder: The Myth and its Meaning in Classical Literature* (New York: Peter Lang, 1992).

Heffernan, Carol Falvo, 'Wells and Streams in Three Chaucerian Gardens', *Papers on Language and Literature*, 15 (1979), 339–58.

Helgerson, Richard, 'The Land Speaks: Cartography, Chorography, and Subversion in Renaissance England', in Stephen Greenblatt (ed.), *Representing the English Renaissance* (Berkeley and Los Angeles: University of California Press, 1986), 326–61.

—— *Self-Crowned Laureates: Spenser, Jonson, Milton and the Literary System* (Berkeley and Los Angeles: University of California Press, 1983).

Hembry, Phyllis, *The English Spa, 1560–1815: A Social History* (London: Athlone Press, 1990).

Henderson, Paula, 'The Architecture of the Tudor Garden', *Garden History*, 27 (1999), 54–72.

—— 'A Shared Passion: The Cecils and their Gardens', in Pauline Croft (ed.), *Patronage, Culture and Power: The Early Cecils, 1558–1612* (New Haven: Yale University Press, 2002), 99–120.

—— 'Sir Francis Bacon's Water Gardens at Gorhambury', *Garden History*, 20 (1992), 116–31.

—— *The Tudor House and Garden* (New Haven: Yale University Press, 2005).

Hendrix, Howard, ' "Those Wandring Eyes of His": Watching Guyon Watch the Naked Damsels Wrestling', *Assays*, 7 (1992), 71–85.

Heninger, S. K., 'The Orgoglio Episode in *The Faerie Queene*', *English Literary History*, 26 (1959), 183–6.

—— 'Speaking Pictures: Sidney's Rapprochement Between Poetry and Painting', in Gary F. Waller and Michael D. Moore (eds.), *Sir Philip Sidney and the Interpretation of Renaissance Culture: The Poet in his Time and in Ours: A Collection of Critical and Scholarly Essays* (London: Croom Helm, 1984), 3–16.

Herendeen, Wyman H., *From Landscape to Literature: The River and the Myth of Geography* (Pittsburgh: Duquesne University Press, 1986).

—— 'A New Way to Pay Old Debts: Pretexts to the 1616 Folio', in Jennifer Brady and W. H. Herendeen (eds.), *Ben Jonson's 1616 Folio* (London: Associated University Presses, 1991), 38–63.

Hieatt, A. Kent, and Prescott, Anne Lake, 'Contemporizing Antiquity: The *Hypnerotomachia* and its Afterlife in France', *Word & Image*, 8/4 (1992), 291–321.

Highley, Christopher, *Shakespeare, Spenser, and the Crisis in Ireland* (Cambridge: Cambridge University Press, 1997).

Höltgen, Karl Josef, 'Sir Robert Dallington (1561–1637): Author, Traveler, and Pioneer of Taste', *Huntington Library Quarterly*, 47 (1984), 147–77.

Hough, Graham, *The First Commentary on The Faerie Queene* (privately published, 1964).

Howarth, David, *Images of Rule: Art and Politics in the English Renaissance, 1485–1649* (London: Macmillan, 1997).

Howe, John M., 'The Conversion of the Physical World: The Creation of a Christian Landscape', in James Muldoon (ed.), *Varieties of Religious Conversion in the Middle Ages* (Gainesville: University Press of Florida, 1997), 63–78.

Howes, Laura K., *Chaucer's Gardens and the Language of Convention* (Gainesville: University Press of Florida, 1997).

Hulse, Clark, *The Rule of Art: Literature and Painting in the Renaissance* (Chicago: University of Chicago Press, 1990).

Humphreys, John, *Elizabethan Sheldon Tapestries* (London: Oxford University Press, 1929).

Hunt, John Dixon, 'Approaches (New and Old) to Garden History', in Michel Conan (ed.), *Perspectives on Garden History* (Washington, DC: Dumbarton Oaks Research Library and Collection, 1999), 77–90.

—— 'Experiencing Gardens in the *Hypnerotomachia Polofili*', *Word & Image*, 14 (1998), 109–19.

—— *Garden and Grove: The Italian Renaissance Garden in the English Imagination 1600–1750.* (rev. edn. Philadelphia: University of Pennsylvania Press, 1996).

—— *Greater Perfections: The Practice of Garden Theory* (London: Thames and Hudson, 2000).

Huttar, Charles A., 'Frail Grass and Firm Tree: David as a Model of Repentance in the Middle Ages and Early Renaissance', in Raymond-Jean Frontain and Jan Wojcik (eds.), *The David Myth in Western Literature* (West Lafayette, Ind.: Purdue University Press, 1980), 38–54.

Imbrie, Ann E., ' "Playing Legerdemaine with the Scripture": Parodic Sermons in *The Faerie Queene*', *English Literary Renaissance*, 17 (1987), 142–55.

Ivins, William M., Jr., 'Artistic Aspects of Fifteenth-Century Printing', *Papers of the Bibliographic Society of America*, 26 (1932), 1–51.

James, Mervyn, *Society, Politics and Culture: Studies in Early Modern England* (Cambridge: Cambridge University Press, 1986).

Jefferson, Ann, and Robey, David (eds.), *Modern Literary Theory: A Comparative Introduction* (London: B. T. Batsford, 1986).

Johnson, A. W., *Ben Jonson: Poetry and Architecture* (Oxford: Oxford University Press, 1994).

Jones, Ann Rosalind, and Stallybrass, Peter, *Renaissance Clothing and the Materials of Memory* (Cambridge: Cambridge University Press, 2000).

Jones, Francis, *The Holy Wells of Wales* (Cardiff: University of Wales Press, 1954).

Kane, Sean, *Spenser's Moral Allegory* (Toronto: University of Toronto Press, 1989).

Kaplan, M. Lindsay, *The Culture of Slander in Early Modern England* (Cambridge: Cambridge University Press, 1997).

Kaske, Carol V., 'The Dragon's Spark and Sting and the Structure of Red Cross's Dragon Fight: *The Faerie Queene* I.xi–xii', in A. C. Hamilton (ed.), *Essential Articles for the Study of Edmund Spenser* (Hamden, Conn.: Archon Books, 1972), 425–46.

—— ' "Religious Reuerence Doth Buriall Teene": Christian and Pagan in *The Faerie Queene*, II.i–ii', *Review of English Studies*, 30 (1979), 129–43.

—— *Spenser and Biblical Poetics* (Ithaca, NY: Cornell University Press, 1999).

Kawachi, Yoshiko, *Calendar of English Drama 1558–1642* (New York: Garland, 1986).

Kay, W. David, *Ben Jonson: A Literary Life* (London: Macmillan, 1995).

Keilen, Sean, *Vulgar Eloquence: On the Renaissance Invention of English Literature* (New Haven: Yale University Press, 2006).

Kernodle, George R., *From Act to Theatre: Form and Convention in the Renaissance* (Chicago: University of Chicago Press, 1944).

King, Andrew, *The Faerie Queene and Middle English Romance: The Matter of Just Memory* (Oxford: Clarendon Press, 2000).

King, John N., *Spenser's Poetry and the Reformation Tradition* (Princeton: Princeton University Press, 1990).

—— *Tudor Royal Iconography: Literature and Art in an Age of Religious Crisis* (Princeton: Princeton University Press, 1989).

Kingsford, Charles Lethbridge, 'Essex House, Formerly Leicester House and Exeter Inn', *Archaeologia*, 73 (1922–3), 1–54.

Kipling, Gordon, ' "He That Saw It Would Not Believe It": Anne Boleyn's Royal Entry into London', in Alexandra F. Johnston and Wim Hüsken (eds.), *Civic Ritual and Drama* (Amsterdam: Rodopi, 1997), 39–76.

—— 'Triumphal Drama: Form in English Civic Pageantry', *Renaissance Drama*, 8 (1977), 37–56.

—— 'Wonderfull Spectacles: Theater and Civic Culture', in John D. Cox and David Scott Kastan (eds.), *A New History of Early English Drama* (New York: Columbia University Press, 1997), 153–71.

Knapp, James A., *Illustrating the Past in Early Modern England: The Representation of History in Printed Books* (Aldershot: Ashgate, 2003).

Kostic, Veselin, *Spenser's Sources in Italian Poetry: A Study in Comparative Literature* (Belgrade: Filoloski fakultet Beogradskog univerziteta, 1969).

Kretzulesco-Quaranta, Emanuela, *Les Jardins du Songe 'Poliphile' et la mystique de la Renaissance* (Rome: Editrice Magma, 1976).

Krier, Theresa M., *Gazing on Secret Sights: Spenser, Classical Imitation, and the Decorums of Vision* (Ithaca, NY: Cornell University Press, 1990).

Kristeva, Julia, *Desire in Language: A Semiotic Approach to Literature and Art*, ed. Leon S. Roudiez, trans. Thomas Gora, Alice Jardine, and Leon S. Roudiez (Oxford: Basil Blackwell, 1982).

Kruger, Steven F., 'Dream Space and Masculinity', *Word & Image*, 14 (1998), 11–16.

Kuin, Roger, 'Sir Philip Sidney: The Courtier and the Text', *English Literary Renaissance*, 19 (1989), 249–71.

Landrum, Grace Warren, 'Imagery of Water in *The Faerie Queene*', *English Literary History*, 8 (1941), 198–213.

Lazzaro, Claudia, 'The Visual Language of Gender in Sixteenth-Century Garden Sculpture', in Marilyn Migiel and Juliana Schiesari (eds.), *Refiguring Woman: Perspectives on Gender and the Italian Renaissance* (Ithaca, NY: Cornell University Press, 1991), 71–113.

Lees-Jeffries, Hester, 'From the Fountain to the Well: Redcrosse Learns to Read', *Studies in Philology*, 100 (2003), 135–76.

—— 'Location as Metaphor: *Veritas Temporis Filia* (1559) and its Afterlife', in Jayne Archer, Elizabeth Goldring, and Sarah Knight (eds.), *The Progresses, Pageants and Entertainments of Queen Elizabeth I* (Oxford: Oxford University Press, 2007), 65–85.

—— 'A New Allusion by Jonson to Spenser and Essex?', *Notes and Queries*, 50 (March 2003), 63–5.

—— 'Sacred and Profane Love: Four Fountains in the *Hypnerotomachia* (1499) and the *Roman de la Rose*', *Word & Image*, 22 (2006), 1–13.

—— 'Sidney's Zelmane and the *Songe de Poliphile*', *Sidney Journal*, 21 (2003), 67–75.

Le Faivre, Liane, *Leon Battista Alberti's Hypnerotomachia Poliphili: Re-cognizing the Architectural Body in the Early Italian Renaissance* (Cambridge, Mass.: MIT Press, 1997).

Lefebvre, Henri, *The Production of Space*, trans. Donald Nicholson-Smith (Oxford: Basil Blackwell, 1991).

Leggatt, Alexander, *Ben Jonson: his Vision and his Art* (London: Methuen, 1981).

Lerner, Laurence, 'Ovid and the Elizabethans', in Charles Martindale (ed.), *Ovid Renewed: Ovidian Influences on Literature and Art from the Middle Ages to the Twentieth Century* (Cambridge: Cambridge University Press, 1988), 121–35.

Leslie, Michael, 'Edmund Spenser: Art and *The Faerie Queene* (Chatterton Lecture on Poetry)', *Proceedings of the British Academy*, 76 (1990), 73–107.

—— 'Gardens of Eloquence: Rhetoric, Landscape, and Literature in the English Renaissance', in Lynette Hunter (ed.), *Toward a Definition of Topos: Approaches to Analogical Reasoning* (London: Macmillan, 1991), 17–44.

—— 'The *Hypnerotomachia* and the Elizabethan Landscape Entertainments', *Word & Image*, 14 (1998), 130–44.

—— 'Spenser, Sidney and the Renaissance Garden', *English Literary Renaissance*, 22 (1992), 3–36.

—— *Spenser's 'Fierce Warres and Faithfull Loves': Martial and Chivalric Symbolism in The Faerie Queene* (Cambridge: D. S. Brewer, 1983).

—— and Raylor, Timothy (eds.), *Culture and Cultivation in Early Modern England: Writing and the Land* (Leicester: Leicester University Press, 1992).

Levin, Carole, *'The Heart and Stomach of a King': Elizabeth I and the Politics of Sex and Power* (Philadelphia: University of Pennsylvania Press, 1994).

Levin, Richard A., 'The Legende of the Redcrosse Knight and Una, or Of the Love of a Good Woman', *Studies in English Literature*, 31 (1991), 1–24.

Lewis, C. S., *The Allegory of Love: A Study in Medieval Tradition* (Oxford: Oxford University Press, 1936; repr. 1959).

Lister, Lalage, *Nonsuch: Pearl of the Realm* (Sutton: Sutton Leisure Services, 1992).

Lockerd, Benjamin G., *The Sacred Marriage: Psychic Integration in The Faerie Queene* (Lewisburg, Pa.: Bucknell University Press, 1987).

Loewenstein, Joseph, *Responsive Readings: Versions of Echo in Pastoral, Epic, and the Jonsonian Masque* (New Haven: Yale University Press, 1984).

Lowry, Martin, *The World of Aldus Manutius: Business and Scholarship in Renaissance Venice* (Oxford: Basil Blackwell, 1979).

Luborsky, Ruth Samson, and Ingram, Elizabeth Morley, *A Guide to English Illustrated Books 1536–1603* (Tempe, Ariz.: Medieval and Renaissance Texts and Studies, 1998).

Lyne, Raphael, 'Grille's Moral Dialogue: Spenser and Plutarch', *Spenser Studies*, 19 (2004), 159–76.

McCabe, Richard A., 'The Masks of Duessa: Spenser, Mary Queen of Scots, and James VI', *English Literary Renaissance*, 17 (1987), 224–42.

McCabe, Richard A., *The Pillars of Eternity: Time and Providence in The Faerie Queene* (Dublin: Irish Academic Press, 1989).

MacCaffrey, Isabel G., *Spenser's Allegory: The Anatomy of Imagination* (Princeton: Princeton University Press, 1976).

MacCaffrey, Wallace, *Elizabeth I: War and Politics 1588–1603* (Princeton: Princeton University Press, 1992).

McCoy, Richard C., *The Rites of Knighthood: The Literature and Politics of Elizabethan Chivalry* (Berkeley and Los Angeles: University of California Press, 1989).

MacDougall, Elisabeth B. (ed.), *Fons Sapientiae: Renaissance Garden Fountains*, (Washington, DC: Dumbarton Oaks, 1978).

—— 'The Sleeping Nymph: Origins of a Humanist Fountain Type', *Art Bulletin*, 57 (1975), 357–65.

—— and Miller, Naomi, *Fons Sapientiae: Garden Fountains in Illustrated Books: Sixteenth–Eighteenth Centuries* (Washington, DC: Dumbarton Oaks, 1977).

McEachern, Clare, *The Poetics of English Nationhood, 1590–1612* (Cambridge: Cambridge University Press, 1996).

McLaren, A. N., *Political Culture in the Reign of Elizabeth I: Queen and Commonwealth, 1558–1585* (Cambridge: Cambridge University Press, 1999).

MacLure, Millar, 'Nature and Art in *The Faerie Queene*', *English Literary History*, 28 (1961), 1–20.

McManus, Caroline, 'The "Carefull Nourse": Female Piety in Spenser's Legend of Holiness', *Huntingdon Library Quarterly*, 60 (1999), 381–406.

MacPhail, Eric, 'Prophecy and Memory in the Renaissance Dream Vision', in Earl Miner et al. (eds.), *The Force of Vision II: Visions in History; Visions of the Other* (Tokyo: International Comparative Literature Association, 1991), 193–9.

McPherson, David, 'Texts and Studies 1974', *Studies in Philology*, 71/5 (1974), 1–106.

Mallette, Richard, *Spenser and the Discourses of Reformation England* (Lincoln: University of Nebraska Press, 1997).

Manley, Lawrence, *Literature and Culture in Early Modern London* (Cambridge: Cambridge University Press, 1995).

Marek, Heidi, 'Narcisse et Salmacis: le thème de l'unité et de la diversité dans *Les Douze fables de fleuves ou fontaines* de Pontus de Tyard', in *Sources et fontaines du Moyen Âge à l'Âge Baroque: actes du colloque tenu à l'Université Paul Valéry, Montpellier III, les 28, 29 et 30 novembre 1996* (Paris: Honoré Champion Éditeur, 1998), 285–301.

Martindale, Charles (ed.), *Ovid Renewed: Ovidian Influences on Literature and Art from the Middle Ages to the Twentieth Century* (Cambridge: Cambridge University Press, 1988).

Mauré, Cécile, 'Mythe et moralité dans *Cynthia's Revels* de Ben Jonson (1600)', *Anglophonia*, 13 (2003), 113–24.

Mazzola, Elizabeth, 'Ethical Dilemmas and Romance Destinations: "Pigeonholes of Oblivion" in *The Faerie Queene*, Book II', *Huntington Library Quarterly*, 61 (1999), 29–52.

Meagher, John, *Method and Meaning in Jonson's Masques* (Notre Dame, Ind.: University of Notre Dame Press, 1966).

Melaney, William D., 'Spenser's Allegory of Temperance: A Study in Comparative Poetics', *Ben Jonson Journal*, 4 (1997), 115–29.

Miles, Rosalind, *Ben Jonson: His Craft and Art* (London: Routledge, 1990).

—— *Ben Jonson: His Life and Work* (London: Routledge, 1986).

Miller, David Lee, *The Poem's Two Bodies: The Poetics of the 1590 Faerie Queene* (Princeton: Princeton University Press, 1988).

Miller, Lewis H., 'A Secular Reading of *The Faerie Queene* Book II', *English Literary History*, 33 (1966), 154–69.

Miller, Naomi, *French Renaissance Fountains* (New York: Garland, 1977).

Montrose, Louis, 'Spenser and the Elizabethan Political Imaginary', *English Literary History*, 69 (2002), 907–46.

Morgan, Gerald, '"Add Faith Vnto your Force": The Perfecting of Spenser's Knight of Holiness in Faith and Humility', *Renaissance Studies*, 18 (2004), 449–74.

Morgan, Louise B., 'The Source of the Fountain-Story in the *Ywain*', *Modern Philology*, 6 (1908–9), 331–41.

Morgan, Luke, 'Landscape Design in England *circa* 1610: The Contribution of Salomon de Caus', *Studies in the History of Gardens and Designed Landscapes*, 23 (2003), 1–21.

Mullaney, Steven, *The Place of the Stage: License, Play, and Power in Renaissance England* (Ann Arbor: University of Michigan Press, 1988).

Nederman, Cary J., and Lawson, N. Elaine, 'The Frivolities of Courtiers Follow the Footprints of Women: Public Women and the Crisis of Virility in John of Salisbury', in Carole Levin and Jeanie Watson (eds.), *Ambiguous Realities: Women in the Middle Ages and Renaissance* (Detroit, Mich.: Wayne State University Press, 1987), 82–96.

Neraudau, Jean-Pierre, 'Autour du *Songe de Poliphile*', in *Images de l'antiquité dans la littérature française: le texte et son illustration* (Paris: Presses de l'École Normale Supérieure, 1993), 73–85.

Nevinson, John L., *Catalogue of English Domestic Embroidery of the Sixteenth and Seventeenth Centuries*, Victoria and Albert Museum Department of Textiles (London: HMSO, 1950).

Nevo, R., 'Spenser's "Bower of Bliss" and a Key Metaphor from Renaissance Poetic', in A. C. Hamilton (ed.), *Essential Articles for the Study of Edmund Spenser* (Hamden, Conn.: Archon Books, 1972), 29–39.

Newton, Norman, 'The Palace of Rhetoric: Geometrical and Architectural Form in Ben Jonson', *Dalhousie Review*, 77 (1997), 23–44.

Nichols, John (ed.), *The Progresses and Public Processions of Queen Elizabeth* (London, 1823).

—— *The Progresses, Processions, and Magnificent Festivities, of King James the First* (London, 1828).

Nitze, W. A., 'The Fountain Defended', *Modern Philology*, 7 (1909), 144–64.

Nohrnberg, James, *The Analogy of The Faerie Queene* (Princeton: Princeton University Press, 1976).

Norbrook, David, *Poetry and Politics in the English Renaissance* (London: Routledge and Kegan Paul, 1984).

O'Connell, Michael, *Mirror and Veil: The Historical Dimension of Spenser's* Faerie Queene (Chapel Hill: University of North Carolina Press, 1977).

Okerlund, Arlene M., 'Spenser's Wanton Maidens: Reader Psychology and the Bower of Bliss', *PMLA* 88 (1973), 62–8.

O'Toole, Michael, *The Language of Displayed Art* (London: Leicester University Press, 1994).

Pardo, Mary, 'Artifice and Seduction in Titian', in James Grantham Turner (ed.), *Sexuality and Gender in Early Modern Europe* (Cambridge: Cambridge University Press, 1993), 55–89.

Parfitt, George, *Ben Jonson: Public Poet and Private Man* (London: J. M. Dent and Sons, 1976).

Parker, Patricia, *Inescapable Romance: Studies in the Poetics of a Mode* (Princeton: Princeton University Press, 1979).

—— *Literary Fat Ladies: Rhetoric, Gender, Property* (London: Methuen, 1987).

Paster, Gail Kern, 'Ben Jonson and the Uses of Architecture', *Renaissance Quarterly*, 27 (1974), 306–20.

—— *The Idea of the City in the Age of Shakespeare* (Athens: University of Georgia Press, 1985).

—— 'Leaky Vessels: The Incontinent Women of City Comedy', *Renaissance Drama*, NS 18 (1987), 43–65.

Pendergast, John S., 'Christian Allegory and Spenser's "General Intention" ', *Studies in Philology*, 93 (1996), 267–87.

Pérez-Gomez, Alberto, 'The *Hypnerotomachia Poliphili* by Francesco Colonna: The Erotic Nature of Architectural Meaning', in Vaughan Hart and Peter Hicks (eds.), *Paper Palaces: The Rise of the Renaissance Architectural Treatise* (New Haven: Yale University Press, 1998), 86–104.

Perry, Curtis, 'The Citizen Politics of Nostalgia: Queen Elizabeth in Early Jacobean London', *Journal of Medieval and Renaissance Studies*, 23 (1993), 89–111.

Perry, Kathleen Anne, *Another Reality: Metamorphosis and the Imagination in the Poetry of Ovid, Petrarch, and Ronsard* (New York: Peter Lang, 1989).

Peterson, Richard S., *Imitation and Praise in the Poems of Ben Jonson* (New Haven: Yale University Press, 1981).

Pevsner, Nikolaus, and Wilson, Bill, *Norfolk 1: Norwich and North-East (The Buildings of England)* (New Haven: Yale University Press, 2002).

Pheifer, J. D., 'Errour and Echidna in *The Faerie Queene*: A Study in Literary Tradition', in John Scattergood (ed.), *Literature and Learning in Medieval and Renaissance England: Essays Presented to Fitzroy Pyle* (Blackrock: Irish Academic Press, 1984), 127–74.

Phillips, James E., 'Spenser's Syncretistic Religious Imagery', *English Literary History*, 36 (1969), 110–30.

Pinkus, Karen, 'The Moving Force in Colonna's *Hypnerotomachia Poliphili*', in Rhoda Schnur (ed.), *Conventus Neo-Latini Hafniensis: Eighth International Congress of Neo-Latin Studies* (Copenhagen: Medieval and Renaissance Texts and Studies, 1992), 831–8.

Polizzi, Gilles, 'Le Devenir du jardin médiéval? Du verger de la Rose à Cythère', in *Vergers et jardins dans l'univers médiéval* (Aix-en-Provence: Centre Universitaire d'Études et de Recherches Médiévales d'Aix, 1990), 265–88.

—— 'L'Esthétique de l'énigme: le spectacle et le sens dans le *Songe de Poliphile*', *Rivista di letterature moderne e comparate*, ns 41/3 (1988), 209–31.

Polizzi, Gilles, 'Le *Poliphile* ou l'*idée* du jardin: pour une analyse littéraire de l'esthétique colonienne', *Word & Image*, 14/1–2 (1998), 61–81.

—— '*Le Songe de Poliphile*: rénovation ou métamorphose du genre littéraire', in Françoise Charpentier (ed.), *Le Songe à la Renaissance* (Saint-Étienne: Association d'Études sur l'Humanisme, la Réforme et la Renaissance, Université de Saint-Étienne, 1990).

Pollock, Zailig, 'Concupiscence and Intemperance in the Bower of Bliss', *Studies in English Literature*, 20 (1980), 43–58.

—— 'The Dragon, the Lady and the Dragon Lady in Book I of *The Faerie Queene*', *English Studies in Canada*, 7 (1981), 270–81.

Power, M. J., 'John Stow and his London', *Journal of Historical Geography*, 11 (1985), 1–20.

Prescott, Anne Lake, 'Evil Tongues at the Court of Saul: The Renaissance David as a Slandered Courtier', *Journal of Medieval and Renaissance Studies*, 21 (1991), 163–86.

—— 'The Thirsty Deer and the Lord of Life: Some Contexts for *Amoretti* 67–70', *Spenser Studies*, 6 (1985), 33–76.

Pugh, Syrithe, *Spenser and Ovid* (Aldershot: Ashgate, 2005).

Quest-Ritson, Charles, *The English Garden: A Social History* (London: Viking, 2001).

Quilligan, Maureen, *The Language of Allegory: Defining the Genre* (Ithaca, NY: Cornell University Press, 1979).

—— *Milton's Spenser: The Politics of Reading* (Ithaca, NY: Cornell University Press, 1983).

Quint, David, *Origins and Originality in Renaissance Literature: Versions of the Source* (New Haven: Yale University Press, 1983).

Rattue, James, *The Living Stream: Holy Wells in Historical Context* (Woodbridge: Boydell, 1995).

Rhu, Lawrence F., *The Genesis of Tasso's Narrative Theory: English Translations of the Early Poetics and a Comparative Study of their Significance* (Detroit, Mich.: Wayne State University Press, 1993).

—— 'Romancing the Word: Pre-Texts and Contexts for the Errour Episode', *Spenser Studies*, 11 (1994), 101–9.

Riddell, James, and Stewart, Stanley, *Jonson's Spenser: Evidence and Historical Criticism* (Pittsburgh: Duquesne University Press, 1995).

Riggs, David, *Ben Jonson: A Life* (Cambridge, Mass.: Harvard University Press, 1989).

Roche, Thomas P., 'The Challenge to Chastity: Britomart at the House of Busyrane', *PMLA* 76 (1961), 340–4.

—— *The Kindly Flame: A Study of the Third and Fourth Books of Spenser's Faerie Queene* (Princeton: Princeton University Press, 1964).

Rockwell, Paul Vincent, 'Writing the Fountain: The Specificity of Resemblance in Arthurian Romance', *Bibliographical Bulletin of the International Arthurian Society*, 42 (1990), 267–82.

Rooks, John, *Love's Courtly Ethic in The Faerie Queene* (New York: Peter Lang, 1992).

Rovang, Paul R., *Refashioning 'Knights and Ladies Gentle Deeds': The Intertextuality of Spenser's Faerie Queene and Malory's Morte Darthur* (Madison, Wisc.: Fairleigh Dickinson University Press, 1996).

Rowe, George E., *Distinguishing Jonson: Imitation, Rivalry, and the Direction of a Dramatic Career* (Lincoln: University of Nebraska Press, 1988).

Rubin, Deborah D., 'Sandys, Ovid, and Female Chastity: The Encyclopedic Mythographer as Moralist', in *The Mythographic Art: Classical Fable and the Rise of the Vernacular in Early France and England* (Gainesville: University of Florida Press, 1990).

Ruutz-Rees, Caroline, 'Some Notes of Gabriel Harvey's in Hoby's Translation of Castiglione's *Courtier* (1561)', *PMLA* 25 (1910), 608–39.

Saccio, Peter, 'The Oddity of Lyly's *Endimion*', in G. R. Hibbard (ed.), *The Elizabethan Theatre V* (London: Macmillan, 1975), 92–111.

Salmon, J. H. M., 'Seneca and Tacitus in Jacobean England', in Linda Levy Peck (ed.), *The Mental World of the Jacobean Court* (Cambridge: Cambridge University Press, 1991), 169–88.

Salmond, Anne, 'Theoretical Landscapes: On a Cross-Cultural Conception of Knowledge', in David Parkin (ed.), *Semantic Anthropology* (London: Academic Press, 1982), 65–87.

Sandler, Florence, '*The Faerie Queene*: A Elizabethan Apocalypse', in C. A. Patrides and Joseph Wittreich (eds.), *The Apocalypse in English Renaissance Thought and Literature: Patterns, Antecedents, and Repercussions* (Manchester: Manchester University Press, 1984), 148–74.

Saunders, Corinne J., *The Forest of Medieval Romance: Avernus, Broceliande, Arden* (Cambridge: D. S. Brewer, 1993).

Schoenfeldt, Michael C., *Bodies and Selves in Early Modern England: Physiology and Inwardness in Spenser, Shakespeare, Herbert, and Milton* (Cambridge: Cambridge University Press, 1999).

Scolnicov, Hanna, *Experiments in Stage Satire: An Analysis of Ben Jonson's Every Man out of his Humour, Cynthia's Revels, and Poetaster* (Frankfurt am Main: Peter Lang, 1987).

Scott-Warren, Jason, *Sir John Harington and the Book as Gift* (Oxford: Oxford University Press, 2001).

Shaheen, Naseeb, *Biblical References in The Faerie Queene* (Memphis, Tenn.: Memphis State University Press, 1976).

Sharpe, Kevin, *Remapping Early Modern England: The Culture of Seventeenth-Century Politics* (Cambridge: Cambridge University Press, 2000).

Shepherd, Simon, *Spenser*, Harvester New Readings (New York: Harvester Wheatsheaf, 1989).

Shibata, Toshihiko, 'On the Palinodial Ending of *Cynthia's Revels*', *Shakespeare Studies* (Tokyo), 10 (1971–2), 1–15.

Shroeder, John W., 'Spenser's Erotic Drama: The Orgoglio Episode', *English Literary History*, 29 (1962), 140–59.

Shuger, Deborah Kuller, *The Renaissance Bible: Scholarship, Sacrifice, and Subjectivity* (Berkeley and Los Angeles: University of California Press, 1994).

Silberman, Lauren, 'The Hermaphrodite and the Metamorphosis of Spenserian Allegory', in Mihoko Suzuki (ed.), *Critical Essays on Edmund Spenser* (New York: G. K. Hall and Co., 1996), 152–67.

—— *Transforming Desire: Erotic Knowledge in Books III and IV of* The Faerie Queene (Berkeley and Los Angeles: University of California Press, 1995).

Sinfield, Alan, 'Sidney and Astrophil', *Studies in English Literature*, 20 (1980), 25–41.

Skretkowicz, 'Symbolic Architecture in Sidney's *New Arcadia*', *Review of English Studies*, 33 (1982), 175–80.

Slights, William W. E., *Ben Jonson and the Art of Secrecy* (Toronto: University of Toronto Press, 1994).

Sluijter, Eric Jan, 'Rembrandt's Bathsheba and the Conventions of a Seductive Theme', in Ann Jensen Adams (ed.), *Rembrandt's Bathsheba Reading King David's Letter* (Cambridge: Cambridge University Press, 1998), 48–99.

Smith, Bruce R., 'Landscape with Figures: The Three Realms of Queen Elizabeth's Country House Revels', *Renaissance Drama*, 8 (1977), 57–115.

—— 'Pageants into Play: Shakespeare's Three Perspectives on Idea and Image', in David M. Bergeron (ed.), *Pageantry in the Shakespearean Theatre* (Athens: University of Georgia Press, 1985), 220–46.

Smith, Irwin, *Shakespeare's Blackfriars Theatre: Its History and Design* (London: Peter Owen, 1966).

Smuts, R. Malcolm, *Culture and Power in England, 1585–1685* (London: Macmillan, 1989).

—— 'Public Ceremony and Royal Charisma: The English Royal Entry into London, 1485–1642', in A. L. Beier, David Cannadine, and James M. Rosenheim (eds.), *The First Modern Society: Essays in English History in Honour of Lawrence Stone* (Cambridge: Cambridge University Press, 1989), 65–93.

Soellner, Rolf, 'The Troubled Fountain: Erasmus Formulates a Shakespearian Simile', *Journal of English and Germanic Philology*, 55 (1956), 70–4.

Spencer, Brian, *Pilgrim Souvenirs and Secular Badges*, Museum of London: Medieval Finds from Excavations in London 7 (London: Stationery Office, 1998).

Spiller, Elizabeth A., 'Poetic Parthenogenesis and Spenser's Idea of Creation in *The Faerie Queene*', *Studies in English Literature*, 40 (2000), 63–79.

Steadman, John M., 'Spenser's *Errour* and the Renaissance Allegorical Tradition', *Neuphilologische Mitteilungen*, 62 (1961), 22–38.

Steele, Robert, *A Bibliography of Royal Proclamations of the Tudor and Stuart Sovereigns* (Oxford: Oxford University Press, 1910).

Steggle, Matthew, 'Horace the Second, or, Ben Jonson, Thomas Dekker, and the Battle for Augustan Rome', in Paul Franssen and Ton Hoenselaars (eds.), *The Author as*

Character: Representing Historical Writers in Western Literature (London: Associated
    University Presses, 1999), 118–30.

—— *Wars of the Theatres: The Poetics of Personation in the Age of Jonson* (Victoria, BC:
    University of Victoria, 1998).

Stephens, Dorothy, *The Limits of Eroticism in Post-Petrarchan Narrative: Conditional
    Pleasure from Spenser to Marvell* (Cambridge: Cambridge University Press, 1998).

Stewart, Alan, *Philip Sidney: A Double Life* (London: Chatto and Windus, 2000).

Stewering, Roswitha, 'Architectural Representations in the *Hypnerotomachia Poliphili*
    (Aldus Manutius, 1499)', *Journal of the Society of Architectural Historians*, 59 (2000),
    6–25.

—— *Architektur und Natur in der 'Hypnerotomachia Poliphili' (Manutius 1499) und
    die Zuschreibung des Werkes an Niccolo Lelio Cosmico* (Hamburg: Lit, 1996).

—— 'The Relationship between World, Landscape and Polia in the *Hypnerotomachia
    Poliphili*', *Word & Image*, 14 (1998), 2–10.

Stocks, Christopher, 'Heroes and Villains: Christopher Stocks on Capability Brown',
    The Independent, 19 Mar. 2005.

Stone, Lawrence, 'The Building of Hatfield House', *Archaeological Journal*, 112 (1955),
    100–28.

Strauss, Paul, 'Allegory and the Bower of Bliss', *Ben Jonson Journal*, 2 (1995), 59–71.

Strong, Roy, *Art and Power: Renaissance Festivals 1450–1650* (Woodbridge: Boydell
    Press, 1984).

—— *Gloriana: The Portraits of Queen Elizabeth I* (London: Thames and Hudson, 1987;
    repr. 2003).

—— *The Renaissance Garden in England* (London: Thames and Hudson, 1979;
    repr. 1998).

—— *Splendour at Court: Renaissance Spectacle and Illusion* (London: Weidenfeld and
    Nicolson, 1973).

Sullivan, Garrett A., *The Drama of Landscape: Land, Property and Social Relations on
    the Early Modern Stage* (Stanford, Calif.: Stanford University Press, 1998).

Summerson, John, 'The Building of Theobalds, 1564–1585', *Archaeologia*, 97 (1959),
    107–26.

Suttie, Paul, 'Moral Ambivalence in the Legend of Temperance', *Spenser Studies*, 19
    (2004), 123–33.

Sutton, James M., 'The Decorative Program at Elizabethan Theobalds: Educating
    an Heir and Promoting a Dynasty', *Studies in the Decorative Arts* (Fall/Winter
    1999–2000), 33–64.

—— 'Jonson's Genius at Theobalds: The Poetics of Estrangement', *Ben Jonson Journal*,
    7 (2000), 297–323.

—— *Materializing Space at an Early Modern Prodigy House: The Cecils at Theobalds,
    1564–1607* (Aldershot: Ashgate, 2004).

Swain, Margaret, *The Needlework of Mary Queen of Scots* (New York: Van Nostrand
    Reinhold Company, 1973).

Sweeney, John Gordon, *Jonson and the Psychology of Public Theatre* (Princeton:
    Princeton University Press, 1985).

—— 'Sejanus and the People's Beastly Rage', in Richard Dutton (ed.), *Ben Jonson* (Harlow: Pearson Education Ltd., 2000), 50–69.

Szépe, Helena Katalin, 'Desire in the Printed Dream of Poliphilo', *Art History*, 19 (1996).

Tait, Hugh, 'Tudor Hat Badge', *British Museum Quarterly*, 20 (1955), 37–8.

Tait, Hugh, 'An Anonymous Loan to the British Museum: 1: Renaissance Jewellery', *The Connoisseur*, 154 (1963), 147–53.

Talbert, Ernest William, 'The Classical Mythology and the Structure of *Cynthia's Revels*', *Philological Quarterly*, 22 (1943), 193–210.

Taylor, Gary, 'The Renaissance and the End of Editing', in George Bornstein and Ralph G. Williams (eds.), *Palimpsest: Editorial Theory in the Humanities* (Ann Arbor: University of Michigan Press, 1993), 121–49.

Tervarent, Guy de Schoutheete, 'L'Origine des fontaines anthropomorphes', *Académie Royale de Belgique: bulletin de la classe des beaux-arts*, 38 (1956), 122–9 + pl.

Thoms, William J., 'Pictures of the Great Earl of Leicester', *Notes and Queries*, 3rd ser. 2 (6 Sept. 1862), 201–2.

Thron, E. M., 'Jonson's *Cynthia's Revels*: Multiplicity and Unity', *Studies in English Literature*, 11 (1971), 236–47.

Thurley, Simon, *Hampton Court: A Social and Architectural History* (New Haven: Yale University Press, 2003).

Tiffany, Grace, *Erotic Beasts and Social Monsters: Shakespeare, Jonson, and Comic Androgyny* (Newark, NJ: University of Delaware Press, 1995).

Tribble, Evelyn B., 'The Partial Sign: Spenser and the Sixteenth-Century Crisis of Semiotics', in Douglas F. Rutledge (ed.), *Ceremony and Text in the Renaissance* (Newark, NJ: University of Delaware Press, 1996), 23–34.

Trippe, Rosemary, 'The *Hypnerotomachia Poliphili*, Image, Text, and Vernacular Poetics', *Renaissance Quarterly*, 55 (2002), 1222–58.

Tudeau-Clayton, Margaret, 'Ben Jonson, "In Travaile with Expression of Another": His Use of John of Salisbury's *Policraticus* in *Timber*', *Review of English Studies*, 30 (1979), 397–408.

—— *Jonson, Shakespeare and Early Modern Virgil* (Cambridge: Cambridge University Press, 1998).

Twyning, John, *London Dispossessed: Literature and Social Space in the Early Modern City* (London: Macmillan, 1998).

Van Dorsten, Jan, *The Radical Arts: First Decade of an Elizabethan Renaissance* (Leiden: Leiden University Press, 1970).

—— 'Steven Van Herwyck's Elizabeth (1565): A Franco-Flemish Political Medal', *Burlington Magazine*, 111 (1969), 143–7.

Van Es, Bart, *Spenser's Forms of History* (Oxford: Oxford University Press, 2002).

—— ' "The Streame and Currant of Time": Land, Myth, and History in the Works of Spenser', *Spenser Studies*, 18 (2003), 209–29.

Vickers, Brian, *Shakespeare, Co-Author: A Historical Study of Five Collaborative Plays* (Oxford: Oxford University Press, 2002).

Villeponteaux, Mary, '*Semper Eadem*: Belphoebe's Denial of Desire', in Claude J. Summer and Ted-Larry Pebworth (eds.), *Renaissance Discourses of Desire* (Columbia: University of Missouri Press, 1993), 29–45.

Vinge, Louise, *The Narcissus Theme in Western European Literature up to the Early 19th Century* (Lund: Gleerups, 1967).

Voss, Paul J., '*The Faerie Queene* 1590–1596: The Case of Saint George', *Ben Jonson Journal*, 3 (1996), 59–73.

Walker, Julia M. (ed.), *Dissing Elizabeth: Negative Representations of Gloriana* (Durham, NC: Duke University Press, 1998).

—— *Medusa's Mirrors: Spenser, Shakespeare, Milton, and the Metamorphosis of the Female Self* (Newark, NJ: University of Delaware Press, 1998).

Wall, John N., 'The English Reformation and the Recovery of Christian Community in Spenser's *The Faerie Queene*', *Studies in Philology*, 80 (1983), 142–62.

Wallace, Andrew, '"Noursled Up in Life and Manners Wilde": Spenser's Georgic Education', *Spenser Studies*, 19 (2004), 65–92.

Wallace, Nathaniel, 'Architextual Poetics: The *Hypnerotomachia* and the Rise of the European Emblem', *Emblematica*, 8/1 (1994), 1–27.

Waller, Gary, *Edmund Spenser: A Literary Life* (London: Macmillan, 1994).

Walls, Kathryn, 'Abessa and the Lion: *The Faerie Queene* 1.3.1–12', *Spenser Studies*, 5 (1984), 3–30.

Walsham, Alexandra, 'Holywell: Contesting Sacred Space in Post-Reformation Wales', in Will Coster and Andrew Spicer (eds.), *Sacred Space in Early Modern Europe* (Cambridge: Cambridge University Press, 2005), 211–36.

—— 'Reforming the Waters: Holy Wells and Healing Springs in Protestant England', in Diana Wood (ed.), *Life and Thought in the Northern Church c.1100–c.1700: Essays in Honour of Claire Cross* (Woodbridge: Boydell Press, 1999), 227–55.

Warner, Marina, *Alone of All her Sex: The Myth and Cult of the Virgin Mary* (London: Weidenfeld and Nicolson, 1976; repr. Vintage, 2000).

Waters, D. Douglas, *Duessa as Theological Satire* (Columbia: University of Missouri Press, 1970).

—— 'Errour's Den and Archimago's Hermitage: Symbolic Lust and Symbolic Witchcraft', *English Literary History*, 33 (1966), 279–98.

Wayment, Hilary, *The Windows of King's College Chapel Cambridge: A Description and Commentary* (London: Oxford University Press, 1972).

Wayne, Don E., 'Mediation and Contestation: English Classicism from Sidney to Jonson', *Criticism*, 25 (1983), 211–37.

Weatherby, Harold L., 'Dame Nature and the Nymph', *English Literary Renaissance*, 26 (1996), 243–58.

—— *Mirrors of Celestial Grace: Patristic Theology in Spenser's Allegory* (Toronto: University of Toronto Press, 1994).

—— '"Pourd Out in Loosnesse"', *Spenser Studies*, 3 (1982), 73–85.

—— 'The True Saint George', *English Literary Renaissance*, 17 (1987), 119–41.

Weber, Burton J., 'The Interlocking Triads of the First Book of *The Faerie Queene*', *Studies in Philology*, 90 (1993), 176–212.

Weinberg, Florence, 'Francesco Colonna and Rabelais's Tribute to Guillaume du Bellay', *Romance Notes*, 16 (1974), 178–82.

Wells, Robin Headlam, 'Spenser's Christian Knight: Erasmian Theology in *The Faerie Queene*, Book I', *Anglia*, 97 (1979), 350–66.

—— *Spenser's Faerie Queene and the Cult of Elizabeth* (London: Croom Helm, 1983).

Wells-Cole, Anthony, *Art and Decoration in Elizabethan and Jacobean England: The Influence of Continental Prints, 1558–1625* (New Haven: Yale University Press, 1997).

Whinney, Margaret, and John Physick, *Sculpture in Britain 1530–1830* (London: Penguin, 1988).

Whittle, Elizabeth H., 'The Renaissance Gardens of Raglan Castle', *Garden History*, 17 (1989), 83–94.

Wiles, Bertha Harris, *The Fountains of Florentine Sculptors and their Followers from Donatello to Bernini* (Cambridge, Mass.: Harvard University Press, 1933).

Williams, Kathleen, *Spenser's Faerie Queene: The World of Glass* (London: Routledge, 1966).

Wilson, Dudley, '*The Strife of Love in a Dreame*: An Elizabethan Translation of Part of the First Book of Francesco Colonna's *Hypnerotomachia*', *Bulletin of the Society for Renaissance Studies*, 4 (1986), 41–53.

Wiltenburg, Robert, *Ben Jonson and Self-Love: The Subtlest Maze of All* (Columbia: University of Missouri Press, 1990).

Wind, Edgar, *Pagan Mysteries in the Renaissance* (Harmondsworth: Penguin, 1967).

Witt, Robert W., *Mirror within a Mirror: Ben Jonson and the Play-Within* (Salzburg: Institut für Englische Sprache und Literatur, 1975).

Womack, Peter, *Ben Jonson* (Oxford: Basil Blackwell, 1986).

Woodhouse, A. P., 'Nature and Grace in *The Faerie Queene*', in A. C. Hamilton (ed.), *Essential Articles for the Study of Edmund Spenser* (Hamden, Conn.: Archon Books, 1972), 58–83.

Woodhouse, Elisabeth, 'Kenilworth, the Earl of Leicester's Pleasure Grounds Following Robert Laneham's Letter', *Garden History*, 27 (1999), 127–44.

Worden, Blair, 'Favourites on the English Stage', in J. H. Elliott and L. W. B. Brockliss (eds.), *The World of the Favourite* (New Haven: Yale University Press, 1999), 159–83.

—— *The Sound of Virtue: Philip Sidney's* Arcadia *and Elizabethan Politics* (New Haven: Yale University Press, 1996).

Yachnin, Paul, *Stage-Wrights: Shakespeare, Jonson, Middleton, and the Making of Theatrical Value* (Philadelphia: University of Pennsylvania Press, 1997).

Yates, Frances, *Astraea: The Imperial Theme in the Sixteenth Century* (London: Routledge and Kegan Paul, 1975).

Yiavis, Kostas P., 'Life-Giving Waters and the Waters of the Cephise: *Fairie Queene* 1.11.29–30', *Classical and Modern Literature*, 19 (1998), 77–82.

Yoch, James J., 'Subjecting the Landscape in Pageants and Shakespearean Pastorals', in David M. Bergeron (ed.), *Pageantry in the Shakespearean Theatre* (Athens: University of Georgia Press, 1985), 194–219.

—— 'A Very Wild Regularity: The Character of Landscape in the Work of Inigo Jones', *Research Opportunities in Renaissance Drama*, 30 (1988), 7–15.

Zaalberg, C. A., *Das Buch Extasis van Jan Van Der Noot* (Assen: Van Gorcum, 1954).

Zender, Karl F., 'The Unveiling of the Goddess in *Cynthia's Revels*', *Journal of English and Germanic Philology*, 77 (1978), 37–52.

Index

Achilles Tatius 93
Acrasia 173, 175–7, 183
Actaeon 10, 11, 37, 71, 75, 136 n. 40, 171,
    186–7, 212–16, 226, 231–2, 237,
    239–40, 244, 252, 259–74, 276, 282
Adam 124 n. 5, 129, 130, 164–5
Adonis 36, 76, 80, 82–3, 92, 98, 99; see also
    Fountain of Adonis; *Figures 7, 9*
Aeneas 36, 86, 88–91, 92, 99, 123 n. 2; see
    also Fountain of Aeneas
Alberti, Leon Battista 46, 97–8
Amavia 172–6, 183
Amoret 136 n. 39, 174, 186–7, 189–91,
    193–4
Amoretti 136 n. 39, 194 n. 70
ampullae 144–5, 147, 154, 166 n. 66; see
    also pilgrimage; *Figure 10*
Anaxarete 80, 175
Anderson, Christy 15 n. 41, 35
Apollo 11, 80, 132–3, 229, 230, 277; see also
    Helicon; Muses; Parnassus
Apuleius 73, 82 n. 35, 216
Archimago 134 n. 32, 135, 155–6, 161 n.
    50, 164–5, 171, 219
architecture 57, 60, 69 n. 1, 85, 95
Arethusa 14, 17, 78, 174 n. 10, 175
Aristotelian physiology 27, 140
Arnold, Janet 204–7
Arthurian romance, *see* romance
Arundel, twelfth earl of, *see* Fitzalan, Henry
Arundel, fourteenth earl of, *see* Howard,
    Thomas
Ascham, Roger 125, 142
Astraea 106, 208, 211, 219–20, 276
Astrophil and Stella 41–2, 79, 87, 96–7,
    98
As You Like It 2
Aubrey, John 33, 281
Auerbach, Erich 25

Bachelard, Gaston 5, 10
Babington Plot 151
Bacon, Francis 238, 268, 280–1
Bale, John 117, 119, 122, 130–31, 141,
    156–7, 168
Baley, Walter 152, 167–8

balm 136 n. 39, 158–9, 161–5, 167–8, 277
baptism
    in *The Faerie Queene* 127, 142–3,
        158–68, 175
    in the *Hypnerotomachia* 59, 63, 65–6, 69,
        72
    liturgy 66, 142–3, 165
Barkan, Leonard 73, 99, 192, 199–200, 216
    n. 66, 261, 269 n. 46, 273 n. 57
Barnes, Barnaby 165
Barthes, Roland 193 n. 68
Bartholomew Fair 210, 230
Barton, Anne 226
Bate, Jonathan 210–11, 218 n. 2, 270 n. 47,
    271
baths 147, 149–52, 157, 159, 167–8, 204
    Bath 147, 149, 150 n. 20, 153–4
    Buxton 147, 149–51, 158
    health benefits of 147, 148–50, 152,
        167–8
    and holy wells 36, 149–52, 155, 167–8
    in *Hypnerotomachia*, 53, 54, 59–60, 73
    Newnham Regis 147, 152, 167–8
    and recusancy 150–2
    writings about 149–50, 151–2, 167–8
Bathsheba 171, 212–15, 220–2
Beaujoyeulx, Baltasar 229
Bednarz, James 223 n. 18, 242
Belphoebe 43 n. 6, 133, 136 n. 39, 186–7
Bennett, Josephine Waters 116 n. 38, 117
Bertie, Katherine, duchess of Suffolk
    206–8
Bevington, David 226–7, 229
Bevis of Southampton 154; *see also*
    romance
bible 36, 105–6, 108, 109, 112, 113, 114,
    115, 116–21, 122, 127, 128, 138–9,
    146, 152, 156, 159, 162, 163, 164, 166,
    167–8, 186, 212–13, 220, 222, 246,
    280, 284
    exegesis and commentary 114, 116, 117,
        118, 128–31, 138, 141, 155, 156, 157
        n. 38, 158, 159, 166
    translation 108, 113, 114–16, 119–20,
        168
    Authorized Version 108, 119–20, 246
    Geneva 119, 129, 138, 158, 212 n. 56

bible (*cont.*)
  Rheims-Douai 114
  Genesis 114–16, 118, 128–31, 139–40, 143
  Exodus 164
  1 & 2 Samuel 212–14, 221–2
  Psalms 65, 73, 108, 162, 191, 194, 211 n. 50, 212
  Song of Solomon 24, 27, 74 n. 16, 108, 140
  Isaiah 162
  Jeremiah 115–16, 128, 131, 143, 168
  Judith 222 n. 17
  Ecclesiasticus 140
  Matthew 154
  Mark 163
  John 74 n. 16, 116 n. 39, 118, 139–40, 146, 154, 158, 162, 163, 166–7; see also *Figure 11*
  1 Corinthians 138, 164
  Ephesians 127, 138
  1 Thessalonians 138
  1 John 158
  Revelation 116–18, 119, 130–1, 141–2, 143, 147, 154, 156–8, 167–8
Biblis 72, 75, 78
Biddle, Martin 255 n. 1, 257 n. 7, 259–66
Bisham 15–16
Blackfriars theatre 220, 236
  company 222–4
  history 223
  repertoire 220, 222–3, 225, 227
  staging 223–6
Bland, Mark 272
blank space 84, 98; see also loss
blood 67, 74, 81, 82, 112, 132–4, 158–61, 163–6, 172–5, 189, 210–11
Boccaccio, Giovanni
  Decameron 76–7
  influence 80, 82, 83; see also *Figure 8*
Book of the Courtier, The, see Castiglione, Baldassare
book-bindings 91, 120–1, 284; see also textiles
Braunmuller, A. R. 228
Britland, Karen 176
Britomart 172, 173, 186–94
Brown, 'Capability' 22, 33
Brown, Sarah Annes 11, 186 n. 48, 200 n. 5, 216 n. 66, 269 n. 46, 273 n. 57
Burghley, Lord, *see* Cecil, William
Burrow, Colin 175
Busirane 108, 189

Buxton 147, 149–51, 158

Calvinism 36, 134, 163 n. 57, 165–7
Cambridge 108, 116, 117, 118
  Corpus Christi College 48, 52
  Fitzwilliam Museum 45
  King's College 4, 129
  Pembroke College 107
  Peterhouse 52
  St John's College 44 n. 8
  Trinity College 42, 59
  University Library 45, 201, 243
Camden, William 16, 109, 150–1, 243, 274, 275–6
Campbell, Oscar 226, 241
Canterbury Tales, The 24; see also Chaucer, Geoffrey
Castiglione, Baldassare 13, 47, 182 n. 34
Caus, Isaac de 41, 95–6
Cecil, Robert 35, 94, 266–7
Cecil, William, Lord Burghley 34, 35, 41, 88, 90, 94, 147, 184 n. 38, 197, 266, 275 n. 66
Cephisus 153, 188
Chamberlain, John 267
Chambers, E. K. 222–3
Charissa 132
Charles II, king of England 256
chastity 16, 64, 74, 80, 89, 131, 137, 140, 143, 172–5, 177, 191, 203, 216, 219, 221
Château d'Anet 20, 191
Chaucer, Geoffrey 5, 24, 30, 135, 161, 246 n. 34
  Canterbury Tales 24
  mentioned by Spenser 135
  Troilus and Criseyde 30
Cheapside 1, 2, 36, 104, 107, 118, 120, 258, 277, 282; see also London
Cheney, Donald 125, 167 n. 70
Cheney, Patrick 135
chivalry 27, 31, 62, 125; see also romance
Ciapponi, Lucia A., *see* Pozzi, Giovanni
Circe 176, 183
Clifford, Rosamund 32–3
Coelia 193
Colet, John 179
Colonna, Francesco 46; see also *Hypnerotomachia*
Comito, Terry 8, 9, 10, 54 n. 3
commonwealth 104–5, 109, 119, 120, 128, 199–203, 219–20, 242, 244, 246–7, 252

Cooper, Helen 27 n. 69, 188
court, the, 24, 25, 32, 37, 41, 48, 112,
    198–203, 216–17, 226, 229, 230–1,
    233, 234–54, 267–9, 276, 282
courtiers 2, 37, 91, 92, 103, 109, 182 n. 34,
    199, 203, 226, 229, 230–1, 232–3,
    234–54, 259, 269–70, 276
creation 11, 22, 23, 131–4, 136, 153–4,
    180
Cullen, Patrick 124 n. 5, 142
Cupid 54, 65, 67, 68, 69–71, 76, 80, 81, 82,
    83, 86, 88, 89, 90, 92, 99, 186–7, 189,
    215, 231, 236, 239, 250, 252, 269, 271
cups 4, 63, 157–9, 173, 176–8, 183, 202; *see
    also* mazer
Curtius, Ernst 22–3
Cymbeline 216
Cynthia's Revels, see Jonson

Dallington, Robert
    life 48, 52
    The Strife of Love in a Dreame 43 n. 6, 46,
        48, 49–50, 55 n. 4, 56, 63, 85, 282
    *A Survey of the great dukes state of
        Tuscany,* 16, 18–19
Daniel, Samuel 51, 276 n. 70
Daphne 175
David 171, 212–15, 220–22, 232, 272; *see
    also* Bathsheba
Davies, Sir John 200
death 76, 80, 82, 83–4, 92, 99, 172–5
deception 115, 126, 130, 135–6, 157, 171,
    173, 179–80, 185, 188, 192
Dees, Jerome S. 189
Dekker, Thomas 250, 276–7, 282
Delves, Sir George 234–6, 255, 259; see also
    Figure 14
desire 10, 27, 29, 44, 53, 55–7, 60, 61, 63,
    64–5, 67–8, 70, 72–4, 75, 77, 79, 81,
    84, 87, 90, 124, 140, 181, 183, 260, 280
Deucalion 153
Devereux, Robert, earl of Essex 34, 35, 37,
    44, 48, 52, 198, 223, 241 n. 15, 247,
    252, 254, 255, 266–76, 277 n. 79, 278
devices 3, 8, 12, 13, 24, 26, 31, 36, 59, 61,
    67, 76, 79, 87, 88, 92, 96, 105, 180, 183,
    198–9, 204–7, 209, 216, 218–19, 239,
    243, 250, 253, 258, 268–9, 281, 282; see
    also *Figures 13, 14*
dew 66, 81, 82, 136, 164, 177
Diana 1–2, 7, 10, 16, 17, 25, 34, 37, 66, 71,
    78, 79–81, 136 n. 40, 138, 171, 173–4,
    186–7, 193, 200, 203–4, 212–17, 231,

239, 248, 252, 257–67, 269–70, 272–3,
    276, 282, 284
Dido 88, 89, 90, 123 n. 2
Dixon, John 117, 158
Donaldson, Ian 268
Donne, John 164 n. 62
dragons 53, 56, 58, 63, 124, 130–3, 153,
    154, 167, 177, 257
dreams 9–10, 28, 53–7, 61, 68, 73, 77, 78,
    80, 83, 84, 136, 165
Dronke, Peter 50, 65
Drummond, William 268
Duchess of Malfi, The 200, 202–3
Dudley, Robert, earl of Leicester 34, 35, 41,
    89, 147, 152, 160–1, 169, 185, 208–9,
    214 n. 61, 215, 235, 263 n. 28, 271, 273,
    276 n. 70
Duessa 36, 118, 123, 126, 136–7, 140–3,
    157–9, 165, 171, 174, 176, 188–9
Duffy, Eamon 166 n. 66
Dughi, Thomas M. 162–3
Duncan-Jones, Katherine 42, 88, 91
Dundas, Judith 184, 251

eagle 162–3
Easter 65–6, 194
Echidna 131–4
Echo 223–5, 231–3, 236, 241, 248, 250,
    251, 252, 269, 271
education 3, 11, 29, 94, 95, 107–8, 119, 123,
    125, 127, 138, 142, 159–61, 179–82,
    185, 186, 193, 201–2, 210–11, 238
Elizabeth I, queen of England 1–2, 3, 48,
    89, 91, 94, 103–12, 147, 152, 159 n. 45,
    169, 185, 197–8, 203–9, 213–14,
    216–17, 218–20, 226, 231, 236, 237,
    239, 241, 242, 246–7, 249–51, 253,
    256, 258, 264–71, 274–6
    Accession Day tilts 267, 268, 276
    Babington Plot 151; *see also* Buxton
    coronation entry 36, 103–11, 118,
        120–1, 128, 146, 159, 197, 206–7,
        218–20, 230, 246, 280
    'cult of' 7, 34
    devices 34, 89, 204–8, 275; see also
        Figure 13
    as Diana 1, 37, 200, 203, 216, 226, 231,
        258–9, 264–6, 267, 269–73, 276; see
        also *Figure 17*
    as fountain 1, 37, 106, 120, 197–8,
        201–8, 219–20, 236, 258–9, 263,
        274–5; see also *Figure 13, 17*
    gifts to, 103–6, 205–8, 216–17, 239

Elizabeth I, queen of England (*cont.*)
  jewellery 204, 206
  portraits 34, 88–9, 106, 185, 197, 205–6,
      207 n. 33, 234, 263 n. 28; see also
      Figure 13
  proposed marriage of 36, 89, 206, 264 n.
      30, 265
  Ridolfi plot 265
  wardrobe 204–8
Elsky, Martin 238, 246–7
Elyot, Sir Thomas 200–1, 238
emblems 2 n. 7, 55 n. 5, 89, 95, 96, 134, 160
    n. 48, 175, 197–8, 205–6, 226
embroidery 120–1, 204–7; *see also* textiles
Endimion 224–9
England 4, 5, 6, 7, 9, 13, 16, 20, 23, 43–4,
    45, 46, 47, 51, 52, 76, 85, 89, 94, 95,
    107–8, 117, 118, 119, 125, 133,
    145–52, 154, 155, 157, 161, 164,
    167–8, 203, 218–20, 254, 273–4, 276,
    280–2, 285
England's Helicon (1600) 2
epic 88, 91, 98, 99, 122, 125–6, 131, 135,
    150
Erasmus, Desiderius 3–4, 119, 168, 209,
    238, 253
  on artifice 178–80, 183
  Colloquies 145–6, 178–80, 183
  Education of a Christian Prince 201–2,
      263
  Enchiridion 36, 122, 126–9, 138–9,
      142–3, 180
  letters 113–14
  Paraphrases 4, 140 n. 50, 163, 165–6, 206
  on pilgrimage 145–6
Essex, earl of, *see* Devereux, Robert
Essex House 215 n. 65, 273, 277 n. 79; *see*
    also Leicester House
Eucharist
  in *The Faerie Queene* 158 n. 42, 159,
      161–8
  in the *Hypnerotomachia* 63, 66, 73
Evelyn, John 282–3
Everswell, *see* Woodstock
Everyman 160
Every Man out of his Humor 223, 229, 240
    n. 12, 242, 249–50

Faerie Queene, The see Spenser, Edmund
Farmer, Norman 92–3
fiction 10, 36, 37, 42, 83, 88, 92–3, 98–9
Fidelia 157–9, 176
fireworks 169

Fitzalan, Henry, twelfth earl of
    Arundel 206, 256–7, 265
Fleming, Juliet 246 n. 34
Fletcher, Anthony 201
folklore 15, 24, 25, 26, 28
fons Bandusiae 134, 200
fontes 113, 119, 121, 171, 211, 280
forests 23 n. 64, 25, 27, 28, 30–1, 62, 80,
    108, 123–4, 128–9, 172, 186, 225–6;
    see also trees
Fountain of Adonis (*Hypnerotomachia*) 54,
    56, 72, 75–7, 78, 82, 83–4, 85–7, 92,
    97–8, 99; see also *Figures 7, 8, 9*
'Fountain of Aeneas' (*Arcadia*) 85–98; see
    also *Figure 9*
Fountain of Venus (*Hypnerotomachia*) 54,
    56, 58, 65, 66, 67, 68, 69–75, 82–4,
    171, 190 n. 56, 192
Fountaine of Selfe-Love, The, see Jonson,
    Ben
Fountayne or Well of Lyfe (1532) 166; see
    also *Figure 12*
fountain(s)
  'antike boyes' on, 59, 177, 183; see also
      Figure 19
  bloody 134, 163, 172–4, 189, 210–11
  Christ as, 74, 146, 163–7; see also *imago*
      pietatis; *Figures 11, 12*
  in cities 1, 3, 4, 13, 19, 104–6, 109–11,
      112, 120, 277, 280
  classical 5, 11–13, 93, 134, 153, 253
  definitions 8, 11 n. 26, 19, 21
  of Diana 1, 2, 7, 200, 204, 216, 239,
      257–66, 270, 282, 284; see also
      Figures 16, 17
  Elizabeth I as, 1, 37, 106, 120, 197–8,
      201–8, 219–20, 236, 258–9, 263,
      274–5; see also *Figure 13*
  in English gardens 93, 281–3
    Bisham 15–16
    Hampton Court 255, 274–6; see also
        Figure 19
    Kenilworth 7, 37, 43, 59, 61, 169–72,
        177–8, 180, 183, 185, 192, 194,
        208–9, 258–9, 275 n. 67, 284–5
    Nonsuch 7, 37, 59, 61, 255–66,
        270–1, 274, 276, 278, 282, 285;
        see also *Figures 15, 16, 17, 18*
    Theobalds 61, 88, 90, 94–5, 99, 284–5
    Trinity College, Cambridge 59
  erotic 24, 27, 37, 55, 59–60, 64, 68, 70,
      74, 82, 136–40, 177–8, 183, 221,
      258, 282

fons Bandusiae 134, 200
fontes 113, 119, 121, 171, 211, 280
giocchi d'acqua, see water jokes
in Italian gardens 3, 6–7, 11–20, 61, 76
maintenance of, 110, 281–2
of Narcissus 10, 24, 73, 83, 191–2, 200, 226, 251; see also *Figure 1*
political 3, 37, 88, 112, 197–204, 205–8, 212, 216, 218–20, 238, 243–7, 257, 281
polluted 115, 119, 125, 128–31, 136, 143, 156, 200, 202, 210–12, 219, 247
puer mingens 56, 59, 61, 63, 69
of Salmacis 10, 37, 71, 75, 137, 192, 212 n. 54, 244–5, 252
Scripture as 106, 114, 120, 179–80, 198; *see also Figures 11, 12, 13*
sexual 70–5, 82, 138, 140–1, 222; *see also* erotic
spiritual 68, 72–4, 106, 114, 119, 120, 121, 127, 136, 146, 155–7, 163–7, 179–80, 197–8, 207, 219–20; see also *Figures 11, 12, 13*
as syncretic, 2, 3, 23, 82, 113, 153, 198, 231, 233
Virgin Mary as, 74
water jokes 19, 59, 61, 183, 185, 262, 265; see also *Hypnerotomachia*, 'Trickster' Fountain; see also *Figure 3*
wine 169, 276–7
Fowler, Alastair 171
Fradubio 136 n. 40, 137, 165, 186 n. 48, 187
Fragonard, Marie-Madeleine 24
France 24, 48
Château d'Anet 20, 191–2
Frazer, James 25, 58
Frye, Northrop 118
Fulke, William 114
Fumerton, Patricia 34, 185 n. 44
fustian 239–40

gardening manuals 20–2
gardens
artifice in, 12, 15, 17–18, 20, 59, 61, 63, 86, 178–80, 261, 281–2
automata in, 19, 183, 185, 261
classical 11–13
enclosed 24, 27, 30, 137, 258–9
in England 3, 5, 7, 8, 16, 21, 23, 36, 43, 44, 93, 95, 280–1
Bisham 15–16
Kenilworth 7, 37, 41, 43, 59, 61,

169–72, 177–8, 180, 183, 185, 192, 194, 208–9, 258–9, 284–5
Nonsuch 7, 37, 59, 61, 254, 255–66, 270–1, 276, 278, 282, 285; see also *Figures 15, 16, 17, 18*
Theobalds 7, 41, 61, 88, 90, 94–5, 99, 184 n. 38, 284–5
Wilton 41, 43, 95–6
Woodstock 31–3
history 5, 6–8, 44, 283
medieval 24, 27, 30, 31–3, 136–7
mottoes and poems in, 34, 35 n. 87, 59, 61, 63, 259, 262–6, 271, 280
Raglan Castle, Gwent 94–5
theory 5, 8–9
Gargaphia 71, 231, 239, 259, 269
Gent, Lucy 42, 43 n. 6, 44 n. 9, 88, 96–7
gods 109
Apollo 11, 80, 132–3, 229, 230, 277; *see also* Helicon; Muses; Parnassus
Cupid 54, 65, 67, 68, 69–71, 76, 80, 81, 82, 83, 86, 88, 89, 90, 92, 99, 186–7, 189, 215, 231, 236, 239, 250, 252, 269, 271
Diana 1, 2, 7, 10, 16, 17, 25, 34, 37, 66, 71, 78, 79–81, 136 n. 40, 138, 171, 173–4, 186–7, 193, 200, 203–4, 212–17, 231, 239, 248, 252, 257–67, 269–70, 272–3, 276, 282, 284; *see also* Actaeon
Mercury 225, 231, 232, 236, 239, 242, 251, 271
Venus 36, 54, 58–9, 64, 65, 66, 69–74, 76, 79, 81, 82, 83, 86, 88, 90, 92, 183, 186–7, 215; *see also* Fountain of Venus
Godwin, Joscelyn 54
Golden Ass, The, see Apuleius
Golden Legend, The 164–5
Goldring, Elizabeth 35, 103 n. 1, 169 n. 3
grail 29
Greene, Thomas 279
Gregerson, Linda 10, 98, 174–5, 185, 188, 193 n. 67
Greville, Fulke 207–8, 217
Gunpowder Plot 151 n. 26, 277 n. 79
Gurr, Andrew 224
Guyon 111, 171–7, 180–4, 186–7, 192–3, 221, 264

Habicht, Werner 230
Hagar 139–40

Hall, Joseph 241
Hampton Court 37, 59, 119, 204, 255, 274–6; see also *Figure 19*
Harbage, Alfred 222–3
Hardwick, Bess of, *see* Talbot, Elizabeth, countess of Shrewsbury
Harington, John 213–14, 216–17, 232, 266, 272–3
Harrison, William 95, 151–2
Harvey, Gabriel 108, 238
hat-badges 5, 146–7, 166 n. 66, 283–4; see also *Figure 11*
Hatton, Christopher 34, 89
Hawes, Stephen 178 n. 22
Hebrus 153–4
Helicon 2, 11, 205, 230, 232, 233, 238, 242, 247, 252, 277; *see also* Apollo; Parnassus; Muses
Henderson, Paula 6 n. 12, 7, 59 n. 9, 94 n. 18, 184 n. 38, 258 n. 12, 275 n. 66, 281 n. 4
Henri III, king of France 229
Henry II, king of England 32
Henry VI, king of England 104
Henry VIII, king of England 256, 263 n. 28, 275 n. 66
Henry IV, Part 1 162 n. 54
Hentzner, Paul 16, 94, 275
Herbert, Mary Sidney, countess of Pembroke 41
Hermaphrodite 72 n. 9, 190–4, 244
Hermaphroditus 10, 71, 75, 137–8, 212
Herwijk, Stephen van 106 n. 13, 197–8, 203, 263 n. 28; see also *Figure 13*
Hesiod 131–3
Heydon, Christopher 43 n. 8, 51–2, 56
Heywood, Thomas 106, 282
Hoby, Sir Thomas 13–16, 17, 20, 47, 61, 282
Holbein, Hans 146 n. 7; see also *Figure 11*
Holywell 151 n. 26
Homilies, Book of 105, 113, 114, 118
Horace 23, 90, 134, 200
Horeb 164
Howard, Thomas, earl of Arundel 283
Hulse, Clark 34
humanism 2, 4, 23, 35, 36, 37, 112–14, 119, 120, 121, 122, 123, 126, 236, 238, 242, 249, 253, 263, 279–80; *see also* individual authors
 political writing 23, 198–203, 210, 212, 216–17, 230, 249
 translation 23, 36, 113–16, 119, 121

Hunt, John Dixon 8, 17, 261, 265
Hypnerotomachia 35–6, 53–99, 171, 172, 174, 175, 183, 190 n. 56, 191 n. 59, 192, 280, 282, 284–5
 authorship 46
 baptism in, 59, 63, 65–6, 69, 72
 criticism 50–1, 54, 55
 desire in, 44, 53, 55–7, 60, 61, 63, 64–5, 67–8, 70, 72–4, 75, 77, 79, 81, 84, 87
 Eucharistic imagery in, 63, 66, 73
 Fountain of the Sleeping Nymph 53, 55, 57, 58–60, 75, 81, 221, 258; see also *Figure 2*
 'Trickster' fountain 53, 59, 61, 69; see also *Figure 3*
 Fountain of Venus 54, 56, 58, 65, 66, 67, 68, 69–75, 82–4, 171, 190 n. 56, 192
 Fountain of Adonis 54, 56, 72, 75–7, 78, 82, 83–4, 85–7, 92, 97–8, 99; see also *Figures 7, 8, 9*
 fountains in, 42, 44, 45, 51, 52, 53–68, 69–84, 85–7, 92, 97–8, 99; see also *Figures 2, 3, 4, 5, 6, 7, 8, 9*
 history 45–7, 50, 52
 illustrations 44, 45, 46, 49, 51, 54, 56, 60, 61, 62, 63, 65 n. 17, 69, 75–7, 86, 87, 96, 282; see also *Figures 2, 3, 4, 5, 6, 7, 8, 9*
 influence 41, 43, 45, 48, 51, 85–99
 marriage in, 66, 72–3
 owned by Jonson 43, 51, 64
 as pagan 58, 64–6, 72, 73, 76, 83
 Polia 46, 51, 54, 57, 61, 63–7, 69–83, 175, 192
 Poliphilus 47, 51, 53–68, 69–83, 87, 175
 reception in early modern England 42 n. 4, 47, 51–2, 56, 64, 85–99
 and the *Roman de la Rose*, 62, 69–70, 73, 83
 ruins in, 58, 59, 67
 and Sidney 42, 43, 44, 46, 48, 50, 75, 77, 79, 85–99; see also *Figure 9*
 Songe de Poliphile 46, 49, 51, 60, 63, 83, 86–8, 95, 96
 specific copies of, 43, 45, 51, 64
 and Spenser 43
 Strife of Love in a Dreame 16 n. 43, 48–9, 51, 63, 75, 85, 88
 structure 44, 50–1, 56, 57, 58, 61, 62, 67, 77, 82–3, 87
 synopsis 53–4
 thirst in, 53, 54–8, 60, 64, 66, 73, 74, 77, 83

translations 16 n. 43, 46, 48–50, 51, 54,
    62, 63, 69 n. 1, 85
voyeurism in, 59–60, 71, 221

iconoclasm 1, 146, 176 n. 15, 184–6
imagination 10, 36, 37, 44, 70, 84, 88, 98,
    99, 113, 114, 284–5
imago pietatis 166; see also *Figure 12*
imitation 17, 75, 76, 98, 131, 134, 172,
    179–80, 201, 202, 237–8, 241, 253,
    261, 266–7, 270
interdisciplinarity 33–5, 185, 253
intertextuality 5, 14, 23, 26, 34, 45, 113,
    116, 117, 121, 122–4, 131, 136, 143,
    154, 171–2, 189, 193, 194, 199, 210,
    253, 279, 282, 284
Ireland 108, 118, 147–8, 158, 214 n. 61,
    234, 266
Italy 3, 5, 6, 7, 11–20, 25, 47, 48, 61, 108,
    283
  Messina 13
  Pratolino 6, 18–20
  Naples 13, 17–18
  Syracuse 14–15, 16–18
  Tivoli 18, 19
  Venice 46, 65, 77, 94, 230
  Villa d'Este 19, 20, 263 n. 27

James I, king of England 119, 202, 246, 256,
    276–7
Jewel, John 115, 119, 131, 168
jewellery 5, 204, 206, 234 n. 2, 236, 239,
    285
Johnson, A. W. 43 n. 7
Jones, John 149–50
Jones, Inigo 41
Jonson, Ben 109, 117, 162 n. 53
  Bartholomew Fair 210, 230
  Conversations with Drummond 268–9,
    274
  Every Man Out of his Humor 223, 229,
    240, 242 n. 12, 249–50
  'First Ode' 272
  *The Fountaine of Selfe-Love, or Cynthias
    Revels* 1, 34, 37, 172, 197–217,
    222–6, 229–33, 236–54, 265–76,
    282
    Argument 236, 239
    date 198, 222–3, 247, 267, 272
    and the earl of Essex 198, 223, 247,
      252, 254, 266–76
    Folio text 198, 199, 223, 230, 232, 253

'Hymn to Cynthia' 248, 249, 271–4
Induction 223, 224, 231, 236–7, 239,
    245, 250
language in, 209, 233, 237–41, 246–8,
    250–51, 253
masques 229, 236, 239, 250–2, 267,
    269
names in, 245, 268–9, 273–4
Palinode 236, 252–3
Prologue 231, 236–8, 242, 250, 253–4
setting 239, 267
staging requirements 223–6, 228
library 43, 64, 117, 162 n. 53, 229, 240
Poetaster 225, 242, 247
Timber, or Discoveries 240–43, 247, 252
Volpone 230
Jordan 153–4
Julius Caesar 210 n. 43
justice 37, 203, 208, 211, 219, 266, 269–70,
    273, 275–6; see also *Figure 19*

Kaske, Carol 116–18
Kawachi, Yoshiko 222–3
Kenilworth 7, 35, 37, 41, 43, 59, 61, 89, 147,
    160–1, 169–72, 177–8, 180, 183, 185,
    192, 194, 208–9, 258–9, 275 n. 67,
    284–5
Killigrew, Henry 169
King, Andrew 154
King, John N. 125 n. 11, 128 n. 19, 133 n.
    29, 139 n. 47, 141–2, 156–7, 159 n. 45,
    176 n. 15, 180 n. 28, 184 n. 42, 197 n. 1
Kipling, Gordon 111 n. 30
Krier, Theresa M. 72 n. 9, 187, 190 n. 56,
    192 n. 64
Kristeva, Julia 99

labyrinths 63, 134, 235
landscape 4, 5, 9, 12, 15, 36, 41, 44, 77, 108,
    110, 113, 122, 131, 146–7, 149, 152,
    154–5, 167, 254, 262, 279–81, 282,
    284–5
  concepts of, 4, 6 n. 12, 36, 44–5, 61, 90,
    98, 112, 147, 154–5, 167, 279–81,
    282, 284–5
  gardening 22 n. 57
  and genre 25, 26, 36, 113, 122, 123, 124,
    125, 131, 192
landscape entertainments 4, 42 n. 4
Laneham, Robert, *see* Langham, Robert
Langham, Robert 169–70, 172, 178, 183,
    185, 194, 259

Langland, William 144, 146, 161
language 11, 108, 112, 135, 155–7, 199,
    209, 233, 237–41, 246–8, 250–1, 253
Languet, Hubert 91
Lavinia 210–11
Lawson, William 21–2
Lefebvre, Henri 110 n. 27
Leicester, earl of, *see* Dudley, Robert
Leicester House 208, 215 n. 65, 273; *see also*
    Essex House
Leslie, Michael 7, 8, 42, 171–2, 183, 261–2
Leucippe and Clitophon 93
Lewis, C. S. 171, 177, 178, 181
locus amoenus 8, 23, 24, 76, 83–4, 136
London 1–2, 103–12, 118, 120–1, 125,
    147, 208–9, 218–19, 267, 276–7
    Cheapside 1–2, 36, 104, 107, 118, 120,
        282
    conduits 36, 104–6, 109–12, 120, 276–7
    history 1–2, 109–11
    idealization of 109
    landmarks 1–2, 36, 104–6, 109–12, 120
    as new Jerusalem 111–12, 121
    as new Rome 108, 111
    as new Troy 111–12
    Paul's churchyard 104
    water-supply 110–11
loss 5–6, 43–4, 47, 51, 98, 110, 285; *see also*
    blank space
Loues Metamorphosis 223–5
'Lumley Inventory' 256–8; see also *Figures
    16, 17, 18*
Lumley, John 255–8, 260–1, 263, 265–6
Lupton, Thomas 150
Lyly, John 223–7, 229
    Endimion 226–9
    Loues Metamorphosis 223–5
Lyne, Raphael 184

MacCaffrey, Isabel 171
MacDougall, Elisabeth 7, 11
Malacasta 188
Malory, Thomas 5, 26–31, 125
manna 164, 167
Manutius, Aldus 45–6
Markham, Gervase 20–2
Martial 277
Martin, Jean 46
Mary I, queen of England 105, 256
Mary, queen of Scots 147, 149–51, 205, 266
    n. 35
materiality 2, 3, 4, 5, 6, 8, 9, 23, 24, 34, 35,
    37, 42, 44, 51, 52, 60, 70, 72, 74, 75, 77,

79, 81, 82, 87, 90, 91, 92, 95, 98, 110,
    118, 120–1, 134, 146, 170–2, 174, 207,
    210, 217, 253, 279–80,
    282–5
mazer 176, 178; *see also* cups
Merchant Taylors' School 107–8
Mercury 225, 231, 232, 236, 239, 242, 251
Merlin 189, 193, 194
metalwork 177–8, 197–8, 214 n. 61
miles Christi 124–7, 137, 139, 142–3
Miller, Naomi 62 n. 15
miracles 29, 145–6, 152, 157, 159, 168
mirror 10, 42, 79, 83, 86, 92–4, 95, 98, 99,
    172, 185, 188, 192–3, 199–200, 233,
    237, 250–1; *see also* reflection,
    speculum
Mirror for Magistrates 93
Montrose, Louis Adrian 34, 264 n. 31
morality 2, 4, 7, 10, 15, 36, 37, 59, 88, 91,
    95, 98, 99, 112, 125, 135, 142–3, 171,
    174, 177 n. 19, 179–85, 192, 199–203,
    209, 212, 215–16, 237–52, 265, 270,
    280, 281–2
Mortdant 173, 175–6
Moryson, Fynes 16, 18, 19–20
Moses 164
Mulcaster, Richard 107–9, 112, 119, 141,
    159, 182, 203, 218, 282
museums 121, 144, 146, 197, 204 n. 22,
    205, 208, 214 n. 61, 234, 283–4
Muses 2, 11, 190, 204, 229, 230, 232, 237,
    277; *see also* Apollo; Helicon;
    Parnassus

Narcissus 10, 24, 73, 75, 79, 83, 97–9, 153
    n. 29, 188–93, 199–200, 212, 226,
    231–2, 233, 237, 238, 240, 244, 245 n.
    33, 248, 251
Narcissus (*c.* 1603) 228, 274 n. 60
narrative 45, 50, 51, 54, 57–8, 60–3, 67–8,
    76, 77, 83, 118–19, 122–4, 127, 137,
    147, 154, 165, 189, 236, 280
Nashe, Thomas 49–50, 108
National Portrait Gallery, London 197–8;
    see also *Figure 13*
Neville, Henry 267
Newnham Regis 147, 152, 167
Nichols, John 151 n. 24, 169 n. 2, 203 n. 18,
    206 n. 29
Nile 132, 211
Niobe 11, 226, 231–2, 252
Nohrnberg, James 163, 176, 191 n. 60
Nonsuch 7, 37, 59, 61, 254, 255–71, 274,

276, 278, 282, 285; see also *Figures 15,
16, 17, 18*
Norden, John 109, 274–5
Norwich 203

obelisks 96, 205, 260, 265, *see also* pyramids
oil 161 n. 53, 164, 165
origin 22–3, 27, 28, 55, 122, 128, 131–5,
156, 166
Orpheus 154
otherworld 27–8, 29
O'Toole, Michael 9
Ovid 2, 5, 10–11, 14–15, 17, 37, 72, 75, 82,
92, 122–3, 153–4, 170, 174–5, 178,
188, 189, 190–2, 210–13, 216, 226,
239, 244, 279; *see also* Sandys, George
Metamorphoses 5, 10–11, 16, 27, 72, 132,
137, 170, 178, 210–11
Adonis 76, 80, 82–3, 92, 98, 99; *see
also* Fountain of Adonis, *Figures 7,
9*
Anaxarete 80, 175
Arethusa 14, 17, 78, 175
Atalanta 92
Biblis 72, 75, 78
Diana and Actaeon 10, 11, 71, 136 n.
40, 171, 186–7, 212–16, 226,
231–2, 237, 239–40, 244, 252,
261, 265, 282
Echo 223–5, 231–3, 236, 241, 248,
250, 251, 252
Narcissus 10, 24, 73, 75, 79, 83, 97–9,
153 n. 29, 188–93, 199–200, 212,
226, 231–2, 233, 237, 238, 240,
244, 245 n. 33, 248, 251
Niobe 11, 226, 231–2, 252
Salmacis and Hermaphroditus 10, 71,
75, 137–8, 191–2, 212, 244–5
Tristia 270–1

pageants 4, 34, 36, 103–12, 119, 125, 128,
159, 206–7, 208, 218–20, 224, 229–30,
246, 268, 276–7
painting(s) 1, 34, 36, 87, 88–9, 90, 91, 92,
94, 97–8, 160–1, 179–80, 185, 204 n.
22, 215, 221, 235–7, 255, 264, 284, 285;
see also *Figure 14*
palimpsest 4, 92, 98, 123, 125, 147, 279, 280
Palmer 172–5, 182–4, 193, 264, 271
Parnassus 11, 241; *see also* Apollo; Helicon;
Muses
Peacham, Henry 160
Peele, George 3, 218–25, 227–30, 282

Arraignment of Paris 218, 220, 225
Descensus Astraeae 106, 208, 218–20
*The Love of King David and Fair
Bethsabe* 212 n. 55, 220–4, 227–31,
243, 253
The Old Wiues Tale 224, 227–8
Titus Andronicus 218 n. 2
pelican 167 n. 70, 258 n. 12, 260, 265; see
also *Figures 15, 18*
Pembroke, countess of, see Herbert, Mary
Sidney
Percy, William 228
Pérez-Gomez, Alberto 57
Petrarch, Francesco 89, 279–80
Petrarchan convention 79, 82–3, 93, 190
Philautia 245, 268–9
Piers Plowman, see Langland, William
pilgrimage 144–8, 151, 154–5; see also
Figure 10
Pinkus, Karen 50
Plato 10 n. 24, 22, 68, 79, 82, 93, 242, 251
Phaedrus 70–2, 73, 75 n. 17, 81 n. 34,
160 n. 46, 190 n. 56
Platter, Thomas 33, 203–4, 256–7, 261–3,
267 n. 37, 275
Pliny, the Younger 5, 12–3
ploughman literature 144, 161
Plutarch 23, 37, 202–3, 209, 210 n. 43, 240
Poetaster 225, 242, 247
poetry 2, 3, 11, 23, 30, 41, 90, 94, 98, 122,
125, 131, 132, 134–5, 154, 190, 199,
232–3, 237–8, 241–3, 246–7,
251–3
Policraticus, see Salisbury, John of
Polizzi, Gilles 51, 73, 83
pollution 110, 115, 119, 125, 128–31, 136,
143, 155–6, 200, 202, 210–12, 219–20,
240–7, 270
Pozzi, Giovanni 45, 54, 66
Prayer Book 121, 142, 165
Prescott, Anne Lake 77 n. 26, 194 n. 70
Priapus 45, 53, 63, 75, 183
Protestant internationalism 197–8, 207–8,
218–20, 266; see also *Figure 13*
Pugh, Syrithe 123 n. 1, 124, 132 n. 25, 137,
174 n. 10, 180, 189
pyramid 51, 52, 53, 56, 58–9, 205, 260; *see
also* obelisk
Python 11, 132–3; *see also* snakes, dragons

'Queen's English' 246–7
Quilligan, Maureen 132
Quint, David 22–3

Raglan Castle, Gwent 94–5
Raleigh, Walter 2
reading 2, 4, 5, 6, 10, 13, 27, 35, 37, 42, 45,
        49, 50, 51, 59, 60–1, 62, 68, 70, 74–5,
        78, 79, 84, 87, 91, 95, 96, 98, 112–14,
        116–19, 120, 122–7, 131, 135, 138–9,
        141–3, 147, 157, 159, 161, 162, 167,
        171–4, 180–1, 184–9, 192–4, 210,
        236, 243, 253, 262–3, 265, 279–80,
        282, 284–5
Redcrosse 2 n. 7, 36, 111, 113, 118, 119,
        122–43, 154–68, 171, 173, 174, 177,
        180, 186, 192–3
'Red Velvet Book', *see* 'Lumley Inventory'
reflection 9–10, 30–1, 36, 42, 73, 74, 83,
        87, 92–5, 97–9, 160, 180, 185, 188–9,
        191–2, 198, 199, 200–1, 233, 237, 241,
        248, 250–1, 282
repentance 2, 118, 160–1, 212–13, 265–6
Revels, Office of the 224, 228–30
Rich, Barnabe 94, 148, 150 n. 21
Ridolfi Plot 265
Ripa, Cesare 160
romance 23–33, 50, 62, 83, 88, 91, 99,
        122–6, 129, 136–7, 142, 153–4, 159,
        167, 178 n. 22, 186, 226
Roman de la Rose 5, 24, 30, 62, 69–70, 73,
        83; see also *Figure 1*
Ronsard, Pierre 73
Ruddymane 173, 175

St Winifred's Well, *see* Holywell
sacraments 36, 51, 57–8, 59, 63–6, 69, 72,
        73, 127, 142–3, 147, 158–68,
        175
Salisbury, John of
        Policraticus 37, 243–7, 253
Samaritan woman 139–40, 146, 154; see
        also *Figure 11*
Sandler, Florence 117 n. 43, 126 n. 14,
        127
Sandys, George
        Metamorphosis (1632) 11 n. 26, 271
        A Relation of a Iourney (1615) 16–18
Scudamour 186, 190–1, 194
sculpture 8, 9, 58, 60, 61, 62, 76, 83, 86–7,
        94–5, 174, 178, 183–4, 185, 190–1,
        192, 216, 256–7, 260–1, 264, 265, 275,
        279, 280, 281
Seth 164
Shaheen, Naseeb 116
Shakespeare, William 3, 200 n. 9, 268, 282
        As You Like It 2
        Cymbeline 216
        Henry IV Part I 162 n. 54
        Julius Caesar 210 n. 43
        Titus Andronicus 3, 209–11, 218 n. 2
        Venus and Adonis 92
Sharpe, Kevin 7 n. 14, 23
Sheldon tapestries 208–9; *see also* textiles
Shrewsbury, countess of, *see* Talbot,
        Elizabeth
Shrewsbury, earl of, *see* Talbot, George
Shroeder, John W. 140–1
Sidney, Henry 206
Sidney, Mary, countess of Pembroke, *see*
        Herbert, Mary Sidney
Sidney, Philip 41–52, 206, 208, 217
        Arcadia 7, 35, 36, 75, 77, 85–99, 172,
                280, 282
                context 41, 89–91
                Fountain of Aeneas 85–98; see also
                        Figure 9
                and English gardens 90, 93, 94–6, 99
                and Greek romance 93
                and portraits 88–9
        Astrophil and Stella 41–2, 79, 87, 96, 98
        career 41, 91
        Defence of Poesie 90–1, 93 n. 17, 94, 96,
                98, 242
Silberman, Lauren 187, 191 n. 57, 193 n.
        66, 194
Siloam 153–4
sleep 28, 30, 31, 53, 55–6, 135–6, 165
Sluijter, Eric Jan 215
Smith, Irwin 225
snakes 124, 128–33, 158, 207, 262; *see also*
        Python, dragons
spectacle 70, 74, 77, 87, 93, 103, 170,
        173–4, 183–4, 190
specularity 10, 98, 173–4, 180, 183–4, 187,
        188, 215–16, 258–9
speculum 93
Spenser, Edmund 106–21, 218–20
        Amoretti 136 n. 39, 194 n. 70
        as English poet, 11, 116, 122, 135, 150,
                274
        Astrophel 92
        life 107–8, 118, 274
        The Faerie Queene 7, 34, 36, 43, 98, 106,
                109, 110, 111–14, 116–19, 120,
                122–43, 144–68, 169–94, 280; *see*
                also individual characters' names
                baptism in, 127, 142–3, 158–68, 175
                and the bible 114, 116–19, 120, 122,
                        127–31, 138–43, 146, 152, 156,

159, 162, 163, 164, 166, 167–8, 186, 191, 194
and Calvin 134, 163 n. 57, 165–7
and Chaucer 11, 135, 161
early readers 158, 162 n. 53
and Erasmus 122, 126–9, 138–9, 142–3, 163, 165–6, 168, 178–80
Eucharist in, 158 n. 42, 159, 161–8
and Horace 134
and Ovid 122–3, 132, 137–8, 153–4, 174–5, 178, 188, 189, 190–2
versification 128, 137
and Virgil 131
Book 1
  opening 123–4
  combat with Errour 114, 124–6, 127–35
  Archimago's hermitage 135–6, 155–6, 165
  Fradubio 136–7, 165
  Abessa 139–40, 159
  dalliance with Duessa 136–42, 174
  Orgoglio 133, 138–9, 141, 157–9
  House of Holinesse 108, 158, 159–61, 193
  Mount of Contemplation 111, 161
  dragon fight 131, 177
  Well and Tree of Life 113, 123, 125, 128, 143, 153–5, 161–8, 173
Book 2
  Fountain of the Chaste Nymph 172–5
  Castle of Alma 108, 111
  Bowre of Bliss 108, 171–85, 187, 192, 280
    gates 172, 176, 178 n. 21
    Genius and Excesse 176–7
    fountain and bathers 171, 172, 174, 177–85, 221 n. 10, 264, 271
    Acrasia 173, 175–8, 183
    destruction of the Bowre 175, 177, 184–5, 187
Book 3
  Proem 185, 194
  Castle Joyous 188, 189
  Britomart looks in the mirror 188, 193
  Merlin's prophecy 189, 193, 194
  Belphoebe and Amoret 133, 136 n. 39, 186–7
  Venus and Diana 186–7
  Paridell 189
  Britomart meets Scudamour 186

House of Busirane 108, 174, 187, 189–90
  the Hermaphrodite 190–4
Book 4
  False Florimell 136
Book 5
  Malfont 135
  Mutabilitie Cantos 147, 186 n. 48, 251, 271
  Letter to Raleigh 123, 124, 182
Prothalamion 109, 273–4
Shepheardes Calender 89, 107, 135, 178, 226 n. 31
A Theatre for Voluptuous Worldlings 46 n. 17, 141
A View of the Present State of Ireland 148, 158
Steadman, John M. 133–4
Stewering, Roswitha 46 n. 15, 66, 67, 68, 75
Stow, John 1, 109–11, 282
Strong, Roy 6–8, 22, 89, 197 n. 1
Suffolk, duchess of, *see* Bertie, Katherine
Sullivan, Garrett 23
Sutton, James 35, 95
syncretism 2, 3, 23, 44–5, 82, 113, 122, 143, 153, 198, 231, 233, 253, 269 n. 46

Talbot, Elizabeth, countess of Shrewsbury 205
Talbot, George, earl of Shrewsbury 149–51
Taylor, John, 'the Water Poet' 96
tapestries 208–9, 235, 284; *see also* textiles
Tasso, Torquato 22, 124 n. 5, 181, 222 n. 17
temperance 171 n. 7, 175, 177, 182, 184, 242, 264
textiles 5, 37; *see also* book-bindings; embroidery; Sheldon tapestries; tapestries
Theobalds 7, 35, 41, 61, 88, 90, 94–5, 99, 184 n. 38, 284–5
Timber, or Discoveries 240–3, 247, 252
Titus Andronicus 3, 210–12, 218 n. 2
Topcliffe, Richard 151, 158
travellers 11–20, 47, 48, 52, 203–4, 279–80; *see also* individual names
Tree of Life 136 n. 39, 158–68
trees 21, 25–6, 30, 56, 85–6, 96, 104–5, 128–9, 165, 225, 230
Tristan 30, 31–3
Troilus and Criseyde 30; *see also* Chaucer, Geoffrey

Troyes, Chrétien de 25–7
Truth the Daughter of Time, see *Veritas Temporis Filia*
Tudeau-Clayton, Margaret 243, 247
Turner, William 149–50
Tuve, Rosamund 163
Tyard, Pontus de 191–2

Una 119, 155, 165, 193
Uriah 212, 214 n. 61, 221–2
Utenhove, Charles 197–8; see also *Figure 13*

Van Der Noot, Jan 46–7, 108, 141
Venice 46, 65, 77, 94, 230
Venus 36, 54, 58–9, 64, 65, 66, 69–74, 76, 79, 81, 82, 83, 86, 88, 90, 92, 183, 186–7, 215; *see also* Fountain of Venus
Venus and Adonis 92
Veritas Temporis Filia 103–7, 109, 112, 128, 146, 159, 206–7, 218–20, 246; *see also* Elizabeth I, queen of England, coronation entry
Victoria and Albert Museum, London 121, 205, 208, 214 n. 61, 283
Virgil 15, 22, 131, 210
Volpone 230

Waldstein, Baron 94, 204, 261–2
Walls, Kathryn 139 n. 48, 140 n. 49, 159
Walsham, Alexandra 146–7, 149 n. 15, 151 n. 26, 155
Walsingham, Francis 34, 208
Walsingham, shrine at 145, 155
water 8–11, 27, 64–5, 92
  depth 9, 73–4
  holy water 64–6, 72, 147

motion 9, 27, 183
surface 9–10, 73–4, 84, 93, 97–8, 172, 188, 192, 200, 211
water jokes 19, 59, 61, 183, 185, 262, 265; see also *Hypnerotomachia*, 'Trickster' Fountain; *Figure 3*
Waters, Douglas 141 n. 54, 156
Watson, Anthony 255–7, 259–61, 262–6
Weatherby, Harold 161 n. 53
Webster, John 200, 202–3
wells, holy 36, 64–5, 144–68
  in England 110, 144–6, 149, 155
  in Ireland 147–9
  in Wales 151 n. 26
  in literature 64–5, 111, 154
  and miracles 144–6, 152, 157, 159, 168
  and patriotism 111, 147, 150, 155, 152, 167
  post-Reformation 146–7, 149–51, 151 n. 26, 167–8
  and repentance 160–1
Wells-Cole, Anthony 51, 208–9, 235 n. 5
Whitney, Geoffrey 205–6
Whore of Babylon 116, 118, 141, 157
Whitehall 203–4, 208 n. 36, 222
Wilton 41, 43, 95–6
Wind, Edgar 76 n. 22, 191
wine 158–9, 173, 175–6, 232, 277
Woodstock 31–3
Worden, Blair 89, 276
Wotton, Henry 268, 276 n. 71
wounds, cult of 166; see also *Figure 12*
wrestling 181–3
Wright, Thomas 240–1
Wroth, Mary 95–6

Yvain 5, 25–6, 29